Memoirs of the Life of Sir John Clerk of Penicuik

PUBLICATIONS

OF THE

SCOTTISH HISTORY SOCIETY

VOLUME XIII

CLERK OF PENICUIK'S MEMOIRS

December 1892

John Clerk

MEMOIRS OF THE LIFE OF

SIR JOHN CLERK

OF PENICUIK, BARONET

BARON OF THE EXCHEQUER

EXTRACTED BY HIMSELF FROM

HIS OWN JOURNALS

1676-1755

Edited from the Manuscript in Penicuik House
with an Introduction and Notes, by

JOHN M. GRAY
F.S.A. SCOT.

EDINBURGH
Printed at the University Press by T. and A. Constable
for the Scottish History Society
1892

CONTENTS

ILLUSTRATIONS

Nos. I., VI., VII., and VIII. are from oil-paintings, Nos. II. and III. from miniatures, No. V. from a pencil-drawing, and No. X. from a copper-plate, preserved in Penicuik House.

ERRATA

Page 8, second line of Note [2], for *masculise* read *masculis e*
22, fourth line of notes, *for* vol. i. p. 1059-60 *read* vol. ii. pp. 1159-60
29, fourth line of Note [4], *for* Boudoin *read* Bowdoin
45, fourth last line, *for* who been bred *read* who had been bred
90, fourth last line, *delete* and
117, fifteenth line of Note [1], *for* Stuckeley *read* Stukeley
131, last line of Note [2], *for* Woodrow *read* Wodrow
139, fourth line of Note [1], *for* Lympandoun *read* Tympandoun
150, sixth line of Note [1], *for* vol. iii. *read* No. II. part iii.
165, second line of Note [1], for *Bibiotheca* read *Bibliotheca*
third line, *for* part i. *read* part iii.
second line of Note [2], *for* part i. *read* part iii.
168, tenth line of Note [2], *for* French *read* English
173, Note [1], *for* Charles Emmanuel II. *read* Charles Emmanuel I.
206, fifth line from top, *for* Queensferry *read* Queensberry

INTRODUCTION

The manuscript which, through the kind permission of Sir George Clerk of Penicuik, is now printed for the use of the members of the Scottish History Society, contains an Autobiography of his ancestor Sir John Clerk, second baronet of Penicuik, the great-grandson of William Drummond of Hawthornden, the poet. Sir John was one of the commissioners for the Union, and a Baron of the Court of Exchequer in Scotland; and his account of his life, extending from 1676 to 1755, embraces a particularly significant portion of our national history. The manuscript contains not only a full record and a carefully weighed estimate of current political events, both at home and abroad, but also much curious information bearing on the material and social condition of Scotland during the period indicated, along with such an account of the Baron's own private tastes, pursuits, and employments, as presents us with a vivid and reliable picture of the daily life of a cultured Scottish gentleman of the first half of the eighteenth century.

The manuscript is contained in a stout quarto volume of 251 pages, in Clerk's own handwriting, preserved in the charter-room of Penicuik House; its battered vellum binding warped and time-stained, and its margins mouldering away with damp, which accounts for the defective condition of many of its writer's marginal notes. I have reprinted it as it stands, adding only some slight and necessary punctuation.

As the author states, the Autobiography is founded upon a journal which he 'was always in use to keep.' The most important portion of this 'journal' that is still accessible consists of two folio manuscript volumes, preserved at Penicuik House, embracing an account of his travels on the Continent from 1694 to 1699; and these have furnished some illustrative footnotes; while the 'Memoirs of a Goat Whey Campaign at Lauers in 1749,' a separate manuscript, printed as Additional Note S., affords further insight into the Baron's method of using his contemporary journal in the production of his more weighed and final 'Account of my Life.' It would have been interesting if the various other portions of his journal to which he refers had been preserved and accessible—such portions as the 'Particular Journal of a little Trip to England' in 1724, in company with Alexander Gordon, to view the Roman Wall, mentioned at folio 141; the 'Diary of all I saw or met with in England' in 1727, when he visited the chief virtuosos in London, and made an excursion to Stonehenge and Wilton, mentioned at folio 148; the 'Journal of what I saw' in a 'trip' to Houghton Hall, Norfolk, and to London in 1733, mentioned at folio 158; and the 'Particular Account' of his visit to the coal-pits at Whitehaven in 1739, referred to in folio 181. We have proof that some of these manuscripts were preserved at Penicuik long after the Baron's death, in an entry in a 'Scroll Inventory of the Contents of the Charter-room,' dated 29th March 1783, which includes the following entry, 'No. 24, Baron Clerk's Travels at home or in England, 1724 and 1733, 3 vols.:' but these have now disappeared; and, after a somewhat careful search among the very voluminous, unclassified contents of the charter-room, I have been obliged to abandon the hope of discovering them.

The manuscript now printed for the first time begins with a brief reference to the writer's ancestry: and he opens the account of his own life by recording that he was born on the 8th of February 1676; a statement, confirmed by the Baptism Register of the City of Edinburgh, which rectifies the initial error of all his biographers, who unanimously give the date as

1684. He received his earliest instruction in the parish school of Penicuik; and then studied in Glasgow University; passing in his eighteenth year to Holland to study at Leyden, where he mainly devoted himself to law. Here he also, under Gronovius, laid the foundations of an extensive knowledge of Roman antiquities, the study of which formed a favourite pursuit during all his life; received instruction in drawing from William Mieris, attaining more than common proficiency; and became a skilful musician: so that, after added practice in Italy, he was able, on his return to Scotland, to affirm that he 'understood pictures better than became his purse, and as to music I performed rather better than became a gentleman.' It seems to have been chiefly his enthusiasm for music, combined with other similarities of taste, that attracted him to Boerhaave, of whom the manuscript contains some interesting particulars, and who was sufficiently a Scotsman in his likings to pronounce 'oat-meal potage,' when eaten with cream, a '*nutrimentum divinum.*' The pair 'lived like Brothers together, while I staid in Leyden,' and they continued to be correspondents during the life of the great physician.

Though possessed of but a slender purse, the young Scottish student set his face steadfastly towards Italy, that holy land of pilgrimage for all interested in the things of art and culture. His journey was contrary to the wishes of his father, 'but the vast desire I had to see a Country so famous for exploits about which all my time had been hitherto spent in reading the classicks, likeways a country so replenished with Antiquities of all kinds, and so much excelling all other countries in painting and musick, I say these things created such a vast desire in me to see it, that I am sure nothing in life had ever made me happy if I had denied my self this great pleasure and satisfaction.'

At Vienna he was introduced at court by Lord Lexington, and enjoyed the musical entertainments to which the Emperor

Leopold I. was so ardently attached. At Rome, again, he moved in the best circles, studying law in a more or less formal way, under Monsignor Caprara, of the Rota, and Monsignor Chaprigni, and music under Pasquini and Corelli, who figure vividly in his pages. At Florence he received especial favours from the Grand Duke Cosmo III., by whom he was appointed a Gentleman of the Bed-chamber. Paris pleased him little after Italy; and in the end of 1699 he returned to Scotland.

The two unpublished manuscript volumes of his *Travels* prove how wisely and diligently he had employed his time while abroad, and how close and thorough had been his study of the history, laws, and manners of the various countries in which he had resided.

In July 1700, he was admitted a member of the Scottish bar: and the efforts of his father to provide a fitting mate for him form a quaint episode in the Autobiography. It may be noticed that the 'Daughter of ——' 'the P——t of the ——n,' to whom he refers in terms the reverse of complimentary, was doubtless Margaret, eldest daughter of Sir Hugh Dalrymple, of North Berwick, Baronet, President of the Court of Session at the time indicated. She was born in 1683, and was married to Sir John Shaw, of Greenock, Baronet, the contract being dated 1st March 1700. The bride finally chosen by Clerk was the Lady Margaret Stuart, eldest daughter of Alexander, third Earl of Galloway, whose bright handsome face, painted by William Aikman, the Baron's cousin, in his youth, fronts us in our Illustration No. VI. Her death so soon afterwards, on the birth of her first son, forms a pathetic page in her husband's Autobiography.

His marriage had introduced him to James, second Duke of Queensberry, his wife's cousin, who proved a warm friend, and was the main cause of Clerk's advancement in life. Through the influence of his brother-in-law, James, fifth Earl of Galloway, he was elected member of Parliament for the burgh of Whithorn, which he represented in the Scottish Parliament from 1702 till the Union, and in the first parliament of Great Britain. His account of the state of the various political parties of the time, and the personal glimpses that he affords of prominent individuals, will be read with interest. The 'Union' Duke of Queensberry figures as 'a very friendly affable man;' the Marquis of Tweeddale is a 'very good man, but not perfectly qualified for court intrigues;' Fletcher of Saltoun is 'a little untoward in his temper and much inclined to eloquence, however a very honest man, and meant well in everything he said and did, except in cases where his humure, passions or prejudices were suffered to get the better of his reason;' John, Duke of Argyll, the young High Commissioner 'behaved himself in a manner far above what cou'd be expected from one of his years.'

About this time Clerk gave utterance to his own sentiments, and also served his political party, by the production of two pamphlets,—one 'against diminishing the antient prerogatives of the crown,' the other an 'Essay upon the intended Limitations' proposed by Fletcher, of which the object 'was to take the patronage of office out of the hands of the Crown and exercise it in the Estates by ballot;'[1] but all my efforts to identify these tracts, in the British Museum, the Advocates', Signet, and Edinburgh University Libraries, in the very extensive collection of contemporary pamphlets at Penicuik House, and in other likely places, have failed.

A commission to inquire into the public accounts and national debt having been appointed in 1703, Clerk, through the influence of the Duke of Queensberry, was chosen a member. Here his thorough and painstaking way of work, of which we saw first indications in the elaborate foreign journals of the youth of twenty, came into play; and he was

[1] Hill Burton's *History*, vol. viii. p. 92 (1873).

the member of commission who was intrusted with drawing up the report which was submitted to parliament in the following year. It is to be noticed that the George Drummond, 'then about 18 years of age,' who 'wrote a good hand,' and acted as Clerk's amanuensis in this work (see marginal note at page 54), was afterwards Provost of Edinburgh, and worthily celebrated as the founder of the Royal Infirmary, and the wise and helpful patron of the University. The commission was continued by the parliament in 1704, and a second report was submitted in 1705.

Clerk was next nominated, on the recommendation of the Duke of Argyll, a member of the council appointed in 1705 to inquire into the trade and commerce of the Scottish nation; and having again proved his ability and 'thorough acquaintance with all the Finances of Scotland, and the whole management of the Lords of the Treasury, and Exchequer of this Country, from the Revolution in 1688 down to the year 1706,' he was 'tho' at this time very young for so great a trust'—indeed, barely thirty—nominated a commissioner for the Union. He was greatly disinclined to accept the appointment; for, careful, keen-sighted politician though he was, he had come to the conclusion that public feeling in Scotland was too determinedly hostile to the Union, and 'doubted not but, after a great deal of expense in attending a treaty in England, I should be obliged to return with the uneasy reflection of having either done nothing, or nothing to the purpose, as had been the case of former commissioners appointed for this end.' But evidently his value as a public servant was fully appreciated by those in power; the strongest pressure was applied to force his consent; Queensberry threatened to withdraw his patronage and friendship if he persisted in declining the proffered honour: so having said, in all sincerity, his *nolo episcopari*, Clerk at length accepted his nomination, and entered upon the weighty duties which it entailed. He was one of the four Scottish commissioners appointed to confer daily with a like number of the English commissioners; and he devoted himself especially to the financial aspects of the Treaty of Union, aspects which, as a glance at contemporary debates and the pamphlet literature on the subject amply proves, were felt by both nations to be of paramount importance. It was at this time that he published his two pamphlets—*A Letter to a Friend*, etc., and *An Essay upon the XV Article*, etc.

Of the negotiations for the Union, the Autobiography furnishes us with a full and well-considered account, which has the interest and the freshness of a record by one who was busily engaged in what he describes, and was thoroughly conversant with all its details; and in the touches, here and there, of more personal reference, we feel that it is an actor in this stirring scene of our national drama who is here taking us by the hand, and introducing us to his fellow-actors and their doings. The passages, in particular, which deal with his two interviews with Queen Anne, if they want the dignity of formal history, have intimate touches of homely and pathetic reality, that bring us close to the time and the scenes.

His opinions upon the Union, and his record of the negotiations that were preliminary to it, have already been incorporated in the pages of the historian; for several of his manuscripts dealing with the subject were placed at the disposal of the Rev. Dr. Thomas Somerville, author of *The History of Great Britain during the Reign of Queen Anne*, by the Baron's grandson, Sir John Clerk, the fifth baronet. In the preface to his *History*, Dr. Somerville refers to 'some excellent treatises' for explaining the scheme of the Union, and refuting the objections of its ignorant and factious opposers, written by Clerk, 'a member of the Scottish Parliament at the time of the Union' who 'devoted himself, with assiduous application, to the study of the momentous questions then in agitation,' and who 'to the accomplishments of a scholar and antiquary' added 'an accurate knowledge of the history and constitution of Scotland.' Doubtless these are the four published pamphlets referred to at folios 48 and 78 of the Autobiography. But the historian also expresses 'great obligations' for the use of 'valuable manuscripts.' 'Those which I inspected, as particularly suitable to my purpose, are [1] short journals of the proceedings of the Scottish Parliament while the Union was depending; [2] observations on [George] Lockhart's *Memoirs*; and [3] a testamentary memorial for the instruction of his own family, giving a concise and perspicuous account of the treaty; and, after the experience of more than thirty years, comparing its effects with the presages and expectations, both of its abettors and opposers, at the time of its formation. From these materials, fraught with private anecdotes, and marked descriptions of the conduct of parties, and the character and intrigues of their leaders, I am able to treat of Scottish affairs with greater precision and certainty than former historians, who, for want of better sources of information, have implicitly relied upon annals and memoirs, of which the authors are unknown.'

Again, at p. 286 of *My Own Life and Times*, Somerville mentions that he had access to the valuable manuscripts 'composed by' Baron Sir John Clerk, 'an influential member of the Scottish Parliament at the time of the Union, and much in the confidence of the Duke of Queensberry, his [her] Majesty's Commissioner.'

None of these manuscripts seem to be now at Penicuik House. Probably the items which I have numbered [1] and [3], are the 'Journal of the proceedings of the Scots and English Commissioners in the Treaty for an Union between the two Kingdoms of Scotland and England, holden at the Cockpit in London, A° 1706, holograph, 3 vols.,' and the 'Observations on the State of Scotland before the Union, and the advantages accruing to Scotland by the union of the two kingdoms, copied by his chaplain,' which figure as Nos. 26 and 69 in the Inventory of 1783, already referred to.

The second item, as we learn from a note at page 156 of Somerville's *History*, was 'a copy of Lockhart's *Memoirs*, with notes in Sir John's own hand, on the margin; upon the back of the title-page, the following words are written in the same hand:—" As these Memoirs are said to have been written by Mr. Lockhart in the heat of party rage, it is no extraordinary matter to find them erroneous in several particulars, which the following notes will demonstrate; yet many of the characters are just, in so far as the author was acquainted with the persons. These notes were revised by me in the year 1738, and again in 1747. I have carefully considered them, and do not only adhere to them, but positively assert, that every particular fact mentioned by me is exactly agreeable to truth; and to my knowledge, I have concealed nothing.—J. C." In a note on the margin of the second page of the preface, Sir John says: "These Memoirs were given out to be copied, and so came abroad; however, the persons abused took little notice of them, and the supposed author abjured them, on many occasions, so that I and others have liberty to animadvert on them, if we please." Thus qualified, the Memoirs become respectable documents of historical facts. By the perusal of this valuable MS., I have not only been enabled to correct many errors and misrepresentations contained in the text of the Memoirs, but have also derived important information with respect to collateral events and transactions, which enter into the Scottish history at the period of this work.' It is much to be regretted that this interesting annotated copy of Lockhart cannot now be found.

The financial skill which he had already so frequently displayed pointed out Clerk as a fitting person to be concerned in the management of the Equivalent of £398,085, 10s. paid by England in consideration of the increased taxation of Scotland and to settle the affairs of the African or 'Darien' Company. He was one of the commissioners appointed to review the calculations for the Equivalent, made by Professor David Gregory of Oxford and the celebrated William Paterson; and he took an important part in the work of the committee, and personally conveyed the £100,000 of retired Bank of England bills to London.

In the negotiations for the Union and the arrangements which succeeded it, Clerk had faithfully served his country and his party, and established his character as a capable and pains-taking public servant: and when the Scottish Court of Exchequer was founded, in conformity with the Nineteenth Article of the Treaty, he received his reward, by being appointed one of its five Barons. During the frequent absences of the Chief Baron he acted as president of the Court. The position was a dignified and remunerative one; and, as it necessitated attendance during only some three months of the year, it afforded ample leisure for the prosecution of the Baron's favourite studies. His appointment was followed by his marriage to Janet, third daughter of Sir James Inglis, first baronet of Cramond, a 'most religious, virtuous woman, and one who, in all respects, might suit my humure and circumstances to rub through the world in a sober and privat state of life.'

From this period the Baron ceases, for the most part, to be an actor in the political life of his time; but his Autobiography proves that he still watched contemporary history with a keenly observant eye, and was personally well acquainted with many of its most prominent figures both in England and Scotland. Lord Bolingbroke is 'a smart clever man, a good schollar, and a great Rake;' Harley is 'the late shuffling, impudent Treasurer;' Mar was 'not only my acquaintance, but my very particular friend;' Lord Lovat was 'a man of a bold, nimbling kind of sense, very vain of his clan, the Frazers, and ready to sacrifice everything to their interest'—hardly the verdict pronounced on him by history, which, however, amply confirms the statement that he 'was all his life a cunning, double man.'

Among the more interesting pages of the Autobiography are those which contain a detailed record of the Rebellion of 1715, and an estimate of the causes out of which it arose. Here the Baron was himself an actor, appearing in arms, along with the Duke of Argyll, before the citadel of Leith, when it was occupied by the Highlanders. He had intended to draw up a more elaborate account of the events of this period, for 'Scraps of a history of the Rebellion 1715, which I intended to have written,' is item No. 30 in the Inventory of 1783.

From the Rebellion we pass to the Mississippi Scheme, into which the writer enters very fully, with the freshness of a contemporary and personally interested authority. He was an 'Adventurer for 200 lbs. stg. of the capital stock, and lost thereby about 400 lbs. stg. However, I reckoned it no small happiness to my Family that I got so well off, for some of my particular friends and Acquaintances in Scotland were quite ruined by it.' He was 'particularly acquainted with Mr. Law,' 'a man full of projects, and of a very fertile clear head.'

Next follow accounts of the attempted invasion from Dunkirk in 1744, and of the Continental wars in which Britain was concerned; and we reach the Rebellion of 1745, which occupies some twenty very readable pages. On the approach of the rebels to Edinburgh, the Baron, then an old man of nearly seventy, retired, with his wife and eldest daughter, to England; but his second son, George, served in the royal army, and James, his eldest son, fought bravely at Falkirk. He returned in time to attend the Prince of Hess, at Holyrood; but, in his absence, the Highlanders, '16 or 20 at a time,' were quartered in Penicuik House, and he was mulcted of 6000 stones of hay and 76 boles of oats, to the value of about £200.

The public events with which the remaining pages of the

Autobiography deal are chiefly those connected with the military operations on the Continent and in America.

But the record which the Baron gives of his own personal pursuits is not less interesting than his remarks upon contemporary national history. Apart from his duties in the Court of Exchequer, his life was very equally balanced between the things of active practical endeavour, and the placid contemplative pursuit of the study of literature, antiquities, and art. He was fond of a country life, and of the employments and relaxations proper to a landed proprietor; a keen sportsman, devoted to riding, fond of angling, never missing 'the pouting' in due season, and enjoying his game of curling in the winter—as is witnessed by his 'stones,' still preserved at Penicuik House. But he derived quite as keen enjoyment from the closest application to all the practical details of the management of his various estates, and was never weary of adding to their acres by purchase, and of improving them by planting and by the development of their minerals. During by far the greater part of his life he resided in the country, riding in, daily, the six or seven miles to Edinburgh, from Penicuik or Mavisbank, when the Court of Exchequer was in session. He was firmly convinced that the first duty of an owner of land is to reside on his estate and exercise the closest supervision over his property and his dependants; and in his 'Scheme of Improvements' referred to in Additional Note R., he is most emphatic in his advice that the owners of Penicuik should always reside there—'We ought to be Strangers at Edinr. and Mavisbank and all other places. God grant that it may be so.' In his earlier years the estate of Penicuik was little more than a bare upland waste—the mansion-house stands more than seven hundred feet above the sea-level; but in 1703, at his father's instigation, he commenced to form plantations; no year passed, during the rest of his life, without some progress being made, in this direction, there and on his other properties; and it is mainly to his labours that the present richly wooded and exquisitely varied appearance of the Penicuik estate is due. His minute and detailed accounts of planting, building, constructing ponds, sinking coal-mines, and other improvements will possess considerable interest for those readers who have studied the material progress and condition of our country. In his various expeditions in Scotland and England he travelled always with open and observant eyes; whether examining the coal-pits at Whitehaven, or drinking 'the Goat Whey' in the Highlands, he was continually noting the capabilities of the country and the social and industrial condition of its inhabitants; and the knowledge which he acquired in this way and in the personal management of his own property, must have rendered him a valued member of the Board of Manufactures, of which he was appointed a commissioner in 1727.

But Sir John Clerk was no mere country laird, wholly immersed in material things; his nature was far too wide, his mind far too cultured, for any danger of this; his 'spirit' in no wise 'lacked all life behind, all stray thoughts, fancies fugitive, all loves except what trade'—and merely practical things—'can give.' There was a wide margin in his life for the quite unremunerative, yet truly satisfying, things of culture, art, and scholarship.

We have seen that he studied drawing in Leyden; and the numerous sketches still preserved, out of a far greater number that he executed while abroad, prove that he used his pencil with a facility and an accuracy rather uncommon in an amateur at the period. The Autobiography contains no indication that he continued the practice of graphic art in later life; but a few sketches preserved among the Clerk papers such as the designs for fountains at Penicuik and Dumcrieff, indicate that the pursuit was never wholly abandoned.

'Music,' he tells us, 'had always great charms with me,' and he continued to be a performer upon the harpsichord till nearly the age of fifty, when his slightly weakened eyesight, necessitating the use of spectacles, warned him to desist. His pen was never idle, as is amply witnessed by the immense number of still existing unpublished manuscripts in his handwriting, and of transcripts by amanuenses, dealing with the great variety of social, political, philosophical, and antiquarian subjects, of which the most important is his Latin history of Britain, frequently referred to in the Autobiography. And these are but the surviving portions of a vast mass of manuscript productions which he destroyed during his lifetime.

Towards poetry, 'both in Latine and English,' he 'had a great inclination,' 'but I curbed as much as I cou'd these salies of fancy, as what I thought inconsistent with the gravity of a judge, and a man of business.' That he restrained his impulses in this direction will hardly be regretted by any one who has perused his manuscript 'poem in Milton's way,' 'The Country Seat.' A somewhat higher level is reached in the lines 'Harmonious pipe, how I envye the bliss,' which he is said to have enclosed in a flute which he sent to Susanna, daughter of Sir Archibald Kennedy, of Culzean, afterwards third wife of Alexander, Earl of Eglintoune (see Anderson's *Scottish Nation*, vol. i. p. 653), and in the lines with which he continued the initial verse of the old song:—

> 'O merry may the maid be
> That marries the miller,'

which will be found in Johnson's *Musical Museum*, vol. ii. p. 129. Among the pieces preserved in manuscript at Penicuik House are 'A Song on Friendship,' 'An Epick Madrigal on Squire Robert's Hunting Expedition, into the North of England, in July 1749,' and a political 'Ballad to the Tune of Faction no More;' and his muse did not disdain the humblest of subjects and occasions, for among the Baron's papers is a curious 'Prologue to Punch's Farce—For the Bairns at Pennycuik, 1731.'

But it was in the study of the classics that he found his constant and never-failing delight. At thirty-two he tells us that 'all my leisure houres were spent in books.' At thirty-eight we find him carefully reading over 'all the Roman Classicks,' and making 'very large excerps, from them all, particularly from Livy and Salust, whom I was chiefly to imitat in my History of Great Britain in Latin.' At seventy-two he records that 'I may truly say that I was never so happy as when learning something out of a book;' he 'read the Greek and Roman Classicks with great diligence, and still discovered new beuties in them;' and we have a pleasing glimpse of the good old man, 'this day being the 19th day of jan., 1748,' 'reading over Horace *De Arte Poetica*, which I am persuaded I have read 50 times before.' The practical and masterful human sense of the great Latin authors was excellently congenial to the Baron's own temperament, and aided in knitting into double strength his stout Scottish nature. When, in 1730, he intrusts his sons Patrick and Henry to the Haddington schoolmaster, he has 'no particular thing to recommend save one, on which all parents ought to joyn with me, that is, that my boys be brought up in the old Greek and Roman way. . . . This sort of Education fitted all their youth to the management of their sacred and civil concerns.' As old age approaches, and he feels the first touches of its frailties, he cheers himself and takes courage as he quotes the '*Obsta*' of Seneca; and the wisdom of pagan philosophers mingles with the counsels of Christianity, as he braces himself to meet the last ills and trials of mortal life.

Sitting so reverently as he did at the feet of the ancients, so devoted a student of their written words, it was natural that he should prize and study such tangible and concrete relics of the past as have been preserved to us from classic times: and his archæological tastes must have been greatly fostered by his residence as a youth in Italy, whose antiquities he describes at great length in his MS. volumes of Travels, and by the instruction of men like Gronovius of Leyden, and Chaprigni of Rome. He was fortunate too, in the fact that both his Midlothian and his Dumfriesshire properties were situated in districts rich in camps and other memorials of the Roman occupation. His excavations at Cramond and various localities near Penicuik, as well as at Middlebie, resulted in the discovery of many interesting remains of antiquity, the majority of which are still in Penicuik House, while some, through the generosity of one of his successors, have gone to enrich the Scottish National Museum of Antiquities. At folios 139-141 of the Autobiography will be found an account, only too brief, of his expedition in 1724, to the Roman Wall, in company with the celebrated Alexander Gordon, author of the *Itinerarium Septentrionale*, of whom he was a most helpful and appreciative patron: and he corresponded upon antiquarian subjects with the Earl of Pembroke, Roger Gale, William Gilpin, Dr. Stukeley, and other leading English virtuosos of the time, through whose influence he was elected a member of the Society of Antiquaries, and of the Royal Society. He was also a member of the Gentlemen's Society of Spalding; and of the Peterborough Society, to which he made a communication on 1st July 1742, regarding 'the unseasonable colds of the late years,' which he conjectures 'to be owing to the great spots on the surface of the sun, many of which are much larger than the whole globe of our earth, which must needs take off both from its light and heat.'[1]

His writings upon antiquities have still a value, though the wider and sounder knowledge on such subjects that is now

[1] Nichols' *Literary Anecdotes*, vol. vi. p. 139.

possible, may lead us to question some of his conclusions, to feel that he is far from infallible in his judgments. Indeed, according to Lockhart,[1] the immortal episode of 'the Prætorium,' in *The Antiquary*, is little more than the simple record of an incident at Dumcrieff in which the Baron played an important part, as related to the novelist by John Clerk of Eldin, the son of Sir John, and father of Scott's close friend, William Clerk; and doubtless 'many traits' of the Baron were 'embroidered on the character of George Constable in the composition of Jonathan Oldbuck.' But, at least, the Baron was a sincere and reverent lover of antiquity, a true antiquary who did much to further the pursuit in our country; and those whose sympathies are rather with things Gothic than with things classic will be grateful to him as the preserver—one is glad to say, not the *restorer*—of Roslin Chapel.[2]

The most adequate idea of the widely varied interests that occupied the Baron may be gathered from his extensive correspondence with Gale—to which I have so frequently referred in footnotes—printed in Nichols' *Bibliotheca Topographica*, (*Reliquiæ Galeanæ*), No. II. Parts ii. and iii. Here we find him discoursing on antiquities of all kinds, on the flight of wild fowls, on comets and eclipses, on coal mines, on Scottish mosses and the 'subterranean Oakes' which they contain, on the Highlanders and their language. Interesting letters, dated 22nd June and 5th August 1743, record the destruction of 'Arthur's Oon,' 'demolished lately here by Sir Michael Bruce of Stonehouse, near Falkirk,' and recommend that 'the Anti-

---

[1] Lockhart seems to have fallen into considerable confusion between the Baron, Sir John, and his son, John Clerk of Eldin.—See *Life of Scott*, pp. 41 and 332 (ed. of 1845), the latter indexed as 'Clerk, Sir John, Antiquarian, anecdote of,' but only Clerk of Eldin's name being mentioned in the text. See also Wilson's *Reminiscences of Old Edinburgh*, vol. ii. chap. xviii., which contains an interesting sketch of the Baron in his aspects as an antiquarian.

[2] See Additional Note O.

quarian Society in London should order a fine print to be made of,' 'for thus a Goth's memory may be preserved as well as the figure of that ancient fabric.' 'We all curse him [Bruce] with bell, book, and candle; but there is no remedy except what we have from some accurate descriptions of it given by Dr. Stuckely and others.' How keen was the Baron's interest in the structure and grief for its demolition is evinced in a copy of an unpublished letter to Gordon, dated 12th April 1754, preserved among the Clerk papers, in which he avers, 'I wish I could have redeemed it at the expence of 1000 guineas.' A restoration of 'Arthur's Oon' was erected by Sir James, his son and successor, near Penicuik House.

So far as I have discovered, the above-mentioned correspondence with Gale comprises all the Baron's letters that have been published; with the exceptions of a letter to Maurice Johnston, dated 11th January 1741-2, containing 'observations on burning of the dead, the British language, obelisks, circular stones, etc.,' published in the *Bibliotheca Topographica*, No. II. Part ii. p. 71; of two long letters on 'the Sepulchres and Funeral Rites of the Ancients in Britain,' addressed to Gale—the first of which was read before the Society of Antiquaries—printed in the appendix to Gordon's *Itinerarium*; of a brief letter to Gale, dated 6th November 1731, on the effect of thunder on trees, and on the discovery of the horn of a deer in the heart of an oak, printed in the *Philosophical Transactions*, vol. xli.; and of three short undated notes—published in the *New Scots Magazine*, November 1829—to James Anderson, editor of the *Diplomata Scotiæ*, etc., furnishing him with introductions to the Chief Baron and to Baron Scrope, and expressing the fear that he should be obliged to decline purchasing a collection of books. 'I have a great family to provide for; and so I fancy I have the same reason to forbear setting up a great library that you have for disposing of one.'

The other printed writings of Baron Clerk are:—

Two pamphlets, published in 1703, and referred to at folio 48 of the Autobiography as 'against diminishing the antient prerogatives of the Crown,' and an 'essay upon the intended Limitations.' As already stated, I have been unable to discover these pamphlets, or to verify their titles.

A Letter to a Friend giving an Account of how the Treaty of Union has been received here, and wherein are contained some remarks upon what has been written by Mr. H. and Mr. R., Edinburgh, printed in the year MDCCVI, 4to, referred to at folio 78 of the Autobiography as a pamphlet, 'under the Title of Some considerations on the Articles of the Union.' It has been usually attributed, in error, to De Foe—see Additional Note G,—Pamphlets attributed to Sir John Clerk.

An Essay upon the XV *Article of the Treaty of Union, wherein the Difficulties that arise upon the Equivalents are fully Cleared and Explained. Printed in the year* MDCCVI, 4to. See Autobiography, folio 78, and note [2] there.

Historical View of the Forms and Powers of the Court of Exchequer in Scotland, 4to. This was written by Clerk and Baron Scrope in 1726, but was not printed till 1820, when it was issued for private circulation by the Barons of Exchequer, under the editorship of Sir Henry Jardine, W.S., the King's Remembrancer. This work is not referred to in the Autobiography.

Dissertatio de Stylis Veterum et Diversis Chartarum Generibus, 4to, pamphlet. This, which contains an engraving of the writing implements of the ancients, bears no date, place of publication, or author's name, but we learn from the *Bibliotheca Topographica*, No. II. Part iii. p. 298, that it was printed in 1731. An abridgment of it, in English, was read before the Royal Society by Roger Gale on 4th March of that year, and printed in the *Philosophical Transactions*, vol. xxxvii. The whole work, in Latin, with the plate re-engraved, was included in the third volume of the Supplements to the *Thesauri* of Grævius and Gronovius, edited by Joannes Polenus, Venice, 1737 fol. This tract is not referred to in the Autobiography.

An Account of the Observations of the late Solar Eclipse made at Edinburgh, on Feb. 18th, 1736-7, by the Honorable Sir John Clerk, Bart., one of the Barons of his Majesty's Exchequer there, and F.R.S., communicated by Roger Gale, Esq., F.S.A., and published in the *Philosophical Transactions*, No. 447, January to May 1738.

Dissertatio de Monumentis quibusdam Romanis in Boreali Magnæ Britanniæ parte detectis anno MDCCXXI, Edinburgh 1750, 4to, with an engraved frontispiece. Written in 1743. See Autobiography, marginal and footnotes to folios 155-56, and folio 193. An account, in English, by the Baron, of the statue of Brigantia and two altars found at Middlebie, had been published by Gordon in the 'Additions and Corrections' to his *Itinerarium*, in 1732.

It is to be observed that the pamphlet *Money and Trade considered* . . . attributed to Clerk in the Catalogue of the Advocates' Library, and in the *Dictionary of National Biography*, was written by John Law. See Additional Note G.

The Autobiography is continued till the end of 1754, the year preceding that of the Baron's death. In its later pages we see its writer suffering under the pressure of domestic calamities and of the increasing infirmities of old age; but striving, not without success, to bear all his ills with calmness, and to possess his soul in patience. In 1742 his son, Patrick, died at the siege of Carthagena. His loss was deeply felt by his father, and it poignantly recalled the death of his eldest son—whom his half-brother especially resembled—which had been the great grief of the Baron in middle life, as the death of that son's mother, Lady Margaret, had been the chief sorrow of his earlier years. The loss of Patrick was followed by that of his twin-brother, Henry, who died in the East Indies, of a lingering disorder, in 1745. The old man himself was attacked by severe fits of sickness; 'they were, I thank God, but very short, but the pins of my Earthly Tabernacle were sadly loused and shattered with them. . . . I did the best I cou'd to conceal these Infirmities from my friends, and especially from strangers, who, I saw, were gaping for my office to some of their Friends. I expect nothing but bad days and bad health, yet I must keep up my mind and do the best I can to appear content; but how can this be when I feel my body a kind of burden to me, and the pleasures I once had quite gone? . . . I strive to amuse myself in different ways, but the efforts I use —for instance, to go a-fishing or shooting—are in a manner useless, so that I am actually dropping into the grave; but happy I am in this, that I resign my life to God who gave it, and only wait patiently till my change come;' and he congratulates himself that he is not like some men of his age that he had known, who 'are angry at all the world.' In 1752 he tells us, 'I began to feel a great languor and a kind of *satietas vitæ*, so that I may say, as Cæsar did, *emori nolle sed de vita nihil curo*;' but in 1753, at the age of seventy-eight, he records: 'I continue to have a great relish for books, tho' I seem to forget as fast as I read. Where then can I have my best refuge but in God himself, to whom I commit all my concerns?' Finally, the Autobiography closes with a curious dietetic note, which has in it a touch of the grotesque that sometimes obtrudes itself so unexpectedly, so incongruously, into the midst of the very gravest things of our poor human life.

No particulars of the Baron during the following year have been preserved, till we come to the final entry in the *Scots Magazine* for 1755: 'Oct[r] 4. At his seat of Pennycuik, Sir John Clerk of Pennycuik, one of the Barons of the Exchequer. He had been Baron since the union in 1707. He is succeeded in estate, and the title of Baronet, by his eldest son, James.'

As will be obvious from even such a slight and imperfect

sketch of its contents as I have been able to give above, the Autobiography contains much of value in connection with the history and condition of Scotland, and the manners and customs of its inhabitants during the first half of the eighteenth century. But the piece of antiquity which it presents most clearly to our view is the Baron himself; it is his picture that is painted in fullest details in the following pages. The Autobiography has all the merit and the interest of a frank and an intimate self-disclosure. It was intended to be read only by his family and a restricted circle of friends; but Sir George Clerk, in consideration of the historical value that increasing years have given to the manuscript, has yielded to the request that he should permit its publication for the use of the members of the Scottish History Society; a Society with whose aims—had he lived to see its establishment—the good antiquarian Baron would certainly have been in most substantial sympathy. It is to be borne in mind that the manuscript was written without the precision and care for style which would certainly have been bestowed had publication been intended; and I cannot doubt that those who peruse it will come—as I have done—to entertain very friendly and kindly feelings for its writer, this stout old Scottish Baronet and Judge.

I have to express my thanks for much assistance received while editing the manuscript, especially from Mr. T. Graves Law and Mr. W. G. Scott-Moncrieff. The notes which these gentlemen have supplied are indicated by their initials. I am grateful to the Dowager Lady Clerk for kindly affording every facility for search among the Baron's unclassified manuscripts preserved at Penicuik House, and to Mr. Thomas Ross for executing a drawing of Mavisbank House specially for this volume. Among the other helpers to whom my thanks are due, for information and aid of various kinds, I may mention the Earl of Southesk, Mr. G. L. Ryder, C.B., the Rev. Dr. W. H.

Goold, the Rev. Father Oswald Hunter Blair, Dr. Richard Garnett, Dr. Thomas Dickson, Dr. A. Rowand, Mr. A. Wedderburn Maxwell, Mr. J. T. Clark, Professor Patrick Geddes, Mr. Archibald Steuart, Mr. J. R. Menzies, Messrs. J. and F. Anderson, Messrs. Winchester and Ferguson, Mr. Victor A. Noël Paton, and Mr. C. Birnie.

J. M. G.

Scottish National Portrait Gallery,
7th November 1892.

THE HISTORY OF MY LIFE

EXTRACTED FROM A JOURNAL I WAS ALWAYS IN USE TO KEEP, AND INTERSPERSED WITH SHORT ACCOUNTS OF THE MOST REMARKABLE PUBLICK AFFAIRES THAT HAPNED IN MY TIME, ESPECIALLY SUCH AS I HAD SOME IMMEDIATE CONCERN IN.

JOHN CLERK.

This Manuscript is never to be lent out, but to remain with my Heirs and Successors, for even things in it which are really trifles, may be of great use to some of my posterity.

THE BIRTHS OF MY CHILDREN BY MY WIFE JENNET INGLIS.

JAMES CLERK, born December 2th, 1709.
HENRY CLERK, born November 27, 1710.
ANNE CLERK, born June 4th, 1712.
BETTY CLERK was born August 10th 1713.
GEORGE CLERK was born October 31st 1715.
JEAN CLERK was born February 5th 1717.
PATRICK and HENRY CLERKS was (*sic*) born October 5th 1718.
MARY CLERK was born August 28th 1720.
WILLIAM CLERK was born March 19th 1722.
JOANNA CLERK was born March 10th 1724.
BABIE CLERK was born October 17th 1725.
JENNET was born 10 Agust 1727.
JOHN was born 10 Decembr 1728.
MATHEW, born 15 March 1732.
ADAM, born May 1737.[1]

N.B.—Having consulted some of the Antiquaries of Wales, for the derivation of the word Penicuik I had an answer on the 5 of March 1745 to this effect:—That ye word Penicuik was an old British name consisting of 3 words, *pen y quick*, which signified Head of a Grove or Wood.

This I take to be the true derivation, for, in some of the Antient writs and charters, the word is written Penicuik.

Some of our Scots Highland Antiquares thought it signified *Mons Cuculi*, for that *cuick* was the Irish name for Cuculus, but then they knew not what to make of *Pen*, and therefore they derived it from *Ben*, a hill, as Ben Lomont; but the old British Etymology is more proper and certain, for *Pen* signifies a Head; besides, the village of Penicuik realy stands at the head of a Grove or Wood. So that the true English of the word *Penycuik* is Woodhead.[2]

---

[1] Douglas mentions only seven sons and six daughters, omitting Mary and William, both of whom died young, and giving only one Henry.

[2] 'The name Penicuik signifies, in the British tongue, Hill of the Gowk or Cuckoo, a circumstance which suggested to a versifier in the *Scots Magazine* the subject of a clever poetical effusion styled "The Gowk and the Mavis."'—Chambers's *Peeblesshire*, p. 483, *note*.

MEMOIRS OF MY LIFE, extracted from Journals I kept since I was 26 years of Age. JOHN CLERK.

Nota.—This book may be read by all my friends in the House of Pennicuik, but is *never to be lent or carried out of the House.*

As these Memoirs can be of no other use but to satisfy the curiosity of my Relations and dependants I shall write them with the same negligence of style that so many trifeling occurrences may deserve, and, with a view to all this, I absolutely prohibite and discharge any of my Posterity from lending them[1] or dispersing them abroad. They are to remain in the House of Pennicuik, or such other place as they can best be keept. *fol.* 1.

Having nothing to boast of as to the Antiquity of my Family,[2] which, by-the-bye, I have always laught at in others, I shall trace my mean Progenitors no farther back than about

---

[1] So marked in the MS.

[2] Douglas traces the Clerks of Penicuik as most probably descended from 'John Clerk, one of the hostages for King David's ransom in 1357 . . . a merchant, and the most considerable man of that town (Montrose). And it appears by their Council books that the Clerks were the chief magistrates of that burgh for some centuries thereafter; of whom are descended the immediate ancestor of his family, viz. :—I. William Clerk, merchant, burgess of Montrose, who lived in the reigns of Queen Mary and King James VI., and, dying about the year 1620, left issue, a son,—II. John Clerk, who was baptised by the Bishop of Caithness at Fettercairn, 22d December 1611.' The last statement is made on the authority of the *Records of the Kirk-Session*, but these are now lost. 'He was bred a merchant, and was a man of parts and spirit.' The Bishop of Caithness at this time was Alexander Forbes, M.A., appointed rector of Fettercairn 1588, 'son of John Forbes of Ardmurdo, descended from Forbes of Brux, obtained his degree at the University of St. Andrews in 1585, promoted to the bishoprick of Caithness in 1606, but held this charge in conjunction and afterwards with the bishoprick of Aberdeen, having been a member of eight out of the ten Assemblies, from 24th April 1593 to 10th November 1602. He died at Leith, 14th December 1617, aged about 53, in 29th min.'—Scott's *Fasti.*

the 1568. At that time my Grandfather's Grandfather, John Clerk, was possessed of the lands of Kilehuntley, a Feu of the Duke of Gordon in Badenoch. He hapned to take part with Queen Mary of Scotland against his superior, and on that account was obblidged to fly that country and take shelter in Aberdeenshire[1] in a little Town called Fettercairn. Here he lived with his Family many years; how he traded I never cou'd learn, but he lived creditably, and was sufficiently able to breed up his son William, a Merchant in Montrose, and to provide him with a good stock.

See ... folio Edition, printed at Edin., ... page 337 ... in which I hav adjected this circumstance.

This William continued a Merchant in that Town so long as he lived, and bred up his son John Clerk,[2] my Grandfather, in the same occupation. | He gave him afterwards a stock and sent him to Paris, where he continued many years, and gained, for those days, a considerable fortune, for he return'd to Scotland in the year 1646 possessed with at least ten thousand lib. ster.

fol. 2.

When he came first home he had no other intention than to return to France[3] after he had established a good correspondence with the merchants of his own Country, but having married my Grandmother, Mary Gray,[4] he by Little and Little found his mind alienated from France, and so resolved to settle here, give over all Trade, and become a Country Gentleman.

The lady I mentioned was Daughter of Sir William Gray,[5] a

---

[1] Fettercairn is situated in *Kincardineshire.*

[2] See Illustration No. II., from a miniature in the possession of Sir George Clerk, dated 1644, painted in oils on a small oval slab of blood-stone. A life-sized copy, by Aikman and another portrait of John Clerk, a full length, stated to be the work of De Wit, are also in the possession of Sir George.

[3] '*Nota.*—My grandfather, John Clerk, upon some disgust in this country, had an intention to have returned again to France, and had actually imbarqued his wife and children for that purpose, but being detain'd by contrary winds in the Road of Leith for some days, he changed his resolution and returned to Edinb^{r}, and afterwards bought the lands of Penicuik in 1654, so near was the family of being French.'—*Isolated note in the Baron's handwriting in the possession of the family.*

[4] See Illustration No. III., from a miniature in the possession of Sir George Clerk, who has also a life-sized copy of it by Miss Ann Forbes.

[5] According to Crawford, Sir William Gray of Pittendrum was son of Thomas Gray of Brighouse. He acquired great wealth as a merchant, and extended the foreign trade of the country. For corresponding with Montrose he was fined 100,000 merks by the Parliament of St. Andrews, and was imprisoned in the Castle and Tolbooth of Edinburgh till the amount was reduced to 35,000 merks,

11

JOHN CLERK

Grandfather of Baron Sir John Clerk

III

MARY GRAY

Grandmother of Baron Sir John Clerk

Cousin of the Lord Gray, and whose son, the Master of Gray,[1] married the Heiress of the family of Gray, from whom the present Lords of Gray are descended.

In 1654 my said Grandfather[2] bought the Baronie of Pennicuik. It had formerly belonged to many Heretors, but the Lairds of Pennicuik possessed the greatest part of it. This was a pretty old famely, but at that time became extinct. They held the Baronie of Pennicuik, or at least the lands they possessed in it, of the Croun paying *in redendo* of 3 blasts of a Horn which continues to this day.[3] There were 3 or 4 more

---

which he paid. A sum of £10,000 stg. was also extorted from him as a loan, and never repaid. He married Egidia, sister of Sir John Smith of Grothill and King's Cramond, Provost of Edinburgh, by whom he had six sons and twelve daughters.

[1] William Gray, Master of Gray, eldest son of the above mentioned Sir William, received from his father 232,000 merks on his marriage to Anne, Mistress of Gray, eldest daughter of Andrew, eighth Lord Gray. He commanded a regiment in the army of Charles II. at the battle of Worcester, and was killed in a duel, near London, by the Earl of Southesk, in August 1660, in the lifetime of his father.—Douglas's *Peerage*.

[2] See Additional Note A, Barony of Penicuik.

[3] The hunting-horns in the arms of the family of Pennicuik of that Ilk have doubtless reference to this tenure; and the crest and one of the two mottoes of the Clerks of Penicuik seem to have been adopted for the same reason. In 1672-76, 'John Clerk of Pennicook' matriculated his arms in the Lyon Register as 'Or, a fess chickie azur and argent betwixt two crescents in chief gules and a Boar's head couped in Base sable: above the shield ane helmet befitting his degree, mantled gules doubled argent Next is placed for his crest issuing out of the Torse a demi-man winding a horn proper The motto on an Escroll, Amat victoria curam.' In this Register Sir George Clerk matriculated, in 1807, the same arms, with the same motto, 'on a compartment below the shield,' but with the addition 'above the crest' of a second motto, 'Free for a Blast,' and of the supporters that are still used,—'On the dexter side a Naked Savage wreathed about the middle with oak leaves holding in his exterior hand a Bow, with a Quiver full of arrows slung over his shoulder and the skin of a wild beast hanging behind his back, all proper; on the sinister side a Druid priest with a flowing beard proper vested and hooded argent holding in his exterior hand a branch of Oak accorned proper.' The second motto, 'Free for a Blast,' was, however, used by the family long before this date. It is the only motto assigned to the Clerks of Penicuik in Douglas's *Baronage*; and it appears alone on the fine *Ex Libris* plate of the family which we print on the final page of this volume (where it may be noticed that the fess is given as 'argent and azure,' instead of 'azure and argent'): and in two ovals of painted glass, preserved in Penicuik House, displaying the Clerk arms, and dated 1675, the motto 'Amat victoria curam,' on a scroll above the crest, has been carefully removed with acid, and the motto 'Free for a Blast' substituted.

...in the Forrest of Duntreath[1] between Edin. and Bredburns, near ... stone still remaining called the ... Stone.

fol. 3.

gentlemen who possessed the rest of the Baronie, as a son of the House of Roslin in Wester and Easter Ravensneuck,[2] a Laird in the Halls,[3] one at Bruntstane[4] and one at Cairnhill.[5] These lands became vested in the persone of a Countess of Eglintoun from whom they were bought. |

There were several Houses in the Baronie, but my Grandfather made choise of the House of Newbiging,[6] which he repaired and made some additions to it about the year 1666, so that at that time, being dressed up with two Battlements covered with lead, it became the best house of the shire of Edin., a great many others were afterwards built which excelled it, but here my Grandfather, my Father, and my self have lived for the most part these many years.

But to return to my Grandmother, Mary Gray. I have been credibly informed that she was a persone of great Vertue and Piety, but died about the Age of 36.

---

[1] 'In the deed, dated 20th February 1591, confirming the succession of Andrew Penycukis to his father, Sir John, the *reddendo* is described as "Six blasts of a flowing horn on the common moor of Edinburgh, of old called the forest of Drumselch, at the king's hunt on the said moor, in name of blench." In every other charter which I have read the number of blasts is mentioned as three. It is not unlikely that a clerical error may be an explanation of this discrepancy.'—Wilson's *Annals of Penicuik*, p. 140. The Buckstone, upon which the proprietor of the barony of Penicuik is bound by his tenure to sit and wind three blasts of a horn when the king shall come to hunt on the Boroughmuir, is on the road between Edinburgh and Biggar, near the entrance to Mortonhall. The tenure is referred to by Sir Walter Scott in 'The Gray Brother'—

'That fair dome, where suit is paid
By blast of bugle free.'

[2] 'This summer I bought from Mr. Sinclare of Roslin the superiority of the lands of Carnhill, Easter and Wester Ravensnuck, all which are parts of the Barony of Pennicuik.' See present MS., folio 154.

[3] Halhous (Halls) is included in the Sasine in favour of the Countess of Eglintoun, 4th September 1647.

[4] The lands of Brunstane were in 1373 granted by Sir David de Penicok to his cousin, William de Creichtoune. They are included in the Sasine in favour of the Countess of Eglintoun, 1st September 1646.

[5] See note above, No. 2. The lands of Cairnhill are specified among those which Dame Jean Ross, Lady Innes, and her niece, Margaret Hepburn, received as heirs-portioners of the Countess of Eglintoun.

[6] See Illustration No. IV., from a drawing by John Clerk of Eldin. Demolished when the present mansion of Penicuik House was erected in 1761, upon a closely adjoining site. Sir John gives a curious account of the estate and old house of Penicuik in a letter to Boerhaave. See Additional Note B.

IV

THE OLD HOUSE OF PENICUIK

She bore my Grandfather at death 16 [1] children, and all of them were very well provided for. I have heard it said that the youngest of them had at least 1200 lib. ster.

My Grandfather lived till his age of 63, and was an excellent occonomist, tho he keept always a very hospitable house.

He was particularly exact in business, and if he had not given over his Trade too soon he might have been immensely rich, for by many of his books which are still in the charter house of Pennicuik [2] he appears to have been a man of great sense and great application to business.[3]

He was a strong little man about 5 foot 5 inches, but in his elder years was vastly troubled with the Gravel, and died of a kind of Palsey.

My Father, John Clerk, was married to my Mother, Elizabeth Hendersone, in the year 1674. She was the only daughter of Mr. Henry Hendersone of Elvingstone, in East Lothian, a Doctor of Physick. | Her Mother was Elizabeth *fol. 4.*
Drummond,[4] Daughter of Mr. William Drummond of Hawthornden,[5] the Historian and Poet, a man of an excellent Genius for the times he lived in. The Doctor's Father was one Mr. Thomas Hendersone, a merchant in Edin., and a brother of the Hendersons of Fordel in Fife.[6]

---

[1] Douglas gives only five sons and five daughters.

[2] Many of these, and many MSS. of the first Baronet, are still in the possession of Sir George Clerk.

[3] 'He also acquired the lands of Wrightshouses, near Edinburgh, upon which he got a charter under the great seal from King Charles II. (chart. in pub. archiv.), *Johanni Clerk de Pennicuik, etc. etc.*, dated 9th March 1664.' These lands passed to his second son, James, who married a French lady, Mary Ricard. —Douglas's *Baronage*. From this charter it appears that the lands of Wrightshouses were granted to John Clerk of Penicuik, with reversion to William Napier on payment of a sum of £10,000 Scots. See Additional Note C, Wrightshouses.

[4] 'Of Elizabeth, the only surviving daughter of Drummond the poet, all that is known is that she married a Dr. Henderson, a physician in Edinburgh, and was dead long before 1711.'—Masson's *Drummond* (London, 1873), p. 459.

[5] In the City of Edinburgh Register, the name of 'William Drummond of Hawthorndane,' the poet's son, appears, under date 2d March 1675, as one of the witnesses to the baptism of Elizabeth, the Baron's elder sister. He survived till 1713, dying at the age of seventy-eight.

[6] There is no account in Douglas's *Baronage* of any Thomas Henderson, a brother of a laird of Fordel.

My Grandfather the Doctor was a very phylosophical man, but a man of good learning and very great piety, for he used always to pray to his patients as well as prescribe Medicines for them. I have seen many Translations of the Psalms by him in Latine verse, and some are still by me.

After his death the lands of Elvingstone fell to me, but lying at a distance from the place I lived in, I sold them about the year 1710.[1]

with the price I bought the Lands of Cammo.

My Mother was a persone of singular vertue and religion, but died in the 25 year of her age, after she had born to my Father 7 children.

With regard to my Father I need say little, for as he was a man of great knowledge and application, he has left a great many journals and writings under his hand which will, I hope, bear testimony to the regard he always had for religion, vertue, and Honesty.

... reasone was when my Grandfather was a Merchant in Paris he ... that a French or foreign Education hurtfull to ... in the tending to corrupt their morals ...

The most remarkable steps of his life were these: having been detained at home by his Father, he did not travel till after he was married, and after he had two sons and a daughter.

About that time, in the year 1679,[2] he was made a Knight-Baronet by King Charles the 2nd.

After that, and particularly after the Revolution in 1688, he was a member of the Parliament of Scotland for the shire of Edin.|

fol. 5.

ruine their Estates.

N.B. the Earl of Lawderdale was Colonel.

He served the shire very often as a justice of peace and Liutenant-Colonel of their Militia Regiment, but never solicited for any publick office.

He managed his affaires with great Frugality, and about the year 1694 he bought the Baronie of Laswade,[3] and some years afterwards the Lands of Utershill, Loanstone, and Pomathorn.

---

[1] In the parish of Gladsmuir. From a copy of the deed of sale, still in the possession of the family, it appears that this estate was purchased by William Law, first Professor of Moral Philosophy in the University of Edinburgh. He figures in the City Records as Mr. Law of Elvingston, and died in 1729.

[2] 'By King Charles II. created a baronet by his royal patent to him,—*et hæredibus masculise corpore suo*, dated 24th March 1679.—Douglas's *Baronage*, p. 422.

[3] 'Anno 1700, acquired the lands and barony of Leswade, in the shire of Edinburgh.'—Douglas's *Baronage*. See Additional Note D, on the Court Book of the Baronies of Lasswade and Loanhead.

He was one of the strongest men in his time, but not tall in stature, being scarce 5 foot 6 inches. He was at times much afflicted with the Gout and the Gravel, but after his age of 60 he got pretty free of both these distempers, by giving over the use of all other Liquids but milk and water. **he was finely made, had proportionable ... and was in his ... a Hercules ... shoulders ... muscles**

He was a pretty good schollar, and exceedingly knowing in Divinity.

Tho he had no great humoure of talking, yet I never knew any body that cou'd talk with greater readiness and propriety.

As he had a very great turn for business, no body wou'd have made a better Lawer than he, if he had been bred to it.

After the death of my mother, which he lamented for many years after, he continued a Widower near to 9 or 10 years, and that he might bring no extraordinary burdens on his family, he married Mrs. Christian Kilpatrick, daughter of Mr. James Kilpatrick,[1] a minister, and of a Gentleman's family. This Lady had several children to my father, and behaved her self on all occasions exceedingly well, and with great affection to me and the rest of my brothers and sisters.

They lived constantly in Pennicuik house till | my Father's *fol.* 6. death, which hapned in the 73 year of his age, 1722. He had what he always wisht for an *εὐθανασία*, for he had a very quiet and easy death. It came upon him by degrees, and tho in appearance he was pretty well, but a little weak the day before

[1] 'James Kilpatrick, recommended to the Session of Carrington or Primrose, in the Presbytery of Dalkeith, by Geo. Lord Ramsay, 1st Jan. 1660, "as a domestic in his own house," was called 15th following, and ord. 28th June thereafter. Deprived by the Act of Parl. 11th June, and of Priv. Council 1st Oct. 1662. . . . At the Provincial Meeting, 2nd Nov. 1687, Mr. Dav. Williamson was appointed to send the letter of the General Meetings for his (Kilpatrick's) return from Ireland; he returned accordingly, on the invitation of the parishioners, in June, and brought his family in Nov. following; was allowed to preach and exercise the other parts of the ministry, by the Committee of Estates, 10th May 1689, without prejudice to the patron's right of patronage; was restored by the Act of Parliament 25th April 1690, was a member of the Assemblies 1690, 1692, and died 4th July 1696, in 37th min., having mortified j^{c} merks to the poor of the par. His funeral sermon was preached on the 5th of said month by his nephew, Mr. Andrew Rogers, min. of Galston, from Matt. xvi. 24. Mr. K. marr. 22d Dec. 1691, Helen Kerr, relict of Mr. Geo. Johnstoun, min. of Newbattle, and had a daugh., Christian, who marr. Sir John Clerk of Penicuik, Bart.'—Scott's *Fasti.*

he died, yet in the night time he sleapt away without the least groan or complaint, tho his Lady and some of my sisters were in the room with him.[1]

The children who survived him were 2 sons and 3 daughters by my mother, and 5 sons and 4 daughters by my mother-in-law, in all 14.[2]

I come now to write the chief occurrences of my own Life.

I was born the 8 of feb. 1676,[3] and have reasone to be thankful to God that tho I be not descended of noble parents or from an Antient Family, yet I am the son of those who bore deservedly a very great name for Religion, Vertue, Honour, and Honesty. I have been at least willing to imitat them in the whole course of my Life, and I hope by the blessing of Heaven these good inclinations will be propagated down to my posterity.

I was put to the school of Pennicuik after my Mother died, and found a very careful master in the persone of one Mr. Alex. Strauchan, only that, according to the bad custome of these times, he was too severe a disciplinarian. I learnt from this never to suffer any man to use my children and young friends as if born to be slaves. Boys who have a Genius for learning ought to be alured to their Books, and those who want this Genius ought to be put to Mechanick occupations,

---

[1] 'Sir John Clerk had often observed in the course of conversation, that it would be a very pleasant thing for a person to fall asleep and not awake till he found himself in Heaven. On the night of his daughter's marriage (to the Rev. Alex. Moncrieff of Culfargie), or that immediately following, while the young couple were still in his house, he retired at his usual hour, and some little time afterwards was followed by Lady Clerk, who found him quite dead, as if in a pleasant sleep, with his head resting on the palm of his hand.'—Seton's *House of Moncrieff* (1891), p. 111. See also folio 127 of the present MS.

[2] Douglas in his *Baronage* mentions only three sons of the 1st Baronet of Penicuik and Christian Kilpatrick, his second wife, viz., James, Robert, and Hugh.

[3] All the biographies of the second Baronet of Penicuik, including that in the *Dictionary of National Biography*, give the date of his birth as 1684. His baptism appears as follows in the Edinburgh City Register, the entry including the names of several notable witnesses:—'26th February 1676, Mr. John Clerk of Pennycook. Elizabeth Henderson. A. S. N. John. Witnesses, Kenneth, Earle of Seaforth; Earle of Perth; James, Lord Corstorphine; Sir Archibald Primrose, Lord Register; Doctor Henry Henderson; Thomas Henderson, Chirurgian=Apothecarie; and James Clerk, Brother-german to y[e] s[d] Mr. John.'

in which they may become far more useful to | humane society *fol. 7.* than if bred schollars.

With this Mr. Strauchan I learnt Latine, and afterwards with another master in the same school I was taught Greek.

one Mr. Pou....

I spent 7 years at this kind of emploiment, but if in the meantime I had learnt to write a tollerable hand, the Memoirs I am now writeing had been more legible. One thing indeed contributed mainly to make me write ill, which was an exercise about that time common in schools, to write long notes of sermons after the Minister. This practise, however, served a little to fix our attention, and keep us from doing worse things.

I was in a habite of writing always fast in order to follow the Ideas of ... mind and this contributed to this bad hand tho ... I have written more than most men in my time as particulary the T... cou'd declare ... a record be ... kept of what I have destroied.

Here, at school, a very great misfortune befell me about my age of Thirteen, for a country man's Horse standing sadled and brideled in my way, I got upon him, and as Boys used to do, I put him to the Gallop, but he proved too headstrong for me. I cou'd not command him, and to be free of a precipice to which he directed his course, I threw my self off, and both broke and disjointed my right leg. I was brought home in a very sad condition, and continued in torture and misery for at least 4 months after. My kind father attended me night and day, and no assistance was wanted that cou'd be procured by either physitians or Chyrurgeons, however, I got no benefite by them till nature perfected the cure, in a word, my leg sweled so sore at first that it could never be set, and the Tibia being not only broken but disjoynted and split, I had several ulcers in my leg, which required a great deal time in the cure. These continued to run for near 6 months, and if it had not been for the extraordinary care| of Mr. Robt. Clerk,[1] my unckle, *fol. 8.* and who was a very expert chyrurgeon, I must have lost my leg. I recovered at last, and contented myself with this reflexion, that my misfortune came from the wise hand of providence in order to curb the vast inclinations I had to rambling and such violent exercises as I cou'd never have indured.

but no bones cam out. These ulcers might have been cured sooner by opening up than by Tents and pledgets as was then the practise. On revising all this in the 73 year of my age,

[1] Fifth and youngest son of John Clerk, first proprietor of Penicuik; was born in 1664, and after studying at home and abroad, practised in Edinburgh with success. He died 1720. His son, Dr. John Clerk, a still more celebrated medical man, President of the Royal College of Physicians, Edinburgh, 1740, acquired the lands of Listonshiels and Spittal, Mid-Lothian. — Douglas's *Baronage*.

I cannot but approve of what is here. it is true that I never had the perfect use of this leg, nor could and ever travel on it above 2 or 3 miles, yet made a shift by help of a good deal ... to make ... most purposes except that of ...cing, for by the help of a Horse I can have to this Age a very ... and was not hindered others in all diversions. About 2 years ago my ... grew weaker, and I ... a constant pain and distrest at the joint in walking about.

After this misfortune I continued near a year with my Greek Master at Pennicuik, and then I was sent to the College of Glasgow.[1]

I studied in that place Logicks and Metaphisicks for two winters, and with great application, but never felt any benefite by them that I was sensible of, on the contrary, I found them so hurtful that I many times afterwards repented my having spent so much of my time upon them, and indeed it cost me as many years to unlairn what I had learnt at Glasgow. It was happy for me that my father come to think that I was doing no good there, and therefor I easily obtain'd his Liberty to go over to Holand, and follow my studies at Leyden.

On the 24 of Octr. 1794[2] I imbarqued on a ship belonging to the Queen's ferry bound for Rotterdam. My Father brought me to the ship and left me with tears, but I was so fond of the voyage that I had very little regard to the distress I left him in.

We sail'd and had very rugh weather, but what was worst, there being a War with France,[3] 4 French Privateers came upon our fleet, which consisted of 90 merchant ships, guarded by two | *fol. 8.* Dutch Frigets of 40 guns each.[4] I know not what had been the event, but being within 50 leagues of the coast of Holand, we made the best way we cou'd to get into the nearest

[1] Among the 'nomina discipulorum tutiæ classis sub præsidio Magistri Jacobi Knibloe qui hoc Anno Academiam intrarunt Februarii 28, 1693,' is 'Joannes Clerk primogenitus Domini Johannis Clerk, a Pennicook.'—*Munimenta Alme Universitatis Glasguensis* (Glasgow, 1854), vol. iii. p. 152.

[2] Clerical error for 1694.

[3] The war between France and the 'Grand Alliance,' of which England and Holland were members. Five months before Clerk sailed for Holland, on the 27th June 1694, the English fleet, under Admiral Rooke, had been defeated in Lagos Bay, by the French under Tourville. The war was terminated by the Treaty of Ryswick, 1697, in which Louis XIV. acknowledged William III., and promised to abstain from countenancing the supporters of James VII.

[4] In the opening of the MS. *Journal of my Travels* Clerk gives a further account of his voyage, and it may be noted that he states the number of ships in the fleet in which he sailed differently here:—'On the 28 of October 1694, being then 18 years of age, I came from Pennycook to the Quean's ferry, where having stayed 3 days for a wind, I went on board a ship called the Dragon, commanded by one Dundass, who set sail for Holland in companie of 58 other merchant ships and two Dutch men of war, the Briol and the Hutson, of 40 guns each.

'After we had been eight days at sea, we discovered on a Sabath morning

ports. It was towards night when the French Men of War got up to us. The Dutch ships were ready to engage them; however, 4 of our coal ships were taken and set on fire in the night time, after their men had been taken out. I was concern'd at the dismal schene, and wisht I had still been at Pennicuik; but then a worse succeeded, for a great Dutch fly boat run a board of us in the dark, and we were within an inch of being broken to pieces. Some of our Masts and riging were damaged, and all our men were on the point of jumping on board the Dutch vessel, as being of far greater bulk and strength than ours; however, it pleased God that we got free of one another at last.

Next morning we found we were on the coast of Zeland, and in a few houres after got safe in to Camphire.[1]

As Zeland is one of the finest little Islands in the world, it gave me very great pleasure, and indeed I found the difference very great from it and the country I had left. I staid in it 3 days and surveyed the fine cities of Midleburg and Flushing. On the 4th and 5th day, by the way of Dort, I came in a large boat to Rotterdam. I staid here only a day or

---

Monsieur Jean Du Bart, with a squadron of five men of war, making down upon us with all the sail he had, but, there being a great calm, we had the good fortune, by the help of our boats, to keep our distance from them till the morning; then a brisk breeze hapned, which, tho' it gave them the advantage of coming up with two of our straglers, yet, the night being come, we made a shift to get quit of them, tho' in great confusion and danger of running down one another.

'We (were) now at this time upon the coast of Holland, and our ships were once in danger of being sunk by a Dutch flyboat, and at another of being stranded upon the shallows near Goeree.

'Our ships that were taken now burned in the nighttime, for we perceived them for 8 hours flaming, their cargoes being coals.

'Our fleet, being thus scattered, was obliged to put into different ports in Holand, and 12 of our ships, the Dragon being one of them, arrived safely in Camphire in Zealand.'

The Jean Du-Bart referred to above was a celebrated privateer, born at Dunkirk in 1650. He served in the Dutch navy under De Ruyter, and afterwards became a corsair against Holland. He gained the favour of Louis XIV., entered his navy, and a medal was struck commemorating his capture of a Dutch convoy of a hundred vessels laden with corn when France was in danger of famine. About 1696 he captured another rich Dutch convoy, and carried fifteen vessels into Dunkirk. He died 1702.

[1] Campvere.

two, and went to Leyden, where I began my studies of the civil law[1] under a very learn'd man, Philippus Reinhardus Vitriarius.[2]

I boarded in the house of a learned German, who taught privately Mathematiks, Phyilosophy, and Musick, one Sarnbuchius.[3] Here I spent my time both profitably and agreeably,

---

[1] In the *Album Studiosorum* of the Leyden University the name 'Joannes Clerk, Scotus, 22, J. Dr.' appears under date of May 14th, 1697, two days after that on which the writer of the present MS. started on his travels in Germany and Italy, as he informs us in his MS. *Journal of my Travels*, vol. i. p. 16. The other Scotsmen whose names are entered in the same year are:—

'Alexander Wodrouw,	Scotus,	22	T.
David Erskine,	,,	22	J.
Samuel Straten,	,,	21	M.
Thomas Hamilton,	,,	20	J.
David Dundas,	,,	22	J.
Franciscus Kinloch,	,,	20	J.
Jacobus Bethun,	,,	20	J.
Johannes Ogilvius,	,,	24	J.
Jacobus Ross,	,,	22	J.
Johannes Murrowe,	,,	20	J.
Joannes Grant,	,,	25	J.
Joannes Kirkwood,	,,	23	M.'

—*Album Studiosorum academiæ Lugduno Batavæ* (*Hagæ Comitum*, 1875). In his MS. *Travels*, vol. i. p. 14, Clerk gives the following account of the University of Leyden:—

'The fabrick of its famous university consists of one building chiefly, with two great halls, one above another, and another of a lesser size on the lowest story. The whole building is by half not so good as an ordinary countrey church. These halls serve only for publick lessons and orations; here are their Graduations and musick made upon any solemn occasion.

'There are 4 professors of Law, 2 of philosophy and Mathematicks, 2 of Divinity, 2 of Eloquence and history, 2 of Physick, one of Ecclesiastick History, one of Botany, one of Anatomy, one of Chymistry; but this number varies sometimes, as the Curators for the University think fit. These professors give their privat Lessons or colleges at their own Lodgings, and have always a large room for that purpose; but all of them are oblidged to make a publick Lesson in their own way once or twice a week in one of the halls above named.

'The chief of the college is called Rector Magnificus, and is chosen from among the professors with consent of the Stadtholder of Holand.

'The Anatomy-hall is reckoned the best of its kind of any in Europe, for its great variety of curiosities.'

[2] Philip Reinhard Vitriarius, born 1647, was professor of law at Leyden from 1682 to the year of his death, 1720. He was the author of *Institutiones juris naturæ et gentium*, *Jus civile privatum*, and other works.—L.

[3] The name is very indistinct both here and in the *Journal*. It may read Zambechius.

for I applied my self very closely to | all the three studies. In *fol.* 10.
the last I was a kind of proficient even before I came to Leyden, for I play'd tollerably on the Harpsecord, and since I was 7 years of age I touched the Violin a little.

As I found that there was no keeping of good and verteous company in either Holand, France, or Italy, and far less in Germany, without as much of the practise of musick as to enable one to bear a part in a Concert, I bestowed a great deal of pains on the Harpsecord, and in a year after was as well qualified to perform my part on that instrument as any Gentleman in Holand. I found that this piece of skill was indeed of very great use to me afterwards in the course of my Travels through Germany, Italy, and France.[1]

As to Mathematicks and Phylosophy, I was more inclined to them than consisted with my health, for I have many times followed them with that application that I have been a whole month without going out of the House or puting on my cloaths. I believe if I had followed the dictats of my own inclination I had studied nothing else, but reasone and my Father's desires, which he reiterated every time he wrote to me, oblidged me often to slacken my pace and attend my civil law colleges.

It hapned, therefore, that in place of following the study of the civil Law for 2 years, which few exceed, I bestowed near 3 years upon it, for after I had studied for 2 years with Vitriarius, I bestowed a year on Professor Voetius.[2] This man I found very distinct, for he keept close to his own Compend on the Instituts and Pandects, but he was far from being such a
Corpus Juris | as Professor Vitriarius was. *fol.* 11

I had likeways colleges from the two famous professors of Eloquence, on History and on Tacitus and Suetonius, these

---

[1] 'To keep these studies from being tediouse to me, I applied my self in my leisure houres to the study of Musick, under the same Zambechius (?), who taught me the speculative part thereof according to the mathematical rules, and the practical part upon the Harpsicord. In both these I made, perhaps, more advance than became a Gentleman.'—MS. *Travels*, vol. i. p. 8.

[2] John Voet, born 1647, professor of Civil Law at Leyden from 1683 to 1713, the year of his death. His principal work was *Commentarius ad Pandectas*, in two vols. folio.—L.

were Pirezenius[1] and Gronovius;[2] the last explain'd all the Roman Antiquities of Suetonius in Dutch, but, as I had frequented much the company of Dutch people, I found no difficulty in understanding him, and reading this Author with pleasure, as I have frequently done since. The notes and criticisms he gave us I took in writeing, which are still in the Library of Pennicuik.

I had likeways a college on Church History from the learned Spanhemius,[3] so that while I staid in Leyden, I never had half an houer to spend in idleness, but diverted my mind by different successive studies.

Amongst other things, I learn'd to drau from Francis Mieris,[4] a very great painter. This proceeded partly from

---

[1] Jacobus Perizonius (Voorbrock), the most learned classical scholar of his age, born 1651, became professor of Greek literature, history, and eloquence at Leyden in 1693. Died at Leyden 1715. His principal works are *Animadversiones historicæ in quibus quamplurima in priscis Romanarum rerum . . . autoribus notantur*, etc. Amsterdam, 1685. *Origines Babylonicæ et Ægyptiacæ*. Leyden, 1711.—L.

[2] James Gronovius, famous philologist, born at Deventer in 1645, came to Leyden in 1658. In 1668 he went into England to collate manuscripts at Oxford and Cambridge, and there made friends with many Englishmen of learning. In 1679 he took the chair of Greek Literature at Leyden, formerly occupied by his father, John Frederick Gronovius. In 1692 he lectured on Eloquence, and in 1702 on Geography. His critical works are numerous—editions of the classics and commentaries—but he is best known for his *Thesaurus Antiquitatum Græcarum*, Leyden, 1697-1702, in 12 vols. fol. His edition of *Tacitus, cum J. Gronovii et variorum notis*, was printed at Amsterdam in 1672, and again in 1685; his *Suetonius, a Salmasio recensitus cum emendationibus*, at Leyden in 1698.—L. Boerhaave also attended the lectures of Gronovius, 'whose stile he has been thought to imitate in some of his earlier orations.'—See Burton's *Life of Boerhaave*.

[3] Frederick Spanheim, a Swiss, was born at Geneva in 1632. In 1670 he accepted the Chair of Theology, which his father had held before him, at Leyden; and in the following year he added to theology ecclesiastical history. He was three times rector of the University, and died at Leyden in 1701. He is credited with sixty-four publications, the most of which were collected in 3 vols. fol., Leyden, 1701-1703.—L.

[4] The name is evidently given incorrectly here, for Francis Mieris the elder died in 1681; and his grandson, Francis Mieris the younger, was only born in 1689. William Mieris, his son, however, was born in 1662, and, at the time when Clerk arrived in Leyden, was practising his art there. In his MS. *Travels* Clerk states simply that 'I resolved, after finishing my studies, to travel into Germany, Italy, and France, and for that reason, that I might travel with the more satisfaction, I studied frequently painting and drawing under the

V

BARON SIR JOHN CLERK

Ætatis 19

inclination and partly from the advice I had from some of my Dutch friends, for all their young Folks learn to drau from their being 7 years of age, and find it vastly useful to them in most stations of Life.

The only relaxation, if it may be called such, was spending my vacations at the Hegue. There I went for about 3 months, each summer I staid in Holand, yet I was far from being idle, for except a few houres of the day in which | I attended *fol.* 12.
the soveraign Courts of Holland as often as I cou'd get admission, I continued in a course of great Application to my studies. Here at the Hegue I learnt both French and Dutch, and, in order to prepare me for a journey to Italy, I had an Italian Master who brought me a considerable length in the language of that country, and which I found afterwards was of great advantage to me.

Such were my occupations in Holand; as for companions, I had no particular one but the famous Herman Bouerhave,[1] he

---

famous Miris'—giving no Christian name—'which I afterwards reaped the advantage of in a sort of pleasure that is not to be comprehended by any body except such who understand a little of this study.' Doubtless his memory had played him false when he came to write the present account of his Life, and William Mieris is the artist to whom he intends to refer and the draughtsman of the pencil portrait reproduced as our Illustration No. v., although the mount of this drawing is inscribed on the back in the Baron's later style of writing—'My picture done at Leyden by Francis Miris.'

At the end of the second volume of Clerk's MS. *Travels* are inserted sixty-two drawings, made, with considerable skill, from pictures, statues, landscapes, etc., during his tour in Italy; and to these he has appended the note—'These following Draughts are a few of many hundreds that have been given away or lost since I returned from my Travels in 1699. They are very incorrect, from the number I used sometimes to make in a day, and from the different times they were drawn.—J. C., 1741.'

[1] Hermann Boerhaave, one of the most celebrated physicians of the eighteenth century, and a man of immense erudition, was born at Woorhout, near Leyden, 31st December 1668. He was originally destined for the ministry, and followed at Leyden the course of theology. He was made Doctor of Philosophy in his twenty-second year, and shortly after this devoted himself specially to medicine and anatomy. He took his degree of Doctor of Medicine in 1693. He had a great attraction for mathematical studies, which are said to have influenced his medical theories. He lectured on medicine at the University in 1701, and was appointed to the Chair of Medicine and Botany in 1709, which he held till 1738, the year of his death.—L. Clerk corresponded regularly with Boerhaave after his return to Scotland, and many copies of his Latin letters are preserved among

Doctor Bouerhaven was about 7 years older than I was; but he had no business then as a phycian.

was then a young physitian, and, as he was a mathematician and phylosopher, I hapned to contract a very great friendship for him. He was likeways a Musitian, so that by a propensity to the same studies we not only lived like Brothers together while I staid at Leyden, but continued a correspondence together while he lived.

He was my physitian likeways on all my little distempers, but perhaps I trusted too much to his skill when I hapned to take the small-pox at Leyden in May 1697; he pretended that he had discovered a chymecal Medicine which wou'd carry off the small-pox before they came to any height. I suffered him to try his medicine upon me after the small pox were broken out on my body, the effect was that in a day or two they were
fol. 13. all purged off. I greu perfectly well in about | a week after. The Doctor from this success was extreamly elated, and promised himself a very great fortune on his repairing to London and seting up upon the success of this single Specifick for the cure of the small-pox, but, to my very great misfortune, this Desease returned upon me about 5 months after with great violence, as I shall afterwards notice.[1] In other respects I keept

---

the Clerk papers. See Additional Note B. He is said to have bequeathed his books to Clerk, but I have not been able to find on any of the volumes, now the property of Sir George Clerk, such marks of possession as would prove that they had formerly belonged to Boerhaave.

[1] 'Considering the *small-pox* as a *cutaneous inflammation*, joined with a *contagious eruption*, and therefore requiring for the most part the general remedies for the former, with those that are esteemed specific in the latter, he was naturally led to such a method as enabled him not only to mitigate the symptoms, and so lessen the danger of this distemper, but sometimes even to *prevent* it also, that is, *its coming to an eruption*, by subduing it on its first attack, when all the symptoms usually preceding the eruption have appeared in a proper subject who had been in the way of infection, in a season when the small-pox was epidemical; and he doubted not that a variolous form might be observed by others, using the like regimen, to be sometimes removed before it produced a variolous eruption. An article respecting this disease concerns the public welfare too much to be suppress, since our author was so unfortunate as to differ in this point from great authorities, from those to which in other cases he paid a considerable deference.—It is the *fatal consequences* which always ensued upon his several trials of *the purgative method in the secondary fever of the confluent small-pox*, although conducted with all the cautions recommended by the patrons of that practice.'—Section on 'Boerhaave's Lectures and Improvements in Physic,' in Wm. Burton's *Account of his Life and Writings* (second edition, London, 1746), pp. 179-80. See also folios 19 and 30 of the present MS.

my health very well in Holand, and indeed I scarse ever had leisure to consider whether I was well or ill.

A little after I recovered of the small-pox in Holand as above I set out for Italy with no other allowance from my Father than a single 100 pounds. The reasone of this was that my journey was contrary to his inclinations; but the vast desire I had to see a Country so famous for exploits about which all my time had been hitherto spent in reading the classicks, likeways a country so replenished with Antiquities of all kinds, and so much excelling all other countries in painting and musick, I say these things created such a vast desire in me to see it, that I am sure nothing in life had ever made me happy if I had denied my self this great pleasure and satisfaction. I knew that the allowance given me by my Father wou'd never answere the third of my expense, but I was resolved to throu my self on the providence of the great Being which had hitherto protected me and provided liberally for me, without ever being at the pains to consider what was to become of me after the money was spent.

There was another great difficulty in my case which as little affected me, namely, that I had no company to go with me, but behoved | to trust my self entirely to strangers, but even in that *fol.* 14.
I had some flattering hopes, and was not deceived.

I set out from Leyden,[1] came that night to Utrecht, and next day I took my place in a Wagon for Nimuegen. I found here two young Dutch men and their mother, who took all possible care for me.

At Nimuegen I fell acquainted with a very good sort of man, an English Officer, who was sent from Flanders to serve the Venetians in the Morea. With this Gentleman, as my country man, I contracted a very great friendship, and, like two Brothers, we proceeded on our journey to Cologn, Treves, Meyance, and Frankfort to Nuremberg.

I do not mention any particulars of this journey, because I have written particular Memoirs of my Travels to which I referr, as they will be found in two volumes in the charter house of Pennicuik.[2]

---

[1] On 12th May 1697, as we learn from the MS. *Travels*.

[2] These two folios of MS. *Travels*, of 271 and 172 pages respectively, are still in

At Nuremberg my good English Friend and I were oblidged to part, for as he was to proceed directly to Venice by the way of Augsburg and Tyrol, I was resolved at all Hazards to go to Vienna by the way of Ratisbone, Lintz, and Passau. My companion did all he cou'd to dissuade me, but nothing wou'd do, I was again resolved to trust my self in the company of strangers.

My resolution did not want success, for, in the coach from
fol. 15. Nuremberg to Ratisbone,| I fell into the company of two young German Lads like my self who were going to the Emperor's Court at Vienna to solicet for emploiments. I was happy in their company, and took boat with them at Ratisbone down the Danube to the cities we intended to visite. In the same boat there hapned to be an Irish or a Scotch Jesuite Father whom I always observed very assiduous about me. As we dined every day, and lay every night on shore, he took great care to provide me with the best pieces of meat at Table, and with the best beds where we lay. This commerce went on for 5 days, which was the time we took up in sailing down the Danube to Vienna, he never discoursed with me but in Latine or Italian till we were in sight of Vienna, then it was he surprised me by asking in plain English how I did, and discovering himself to be my country man. I was overjoyed at this discovery, but cou'd not find out why he keept it so long in the dark, nor had he, I believe, any reason for it, but a meer whime, to surprise me the more when he found that I had nobody to look after me,—in short, he was exceedingly kind and useful to me while I stayed at Vienna, for he belonged to

---

the possession of Sir George Clerk. They not only contain a full account of his travels, but also elaborate descriptions of the remains of antiquity, churches, libraries, etc., that he visited, and careful estimates of the manners, customs, and government of the various countries that were included in his tour. Clerk frequently in after years revised this *Journal of my Travels*, which was the production of his youth; but he would never consent to its publication, and in 1741 he prefixed to the first volume an even more stringent '*Caveant Posteri*' than that which the present *Account of my Life* bears. That his reason was chiefly the imperfect style of the MS. may be gathered from the statement with which the '*Caveant*' concludes:—'They' (the volumes) 'contain nothing but Truth, tho' told in a pureile way;' and from the note with which the first volume ends:—'I revised this volume in 1753, but disclaim the Printing of it, as it was written by me *when I was not well acquainted with the Language I wrote in.*'

the College of Jesuits in that city. His conversation never turn'd on religious matters, for I suppose he found out by the way that I wou'd be very much inclined to laugh at all such attempts. He therefore laid out himself to explain the manners of Germany, and what I was to observe at the Emperor's Court; all which furnished| me with a great deal more knowledge of the *fol.* 16. city and court of Vienna than I cou'd have attain'd to during the little time I cou'd allow myself to stay there.

While I staid at Vienna, I was introduced by my fellow-traveller to the Lord Lexington,[1] then Envoy from King William of Great Britain to the Emperor.[2] He made me very welcome, and oblidged me to dine with him every day so long as I staid in the place. I was always with him at the Emperor's Leves and Drawing-Rooms. He introduced me to him, and when the Emperor understood from him that I was a great lover of Music, he invited me to his private opera, keept in the Imperial Garden of the Favretti, where the Emperor always resided, about 3 quarters of a mile from Vienna. The Assembly there was very great, and I believe no Court in Europe cou'd afford a Traveller a more magnificent appearance. The Emperor and Empress,[3] two

[1] Robert Sutton, son of Robert, first Baron Lexington, and his third wife, Mary, daughter of Sir Anthony St. Leger, Knight. He succeeded as second Baron in 1668; was Envoy-Extraordinary to the Court of Vienna, and Ambassador-Extraordinary to that of Spain, and for the Treaty of Ryswick. He died in 1723, when the title became extinct, and the Sutton estates passed to his grandson, Lord George Manners.

[2] Leopold I., Emperor of Germany, second son of Ferdinand III., and his first wife, Mary Anne, daughter of Philip III. of Spain. He became king of Hungary in 1655, king of Bohemia in 1656, and emperor in 1658. In 1683 he fled from Vienna on the approach of the Turks, and the city was only saved by John Sobieski, king of Poland, who forced them to raise the siege. The Emperor died in 1705.

[3] Eleonora Theresa, daughter of Philip William, Elector Palatine, the Emperor's third wife. She was born in 1655, was educated as a strict Catholic, and led a life of extreme austerity and self-denial. 'These religious practices did not divert her from the duties of wife and empress. She complied in appearance with the taste and inclinations of her husband, frequented the opera with the Psalms bound like the books of the performance, and exerted her skill in music for his solace and amusement. . . . On the death of her eldest son Joseph, she was intrusted with the regency; and after conducting the reins of state with vigor and prudence, in the short but critical period which elapsed before the arrival of Charles, she resigned her power without regret to resume her darling

sones, Ignatius[1] and Charles,[2] and 3 daughters,[3] with his sister,[4] the Queen of Poland, sat in the fore part of an amphitheater dressed up with boughs of Trees, Green Leafs, and flowers. The Ladies sat behind in 8 or 10 Artificial Benches, and, to the best of my observation, about 4 or 500 without any mixture of men amongst them. The schenes were little real palaces of Timber, and finely painted with all the ornaments of Architectory, the Musick was very grand, viz., two Herpsecords, one on each side, 4 Great Bass violins, as many Lutes and Theorts,[5] and above 30 violins and other instruments. The actors or singers were mostly Italians, for as his Imperial Majesty was himself not
fol. 17. only fond | of Musick to distraction, but a performer himself

course of life. . . . She turned the Psalms into German verse, and set them to music; and besides numerous versions of devout and edifying works, translated from the French *Pious Reflections for every Day of the Month*, which was printed at Cologne. Died 1720.'—Coxe's *House of Austria*, vol. i. p. 1059-60. (London, 1807.)

[1] No doubt Joseph, eldest son of Leopold I., and afterwards Emperor Joseph I., is here meant. He was born 1678, and died 1711. He is referred to by Clerk in his MS. *Travels*, where he describes his first sight of the Imperial family in the church of St. Laurence, at a ceremonial where one of the Court ladies was admitted as a nun:—'First came the Emperor, a very little man, with the uggliest face in the world, after him next his eldest son, Joseph, the King of the Romans, who was a pretty tall youth, of about 19 years of age, next to him followed his brother Charles, Arch Duke of Austrie, a boy about 14 years of age; all these being clad in black. The Empress, with 3 princesses, her daughters, came next. She made but an indifferent appearance, tho' covered with jewels; yet her daughters, the eldest of whom seem'd about 15, lookt tolerably well. After them next the Queen Dowager of Poland, who is the Emperor's sister.'—MS. *Travels*, vol. i. p. 56.

[2] Second son of Leopold I., afterwards the Emperor Charles VI. Born 1685; crowned Emperor 1711; died 1740.

[3] Mary Elizabeth, born 1680; became Governess of the Netherlands; died 1741. Mary Anne, born 1683; became wife of John VI. of Portugal; died 1754. Mary Magdalen, born 1689; died 1743.

[4] Eléonora Josepha, daughter of Ferdinand III. and his third wife, Maria Leopoldina, daughter of Leopold of the line of Tyrol. She married Michael Viesnovitsky, king of Poland, and after his death became the wife of Charles, Duke of Lorraine. Died in 1697. Her grandson Francis again united the houses of Lorraine and Austria by his marriage with Maria Theresa.

[5] The Theorbo, a large double-necked lute, with two sets of tuning pegs, the lower set holding the strings, which lie over the fretted finger-board, while the upper are attached to the bass strings, or so-called diapasons, which are used as open notes.—Grove's *Dictionary of Music*.

on the Herpsecord, he took care to entertain all the best Musitians that Italy cou'd produce, and they were all provided with the best salaries and offices at his court that any way suited their occupations.[1] His Capelmasters were Italian, and all his operas and comedies were in this Language; there was indeed very little else spocken at Court, and in Vienna there seem'd to me more Hungarians and Italians than Germans.

While I staid here I made several excursions, but my greatest entertainment was in the Imperial Library and Galleries, for both these were admirably furnished with Books and pictures.

After having satisfi'd myself with every thing worth seeing at Vienna, and about 20 miles round it in the confines of Hungary, I began to think of seting forwards on my journey to Italy, and without giving my self the least truble about the company I was to travel with, I took my place in a chaise for Venice, through the countries of Stiria and Carmathia. I was growen very hardy in interprises of this nature, for I had neither Governour, servant, nor companion of my own country to take care of me, and I had not monie sufficient to wait the opportunities of others. I set out, however, with a young Gentleman in the chaise with me who hapned to prove as much for my purpose as if I had made choise of him. He was a nepolitan of Fundi, who had travelled this road once before, so, after some few ceremonies at first, | we became as familiar as if we had been bred up together. We were 21 days in our journey, sometimes, or rather once every day, in snow, though it was in the month of Agust, and sometimes roasted with the heat of the sun.

I saw the Emperor's gold mines at C..., which I found nothing else than ... or layer of ... and sand, which being ... up from a deep, was washed in a vessel, and the gold dust got up.

I was then 20 years of age.

fol. 18.

[1] Clerk calls the Emperor 'the greatest Lover and judge of musick that perhaps any great man in the world is. He not only sings and plays on the Herpsecord, but he composes very well both for the Chapel and chamber, for I have heard admirable things of his making, both for humure and Art. At his Court it was an ordinary thing for him to sit down and entertain the company with his Musick, singing and playing very finely; but I confess this sight was so shoking to me that it had like to have spoiled all my inclination to performing my self, if it had not been that I forsaw I was not to be rich enough to purchase Musick any other way than what I made by my self, especially in my oune Country, where at this time there is no such thing. Nothing cou'd be more rediculouse than the odd figure the poor old Emperor made on such occations.'—MS. *Travels*, vol. i. pp. 59, 60.

These sudden alterations produced bad effects on my health, so that if it had not been for the great civilities of this Gentleman I must have lain by the way.

I parted with him at Venice with great reluctancy, and so was again put to my shifts as before. I doubted much if ever after I should find a companion to my taste, and so it hapned, for on leaving Venice, where I saw everything commonly seen by Travelers in the Autum, I set out with a Dutchman to Rome, by the way of Padua, Ferrara, Bolognia, Rimini, Pesaro, Ancona, Loretto, Feligno, Spoletti, Narni, Tarni, and Utricoli.

One Meyder ... and bred in the East Indies.

This companion of mine proved a meer brute, tho' he came into Italy with an intention of improving himself. He was constantly drunk, and never minded any thing but to enquire about the best Taverns, eating, and wine. I suffered many inconveniences with him, for his debaucheries and blasphemies often raised mobs upon us, so that my only employment by the way was to get him carried from one Town to another, and to take care of his persone and monie when I found him dead drunk, sometimes by the way, for he used frequently to leave me and go post to some famouse Tavern, where he drank till I came up with him. He beat the priests for denying him the use of flesh on fridays, and did all the mischivious tricks that ever entered into the head of a Madman. |

fol. 19. I got happily quit of him at last, when I came to Rome in September 1697, and wou'd never see him more.

I was not in this city above 3 days when I again fell into the distemper of the small-pox, which Doctor Bouerhaven thought he had cured me of about 4 months before in Leyden. It came upon me with the same symptoms, but with greater violence than before; however, it pleased God to provide me there with a friend, one Father Cosimo Clerk,[1] who provided

[1] The following account of Father Cosimo appears in the MS. *Travels*, vol. ii. p. 61 :—'About the end of this month (October) arrived at Rome from Florence one father Alexander or Cosimo Clerk, whose father was an advocate in Scotland, one Mr. William Clerk. This man was in his time an officer in the French army, but falling under some misfortunes he left the service, came to Florence, and turned a Religiuse of the Franciscan order. This it seems was his choise, that he might ingratiate himself with the great Duke, who was likewise of this order since the separation between him and his Duchess. The father was allowed by

all necessaries for me, and never left me either day or night till I was perfectly recovered. This disease, however, took up a long time, for after the violence of the distemper was over I broke out in Boils, and had successively three Feavers, each of them very severe. I had a very good physitian, one . . . . . .[1] who was the most eminent man of his profession then in Italy, but I found no kind of tenderness in the treatment he gave me, whether or not he lookt upon me with contempt because I was not of his religion I cannot tell; but, if it was this, the thing seem'd the more extraordinary to me that I never yet had known any physitian who had any religion at all.

But whatever was wanting in this man, others whom I never saw, nor ever was to see, did abundantly compensat, for all the nuns, who resided in the neighbourhood of the street I lived in, sent every day to see how I was, and always brought me very considerable presents of medicines as they pretended for my desease, and of wines, Biscuits, and confections for the entertainment of such who came to see me. The Ladies of the Society of the Touer di Spechio[2] were my chief Benefactors. These are a sort of Ladies who are allowed sometimes to go abroad, and to marry if they think fit. I went after my | recovery to wait on them and thank them, [as I did afterwards.] *fol.* 20.

---

the Duke to assume the name of Cosimo after himself, and indeed in all things he treated him as his sone. He might not be above 34 years of age when he came here, tho he was charged with several matters of importance at the Court of Rome. . . . He carried nothing of Religion about with him but his gown, cord, and beads.' William Clerk was admitted an advocate on the 23d January 1663, and re-admitted in 1676, but the minutes contain only the name and date, and give no particulars of his family. One of the drawings inserted at the end of the second volume of the MS. *Travels*, an outline sketch in pen and ink of a seated friar addressing two others, and marking off the heads of his discourse upon his fingers, is inscribed 'Padre Cosimo and his Brother Monks at St. Piero Montorio, 1698.'

[1] The name is omitted in the MS.

[2] The convent of Tor di Specchi, of the Oblates or Collatines, founded in 1425 by St. Frances of Rome; who was born in 1384, became Superior of the convent in 1437, died 1440, and was canonised by Paul V. in 1608. 'The Oblates of Tor di Specchi are not, strictly speaking, nuns; they take no vows, and are bound by no obligations under pain of sin; they are not cloistered, and their dress is that which was worn at the period of their establishment by the widows of the Roman nobles.'—Lady Georgiana Fullerton's *Life of St. Frances of Rome*, p. 107.

They accepted my visits with great civility in their chapel and in a publick room. How these acts of charity and civility were done to a young stranger I know not, but I supposed they heard that I was a young man in distress near their Monasteries, which was enough for charitable Italian Ladies.

I had at the same time many visits from Priests and Friers in order to convert me, and in the danger of Death to pray for me, but my cousin, Father Clerk, who attended me, and who never trubled his head with Religion of any kind, took off a little of the burden and disquietude I had felt on these occasions. He pretended that he was constantly employed about my soul-concerns, so that there was no need for them to take any truble about matters that were in so great forwardness already. However, my Friend, it seems, had had his fits of devotion, for tho' he was bred a Sojer, and had been employed as a Captain in the French service in Flanders about the year 1793,[1] he took it in his head to turn a Religuse in Italy. When he came to Florence, the great Duke of Tuscany, finding him a smart man, took a likeing to him, and though he had joined himself to the Franciscan Friers, he sent him to Rome to manage some of the Florentine affaires at that Court.

It was therefore in the station of an Envoy that I found him, and in this character he did me very great services. He introduced me in the first place into the acquaintance and protection of the Great Duke, and from whom I received some very kind letters, which I still preserve at Pennicuik. He made me acquainted with most of all the Forraign Ambassadors and great people at Rome.|

fol. 21. I was received with great civilities wherever I went, as the Relation of so great a man as Father Cosimo, and so great an intimat of the great Duke: he not only furnished me with money, but keept a coach and 2 servants for me. This I found a very great conveniency for me, but it was no less for the Father. He gave out that he was my near relation, sometimes my Unckle, and no doubt it did him some service that by the Equipage I keept it appeared that I was a Gentleman of whose family he was a branch.

As a Franciscan Friar he could not keep a coach for himself, wherefor I put it under my name.

[1] Evidently a clerical error for 1693.

Thus we went on, I supported the Father's dignity, and he supported my credite, without any expectation of a return, except to oun him as my patron and Tutor, as well as my near Relation. He seemed indeed sent by the providence of God as my Tutelary Angel by a thousand good offices he did me at all times and in all places.

After my recovery from the small-pox, I applied close to the study of the civil Law, and by means of my good Father Cosmo, I was allowed the conversation of Monsignior Caprara,[1] one of the Judges of the Rota. He took great pleasure to have several young Gentlemen about him to assist in reading his papers, and I was always welcome to him.

I had likeways the constant friendship and company of one Monsignior Chaprigni, a learned Antiquarian and phylosopher. He keept weekly Assemblies of Virtuosos at his House, and I was admitted to be one of the number. Besides these, we had likeways at his house privat Assemblies thrice a week, and in these we discoursed of all new discoveries in Literature and Antiquities. Some made orations in Latine, and some read verses in Greek, Latine, and Italian, of their own compositions.| *fol.* 22.

This gentleman, for his knowledge and singular qualifications, was one of the worthiest men I ever knew; but to my very great loss and misfortune he died before I left Rome. All his valuable things he distributed by a Testament amongst

A perfect old Roman, as was likeways the above named judge of the Rota.

1 'This man, for all moral virtues, might justly be compared to the best of the old Romans, he was about sixty years of age, and affected to live in Cicero's way at his villa Tusculana, for Montsignior Caprara's chief delight seem'd to be in instructing young gentlemen that pleased to wait on him at such set times as he appointed. There were a good many of us who enjoy'd this happiness without any expense, for it was not his manner to receive anything from us. We met thrice a week in a great room where he lived; each of us was provided with copies of all the printed cases on the civil and canon law that lay before the Rota, these we read in the most exact manner we could. Montsignior did not always attend us, but came within an hour before we broke up, and allowed us to ask him all manner of questions in relation to them, for if we did not, he was sure to examine us so strictly in all the circumstances of such cases that nothing must escape us. After it appeared to him yt we had really gone through the circumstances of any case, he used then, with great humanity, to ask our opinion and gave his owne, but always with such caution that it was not easy for any of us to discover what side he had taken in judgement. This learned man in particular pretended great friendship for the Inglesi, as he called all us of Britain, yet no body except myself used to attend his assemblies.'—MS. *Travels*, vol. ii. pp. 74-5.

his friends and acquaintances. Nor was I forgot amongst the rest; for he left me a head of Cicero, a busto of Otho, and a little statue of Diana of Ephesus, with a few other things, which are now at Pennicuik house.[1]

As Monsieur St. Everemont calls it.

My two great diversions at Rome were Musick and Antiquities. I excelled to a fault in the first, but the practise of musick gave me easier access to the best company in Rome than other strangers had. My masters were Bernardo Pasquini,[2] a most skilful composer and performer on the Organ and Harpse, and Archangelo Correlli,[3] whom I believe no man ever equaled for the violin. However, as I bestowed most of my time on the Harpsecord and the knowledge of musical compositions, I profited but little on the violin.

N.B. 'Tho I was always a Lover of Musick, yet the Life of Nero by Suetonius disgusted me

While I staid at Rome I fell into great friendship and intimacy with Wrotesly Russel, Duke of Bedford,[4] and with him I travelled to Naples and many other places in the neighbour-

[1] Still in the possession of Sir George Clerk.

[2] Bernardo Pasquini, a Tuscan, born 1637, died 1710. Came to Rome as a young man, and was appointed organist at Sta Maria Maggiore. The German musician Matheson relates that on visiting the Teatro Capranica in 1679, when an opera was produced in honour of Queen Christina of Sweden, he was 'much struck at finding Corelli playing the violin, Pasquini the harpsichord, and Gattiani the lute, all in the orchestra.'—Grove's *Dict.*—L. In his MS. *Travels*, vol. ii. pp. 62-3, Clerk mentions that the first visit he made in Rome was to Pasquini, 'for I had heard such wonderful accounts of his performances on the organ or Herpsecord that I had no patience till I heard him. . . . I continued with him all the time I lived in Rome for an hour or two every day, and had many things composed for me by him.'

[3] Arcangelo Corelli, a great violinist and composer, born at Tusignano in 1653, settled at Rome in 1681, where he lived in the palace of his friend and patron, Cardinal Pietro Ottoboni. He died in 1713. There is a statue erected to him in St. Peter's, with the inscription, *Corelli, princeps Musicorum.*—L. In the MS. *Travels*, vol. ii. pp. 67-8, is an interesting and enthusiastic account of Corelli and his playing. '. . . He gains a great dale of monie, and loves it for the sake of laying it all out on pictures, and indeed few private men in the world has (*sic*) such a noble collection of the best originals, from Raphael down to Carolo Maratti. He seldom teaches any body; yet, because he was pleased to observe me so much taken with him, he allowed me 3 lessons a week during all the time I stay'd at Rome. . . . He was a good, well-natured man, and on many accounts deserved the Epithet which all the Italians gave him of the divine Arc Angelo.'

[4] Wriothesley, eldest son of the celebrated patriot William Lord Russell. Born 1680; married, in 1695, Elizabeth, daughter and co-heir of John Howland of Streatham; succeeded his grandfather as second Duke of Bedford, 1700; and died 1711.

hood of Rome. In his company I participated of the great honours which the Duke de Medina Cœli,[1] viceroy of Naples, did him. It hapned at that time that the Duke's unckle, Admiral Russel,[2] commanded a great squadron of English Men of War in the Mediterranean. I came on that occasion to understand that whichever prince | can command the Mediterranean, must have all the Kingdoms and States of Italy under great subjection.[3]

exceedingly ... where his Talents are presented. The ... excelled, ... nobody ... esteem'd, but could with skill touch some instrument; this kind of success is never to be coveted.

fol. 23.

In December 1698 I left Rome at the earnest desire of my Father, and I return'd homewards by the way of Florence in company with my constant friend padre Cosimo, and was received by the Great Duke[4] with greater marks of distinction than his Highness used to bestow on strangers.

He received me uncovered, and when he put on his Hat, he oblidged me to be covered. I was not a little out of countenance at this, but I behoved to obey him; yet after I was covered, I took off my hat again, and he continued covered as if he had not observed me. His discourse turn'd on the

[1] Viceroy of Naples 1698; died 1710.

[2] Edward Russell, grandson of Francis, fourth Earl of Bedford. Born 1651, celebrated for his victory over the French, under Tourville, at La Hogue in 1692; created Earl of Orford 1697; died without issue in 1727, when his honours became extinct.

[3] As Clerk was in Rome from September 1697 till December 1698, he must have been there on that

'February Twenty-Two,
Since our salvation Sixteen Ninety-Eight,'

when the execution of Count Guido Franceschini and his four accomplices,

'opposite the church
Under the Pincian gardens green with spring,
'Neath the obelisk 'twixt the fountains in the Square,'

was the sequel to the tragedy upon which Browning has founded *The Ring and the Book*. In the MS. *Travels*, however, we find no reference to the matter; but we have glimpses of Innocent XII., the Pope of the poem, for Clerk records that he was present in the spring of 1698 at the ceremony of Washing the Feet in the Vatican by this Pope, and at his celebration of Mass on the Festival of St. Peter, when 'the musick was exceedingly divine, being the compositions of the famous Palestrina.'

[4] Cosmo III. Born 1642; succeeded his father, Ferdinand II., as Grand Duke of Tuscany in 1670; died 1723. His portrait, by John Smibert, the friend and painter of Allan Ramsay the poet, a crayon drawing executed a few years later, is in the Boudoin College, Brunswick, U.S., and is reproduced in the Rev. F. H. Allen's *Bowdoin Collection* (Brunswick, 1886). It shows an astonishingly grotesque and uncouth countenance.

affaires of Britain, and on the war, and at last on Religion. I had the honour of two Letters from him at Rome on this subject, but he found that I had no great humure to be his convert, so that all discourse on this head was soon broken off. He desired me frequently to come to his Court, and to oblidge me the more, he gave me a patent under the privy seal, signed by him self and his Secretary of State, the Marquise de Ricardi, appointing me a Gentleman of his Bedchamber, which patent lies now in Pennicuik Charter Room; and to heap more obligations upon me, he ordered his Great Library keeper, Signior Malizabechi,[1] to attend me at all the Libraries in Town.

These great honours were conferred on me not from any merite his Highness discovered in me, but purely to shew the regard he had to my friend the Padre, whom indeed he spoke of with great affection and respect.

After I had satiated my self with the Court and curiosities
fol. 24. of Florence, I took | my leave of the Great Duke in order to go to Leghorn, and was presented by him with a Box of chymical medicines,[2] still at Pennicuik, and with all the variety of wines and sweetmeats which his country produced.

By the way a good hearty Polish Bishop who was in our company, helped well to drink off my wines, otherways I must have left them behind me.

My good Padre wou'd still accompany me, and accordingly we came together to Pisa, where we staid a day or two, and from thence to Leghorn.

I staid in this last place only two days, and was greatly regalled by the Gentlemen of the English Factory, who it seems lay under very great obligations to my Religious Friend in certain negotiations he manadged for them at the Court of Florence.

---

[1] Antonio Magliabechi (1633-1714), 'doctor inter bibliothecarios sed bibliothecarius inter doctores,' a man renowned alike for his learning and his slovenly habits. He himself was a great collector, and before his death laid the foundation of the Magliabechian Library for the public use.—L. Pp. 138-140 of the second volume of the MS. *Travels* are occupied with a very curious and minute account of Magliabechi's eccentric appearance and manners, his squalid dress, and the extraordinary dwelling, filled with nothing but books, where he lived alone, without even a servant ('for when he keaped any they used to steal his books'), subsisting upon eggs, bread, and a flask of wine, which were brought to him once a week.

[2] This is still in the possession of Sir George Clerk.

After I had taken my place in a little vessel for Genua, I took leave of my Guardian Angel, who left me with tears.

This guardian Angel of mine was a vastly clever Man, and of great address, for he gained the affections of every body he had a mind to work upon, with his ... parts he might ... have aspired to the greatest dignities of the church of Rome, but as at that time he had no Religion at all, he was at last discovered by the Zealots, and lost all credite with them about two ... after I left Rome.

At Genua I staid about a week, and having brought there some recomendatory letters, I was entertained with great Civility at one of the Assemblies, where there was Musick and Gameing. I participated a little of the first, tho' I found that it was not the best place in Italy for Musick; but as to Gameing, I never had any likeing for it; wherever I came, however, I found that neither in Italy nor Germany any man cou'd be acceptable in an Assembly who neither was a Musitian nor a Gamester.

At one of these Assemblies the Lady of a certain noble Genoese entertained me with more than ordinary civility; and as a good deal of freedom is used in their city, I waited on my Lady to her House. Next morning | I received a Letter from fol. 25. her desiring me to see her often, and accordingly I went for once, and was met at the door by no fewer than 8 children, tho' she was then but about 25 years of Age. The Lady repeated her civilities to me, and least I had been engaged in a foolish Amour with her, I resolved to leave the place as soon as possibly I cou'd.

The Italian Ladies seldom fail to make up to those Travellers who come from England, or any place in Britain; for as they have a fixed opinion about them that they are all very rich, they never fail to expect valouable presents from them; [they] indeed do often [meet] with such [civilities]. My Friend the Duke of Bedford was on this account much in their favours.

As it was Winter, I cou'd not think of traveling into France by land, through Savoy, and therefor I took a place in a Feluca bound for Marseiles.

These vessels are so small that they can only coast it, so that the Company, which consisted of a young Spanish Gentleman and his Lady, from Milan, a French merchant, and my self, with 4 seemen, lay ashore every night, and for the most part dined ashore.

We came the first night to Savona, where I found that the young Spanish Gentleman had no inclination that I should make up any acquaintance with his Wife, but she, on the other hand, took more than ordinary pains to make me one of her Gallants. Her endeavours indeed served to divert me, but I found that she was one of the leudest women that ever her sex produced, tho' she cou'd not be above 15 years of Age. The Husband was a young Officer, and far from being a weak man, but as he had married her only about 6 months before, he was madly fond of her, so that he did not much discover her faults.

And I think she did not take much pains to hide them. I was every day in peril of my Life from his jealousy and her *fol. 26.* Follies in the Spanish way, but I was always on | my guard, and very careful not to put any afront on him. One day I thought we had been fairly quit of them both, for as she was diverting her self on the side of the boat she fell into the sea near Vila Franca, and had certainly perished if the poor Husband, in the outmost dispaire, had not throuen himself into the sea after her, and by swiming saved her Life. However, the creature was not a bit the better for the danger she had escaped, but continued as Frantick as ever. We were detained some days at Villa Franca on account of a great storm, and I took the freedom to ask her what she was to do at Barcelone, where she was going, since it appeared evident to me that one man cou'd not content her. She frankly acknowledged this, but said she wou'd go into a Monastry, where she wou'd be restrained from seeing men and committing extravagances. I asked her likeways what was the reasone she was not contented with her own Husband, who was a very pretty young man. She said she had two reasons, first that he was her Husband, and she did not care to be tied to any body, and next because he was too fond of her and too frequent in his caresses.

This poor man was certainly the worst married of any man in Life, tho' he merited from this leud creature much better treatment. He was so madly fond of her that he used with [pleasure] to relate his courtship of her and how he spent his Evenings with a Guitar in the Spanish way, under her windowes.

I have mentioned this affaire as an Instance of the frailty and inconstancy of the women of that country, for if any body had told me all I knew of this poor young creature, I cou'd not possibly have believed them.

We continued our voyage together till we came into the Gulfe of Lions, or Thulon. We designed to have sailed over it before night, and to have taken up our quarters on the *fol. 27.* South-west side of it, but a | great north wind springing up, we were drove out to sea, and miserably tossed about till midnight. The wind began then to slaken, and to avoide falling into the hands of the Algerians, we made towards the French coast, but in this task we sprung a leke, and with the greatest difficulty got near a sand bank, where we stuck. It was then very dark, we had no thought of being so near the shore as we found our selves next morning, wherefor we gave up all hopes of Life.

In this dismal plight we were in the outmost confusion—

some cried, some prayed, but I observed that our Spanish Lady shewed more Courage than her Husband. A great many vous were made by my companions to this and the other Virgin Mary or Saint upon being delivered from the danger we were in, but she made no vous, as I believe she was conscious of not keeping them. It was our great happiness that there was no Tide where we were, so that when day appeared to break we had suffered no other Harm than what a cold night produced. We had sitten in water to our knees, but finding we were within a stone's cast of the Land, we found no difficulty in geting a shore.

or that the Saint wou'd not hear her.

This hapned on the 7 of January 1699.

Here we left our boat to be refitted by a Carpenter from Marsailes, and by the help of some Asses got safe to this city.

I staid at Marsails but a few days, for I left my Spanish Gentleman and his Lady to pursue by Land their journey to Barcelona, while I and my French companion proceeded on the Road to Lions.

In our way, as I lay at Orange, I hapned to be agreably surprised about midnight with singing of Psalms, for it seems my Landlord was a Protestant, and had ventured to live there, tho' most part of all the Protestants of that country hapned to be banished out of France some years before. | Nothing hapned to me remarkable either in Avignon or Lions, where I staid about a week, wherefor I took my place as one of eght in the stage coach called the Diligence, and came to Paris about the end of january 1699.

I wou'd not have mentioned these ... but that in the ...ence of the Wor ... I look upon it as an advantage to ... that there are men and women of ... characters.

fol. 28.

In this City and at Versailes I saw a compend of all the splendour and vanities of the world. The king, Louis Le Grand,[1] as he was called, was always under the Government of some Woman or other, and vastly intoxicated with the flatteries of those about him at that time. His son, the Dauphine,[2] was not only alive, but three of his sons, the Duke of Burgundy, the Duke of Anjue,[3] afterwards King of Spain, and the Duke of Berry: the youngest of these seem'd not to be under fourteen years of age. Old Lewis was a big black sensual man, who

[1] Louis XIV., born 1638; succeeded to the crown 1643; died 1715.

[2] Louis the Dauphin, born 1661; died 1711.

[3] Born 1683; assumed the crown of Spain, in virtue of the will of Charles II., 1700; died 1746.

had given a great deal of disturbance to Europe, and was like to give a great deal more.

N.B.—My Lord Stair a Relation ... when he was Ambassador at the court of France in ... this great ... dye of a Gangrene in his leg, and left ... bed with his ... exposed in little better condition than a Dog, for all the court deserted him and went to the Duke of Orleans.

Paris was agreeable to me only for the conversation I found there, but was far from giving me that entertainment I had at Rome. Every thing I saw seem'd only to be a copy from some great Original I saw there, Houses, palaces, villas, Gardens, statues, pictures, were all mean in comparisone with what I had observed in Italy. Versailes and its gardens I found excelled in bulk and extent any thing I had ever seen before, but they seem'd at best but awkward imitations, and at last I wearied so much of them that I was not at the pains to go any where out of Paris. Operas and comedies here, Musick, and all entertainments except Dancing, displeased me exceedingly. |
fol. 29. At this last exercise I thought the French excelled all others, so that the greatest Encomium I cou'd bestow on a French man was to allow that he was a good dancer, that is, his aire and motion in a Dance was agreable to me, or possibly to any British man, but to no body else, for neither the Italians nor Spaniards wou'd allow the French any other agreable gesture or mien but what became a Monky more than a Man.

I staid at Paris for some months, but had wearied exceedingly if it had not been for the Company of Signior Capri, the Mathematician, whom the King of France had brought from Bolognia. There was likeways there one Mr. Glover,[1] a Scotsman, who was a very great phylosopher, and otherways a most agreeable companion. With these Gentlemen, and a few others, I liv'd 'till the Month of june, when I set out for Bruxelles, to return home by the way of Holand.

I visited by the way several great cities, as Mons, Cambrey, and Valencienes, but found them chiefly remarkable for their fortifications. After I had observed all the curiosities of Brussels, I went to Antwerp, which in former times had been the chief city of the Low countries for Trade and Manufactories, but now in absolute decay. Several things here gave

[1] 'While I staid in Paris I followed for the most part the study of Mathematicks under one Glover, who came to my House.'—MS. *Travels*, vol. ii. p. 170. Probably the 'Sieur Jean Glover, Ingenieur, Gentlehomme Ecossois,' who was author of *La Rone Arithmetique*, 8vo, Paris, 1699, and of *Nouvelle Mannière d'Executer des Loteries*, 8vo, Paris, 1705.

me great pleasure, particularly some churches and pictures by Rubens. However, I found I had left all the best things of this kind at Rome and in other cities of Italy, therefor I made all the dispatch I could 'till I arrived in Rotterdam. |

Even some of the best things of ... are in Italy [Rubens after he came

In Holand I trifled away 3 months in making visits to my *fol. 30.* friends and old Acquaintances there. I was constantly with Doctor Bouerhaven while I staid at Leyden, and found he had made a very great progress in physick and chymy. What I admired most of his Genius was, that tho' he was a big clumsey man, with fingers proportionable, yet from the time I had left him in Holand, he had acquired a dexterity in playing on the French Lute above all men I had ever heard. As I had acquainted him with my case when the small-pox recurred upon me at Rome, he frankly ouned that he had tri'd his experiment on others, but that it wou'd not do; for tho' his medicine retarded and purged off the infectious morbifick matter of the small-pox for a time, yet it had always recurred with worse symptoms than before. The Doctor was an assiduous attender and performer at Concerts of Musick, and both he and I were at least on this account acceptable in all the best companies at Leyden, Amsterdam, or elsewhere. Holand and its inhabitants entertained me likeways so well in other respects, that with a much smaller allouance than I was to expect in Scotland, I cou'd have lived there all my life; but my Father, by reiterated commands, oblidged me to leave it and go over to London. I was very unlucky in the passage boat, for a great storm drove | it back to the Briel; but in a *fol. 31.* few days afterwards I had a safe passage to Harwich, from thence I went to London, where I staid but a few days, and by journey riding, in company with my Unckle, Mr. William Clerk,[1] I arrived in Scotland on the 2 of novem^r 1699, after I had been 5 years abroad.

and saw some of the antient Greek statues, he found that till then he had not known the *perfectissima naturæ.*

N.B.—The Doctor had been very happy in his oun conceit, if at this time he had found the Art of inoculating the small pox which has since obtain'd such great success, and was even then practised in all the Turkish Empire, particularly at Constantinople.

As I passed from Hadington to Lonhead, on my way to Pennicuik, I found my Father there, who received me very kindly.

I was but a few days at home when I fell sick, for it seems

[1] Third son of John Clerk, first proprietor of Penicuik, 'bred to physic, a man of singular humour, and a remarkable traveller.' He died unmarried.

the Aire and diet of my Country did not agree with me for some time.

After my recovery I fell again to the study of the civil law, in order to be received into the faculty of Advocates at Edr, and in the meantime I took impartial pains to discover what advantages I had received by my 5 years absence abroad, and to make suittable improvements.[1] On my side of the account I had studied law with some mathematicks and phylosophy; I likeways spoke Dutch, French, and Italian pretty readily. I had acquired a little more knowledge of the world; but to ballance all this I found I had spent 5 years of my youth to no great purpose, for 2 or 3 years had been sufficient for all the real good I had done my self. I had likeways spent at least 600 lib. Str. more than my Father knew of, which gave me a very great deal of truble for many years after.

I have heard [that] myGrandfather when he lived at Paris, as a merchand had a bad opinion of the Gentlemen that came there. I believe he was in the right, and [that] no young Boy ought to stay there more than a year or two at most. My Father did best who staid in Holand and France but a few months.

But to return to my studies of the law, they proceeded so well with me, and I recovered so easly what I had lost by my travels in Germany, Italy, and | France, that I passed both the privat and publick examinations with some applause, being afterwards admitted an Advocat.[2] The next consideration was how to gain a little experience in the practise of the Law. This I found very difficult, for I had a natural bashfulness, which I cou'd not conquer; and I found it always easier for me to please others on what I said than to please my self. However, this went in part over by my being constantly in publick business, since the year 1703, as will be afterwards

fol. 32.

---

[1] His MS. *Travels* concludes as follows:—

'*N.B.* my Improvements abroad were these.

'I had studied the civil Law for 3 Winters at Leyden, and did not neglect it at Rome, by which means I passed Advocat by a privat and publick examination some months after my arrival, with great ease and some credite.

'I spoke French and Italian very well, but particularly Dutch, having come young into Holand, and keept more in the company of Holanders than those of my own Country.

'I had applied much to Classical Lairning, and had more than an ordinary inclination for the Greek and Roman Antiquities.

'I understood pictures better than became my Purse, and as to Musick, I rather performed better, particularly on the Herpesecord, than became a Gentleman.

'This to the best of my knowledge is a faithful account of myself.

'John Clerk.'

[2] He was admitted an advocate on 20th July 1700.

showen. However, as the same bashfulness was, it seems, part of my constitution, it never left me to this houer; for tho' I have had many occasions to speak in publick, not only as a Baron of the Exchequer, but frequently as head of the Court, I never spoke but against my inclinations, and indeed it has been my constant choise rather to hear others than speak my self, even in privat conversations. The Talent of Copiousness and Loquacity I abominated in all my acquaintances, and therefor cou'd never think to practise it my self.

I was about 24 years of age when I was admitted an Advocat, and a little after my Father tried all the ways he cou'd think of to have me marry with some prospect of real advantage with regard to my Fortune. He had projected a Wife for me, the Daughter of ———,[1] but the Lady was not to my taste, and indeed it was happy for me to have stopt short in this Amour, for she proved the most disagreable woman I ever knew, 'tho otherways a nise enough conceity woman. | the P—t of the ... —n.

The next attempt my Father made was for the Daughter of a certain Lord, afterwards an Earle,[2] but before I made any advances that way, I found that she was engaged to a neighbouring Gentleman, Mr. C. of O., to whom she was afterwards married, and proved a very good Woman for the short time she lived. The third attempt of this kind was indeed a choise of my own, Lady Margaret Stuart, the eldest sister of the Earl of Galloway.[3] This young lady was a very handsome woman, and for the most part bred up in Galloway, a stranger to the follies of Edin., and one with whom I thought I cou'd be very happy. She was about 22 years of Age, and was the daughter of very honourable and verteous parents, Alexander, Earl of Galloway,[4] and Lady Mary Douglass, eldest sister *fol.* 33. Earl of H—d. Lady Margaret Stuart.

[1] There are blanks here in the MS.

[2] John, second Lord Carmichael, created Earl of Hyndford in 1700. His eldest daughter Beatrice married, in 1700, John Cockburn of Ormiston, the well-known agricultural reformer, eldest son of Adam Cockburn, Lord Justice-Clerk.

[3] She was sister of James, fifth Earl of Galloway. See Illustration No. VI., from a portrait by Aikman, in the possession of Sir George Clerk, who also has a wax cast of her face, taken after death.

[4] Alexander, third Earl of Galloway, and his wife Lady Mary Douglas, eldest daughter of James, second Earl of Queensberry.

of William, Duke of Queensberry. We contracted a friendship and familiarity with one another in the space of 5 or 6 months that her Brother brought her to Edin. to see her Friends. My Father was exceedingly pleased with the match, but wou'd contract very small things for a Lady of Quality to live on, viz., about 4000 ms. Scots yearly for our support during his life, and 4000 ms. for a joynture in case I hapned to die before her. The Earl her Brother scrupled much at this, because she was provided to 2000 lib. ster. of portion and something more, which had been saved to her in her minority. However she was resolved to take her hazard, and we were married with the consent of all parties, on the 6th of March 1701.

He was satisfied with the jointure, but displeased with our present provision.

About two weeks after, we were carried out by my Father to Pennicuik, where we lived all very happily together till the month of | novembr. I had waited in the Summer Session at Edn. as an Advocat, and in the begining of Winter we took a lodging in Town, partly to attend the Session, but chiefly that my Wife inclined to have a House of her own since she found herself with child.

fol. 34.

My Father gave us a sufficiency of money to furnish up our little House in a very handsome way, and so I commenced the head of a Family, being then about 25 years of Age.

I should have noticed a circumstance preceeding my Marriage, which in reality laid the happiness of my whole Life, and which was this. The Parliament of Scotland, which met on the 29 Octr 1700, by appointment of King William, had for his Majesty's high Commissioner James Duke of Queensberry,[1] who was Cousin German to the Earl of Galloway and Lady Margaret Stuart, my future Spouse. My Father hapned to have the honour of his acquaintance as a Member of Parliament, and on the same account was frequently with him. The Earl of Galloway had acquainted him of our intention, and upon this notice his Grace invited me once and again to dine with him. As he was a very friendly affable man, I had the

[1] The second Duke of Queensberry, and first Duke of Dover, born 18th December 1662. He 'represented the king as high-commissioner to the parliament of Scotland, 1700, acquitting himself so much to his Majesty's satisfaction that he was nominated a Knight of the Garter 18th June 1701, and installed at Windsor 10th July following.' He died 6th July 1711.

VI
LADY MARGARET STUART
First Wife of Baron Sir John Clerk

good fortune of coming into favour with him. He spoke to my Father about the match, and pressed him to enlarge the yearly allouance he proposed to give us. My Father it seems contented him by telling him I was to get all he had except very moderat provisions for my Brothers and Sisters, whereupon he gave his consent to my marriage. To this alliance, therefor, I owed the greatest felicity of my Life, as will appear in the sequel of this account.

After my Wife and I had been settled in our House for a few weeks I fell ill of a cold. My Wife was anxiously concerned about me, | which gave me more truble than my desease, *fol.* 35. and to add to my afflictions it seems, God was to deprive me of this valouable woman, for she fell into labour, and a few hours after being delivered of a son, she died to the unspeakable grief of every Body who knew her.

The best account I can give of her death is this. On the 20 of Decembr 1700,[1] about midnight, her pains came upon her. I was then oblidged to leave her Room, being every way in great distress, but she took leave of me with a seeming satisfaction, and said she hoped that she cou'd be in no danger.

Towards the morning, when she felt her pains coming fast upon her, she sent for my Father, for he was then in his own Lodging in Edin., and beged he wou'd pray for her, since she was assured that she was dying. He accordingly prayed very fervently for her, having a great regard to her, but encouraged her all he cou'd by telling her that there was not one bad symptom about her. Still she persisted that she was steping into Eternity, for it seems she felt some of these symptoms in child bearing of which her Mother, Lady Mary Douglass, died.

At least she [lost] heart after they ... and her [mother] ... born 12 children ...

About 7 in the morning she was brought to bed of a Son, to the satisfaction of all about her, but when every body had run into my Room to carry me the good news, she fell into fainting Fits, and on recovering a little out of them, she sent to acquaint me that she found her self dying, and therefor wanted to see me. This was a terrible shock to me, being at that instant very ill and in bed, however, I got quickly up, and by the assistence of some of the women I stagered into my dear Wife's

[1] A clerical error for 1701, the year stated in Douglas's *Peerage*, where, however, the day is given the 26th December.

Room, to whom it pleased God I should make my last Visite. |
fol. 36. I fell on my knees on her bed side, and prayed that God wou'd spare her, but she interrupted me with these words, *My dear Life, I must leave you, but I am hopeful that I shall be happy, and that God will be merciful to my Soul. Live and take care of our poor Child.* She would have said more, but my Father, judging that she wou'd be much the worse by speaking, carried me from her, and I was never blest with the sight of her any more.

... the most melancholy Schene that ever hapned to a poor young Man exalted to the highest degree of his wishes, and in a few houres throuen down into a Gulph of the greatest misery.

No Tongue can express the sadness of my condition. I returned to bed, but in such a plight as no body cou'd well decern whither I was dead or alive.

A little while after, her Brother, Colonel Stuart of Sorbie,[1] came to see her, to whom she said, taking him by the hand, Dear John, farewell, for I am just steping into Eternity.

Tho she seem'd to me extreamly fond and anxious to have a son, yet she choised not to call to see him, but recommended him with great earnestness to my Father and all the Friends about her.

We had called for one of the chief Physitians in Town, one Doctor Hackete,[2] and two of the chief chyrurgeons, my unckle Robert Clerk, and one Mr. Hamilton,[3] a man much emploied in Midwifery. They took all the pains about her they cou'd think of, but I am afraied they were too hasty in their operations, by which she lost a vast deal of blood. The placenta, it seems, was adhering to the uterus, and this they thought themselves oblidged to bring away by force. They encouraged her afterwards with hopes that she wou'd be very well, but
fol. 37. she was positive that she was dying, | and therefor gave herself up intirely to prayer. Mr. Meldrum,[4] a very pious Minister in

---

[1] Brigadier-General the Hon. James Stewart of Sorbie, third son of Alexander, third Earl of Galloway. He died at Scobie, 22d April 1748.

[2] Dr. James Halket was an original member of the Royal College of Physicians, Edinburgh, at its incorporation on St. Andrew's Day, 1681. He was elected President of the College on 30th November 1704.

[3] James Hamilton, elected a member of the Royal College of Surgeons, Edinburgh, on 3d October 1695, and President 1702-3.

[4] The Rev. George Meldrum was Regent of Marischal College, Aberdeen, and in 1658 was elected by the Town Council minister of the second charge in Aberdeen. He was deprived by the Acts of Parliament 11th June, and of Privy

Town, came to see her, at which she expressed the outmost satisfaction, and tho he wou'd not allow her to speak, she expressed great fervency in prayer by her eyes and hands lifted up to heaven.

In the meantime her Doctors were not despairing of her recovery, wherefor, it being Sunday, 21 of Dr, some of her Friends went to church, and those who staid at home continued to keep her quiet, so far as her intollerable pains wou'd allow her.

From 9 to 10 in the morning these pains increased, and her cries were so piercing to me in the next Room that it wou'd be very difficult for any body to conceive the vast agony they put me in.

About half an Houer after Ten the Doctor came to me and acquainted me that my dear Wife was indeed very ill and in great danger. I took his visite as from a Messenger of Death, and therefor did the best I cou'd to prepare my self for the heavy stroke that was to befall me, and indeed the greatest comfort I had at the time was that I my self was very ill, and was in hopes soon to follow her.

About eleven I was informed that she turned her self in bed with the same easiness as if she had been in health, and calling on God to receive her soul, she never spoke more. Thus I lost the best woman that ever breathed Life, for besides many

I may say with Horace: Ergo...perpetuus sopor

Council 1st October 1662; suspended by the Synod 24th October after till 1st January next, for not subscribing canonical obedience, and deposed by the Bishop and Synod the same month. Having been accused of seditious carriage, he was summoned before the Privy Council 16th December succeeding. On taking the oath of allegiance and declaring his readiness to comply with Episcopacy, he was recommended by them to the Primate, in order to his being reponed, which was done accordingly. He was Rector in Marischal College ten times, and was deprived of his charge in 1681 for not taking the Test. He was admitted minister of Kilwinning in 1688, and was transferred to the second charge of the Tron Church, Edinburgh, in 1692; elected Moderator of the General Assembly in 1698, and again in 1703; and Professor of Divinity in the University in 1701. Died 18th February 1709, in the seventy-fifth year of his age and fifty-first of his ministry. He was a 'learned, pious, and laborious minister, had great abilities for his office, having a most sweet, plain, pathetick way of preaching, yet very pungent and affectionate in his application of doctrine, being of a godly and upright conversation, and a large compass of solid knowledge.' Several of his sermons and pamphlets were published.—See Scott's *Fasti*.

Urguet! cui Pudor, et Justitiæ soror Incorrupta *fol.* 38. Fides, nudaque Veritas Nunquam (*sic*) inveniet parem.

Tho she hated to be talkative, she was the most eloquent woman when she behoved to talk that ever I knew in my Life, she was far from being censorious, but so great a mimick that where there was any thing singular in any body's voice or gesture, she cou'd imitat it to a surprising degree.

My Father, who was vastly fond of him, wou'd have taken him to Pennicuik, but as he was only child of his [son] he shuned to ... least any misfortune had hapned to ... because he keept ... very well under the care of so kindly a woman as Lady Carrny, my [aunt] was.

excellent qualifications which admirably fitted her to be my Wife, she was a person of vast piety, was much acquainted with the Scriptures, and | unweariedly assiduous in her duty to God. She was sober and plain in her diet, dress, and vastly inclined to acts of charity, suitable to what she had to bestow. She was prudent and frugal, a persone of excellent sense, and no body cou'd give a better advice in most things.

I had therefor good reasone to bewail her loss, and envy the Grave which divided me from her. I courted sickness and death at that time, and for many months after, more than ever I had courted Life in the greatest height of my prosperity.[1]

My father likeways shewed no less concern for her, and with many tears lamented her death.

Some houres after this heavy misfortune I was carried into Rooms in the next house, for my sickness and affliction made me so weak that I cou'd not stand on my feet.

My poor unfortunat Son,[2] like a phenix from the ashes of his mother, was carried away by the Lady Carrnie,[3] a sister of my Father, with whom he staid for several years, till he was fit for the school.

In the mean time preparations were made for my Wife's interrment, which my Father and I appointed to be in our burial place at Pennicuik. This last ceremonie was perform'd by coaches from Edin., on the 24 of december, and she was laid in a coffin of lead near to my Mother.

It was afterwards the least part of my truble to see my little family, so lately set up, all dispersed, and every one of us, except a single servant to wait on my self, sent to different places.

My Wife had an only Sister, Lady Henretta Stuart,[4] whom she fondly loved, and who staid with her from our coming to

---

[1] At folio 38 of the MS. is inserted a poem of fifty-three lines, in Clerk's handwriting, titled, 'Some Verses on the Death of my dear wife, Lady Margaret Stuart, who died in childbed, 21 December 1700, aged 22 years,' inscribed before his signature, 'Sic lugens cecini, 20 feb. 1701.'

[2] See Illustration No. VII., from a portrait by William Aikman, in the possession of Sir George Clerk.

[3] Margaret, eldest daughter of John Clerk, the first owner of Penicuik. She married William Aikman of Cairny, and was mother of William Aikman, the portrait-painter, who sold the property when he started for the Continent to study art.

[4] Lady Henriet Stuart, youngest daughter of Alexander, third Earl of Galloway.

VII
JOHN CLERK
Eldest Son of Baron Sir John Clerk

VII

JOHN CLERK

Eldest Son of Baron Sir John Clerk

Town to her death. This young lady, with unspeakable sorrow, went | likeways to another house, and sometime afterwards to Galloway. The Earl, her Brother, was then in that country, and was in the deepest affliction for his sister, without the opportunity, which he regretted much, of paying his last duty to her.

N.B. This young Lady was 3 years younger than my Wife, and was afterwards married to the Earl of Glencairn.[1] *N.B.* She is still alive, 26 Dr. 175[3].

fol. 39.

After my Wife's death, I lived in Edin., retired from all mortals, for I never went any where but once every third day to see my son, who was extreamly like his mother and the family of Galloway. I recovered weakly from the indisposition I was in, and even the small degree of health I enjoyed was disagreable to me. My Father saw me often, and took much pains to comfort me, but to little purpose, for I got no rest in the night time but by taking pretty large doses of Laudanum, and at last, by meer mismanagement of my self, I fell into a Hectique Feaver. It was then the month of May, when the country Aire was in its perfection; by my Father's advice, therefore, and that of the Doctors about me, I retired to Pennicuik.

Here I grew better by a kind of milk and vegetable diet, and at last recovered perfectly.

In my melancholly situation I was much oblidged to the Earl of Galloway and Colonel Stuart, my Wife's Brother. They kept a close correspondence with me, and ever after did me all the good offices that were in their power.

I was no less oblidged to the Duke of Queensberry, their Cousin, who always treated me as if I had been his Son, as will afterwards more particularly appear.

I spent the remainder of the year 1701 in great solitude, being seldom in Edin., and I lived for some months in the year 1702 | much in the same way, and for the most part at Pennicuik with my Father.

1701.

fol. 40.

In June 1702 the Earl of Galloway came to see me at Pennicuik, on his way to Edin., being called to attend the Parlia-

[1] William, twelfth Earl of Glencairn, succeeded his father in 1704. He supported the Treaty of Union, was sworn a Privy Councillor, and appointed Governor of Dumbarton Castle. Died 14th March 1734. The date of his marriage to Lady Henriet Stuart is given by Douglas as 20th February 1704. (Compare folio 52 of this MS.) She survived till 21st October 1763, when she died in Glasgow in her eighty-first year.

ment. The sight of him revived all my sorrows, and I believe our meeting had the same effect on him, for he never spoke of his sister but with Tears.

I went with him to Edin., and in his company attended the Duke of Queensberry, who was then the High Commissioner to the parliament. His Grace made his compliments of condolence on the death of his Cousin with great civility and humanity. I made him such returns as I thought suitable, and from that moment he took a resolution to advance me to every station in the Government of Scotland that he thought proper for me.

His Grace was a compleat Courtier, and partly by art, and partly by nature, he had brought himself into a habite of saying very civil and oblidging things to every body. I knew his charecter, and there for was not much elated with his promises. However, I found afterwards that there was nothing he had promised to do for me but what he made good.

After this, his Grace not only allowed me, but desired me to attend him in Parliament, which I constantly did 'till its dissolution.

The chief design of this session of Parliament was to recognize the Authority of her Majesty Queen Ann on the death of her predecessor, King William, and to impouer her to nominate Commissioners for a Treaty of Union between Scotland and England. |

fol. 41. The Duke got these two points setled to his satisfaction by the 1 and 7 Act of this session 1702; he likeways induced the parliament to write a letter to her Majesty in relation to the union, which, by the bye, shews that all the people of Scotland were to expect a Treaty of Union in due time, and consequently were to prepare such instructions to their Members of parliament as they thought fit.

In consequence of the above Act impowring the Queen to name Commissioners for a Treaty of Union, they were accordingly appointed; but upon meeting with the Commissioners for England to the same effect, they came to no final resolutions; this great work therefor fell to the lot of other Commissioners appointed in the year 1706, of which number I hapned to be one.

Upon the rising of the parliament of Scotland, about the end of June 1702, the Duke of Queensberry took journey for London, and his cousin, the Earl of Galloway, and some others of his Friends, waited on him to Dunbar. I was permitted to be one of the retinue, and, after taking leave of the Duke, I returned with the Earl to Pennicuik, and from thence in a day or two I waited on him to the Lead hills on his way to Galloway.

I return'd afterwards to Edin., and as an Advocate waited on the Court of Session till the vacation in August.

From the beginning of this Month till the first of november I continued at Pennicuik, but still in a very melanchollý and solitary way. In the mean time, I found | that my appointed *fol.* 42. time of Death was not come; for tho' I both wished for it and stood prepared for it, with a full resignation to the great Author of my being, yet I found that some of my Maladies went off by degrees. My late heavy loss, however, came houerly into my mind, which I found, in spight of all my endeavours, nothing but Time cou'd remedy.

I often reflected on these words of Horace—Durum: sed levius fit patientia quidquid corrigere est nefas.[1]

During the Winter session I lived very retiredly, studied hard, eated and sleept little, and yet it pleased God to recover me perfectly, and to furnish me with a good stock of Health.

In March 1703 I return'd to live with my Father in Pennicuik, and about this time fell exceedingly into the humure of planting and makeing of nurseries.

My Father observing this, devolved upon me all his concerns this way, and I began my first plantations on the south side of the House of Pennicuik, near the Water of Esk, at an old coal hole on the Brae, to which, from Don Quixote's cave, we gave the name of Montesina's Cave.[2]

About this time likeways I was made very happy by the return of my second Brother, called Henry,[3] who been bred a sea man in the East Indies, and, as there was always great love and friendship between us, we never parted till Death seperated us in the year 1715.

---

[1] Od. i. 24.

[2] This still exists in the bank at the north of Harlaw Loch.

[3] Henry Clerk, second son of Sir John Clerk, first Baronet of Penicuik, died unmarried in 1715. See folio 101 of this MS.

While I staid at Pennicuik in Aprile 1703, an incident hapned to me which contributed very much to my future
fol. 43. Advantages, | for a new Parliament being called to meet in May thereafter, I found no difficulty, by the interest of the Earl of Galloway, to get my self chosen for the Burgh of Whithorn in Galloway as its representative.[1]

This Parliament began on the 6th of that month, the Duke of Queensberry being appointed her Majesty's Commissioner. It began with the usual procession from the Abey of Holyroodhouse to the Parliament House in Edin. The Lords, Barons, and representatives for the Royal Burrows, made a very grand appearance, and such as I never saw the like in any foreign place. The last solemnity of this kind, I my self had occasion to see, in the year 1686, when the Father of this Duke of Queensberry was High Commissioner. I was then a very young Boy, and had not the least apprehension for many years after that I should make one at the next Cavalcade of this kind.

Rideing the Parliament.

A convention of Estates followed the Revolution by King William in 1688, which was afterwards turned into a parliament, and continued 'till the Death of that King in 1702. The same parliament continued to sit upon the accession of Queen Ann to the Crown, and was not dissolved till the year 1703, when the new Parliament was called.

I need not describe the solemnity of the above Cavalcade;[2] only, with regard to my self, I was mounted on a fine gray pad belonging to the Duke of Queensberry, and equipt with
fol. 44. black velvet | accoutrements, as all the representatives of the Royal Burrows were.

---

[1] He represented Whithorn in the Scottish Parliament 1702-7, and in the first Parliament of Great Britain, 1707-8.

[2] See *Extracts from the Registers of the Privy Council of Scotland, and other Papers connected with the Method and Manner of Ryding the Scottish Parliament*, MDC-MDCCII.'—*Maitland Club Miscellany*, vol. iii., 1843. A series of three drawings representing the cavalcade in 1685 is preserved in the Advocates' Library; the first and third being drawings by Chalmers, herald painter to James VII., the second a drawing by Horace Walpole from the original, now lost. The series was reproduced in a set of engravings dedicated to David, Earl of Buchan, by Alexander Kincaid. A less accurate portrayal of the pageant at the opening of the Scots Parliament is engraved in Gueudeville's *Atlas Historique* (Amsterdam, 1708).

We proceeded to the Parliament House, where the Duke, having had his Commission read, made us a fine speech after the House had been regularly constituted, as the custom was. The Earl of Seafield,[1] afterwards Earl of Finlatere, adjourned us for a day or two by another speech, and we returned all back to the Abey in the same formalities we came to the Parliament House. There we were splendidly entertain'd by his Grace, and I was for the most part always at dinner with him while the parliament continued to sit.

as Chancellor.

I have throuen togither some observations on this session of Parliament in another Manuscript book, so shall say little here. It was divided in 3 factions, who, as they had different views, drove different ways. The first was what was called the Court party; they were for supporting the Crown and the Credite of the High Commissioner, consequently they were for giving moderat subsidies for supporting the Government against the insults of the French, with whom we were, at that time, in war. They had the union of the two nations in view, because they not only considered it as the happiest thing that cou'd be brought about for the Interest of Great Britain, but because it was expressly recommended to them by the Queen. The second faction was that of the Jacobites; they were to thwart and disturb the Administration at any rate. The third faction was what went under the name of the | Squadrone Volante. These consisted of about fifteen Lords and Gentlemen, all Whigs in their principles, but who herded together, and keept little or no communication with the Duke of Queensberry and his Friends. They were for opposing every thing which they durst oppose, but to keep firmly in their view the succession of the Crown in the House of Hanover. They pretended to be great Patriots, and to stand up chiefly in defence of the rights and privileges of the subjects; in a word, the publick good and the liberty of the subjects were still in their mouths, but in their Hearts they were known to have Court preferments and places in the chiefest degree of veneration. These were the springs and motives of all their Actions, which appeared in a hundred instances thereafter. However, by the bye, I

fol. 46.

A true description of Modern Patriotism.

[1] Viscount Seafield, fourth Earl of Findlater; see note, p. 62.

must say that such a Squadrone Volante in any Parliament seems to be always a happy means in the hand of Providence to keep the several members of an Administration in their duty, for people in great power seldom fail to take more upon them than falls to their share.

The chiefs of the Squadrone Lords were the Dukes of Montrose[1] and Roxburgh,[2] the Earls of Rothess[3] and Hadington,[4] all these young men of about 24 years of Age; but the chief of all, at least the man under whose name they principally voted, was the Marquise of Twedale,[5] a very good Man, but not perfectly qualified for Court intrigues. |

fol. 47. Amongst their Gentlemen was one Mr. Fletcher of Saltoun,[6]

---

[1] James, fourth Marquis of Montrose, succeeded his father in 1685. In 1705 he was appointed Lord High Admiral of Scotland, and in 1706 President of the Council. For his steady support to the Union and the Protestant Succession he was created Duke of Montrose in 1707. He was appointed Keeper of the Privy Seal in 1709, and re-appointed in 1716; and in 1714 he succeeded the Earl of Mar as a principal Secretary of State. Died 1742.

[2] John, fifth Earl of Roxburghe, succeeded his brother in 1696. In 1704 he was appointed one of the Secretaries of State, and for his promotion of the Union and the Protestant Succession he was created Duke of Roxburghe in 1707. Having distinguished himself during the Rebellion of 1715, he was constituted Secretary of State for Scotland in 1716. Died 1741.

[3] John, seventh Earl of Rothes, succeeded his mother in 1700. He was Keeper of the Privy Seal in 1704, in 1715 was very active against the rebels, and fought at Sheriffmuir. Died 1722.

[4] Thomas, sixth Earl of Haddington. Born 1680, a younger brother of the Earl of Rothes; in 1687 he had a charter of the earldom of Haddington, and succeeded his father, Charles, the fifth Earl. He fought with great courage at Sheriffmuir, 15th November 1715, when he was wounded and had a horse shot under him. He occupied himself greatly in planting and improving his estate of Tyninghame, and died 28th November 1735.

[5] John, second Marquis of Tweeddale, born 1645, was Colonel of the East Lothian regiment raised to suppress the rebels on the invasion of Scotland in 1685 by the Earl of Argyll, and he was High Treasurer of Scotland in 1695. He succeeded his father in 1697, was High Commissioner to the Scots Parliament in 1704, and succeeded the Earl of Seafield as High Chancellor of Scotland in that year. He married, in 1666, Lady Anne Maitland, only child of the Duke of Lauderdale, and died in 1713.

[6] Andrew Fletcher of Salton, the celebrated patriot, son and heir of Sir Robert Fletcher, born 1655, died 1716. The following opinion of our author upon Fletcher is quoted in a note in Somerville's *History of Great Britain during the Reign of Queen Anne* (London, 1798, p. 204), 'from Sir John Clerk's MS. notes on Lockhart's *Memoirs*,' pp. 71, 156:—'Mr. Fletcher's schemes had but

a Man of Republican principles, who had spent his youth in Holand, had been forfeited under the late King James, but afterwards restored under King William by Act of Parliament. He was a man a little untoward in his temper, and much inclined to Eloquence. He made many speeches in Parliament, which are all printed, but was not very dexterous in making extemporary replies. He was, however, a very Honest Man, and meant well in every thing he said and did, except in cases where his humure, passion, or prejudices were suffered to get the better of his reasone.

N.B. These Speeches are to be found in the 38 volume of ... pamphlets, a book in 12°.

The above mentioned Factions rubb'd upon one another and with great severity, so that we were often in the form of a Polish diet, with our swords in our hands, or at least our hands at our swords. In all this struggle, therefore, there was no great good done, so that I am persuaded we had spent our time at home more to the benefite of the nation.

In this session, to silence the murmurs of some splenetick people, and those who were Ennemies to the last administration under King William, an Act past impowering certain Commissioners to enquire into the publick accompts and debts of the nation. I had the honour to be chosen one of them, I suppose by the Duke of Queensberry's recommendation. At this time, being in an humure of scribling, and debates rising very high about | Limitations on the Crown to take place after *fol.* 48. her Majesty's decease, I took upon me to write two Pamphlets, one against diminishing the antient prerogatives of the Crown, the other an Essay upon the intended Limitations. Both were well received by those of my own sentiments, others were pycked at them; but few ever discovered that I was the Author.[1]

There was likeways a notable Act concerted this Session of parliament, intituled Act for Security of the Kingdom; but it was refused the Royal assent till the subsequent session of Parliament, of which hereafter.

By this Act all the people of Scotland were to be armed,

very little credit, because he himself was often for changing them, though in other respects a very worthy man. It used to be said of him that it would be easy to hang him by his own schemes of government, for if they had taken place he would have been the first man that would have attempted an alteration.'

[1] I have been unable to identify these two pamphlets.

and a provision made that on the event of the Queen's death, the persone chosen in England to succeed her should not succeed to the Crown of Scotland, unless certain conditions should be granted by the English to the Scots, such as a free communication of Trade and the Liberty of the Plantations, etc.

From the rising of the Parliament, which was about the end of September 1703, I retired to Pennicuik, and applied very closely to my studies, especially to the law and practise of Scotland in all its several Courts, for I was resolved that the favours which some of my Good Friends had heaped on me should not be thought entirely throuen away, and in pursuance of which I return'd to Town about the begining of Novembr, and joined with those Commissioners who had been appointed in the last session of parliament to state and *fol. 49.* examine the | publick accompts.

This affaire opened up to me a very great scene of Business, for all the Books of the Privy Council of Scotland, all those of the Exchequer and Treasury, all the Accompts of the Customs, Excise, and every Branch of the publick Revenue, with the Books that concern'd our Army, all our Garisons and military affaires, were to be laid before us, and perused with that accuracy as to lay a proper state of them before the next session of Parliament.

The Commissioners appointed for this end were 5 of each state, the Earles of Galloway, Noresk,[1] Balcarras,[2] and Dunmore,[3] with the Viscount of Stair[4] for the nobility; Sr Rob.

---

[1] David, fourth Earl of Northesk, succeeded his father in 1688, and was sworn a Privy Councillor 1702. He supported the Treaty of Union, and was chosen a Scottish representative Peer in 1708, and re-chosen 1710 and 1713. Died 1729.

[2] Colin, third Earl of Balcarres, succeeded his brother in 1659. He was imprisoned for raising troops for the restoration of James VII.; and on the failure of Sir James Montgomery of Skelmorly's plot, in 1690, he retired to the Continent, returning in 1700. In 1715 he joined the Pretender's standard, and after the insurrection was quelled was confined in his own house till the Indemnity. Died 1722. His *Account of the Affairs of Scotland relating to the Revolution of* 1688 was published in 1714.

[3] Charles Murray, second son of John, first Marquis of Atholl, was created Earl of Dunmore in 1686. After the Revolution, he was imprisoned, in 1692, along with the Earl of Middleton. On the accession of Queen Anne he was sworn a Privy Councillor, and supported the Union. Died 1710.

[4] John Dalrymple, second Viscount of Stair. Born about 1648: created Earl of Stair, 1703; died 1707.

Dundass of Arniston,[1] Sir John Lauder of Fountainhall,[2] John Haldan of Glenegles,[3] and William Seaton younger of Pitmeden[4] for the Barons; Colin Campbel,[5] Mr. Dougal Stuart,[6] Sir David Cuningham,[7] Mr. Robt Fraser,[8] and my self, for the Burrous.

After our first meeting, the business was all devolved on four of us, Mr. Dougal Stuart, Advocat, Mr. Robt. Fraser, Advocat, Mr. William Seaton of Pitmedden, my self, and some times, tho seldom, the Viscount of Stair, afterwards Earl of Stair.

---

[1] Robert Dundas, second Lord Arniston, eldest son of Sir James Dundas, first Lord Arniston, and his first wife Marian, daughter of Robert Lord Boyd. He was admitted a Senator of the College of Justice in 1689, and died 25th November 1726. (See *Arniston Memoirs.*) His eldest surviving son was the first Lord President Dundas.

[2] Sir John Lauder of Fountainhall passed advocate in 1668, and was counsel to the Duke of Monmouth at his trial in 1686. He was appointed an ordinary Lord of Session in 1689, and a Lord of Justiciary in 1690, and created a Baronet of Nova Scotia in 1690. Died 1722. His wife was Margaret, second daughter of Sir Alexander Seton, Lord Pitmedden.

[3] John Haldane succeeded his father Mungo Haldane, M.P., of Gleneagles, in 1685. He was one of the members for Perthshire in the Convention of 1689, his seat being declared vacant in 1693, because he had not signed the Assurance. He was M.P. for Dumbartonshire 1700-2, and for Perthshire 1702-7, and in the first Parliament of Great Britain 1707-8.

[4] Son of Sir Alexander Seton, first Baronet of Pidmedden, whom he succeeded in 1719, and brother-in-law of Sir John Lauder of Fountainhall. He represented the county of Aberdeen in the Scots Parliament from 1702 till 1706, and was a Commissioner for the Union. He was author of *The Interest of Scotland, in Three Essays*, 8vo, n.p., 1700; *Some Thoughts on Ways and Means for making this Nation a Gainer in Foreign Commerce*, 8vo, Edin. 1705; *Speech . . . on the First Article of the Treaty of the Union*, 4to, Edin. 1706; and *Scotland's Great Advantages by a Union with England*, 4to, n.p., 1706. Died 1744.

[5] Colin Campbell, son of John Campbell of Woodside, represented Renfrew in Parliament 1702-7; died 1746.

[6] Dugald Stewart, younger brother of James, first Earl of Bute, passed advocate in 1694; was M.P. for Rothesay 1702-7; for Perthshire 1708; and Buteshire 1708; he was appointed a Lord of Session and Justiciary 1709, as Lord Blairhill; and died 1710.

[7] Sir David Cunyngham, son of David Cunyngham of Milncraig, co. Ayr, and of Livingstone, co. Linlithgow, was admitted advocate 1673; was M.P. for Lauder 1702-7; created a Baronet of Nova Scotia 1702. He married (first) the Hon. Isabella Dalrymple, youngest daughter of James, first Viscount Stair; (second) Elizabeth, daughter of Sir Robert Baird, Bart., of Saughton Hall. Died 1708.

[8] Robert Fraser was admitted advocate 1686, and was M.P. for Wick 1702-7.

We began with the funds of Cess, Customs, and Excise, from the year 1689 to the year 1701.

After having stated and considered the charges and discharges relative to each year, and made proper observations about the application of the money, we proceeded to the Grants of Herth money and Pole money,[1] and brought all who had been concern'd in the several Branches of the Revenue before us.

fol. 52. We found in the course of our Enquiries | that very great abuses had been committed, for still a considerable part of the money remained in the rapacious hands of those who had collected it.

We finished our Enquiry in about 6 months, for we came to be weary of our office of Inquisiton. I had the fatigue of drawing up the Report from the several books and papers laid before us, which, after being approven of and signed by all the Commissioners, was laid before the Parliament.

Here I make a vain figure, but what can I do in order to tell the truth. These Egotisms I cannot help, other-ways this account of my Life must be vastly defective. These facts I thought fit to notise in order to appologise for ... other ... of ... may hereafter ...

This session of parliament met on the 6 of July 1704, the Marquise of Twedale being her Majesty's High Commissioner. He, it seems, had undertaken great things, and particularly to get the succession to the Crown of Scotland setled on the House of Hanover, with an oath of abjuration enacted against the Pretender, the son of the late King James the 7th, who had taken upon him the stile and tittle of King of Great Britain, or if these projects cou'd not succeed in parliament, he was at least to please those Members of the last session of

[1] Hearth money and Poll money were special taxes imposed by the Scottish Parliament towards the end of the last century to meet arrears due to the country and the army. Hearth money was apparently first imposed by an Act passed in 1690, when a tax of fourteen shillings Scots was levied upon each hearth in the country, the only exception being those of hospitals and of paupers in receipt of parochial relief. From a report lodged in 1704, it would appear that this tax had realised £151,921, 8s., and that over eight thousand hearths had been exempted under the statute.

Poll money seems to have been first imposed for the relief of heritors and others who were liable for supplies; but in 1691 an Act was passed imposing six shillings Scots upon every one per head, except paupers and the children under sixteen of the poorer class living in family with them, and in addition a scale of payment fixed according to the rank and means of the individual. The money so raised was, as in the case of the hearth tax, for arrears due to the country and army.—M.

parliament who had carried on the above mentioned Act of Security.

By these projects, the Duke of Queensberry and his Friends were laid aside, for as the Hannoverian interest prevail'd greatly in the Court at London, there was a necessity to give them all manner of satisfaction who pushed for the immediat settlement of the aforesaid succession.

The Queen her self, and some few about her, particularly her prime ministers, the Earl of Godolphin[1] and the Duke of Marlebrugh, were far from approving of the sd measure, for | tho they saw that there was no real security for the Revolution or Whig interest without such a settlement, yet they wanted to have it done by means of an Union of the two Kingdoms.

fol. 51.

But on passing this Act of Security[2] the clause relating to the liberty of the plantations was by some trick or other left out, for tho it was voted and agreed to, as will be found in the Minutes of the sd session in the laigh parliament house, and tho it was perhaps read with other clauses in the Act in order to have the Royal assent, yet it seems it never had it ... in none of the [p]rinted Acts does it appear, tho by the bye it was chiefly to obtain the benefite [of] the plantations [that] the union was agreed to in Scotland, at least it was the

In the progress of the session of parliament a trial was made to settle the above mentioned succession with a great many limitations on the Crown, such as that no Officers of State should be created without consent of parliament, and, in a word, that all powers of any consequence should be taken out of the hands of the sovereign, according to what had been done in the last session of parliament in relation to peace and war.

These projects cou'd not take effect, so that the Act of Security formerly concerted and agreed to was passed, and had the Royal assent.

In this session the Report above mentioned from the Commission of the publick accompts, as it was drawn up by me, was ordered to be printed; it was contain'd in 21 pages, and will be found in the Minutes of this session of parliament in the Advocats Library. It took the Parliament up several days, and I and the three Gentlemen principally concerned in it had the thanks of the House, and each of us 200 lib. ster.

Another Act past in this session for continuing our Commis-

[1] Sidney, first Earl of Godolphin, born 1645. In 1679 he was appointed Lord of the Treasury, and in 1684 Secretary of State and head of the Treasury, a position which he again held 1690-96, 1700-1, and in 1702, when he became Lord High Treasurer. He actively promoted the Union, and in 1706 was created Viscount Rialton and Earl of Godolphin, and constituted Lord High Treasurer of Great Britain. In 1710 he was deprived of his offices; and he died in 1712.

[2] See Additional Note E,—Act of Security and Liberty of Plantations.

chief instrument used for the settlement of the question.

... Report will serve [to] give the best idea [of] the publick Funds [of] Scotland from the year 1690 to 1704 that can be had any where.

fol. 52.

N.B. In drawing [th]e two Reports, one [Ge]orge Drummond, [was] my Amanuensis. [He] was afterwards one of the Commissioners, first of the Customs and afterwards of the Excise; he was then about 18 years of Age, and wrote a good hand.

sion, and accordingly we laboured in this affaire till the next session of parliament, when we brought in another Report, drawen likeways by me, but not so long as the former.

During the intervals of parliament I was for the most part at Pennicuik.|

In November 1704 my Sister-in-Law, Lady Henretta Stuart, was married to the Earl of Glencairn.* He was of a very antient family, and a man of excellent sense at that time, tho in low circumstances. We who were her Friends cou'd have wisht her better disposed of, for she was an extraordinary persone, and afterwards proved the greatest happiness and support of this family that possibly cou'd have come into it. My Father presented the Bride with a large piece of Plate, and I waited on her to Falkirk on her way to the Earl's House of Finliston. I parted with her with great truble, on account of the Friendship that had always been cultivated by us since our first acquaintance.

On my return to Edin. I was oblidged to apply to the Affaires remitted to the Gentlemen of our Commission, and indeed most things that were to come before the next session of Parliament were brought before us, particularly some projects for supplying the defect of money, which at that time seem'd to be very scarce over all the country of Scotland.

* This Earl fell afterwards into a habite of Drunkeness, and used to treat her ill.

In Aprile 1705 I resolved to make a visite to My Ld Galloway at his House in that country. I had the happiness of my Father's company to the Lead hills, for he hapned to be appointed as a Ruling Elder to try, with a committee of Ministers, to reconcile one Mr. Hepburne,[1] a Cameronian Minister and his Followers to the Church of Scotland, from whose principles he had receded. I found afterward that this Committe had not been successful, for all the Cameronians were a wild, vain, and conceited sett of men. Instead of minding their business as Farmers or Manufacturers,| they amused themselves chiefly with their own schismatick sholastick divinity and Acts of the General Assemblies. Mr. Hepburn flattered their absurdities by calling them the Remnant of God's people, for the old Presbyterian forms of

N.B. The Cameronians were partly a Roguish, partly an Enthusias- *fol.* 53. tick set of men and women, who placed their Religion of meer trifles, or at best in

[1] See Additional Note F,—James Hepburn.

doctrine and discipline were laid down by them as standards in things agreeable to their own fancies. In other things they differed widely, as being pieces of necessary Reformation which they endeavoured to introduce. The meeting of the above mentioned Comitee was at Sanchar, and, as I was informed, thither came most of all the Cameronians in Scotland, to the number of 3 or 4000. Their disputes were managed in the Kirk, and I think much on the same way as most of the old General Councils.

hearing of discourses and sermons; such were always liked in proportion to their length, and none pleased save what were very long.

In Galloway I was very kindly used by the Earl and all his friends, and some of them went from thence with me by Aire and Irvin to Finliston, where we made a visite to the Earl of Glencairn and his Lady, whom I mentioned above.

I must likeways notice that I was very civilly entertained by the Town of Whithorn, which I represented in Parliament.

I ought to mention here a very remarkable deliverance I had at the sea side near Glasetoun, the House of the E. of Galloway. As I was at sport alone on the shore the sea inclosed me between two Rocks. This was occasioned by a strong Tyde and a very high Wind, so that I was oblidged to make my escape by climbing a High Rock, with very great danger. My rashnes was much condemned by | the neighbouring Gentlemen, but keen Hunters are never very circumspect in their conduct. *fol.* 54.

After staying with my friends at Finlistone for 8 days, I returned back to Edin.

We of the Comitee of Parliament for the publick accompts continued our applications to the matters remitted to us till the Parliament met in September 1704.[1]

John, Duke of Argyle,[2] a youth of about 23 years of age, was appointed her Majesty's High Commissioner, and in this station behaved himself in a manner far above what cou'd be expected from one of his years. I had the good fortune to be very well with him, and from thence derived several pieces of

---

[1] Clerical error for 1705. The Parliament reassembled on 4th September, three days after they had passed the Act for appointing Commissioners for the Union.

[2] John, second Duke of Argyll, born 1678. He succeeded his father in 1703, and was created Earl of Greenwich 1705. He distinguished himself in the continental wars under Marlborough, commanded at Oudenard and Malplaquet, and engaged the rebels at Sheriffmuir. In 1719 he was created Duke of Greenwich. Died 4th October 1743.

favour which I met with at that time, and ever after from himself and his Brother Ld Archibald Campbel.[1]

N.B. This Lord Archibald Campbell, was afterwards a very remarkable man, under the title of the Earl of Illay, and on his Brother's death in 1744 he became Duke of Argyle.

In this parliament, by the Duke's interest, I was chosen one of the Council of Trade,[2] as by the 3^d Act of this session. Another great benefite I received from him was to get the second Report of the Commissioners of the publick accompts read and considered in parliament, and a new Gratification of 200 lib. str. was given to me and 3 other Gentlemen, who had been chiefly emploied in preparing the Report.

A 3^d great Benefite I received by my intimacy with the Duke and his brother was to be recommended to the Queen for one of the Commissioners to be appointed by Her Majesty for the Treaty of Union between England and Scotland. I must acknowledge, indeed, that my good friend the Duke of
fol. 55. Queensberry contributed chiefly to these favours | which I received, for he had recommended me to the Duke of Argyle; and at London, by his interest with the Queen, and the prime minister, the Earl of Godolphin, he procured, unknouen to me, the Honour of being a Commissioner in the above-mentioned great Transaction.

But to return to the affaires before the Parliament of Scotland, the chief business was to pave the way for the Treaty of Union. An Act for this purpose was concerted with great difficulty, for the main opposition was not only from the Jacobites, but from a party of Whigs of about 16 in number, who had for their chiefs the Dukes of Montrose and Roxbrugh and the Marquise of Twedale. These, as before mentioned, went under the name of the Squadrone Volante, their business

[1] Born 1682. He served under Marlborough; in 1705 he was constituted Lord High Treasurer of Scotland; and in 1706 was created Earl and Viscount of Islay. In 1710 he was appointed Lord Justice-General of Scotland. He exerted himself against the rebels in 1715, and was wounded at Sheriffmuir. In 1721 he was appointed Lord Privy Seal in Scotland, and in 1733 Lord Keeper of the Privy Seal. In 1743 he succeeded his brother as third Duke of Argyll. Died 1761.

[2] This Council of Trade was appointed 'to enquire into and Examine the present State and Condition of the Trade and Commerce of this Nation, how the same is Managed and Regulate. And after the said Enquiry and Information is so taken, to prepare such Overtures and Proposals as they shall judge most proper and convenient for the Encouragement and Advantage of Trade, to be laid by them before the next Session of Parliament, etc.'

being sometimes to joyn the Court party, sometimes the Jacobite party, as was most for their Interest. The Duke of Hamiltone[1] was the head of the Jacobites, and, indeed, a man every way fitted to be the Head of a popular discontented party. He was a man of courage, and had a great deal of natural Eloquence, with much affability in his temper.

The reasonings on the Act for the above Treaty turn'd chiefly on Limitations and conditions to be put on the Commissioners, but the chief opposition proceeded from this, that both those of the Squadrone Volante and of the Jacobite party knew that when the States of Parliament came to choose their | Commissioners all of them wou'd be excluded; however, *fol. 56.* at last, to put an end to Disputes, it was agreed that the nomination of these Commissioners should be left to the Queen. This was a proposal of the Duke of Hamiltone, who from that piece of independence expected the Honour of being appointed by the Queen, but in this he was disappointed, for the Ministry in England and Scotland found, by former miscarriages in Treaties of Union, no good cou'd be expected from Commissioners who were not sincerely disposed to drop minute things for the sake of attaining what was principally in view, the good of both nations, and the settlement of the Succession to the Crown in the Protestant Line, in the meantime. I knew that this Duke was so unlucky in his privat circumstances that he wou'd have complied with any thing on a suitable encouragement. He was not only descended of the Royal Family of the Stuarts, but under particular obligations to the Royal Brothers, King Charles and King James, however, he cou'd easily have been convinced that since the succession to the

[1] James, fourth Duke of Hamilton, born 1658. He was appointed Ambassador Extraordinary to France by Charles II. in 1683, and James VII. appointed him to the command of the first or royal regiment of horse, and bestowed on him the forfeited estates of Cultness, North Berwick, and Goodtries. He was implicated in Sir James Montgomery of Skelmorly's plot for the restoration of James VII., and was imprisoned in the Tower. In 1698 his mother resigned her dignities into the hands of the Crown, and he was created Duke of Hamilton by King William. He voted against every article of the Treaty of Union. In 1711 he was created an English Peer as Duke of Brandon. He was slain in a duel with Charles, Lord Mohun, in 1712, when about to start for France as Ambassador-Extraordinary.

Crown of England had been for several years past, to wit, in the Regn of the late King William, setled on the Family of Hannover, it wou'd be next to madness to imagine that the Scots cou'd set up a seperat King, or force any King on England but the persone already chosen by that nation.

The nomination being left to the Queen to name Commis-
fol. 57. sioners, she submitted | this entirely to her Ministry, particularly to the Earl of Godolphin, her prime Minister, and to the Dukes of Queensberry and Argyle.

I hapned, therfor, to be one of those appointed by these noble Dukes, tho' at that time very young for so great a Trust. What moved them chiefly in my favours was the pains I had taken in the Commissions for examining the publick accompts, by which I had a thorough acquaintance with all the Finances of Scotland, and the whole management of the Lords of the Treasury and Exchequer of this Country, from the Revolution in 1688 down to the year 1706.

This choise, however honourable to me, was very far from giving me the least pleasure or satisfaction, for I had observed a great backwardness in the Parliament of Scotland for an union with England of any kind whatsoever, and therefor doubted not but, after a great deal of expense in attending a Treaty in England, I should be oblidged to return with the uneasy reflexion of having either done nothing, or nothing to the purpose, as had been the case of former Commissioners appointed for this end. I was, in short, upon the point of refusing the Honour conferred upon me, and the rather that my Father, whom I always considered as an Oracle seldom mistaken, seemed not to approve of it. However, as at last he grew passive, and that the Duke of Queensberry threatned
fol. 58. to withdraw all friendship for me, I suffered my self | to be prevailed upon, and to take journey for London with other Commissioners, and arrived there on the 13 of Aprile 1706.

I judge it needless for me here to narrate what was transacted by the Commissioners for both nations, every thing having been already published by the authority of the Parliaments of Scotland and England; however, I shall take notice of a few things relating to this great Transaction.

The Commissioners of both nations met in different apartments in the Royal palace of Westminster, which commonly goes under the name of the Cockpit. There was one great Room where they all met when they were called upon to attend the Queen, or were to exchange papers, but they never met to hold conferences together except once, when the number of the Scotch Representatives for the two Houses of the British Parliament came to be debated, all their transactions were reduced in writings concerted in seperat apartments. When proposals or Conditions of the union were to be made by the English Commissioners, the Scots were desired to meet them in the great Room, and their proposals were given in by the Ld Chancellor, or the Keeper of the great seal, who was at that time the Lord Cooper,[1] and when the Commissioners for Scotland had any thing to propose, or had answers to be made to the Commissioners of England, these were presented by the Ld Seafield, then Chancellor for Scotland.

Sometimes the Scots Commissioners met | at the Houses of *fol. 59.* the Secretaries of State for Scotland, who were then the Earls [Marginal note here, but evidently intentionally obliterated.] of Mar[2] and Loudon,[3] the first a most famous Man at the head of the Rebellion in Scotland in the year 1715. He was then very forward for the union and the settlement of the succession in the Protestant family of Hannover, but towards the end of Queen Ann's Reign, in 1713, was as forward for the dissolution of the union, and being on that account and other reasons hated by King George the first, he turn'd Jacobite and

[1] William, first Earl Cowper, son of Sir William Cowper, Bart., was called to the Bar in 1688, and in 1705 succeeded Sir Nathan Wright as Lord Keeper of the Great Seal. He was appointed Lord Chancellor in 1707, and again in 1714, and resigned the seals on the removal of Lord Godolphin from the Lord High Treasurership. He was created Earl Cowper in 1718, and died in 1723.

[2] John, eleventh (Erskine) Earl of Mar, succeeded his father in 1689. In 1706 he was appointed one of the Secretaries of State for Scotland, in room of the Marquis of Annandale, and in 1713 one of the Secretaries of State for Great Britain. He signed the proclamation of George I., but in 1715 proclaimed the Pretender at Braemar. On the dispersion of the rebels he retired with the Pretender to the Continent, and his estates were attainted. Died at Aix-la-Chapelle 1732.

[3] Hugh, third Earl of Loudoun, succeeded his father in 1684. He was sworn a Privy Councillor in 1697, and appointed one of the Commissioners of the Treasury in 1704, and one of the Secretaries of State for Scotland in 1705. Died 1731.

Rebel, after he had taken the usual oaths to the Government and used all the subterfuges and subtilities of a Courtier to ingratiat himself with the Hannoverian Ministry in 1714.

The first grand point debated by the Commissioners for Scotland amongst themselves was whether they should propose to the English a Federal union between the two nations, or an Incorporating union. The first was most favoured by the people of Scotland, but all the Scots Commissioners, to a Man, considered it rediculous and impracticable, for that in all the Federal unions there behoved to be a supreme power lodged some where, and wherever this was lodged it hencefurth became the States General, or, in our way of speaking, the Parliament
fol. 70. (sic) of Great Britain, under the | same royal power and authority as the two nations are at present. And in things of the greatest consequence to the two nations, as in Councils relating to peace and war and subsidies, it was impossible that the Representatives or their suffrages in both nations cou'd be equal, but must be regulated in proportion to the power and richess of the several publick burdens or Taxations that cou'd affect them; in a word, the Scots Commissioners saw that no Union cou'd subsist between the two nations but an incorporating perpetual one. But after all the truble we gave ourselves to please the people of Scotland, we knew at the time that it was but losing our labour, for the English Commissioners were positively resolved to treat on no kind of union with us but what was to be incorporating and perpetual.

In the great Room above mentioned, was a long table, sufficient to hold all the Commissioners for both kingdoms, being about 50 feet in length. At the head of the Table, under a Canopy, was placed a large chaire, ornamented with gold lace and crimsone velvet, for the Queen, when she desired to come amongst us. On her left hand sat the Chancellor of Scotland, and on her right hand the keeper of the great seal, the L[d] Cooper, afterwards Chancellor of England.

The Queen came amongst us three several times, once at
fol. 71. our first or second | meeting, to acquaint us of her intentions and ardent good wishes for our success and unanimity in this great Transaction. At about a month thereafter she came again to enquire of our success, and had most of our Minutes

read to her, and for the last time to approve of what we had done. I endeavoured in all my conduct at this Treaty to acquit my self with the outmost duty to my Country, and for this end gave the greatest application possible to understand all the parts of the English Constitution, and particularly what related to their Debts and publick Taxes, to their Trade and all their Finances, comparing them with these of the people of Scotland, with which I was well acquainted, as having been for two full years a Commissioner of the public accompts in Scotland as above.

On these accounts, I was chosen by the Commissioners of Scotland for the Union to be one of four who were to conferr dayly with the like number of the English Commissioners in relation to the papers given in by both sides which were to be entered into our Minutes, for some of these papers needed some explications and alterations in order to be entered into these minutes agreeable to the sense of the respective Commissioners. I was likeways intrusted with another province by the Commissioners for Scotland, which was to review the Calculations made for the Equivalent to be paid to Scotland |
for bearing their share of the Debt of England, which were fo. 72.
afterwards to be considered as the Debts of Great Britain. These calculations were chiefly made by Doctor Gregory,[1] professor of Mathematicks in the College of Oxford, and a certain great accomptant and projector, one Patersone,[2] from Scotland, but bred in England from his infancy.

---

[1] David Gregory, born 1661, at Kinardie, Aberdeenshire; Professor of Mathematics in Edinburgh University, 1683-91; appointed Savilian Professor of Astronomy at Oxford, 1691, through the influence of Newton and Flamsted; died 1708.

[2] William Paterson, the celebrated financier, founder of the Bank of England, and projector of the Darien Expedition. Born about 1660 at Skipmyre, Tinwald, Dumfriesshire; died 1719. He was a warm promoter of the Union, and is believed, on good grounds, to have written the *Inquiry into the Reasonableness and Consequences of an Union with Scotland*, published in 1706. His biographer, Mr. S. Bannister, states that Mr. Bower was associated with Paterson and Gregory in the above-mentioned calculations, that they each received £200 sterling for their work, and that the Parliament of Scotland moved and carried a resolution 'to recommend Mr. Paterson to Her Majesty for his good services.'

In the almost total absence of information regarding the early life of Paterson, the statement of Clerk that he was 'bred in England from his infancy' may be regarded as a minute addition to his biography.

All this time I neglected not to cultivat that Friendship with the Duke of Queensberry, my Patron, which he had always shown me. I was frequently at Kensington with him, where the Queen keept her Court, and I twice saw her in her closet, to which the Duke was always admitted, being nominated Commissioner by her Majesty for representing her in the inseuing parliament of Scotland.

One day I had occasion to observe the Calamities which attend humane nature even in the greatest dignities of Life. Her majesty was labouring under a fit of the Gout, and in extream pain and agony, and on this occasion every thing about her was much in the same disorder as about the meanest of her subjects. Her face, which was red and spotted, was rendered something frightful by her negligent dress, and the foot affected was tied up with a pultis and some nasty bandages. I was much affected at this sight, and the more *when she had occasion to mention her people of Scotland*, which she did frequently to the Duke. What are you, poor mean like
fol. 73. Mortal, thought I, | who talks in the style of a Soveraign? Nature seems to be inverted when a poor infirm Woman becomes one of the Rulers of the World, but, as Tacitus observes, it is not the first time that Women have governed in Britain, and indeed they have sometimes done this to better purpose than the Men.

Especially Q. Elizabeth.

But to return to the Treaty of Union, the Articles were at last agreed to, sign'd, and sealed, by all the Commissioners, the 22 of July 1706. They were afterwards presented to the Queen at her palace of St. James, before a very numerous Assembley. The Lord Keeper of the Great Seal of England presented his copy to her Majesty, after making a handsome speech. That on the part of the Scots was presented by our Chancellor, Lord Seafield,[1] whose speech excelled the other so

---

[1] James, second son of James, third Earl of Findlater, was born in 1664. He studied law, and was admitted advocate 16th January 1685, was appointed Solicitor-General in 1693, and Secretary of State 1695. On 28th June 1698 he was created Viscount Seafield, and in the same year was President of the Scots Parliament. In 1702 he was constituted Lord High Chancellor of Scotland, and again in 1705. He succeeded his father as fourth Earl of Findlater in 1711, and died in 1730. It was he who remarked on the rising of the Scots Parliament for the last time, 'Now there is an end of an old song!'

far that it was spoken without Hesitation, whereas that of the L[d] Keeper was miserably mangled in the delivery, and at last he was forced to draw it out of his pocket and read it. However, as he was a very eloquent man and a great Lawer, he was so conscious of his own merit that he never changed colloures at his accident, but first stopt a little, and then read his speech from a paper with great composure of mind, while all the Audience was in the outmost pain for him.

To these Speeches, and the Commissioners on both sides ranged on the Queen's right and left hand, her Majesty made a very handsome Return, with a very | graceful pronountiation *fol. 74.* and tone of voice. After this great Transaction was brought to a conclusion the Commissioners on both sides left the Court, and I, with some of my country men, returned to Scotland. But before I left London I was advised to take my leave of the Queen which I did at Kensington. I was introduced to her by the Earl of Loudon, one of our Secretaries of State. She received me in her closet in the same homely way as before, for she had again fallen ill of the Gout. She spoke to me with great complacency, wished me a good journey, and in several warm expressions desired I might make it my business to recommend the Union to her people of Scotland.

I came down the Western Road and found my Father at Moffat. Here we had some Game on the moors for a few days, and at length I came to Edinburgh.

For the moneths of Septemb[r] and October I staid for the most part with my Father at Pennicuik, always poring on Books, except sometimes when I followed my diversions of fouling and fishing.

The Duke of Queensberry having been appointed her Majesty's Commissioner for the ensuing Parliament, he arrived in Scotland in November.

I need not narrate here what was done in this Parliament, there being a very exact History published of it by one Daniel Defoe,[1] who was sent to Scotland | by the prime minister of *fol. 75.*

[1] De Foe was a warm advocate of the Union, and wrote much to promote it. On the recommendation of Harley he acquired the patronage of Lord Godolphin, and, as he tells us, was taken into the service of the Queen 'to be employed

This History of the Union deserves to be read, it was printed in folio. There is not one fact in it which I can challenge.[1]

England, the Earl of Godolphin, on purpose to give a faithful account to him from time to time how every thing past here. He was therefor a Spy amongst us, but not known to be such, otherways the Mob of Edin. had pulled him to pieces.

The Commissioners, on their return to Scotland, fancied to themselves that as they had been doing great service to their Country in the matter of the Union, so they wou'd be acceptable to all ranks and degrees of people, but after the Articles of the Union were published by order of Parliament, such comments were made upon them, by those of the adverse party, that the Mob was almost universally set against them.

Under these hardships and misrepresentations the Articles of the Union were introduced into the Parliament of Scotland. The bulk of the nation seem'd altogether averse to them, nor indeed cou'd they expect a better usage, considering who they were who were determined at any rate to oppose them, for first there were a great many disoblidged Courtiers and self-conceited Men who cou'd relish nothing but what was of their own contrivance.

Next were a vast many of the Episcopal persuasion, who hated the Union meerly because of a first intention which many of the members of Parliament had of making the presbeterian Government and its security the basis of any Union

---

in several honourable though secret services,' whose exact nature he does not specify, merely remarking that 'I had the happiness to discharge myself in all these trusts so much to the satisfaction of those who employed me, though oftentimes with difficulty and danger, that my Lord Treasurer Godolphin, whose memory I have always honoured, was pleased to continue his favour to me, and to do me all good offices to her majesty, even after an unhappy breach had separated him from my first benefactor.'—*Appeal to Honour and Justice*, p. 14.

De Foe kissed the Queen's hand on leaving for Scotland in the autumn of 1706, where he remained till the beginning of 1708. He was frequently in attendance at the various Committees of Parliament, and aided in some of the calculations in connection with imposts, etc. During the riot in Edinburgh on the 23d October 1706, he tells us that 'the author of this had his share of the danger in this tumult, and, though unknown to him, was watched and set [on] by the mob, in order to know where to find him, had his chamber windows insulted, and the windows below him broken by mistake. But by the prudence of his friends, the shortness of its continuance, and God's providence, he escaped.'—*History of the Union*, p. 239 (ed. of 1786).

[1] The first edition of De Foe's *History of the Union of Great Britain* was published in folio, at Edinburgh, in 1709.

between the two Nations, for tho there was no express Article concerted by the Commissioners of the Treaty to this effect, yet it had been commen'd upon, and agreed as the only Expedient to bring | over the ministers of the church of Scot- *fol. 76.*
land, to give the Articles of the Union so much as a hearing; and, indeed, this was all they cou'd procure at first, for as the security of the church of England was to follow of consequence, many of the clergy of Scotland grew jealous of their neighbouring clergy, and endeavoured to instill notions in their Breatheren that such a security given to the church of England was contrary to the principles of their forefathers, who had strenuously supported the Solemn League and Covenant.

Another set of Enemies to the Union were the Jacobites, and as these were very numerous even in the Parliament of Scotland, they cou'd not think of imbracing a system for the union of the two kingdoms wherein the succession to the Crown was to be settled on the House of Hannover, to the perpetual exclusion of all the successors of the late King James.

I do believe that the generality of the members of the Parliament of Scotland had been of the same mind, if it had consisted with reasone to delay the settlement of the succession of Scotland on the same family on whom the English, before the death of the late King William, had settled their crown, for to all thinking Men it appeared evident that sooner or later the Scots behoved to come into the same succession, or expect to see their Country a schen of bloodshed and confusion, for it was impossible for the Scots to make choise of a different king from the persone who was to succeed to the Crown of England, but this I need not truble my self | to explain here. *fol. 77.*

From the above mentioned differences amongst the several parties in Scotland nothing was left to the Commissioners of the Union and to the Ministry of Scotland, than firmly to resolve amongst themselves how to act and leave the event to the providence of God.

Honour, Honesty, and a firm persuasion that they had been acting a faithful part for the interest of their Country, left no room to doubt what they were to do, and therefor they resolved to adhere to the Transaction they had made with the Commissioners of England, and leave it to Members of Parliament to act such a part as they thought best for the interest of their Country.

With these Resolutions the Duke of Queensberry proceeded, and 'tho some additions were made to the Articles of Union, particularly what related to the Settlement of the Presbyterian Government, yet after much debate and opposition these Articles were approven of that seem'd to be best understood, others suffered some alterations, particularly that which related to the Excise, but in my opinion few or no alterations were made to the better.

I had discharged my duty in London, and so became entirely passive as to what should happen in the Parliament of Scotland; however, to vindicat the proceedings of the Commissioners as to things not well understood in Scotland, I wrote
fol. 78. two pamphlets. One went under the Title of Some considerations on the Articles of the Union.[1]

The other was for explaining the 15 Article in relation to the Equivalents to be paid to Scotland on account of subjecting ourselves to the payment of the debts of England.[2]

These pieces were known to be mine, but procured me no hatred from the other side who opposed the Union, and I had the thanks of those who were wellwishers to it.

Before the parliament ended I was chosen one of the 45 Members who were to represent Scotland in the first parlia-

---

[1] See Additional Note G,—Pamphlets attributed to Sir John Clerk.

[2] *An Essay upon the XV. Article of the Treaty of Union, wherein the Difficulties that arise upon the Equivalents are fully Cleared and Explained. Printed in the year MDCCVI.* (twenty-eight pages). There is no copy in the British Museum, but there is one in the Advocates' Library, which appears in the catalogue under 'Union,' and is there correctly attributed to Clerk, under whose name it is indexed in the supplement. It is not, however, included in Halkett and Laing's *Dict. of Anonymous Literature.* In his *History of the Union*, pp. 432-4, De Foe makes a long extract from 'page 200' [should be p. 13], of this pamphlet, ascribing it to 'Mr. Baron Clark, whose judgement I think I may be allowed to appeal to, and who was a witness to and present in Parliament at all these debates.' Again, at p. 395, De Foe quotes from this pamphlet, pp. 4 and 5, various answers to the question, 'Why should Scotland concern itself in paying England's debts at all?'—'as they were argued in the House, and after made public by an honourable member of the Parliament, now Baron of the Exchequer in Scotland, Mr. Clark of Pennycook.'

ment of Great Britain. I had no hand in the honour conferred upon me, but the Duke of Queensberry insisted that I should be one on the List of those who were appointed, and as an incitement to me he offered me a place in one of his coaches to London, which I accepted of, and set out with his Grace on the 2d of Aprile 1707.

A very splendid Retinue accompanied his Grace to Dunbar, but except my self, and a few of his own family in two coaches, he allowed no body the favour of waiting on him to Berwick. I wished that the case had been otherways, for then his country men wou'd have been Witnesses to a quite different Reception which his Grace had in all the Towns of England situated on or near the Road to London than what he had in Scotland.

In Berwick he was received with great pomp and solemnity, as he was likeways at Newcastle, Durham, and other cities, for amidst the joyful acclamations of all the people he was received by all the Magistrates of the cities where he past, and by all the nobility and gentry of the several counties, with the same if not greater Honours than I believe had been paid to *fol. 79.* the Queen her self.

He was complimented and feasted wherever he went, and when he came within 20 miles of London the whole city turn'd out to meet him.

At Hartfoord his Grace was attended by above twenty Members of the parliament of Scotland, who had taken post before him on purpose to make their Court to the Queen and the Ministry of England, but Her Majesty refused to see or hear any body, 'till the arrival of his Grace. At Barnet he was met by the Ministry of England and most of the nobility then attending the two Houses of Parliament. Their Retinue consisted of 46 coaches and above 1000 Horsemen.

When the Duke arrived at his House in London, the Lord High Treasurer Godolphin, at the head of all the Queen's Ministry, waited upon him, and that same night he waited on her Majesty, by whom he was received with high acknowledgements of his great services.

I staid with the Duke in London about 2 months, in which time the Commissions for managing the Equivalent appointed by the 15 Article of the Treaty of Union, with the Commissions

for managing the Customs[1] and Excise[2] in Scotland were concerted. I might have been a Commissioner in any of the two last, but the Affaire of the Equivalent requiring persons of known fidelity, I was in some measure compelled to accept of
fol. 80. it, not without a positive promise from the Duke that I should be afterwards better provided for.

On the 1 of May 1707 the Union of the two Nations, as had been agreed to, took place. That day was solemnized by her Majesty and those who had been members of both Houses of Parliament with the greatest splendour. A very numerous procession accompanied the Queen to the Cathedral church of St. Paul, at least 3 or 400 coaches. The Bishops and Peers sat in Galleries on her Majesty's right hand, and the late members of the House of Commons of England, with such as had been chosen to represent the Commons of Scotland in the first British Parliament, were on her left hand. I think there were not above half a dussan of the Scots commoners then in London, and amongst these I had the happiness to be present at this solemn piece of Devotion.

A sermon was preached by the Bishope of London,[3] and prayers of Thanksgiving were very heartily put up for the success of the Union, at least no body on this occasion appeared more sincerely devout and thankfull than the Queen her self. A fine piece of Musick closed the solemnity, and we return'd back to the Court at St. James's palace in the same order we came to the Cathedral.

On this occasion I observed a real joy and satisfaction in the Citizens of London, for they were terribly apprehensive of confusions from Scotland in case the Union had not taken place.

---

[1] Sir Alexander Rigby, James Isaacson, Lionel Norman, Sir Robert Dickson, Bart., and William Boyd were appointed Commissioners for the management of the Customs; and about the end of April 1708, Lionel Norman, Jessop Bougton, John Colquit, John Sewell, and Warwick Arthur were sent to Scotland to regulate the collection of the duties and instruct the Custom-house officers. See Defoe's *History*, pp. 575-76.

[2] Alexander Wetherburn, John Montgomery, John Whittham, David Ross, and Alexander Forbes, were appointed Commissioners of Excise. See De Foe's *History*, p. 585.

[3] Henry Compton, Canon of Christchurch, appointed Bishop of Oxford 1674, and transferred to London 1675; died 1713.

That whole day was spent in feastings, ringing of Bells, and illuminations, and | I have reasone to believe that at no time Scotsmen were more acceptable to the English than on that day. *fol.* 81.

About the end of May I returned back to Scotland. Some time after this the equivalent stipulated to Scotland by the above mentioned 15 Article of the Union was sent down, viz. 398085 lib. 10 sh. ster. 100,000 lib. str. came in specie, and the rest in Exchequer Bills, which was lodged in the Castle of Edin.

The Commissioners appointed for manadging the same,[1] according to the 15 and 16 Acts of the last session of the Parliament of Scotland, immediately began to make the proper distributions, and particularly to refound the capital stock of the Indian and African Company in Scotland, the rest of the publick debts of Scotland succeeded, so that in a few months most of the Equivalent money was disposed of.

The first Parliament of Great Britain was appointed by her Majesty to meet at Westminster in —— ——[2] thereafter. Thither all those who had been chosen to represent Scotland repaired, and I amongst the rest should have gone, but was oblidged to attend at Edin. for 2 months longer, to exchange above 100,000 lib. in Exchequer Bills, which had fallen into a discount of 5 pr. cent. 3 other gentlemen were detained with me for the same purpose, being appointed by the Directors of the Bank of England to take in these Exchequer Bills and draw Bills on the sd Bank payable at sight.

This was an affaire of great trust, however it was manadged with the success that was necessary for the credite of the Bank. I carried up the retired notes with me to London in february 1708, and received the thanks of the Directors of the Bank. *fol.* 82.

these amounted to about 100,000 lib. str.

I went up post, but near Anwick, the way being covered with ice and snow, my Horse fell with me, by which I unfortunately brok my collar bone, however I recovered in a few days so as to be able to travel in a Coach, and got to London with much pain in two weeks.

---

[1] Twenty-five Commissioners were appointed. See De Foe's *History*, pp. 586-87, also pp. 589-92.

[2] A blank here in the MS. The Parliament met 23d October 1707.

I attended the House of Commons till the close of the session of Parliament in May, and observed with pleasure the Happy union that appeared between the Scotch and English members of parliament in both houses, happy presage of what I expected from the Union.

I am again as in ... sensible that in reading several things here and in other parts of this book some may ascribe ... to vanity, but I declare the case with me

Amongst other Acts past in this session of parliament there was one for constituting a Court of Exchequer in Scotland on the footing of that in England, conform to the 19 Article of the Treaty of union.[1]

The judges in this Court were not to exceed five, one Lord Chief Baron, and 4 other Barons. My good friend the Duke of Queensberry took care that I should be one of them.[2] The

[1] The old Scottish Court of Exchequer included a treasurer, a treasurer-depute, and certain lords of Exchequer, whose number was fixed by the Crown. This continued until the creation by 6 Anne c. 26 of the new and, in its constitution, terms, etc., essentially foreign tribunal of which Sir John Clerk formed a member. It consisted of a chief and four ordinary Barons, who seem to have been remunerated upon a more liberal scale than their brethren of the Court of Session. In 1779 the Lord Chief Baron had a salary of £2000 a year; one of the other Barons of £1200; a third of £700; and the remaining two £750 each. English barristers were eligible for the judicial appointments, and might plead before this Court. After the passing of the Reform Act it became the object of various legislative experiments. The number of its judges were reduced. Provisions were made by 2 and 3 Will. IV. for the transfer of its duties to the Lords of Session after the death or retirement of the last remaining Baron. These provisions were carried out by 2 and 3 Vict. c. 36, but the Court as a distinct jurisdiction continued to exist, although without special judges, until, by 19 and 20 Vict. c. 56 (1856), all that remained was finally merged in the Court of Session.—M. Baron Clerk states that his salary was 'about £500.' See folio 245.

[2] In our Frontispiece, from an oil-portrait by William Aikman, in the possession of Sir George Clerk, Sir John Clerk appears in his robes as a Baron of the Court of Exchequer. Regarding this official costume we may quote the following passage from Clerk and Scrope's *Court of Exchequer*, p. 127:—'From this section' (. . . 'the said Chief Baron and Barons shall use and wear such robes and habits as the Chief Baron and Barons of the Court of Exchequer in England do use and wear, or such other robes or habits as her Majesty, her heirs or successors, shall appoint . . .' in 19th Article of Union) 'observe . . . As to the Robes and Habits which the Barons of Exchequer in Scotland are to wear, they consist only of black cloth Gowns and silk Scarfs of the same colour; which, though different from the habits of the Barons of Exchequer in England, yet in regard they were appointed by her late Majesty Queen Anne, who instituted the Court, it is probable they may continue so to be the habits of the Barons of Scotland in all time coming.'

In addition to this portrait of Baron Sir John Clerk, and the juvenile one reproduced in our Illustration No. v., there are two others in the possession of

Earl of Seafield, afterward Earl of Finlater, late Chancellor of Scotland, was appointed Ld chief Baron, one Mr. Smith,[1] at that time one of the Barons of the Exchequer in England, Mr. Scroop,[2] a councellor at Law, and Mr. Maitlan,[3] an Advocat in Scotland, made up the number. 3 of us, to wit the chief Baron, Baron Maitlan, and my self, understood | the Laws and Customs of Scotland, but were very unskilled in the Laws of England, therefore, to remedy this defect, Mr. Baron Smith and Mr. Scroop were appointed.

fol. 83.

We were all sensible that to qualify us for being Barons in Scotland we behoved to understand both the Scotch and English Laws, but as this was not to be expected, we did the best we cou'd to learn from one another, and in the mean time to act with uprightness and assiduity, which are the chief Qualifications of judges in any Court.

is quite other ways, for to avoid this imputation I have actually passed over a great many things I might have said. I hate Egotisms if I do not avoide them, but as this account of my own Life is not to be published, I must use them or throw away my pen.

Before I left London I was introduced to take leave of her Majesty by the Duke of Queensberry, then appointed one of the principal secretaries of State. I returned her Majesty thanks for the honour she had done me in appointing me to be one of the Barons of Exchequer of Scotland. She was so good as to make me a very handsome reply, and, admiting me to kiss her hand, she wished me a good journey to Scotland. I cannot remember this incident without making this reflexion, as I have done before, that tho' this Great Queen had in her short reign, I mean to the year I saw her, made a very glori-

not Secretary for Scotland only, but for foreign affaires.

Sir George Clerk, both by Sir John Medina. A fifth portrait is engraved by D. Lizars in the *Scots Magazine* for June 1802, 'from the painting in the possession of John Clerk of Eldin.'

[1] James Smith became Chief Baron of the Court of Exchequer in 1708, see folio 85 of the present MS. In 1722 he founded and endowed the English Episcopal chapel in Blackfriars Wynd, Edinburgh, for a clergyman qualified by taking the oaths to Government. This building was demolished in 1822. He died in 1726.

[2] John Scrope. Died about 1752. See folio 248. In 1726 he and Baron Sir John Clerk produced an *Historical View of the Forms and Powers of the Court of Exchequer in Scotland*, which was edited by Sir Henry Jardine, W.S., King's Remembrancer, and published for private circulation by the Barons of Exchequer in 1820.

[3] Alexander Arbuthnott, second son of Robert, second Viscount Arbuthnott. He was admitted an advocate 18th December 1697, and was Member of Parliament for Bervie 1702-4. In 1704 he married Jane, eldest daughter of Sir Charles Maitland, and heiress to her brother Sir Charles Maitland of Pitrichie, and on succeeding to the Maitland estates he assumed the name, and was styled 'Maitland of Pitritchie.'

ous figure in Europe by her Armes and Fleets abroad, and even in bringing about the union of the two Kingdoms, which cou'd never be accomplished by any of her predecessors, tho' she was in all respects Arbitrix of peace and war in Europe, and by her sovereign Authority held the Balance of Power in her hands, yet at the time I was introduced to her to receive
fol. 84. her commands for Scotland, | she appeared to me the most despicable mortal I had ever seen in any station. The poor Lady, as I saw her twice before, was again under a severe fit of the Gout, ill dressed, blotted in her countenance, and surrounded with plaisters, cataplasims, and dirty-like rags. The extremity of her pain was not then upon her, and it diverted her a little to see company with whom she was not to use ceremonies, otherways I had not been allowed access to her. However, I believe she was not displeased to see any body, for no Court Attenders ever came near her. All the Incence and adoration offered at Courts were to her Ministers, particularly the Earl of Godolphin, her chief Minister, and the two Secretaries of State,[1] her palace of Kensington, where she commonly resided, was a perfect solitude, as I had occasion to observe several times. I never saw any body attending there but some of her Guards in the outer Rooms, with one at most of the Gentlemen of her Bedchamber. Her frequent fits of sickness, and the distance of the place from London, did not admit of what are commonly called Drawing-Room nights, so that I had many occasions to think that few Houses in England belonging to persons of Quality were keept in a more privat way than the Queen's Royal Palace of Kensington.

I returned to Scotland about the end of May, and continued
fol. 85. at Pennicuik | for some days.

About that time preparations were making in Scotland for the Election of Members of Parliament to serve in the ensuing session. The Duke of Queensberry on this occasion bestired himself to get two of his friends chosen for the shire of Dumfrise, and for the brughs of Dumfrise, Kirkcubright, Anan, Lochmaben, and Sanchar, according to the plan settled by the

[1] Probably he here refers to Harley, Secretary of State for the Northern Department, 18th May 1704 to 13th February 1708, and St. John, Secretary at War, 20th April 1704 to 14th February 1708.

Articles of Union. To assist his Grace, I was desired by him to visite his friends in these places, which I did for several days, and was not unsuccesful.

In June all the Barons met at Edin., and the Court of Exchequer was then constituted. We assisted one another with our advice, and what knowledge of the laws we had attained in either nation, so that every thing was transacted amongst us with great friendship and unanimity, as well as justice.

The chief Baron having always daubled in politicks, tho' often in an auckward way, was so far imposed on by the Ministry of Great Britain at that time as to be persuaded to lay down his Commission in order to qualify himself the better to be chosen one of the sixteen peers for Scotland. This plot against him was that the prime minister and his friends might appoint one of their own nation to succeed him. Accordingly Mr. Baron Smith was made Chief Baron, | and the Earl of *fol. 86.* Finlater and Seafield, upon the first occasion, got himself elected one of the sixteen peers.

Mr. Baron Smith was indeed vastly superior to the Earl in learning, wisdom, and discretion, so that we who were his Brethren in the Exchequer lived very happily with him. His place being now vacant as an ordinary Baron of the Exchequer, Mr. George Dalrymple, Advocat,[2] and Brother to the Earl of Stair, succeeded to him.

he died in 1726 and was succeeded by one Baron Lant[1] likeways one of the English Barons of Exchequer in Scotland. This I have reasone to believe will generally be the case, for few Scots men will ever arrive at the office of Chief Baron in Scotland.

By the constitution of our Court, we had only 4 Terms or sessions in the year, and few of them exceeded 3 weeks, so that nothing cou'd be better calculated for my humure than the office I enjoyed. I had a great deal of time on my hands, and this I always spent to my own satisfaction. I was naturally studious, and often laborious this way, so that, except the time I spent at my favourite diversions of shooting and fishing in the country, all my leisure houres were spent in Books. Musick had always great charms with me, but this was so far

but this humure for Musick

[1] Matthew Lant was appointed Chief Baron in succession to James Smith, 29th June 1726. See folio 150.

[2] George Dalrymple of Dalmahoy, third son of John, first Earl of Stair. He married Euphame, eldest daughter of Sir Andrew Myrton, Bart., of Gogar; and their eldest son became John, fifth Earl of Stair.

went off as I began to want spectacles, about the 48 year of my age, for I gave over the practise of it entirely about that time.

from hindering my application to Books that on the contrary it was thereby the more promoted, as it keept me often at home when I had sought for relaxation abroad. My favourite instrument was as formerly the Herpsecord, because it furnished me at pleasure all the parts of an entire concert of Musick. |

fol. 87. Amongst my studies the Greek and Roman Literature chiefly delighted, except now and then when phylosophical or mathematical learning required my attention.

The Laws of both nations claimed my particular care, as I was a Baron or Judge in a soveraign Court, and therfor during the Terms of the Exchequer I applied my self very seldom to any other study.

In the years 1709 and 1710 I began to make nurseries at Pennicuik, for in the seasons of planting, which were in February and March, my Father devolved all his care upon me. I was not unsuccessful in these nurseries, for out of these most of the Beuties about Pennicuik house were drauen.

Being now oblidged to live up to the strict character of a judge, my Father insisted with me that I should again enter into a married life, and the rather that I had but one child by my deceased wife, Lady Margaret Stuart. This was a Boy of a vast deal of spirite, however, my Father and Friends were desirous that I should not trust too much to his life.

I, to comply with their wishes, led my thoughts in an overly way upon two Ladies, one was a young Lady of great Quality, and consequently most improper for my circumstances, as my Father had settled a good part of his Estate on the son I had by my late wife. The other was a lightheaded Beuty, and consequently as improper for me as the other.[1] |

My Father hapned to be averse to both these projects,

---

[1] There are blanks in the MS. and the notes here. The second lady here referred to may possibly have been Susanna, daughter of Sir Archibald Kennedy, of whom Clerk is said to have been a suitor. He presented her with a flute, in which was concealed a copy of verses beginning—

'Harmonious pipe, I languish for thy bliss,
When pressed to Silvia's lips with gentle kiss,'

which are given by Chambers in his *Traditions of Edinburgh*. She became the third wife of Alexander, ninth Earl of Eglintoun. Ramsay's *Gentle Shepherd* was dedicated to her in 1726 by Hamilton of Bangour, and Boyse also addressed her in verse. She died in 1780, aged ninety-one.

VIII
JANET INGLIS
Second Wife of Baron Sir John Clerk

wherefor I prevailed very easily with my self to drop them, and indeed I found afterwards that both the Ladies who touched my fancy at that time had made me very unhappy, for one of them proved a very bad Woman, and the other very little better, but their names I here burry in silence.

My third attempt was in reality my first, for by some secret charm or order of divine providence I settled my thoughts on Mrs. Jennet Inglis of Cramond.[1] She had been educated under a most verteous mother, daughter of Sir Patrick Houston, and was her self what I always hope to find her, a most religious verteous woman, and one who in all respects might suit my humure and circumstances to rub through the world in a sober and privat state of Life.

After I had acquainted my Father of my design, which he approved of, and after haveing gone through a few formalities of Courtship, we were married the 15 of Feb. 1709. My Wife was then about 22 years of age, and I about 32, and we were so happy as to have the consent and approbation of our Friends on both sides.

After I was married I lived for some days at Edin. in hired lodgings, and afterwards with my Father at Pennicuik House, till Whitsonday, at which time I furnished a House in Town.

On the 2 of december it pleased God to give us a sone, whom we christned James,[2] after my Wife's Father.

While I lived thus in Quietness, and in all the prosperity of Life my Heart cou'd desire, I fell ill of a great cold in | Aprile *fol.* 89.
1710. My desease was contracted as I thought by the Dampness of a House in the Cowgate, where I lived. I went out to Pennicuik in hopes of recovering in my native Aire, but my desease did not abate, so that in all appearance I languished in a consumption. This gave a very great cheque to my Felicity, and brought much truble and anguish on my Wife and Father. I tried several Doctors and medicines in

[1] Third daughter of Sir James Inglis, first baronet of Cramond, who died in 1688. See Illustration No. VIII., from a portrait by Sir John Medina, in the possession of Sir George Clerk.

[2] He succeeded his father as third baronet in 1755; married Elizabeth, daughter of the Rev. John Cleghorn, M.A. (ordained minister of Burntisland 1701, and of Wemyss 1711, died 1744); and died, without issue, 1782.

vain, my cogh and hoarseness incressed, but my strength keept up so well during the moneths of June and July that I attended the Court of Exchequer, as formerly. I began, however, to dispaire, and therefor as my last shift I resolved to take a journey into England the length of Bath. I left my Wife at her Brother's House[1] in Cramond, under great affliction, and tho' I was very doubtful if ever I should see her again, yet by some secret and irresistible impulse I set forwards on my journey. My Father accompanied me for the first day, but I was able to travel no further than Drummelzier on Tweed, which was about 12 miles from Pennicuik. I got the next day about 12 miles further by the way of Moffat, and so by slow journies to Carlyle. Here I found sensibly my desease abating, and that by Riding I might sooner attain to a cure than by any medicines whatsomever.

I traveled with two friends, one Major Leblanc, a French man, and one Mr. Robert Clerk, they were both very agreable companions, so that I got to Bath in a very agreable way, tho' *fol. 90.* the Weather was very | rainy and inconstant. I undertook this journey contrary to the advice of my Physitians at Edin., for they all agreed that the Bath Water wou'd prove hurtful to me. I found it indeed such, however, the change of Aire and place contributed much to my recovery.

While I was at Bath I made an Excursion to Bristol, where I visited my good Friend and Brother Mr. Baron Scroop, who lived there. While I staid with him I was advised to use the Bristol waters, as more useful in all appearances of faulty Lungs, but as I took this to ... nothing but a ...

I staid in Bath about 6 weeks, and afterwards came to London by the way of Oxfoord and Windsor. I found my self a great deal better, however, instead of the satisfaction I expected to find in London by seing my dear Friend and worthy Patron the Duke of Queensberry in perfect health, I found him dying; however, I had the consolation to see him every day while I tarried in London.

About this time a vacancy hapned in the Court of Session by the death of the Earl of Lauderdale,[2] one of the Lords, and I was much importuned by the Earl of Mar, at that time Secretary of State for Scotland, to accept of the vacant office. I do believe if my health had permitted me I had accepted it,

[1] Sir John Inglis, second baronet of Cramond.

[2] John, fifth Earl of Lauderdale, passed advocate 30th July 1680, was appointed a Lord of Session as Lord Ravelrig 1st November 1689, and died 30th August 1710.

but the Duke of Queensberry refused to give his consent, as it wou'd be attended with a great deal more of fatigue than the office I enjoyed in the Exchequer; I followed his advice, and as yet have found no cause to repent it.

I placed all confidence in riding, which succeeded.

The Duke, on the prospect he had of his death, recommended his son and Family to me, and oblidged me solemnly to promise that I should never be wanting to assist them.

This was the only reasone of my taking the truble afterwards of being one of his Commissioners.

I parted with him at last, and took journey for Scotland, never more to see him, which accordingly hapned, for he died a few weeks after, much honoured and regreted. |[1]

In returning to Scotland nothing remarkable hapned by the *fol. 91.* way. My Cogh was not much abated, however, I recovered my strength daily, and arrived at Pennicuik 2 Octr. 1710, where I found my Father, my Wife, and other friends, in good health, and as I had reasone to believe, all overjoyed to see me in much better plight than when I left the place.

I staid at Pennicuik about 2 weeks, and then went to Edin., where I lived in my own House at the head of blackfrier Wynd.[2] Here I may notice that this House was built, anno 1552, by Thomas Hendersone, merchant, and a cadete of the Family of Fordel, and my mother's Grandfather.

I began, on my return to Edin., to put in practise the Advices given me by my Physitians at Bath for the recovery of my health.

The chief of their prescriptions was to drink Aple Tea, and to abandon the use of all fermented liquors. I made the Aple water my chief drink, and for a month I took 12 gutts or drops of the Elixar Proprietatis[3] cum spiritu sulphuris in a little sack every morning, but that which recovered me perfectly, and I may say within the space of an Houer, was a porrenger of Broth made of a knee piece of good beef, with Hartshorn in it, and the fat well scimed off. No sooner I took this with a Tost of Bread for breakfast than my cogh and spiting left me, and never returned with its former violence. I can explain this miraculous kind of cure to nothing but this. My riding in England had prepared my body for a cure, so that nothing was wanted | but to give the Blood that strength *fol. 92.*

The journey on Horseback which I made into England prepared my body for a cure, and will always have the same effect on others, tho perhaps its good effects do not instantly appear; however, it is certain that Riding will do a great deal of mischief if the Lungs are really vitiated or ulcerated, which it seems mine were not, for I never [co]ft up from my breast any purulent matter, [as] those do who [ha]ve their Lungs [ulcera]ted.

Kitchin physick.

[1] According to Douglas he died in Albemarle Street, London, 6th July 1711.
[2] See Additional Note H.
[3] See Additional Note I.

and consistency as to keep the serum in its ordinary channel, and not to be seperated from it so as to be throuen on the Lungs, from whence proceeded the perpetual cough. But whatever was the cause, 'tis certain that my Cure was instantaneous. I continued this kind of breakfast for this whole Winter-seasone, and grew as healthy and strong by it as ever. This I mention with great gratitude to God for discovering to me the only Medicine which restored my health. I was brought to the brink of dispaire, and laid my account that a few Months wou'd put an end to my infirm Carcase, but this simple cure of my own invention wrought like a charm upon me.

To this great blessing of recovering my Health, God was pleased to add two more, for my Wife was brought to bed of

See *folio* 101.

a second son, on the 26 nov. 1710, whom I christned Henry,[1] after my mother's Father, and I likeways happily fell upon a very convenient Villa for me, the House and lands of Cammo,[2] in the parish of Cramond, about 4 miles distant from Edin., by this purchess I had a very agreable retirement and abundance of Exercise in riding between Edin. and my House in the Country.

During the months of november and decemb^r^ 1710, and january and february 1711, I attended the Court of Exchequer, but in March thereafter I went to Pennicuik, and began all the plantations to be seen there near the Water of Esk. My Father had made some nurseries, and I greatly incressed them, so that I had plenty of Trees | to thicken up all the Woods about Pennicuik Town, and plant the Braes on the north and south sides of Esk, near the House.

Nota. This year, 1754, after many years labour, I finished all my plantations at Pennicuik.

fol. 93.

In summer that year I attended the Court of Exchequer, and sometimes my diversions of shooting and fishing. Nothing remarkable occurred to me or my Family till the 4 of june 1712, that my eldest Daughter Ann[3] was born.

tho I loved all my children very much, yet I was particularly fond of this girle.

About this time the publick Administration of the Affaires of Great Britain was quite changed. The Earl of Godolphin

[1] In *MS. Family Register*, and in *Births of My Children* at beginning of present MS., the day is entered as the 27th. He died of smallpox December 1714 (compare *Register* with present MS. folio 100).

[2] See Additional Note K,—Cammo.

[3] She died unmarried.

and the Duke of Marlebrugh began to decline in the Queen's favours, tho' they were the only supports of her great Reputation in Europe.

This, as I conceived, hapned chiefly from a disgust the Queen took to the family of Hannover, on which the succession to the Crown of Great Britain and Ireland had been settled. This kind of disgust is common amongst princes when their subjects begin to make more than ordinary Court to their successors, and when the people begin to adore the rising sun. The princess Sophia,[1] mother of the Hannoverian Family, was the grand daughter of King James the 6 of Scotland and first of England, and on her the succession to the British Crown was, on the death of Queen Ann, immediately to devolve. This woman was at that time past 60 years of Age, and otherways no extraordinary Lady for parts; however, some in England carried their respects for her so far as to talk of bringing her over to England in the Queen's life time. This galed her Majesty exceedingly, so that she began to despise her Ministers in England, and to project ways of bringing about a peace, | to the prejudice of her Alies abroad and the *fol.* 94. common cause of Europe. The French were now upon the point of being humbled and granting every condition of a peace that cou'd be asked, but this alteration in Queen Ann's affections for the House of Hannover soon discovered that there was no better way left to humble the said House and all its supporters as to give new life and vigour to France. To break the Union of the Two Kingdoms, by which chiefly the succession was settled, and at last to call in her Brother the pretender, as he was usually called, in order to protect her.

These were very difficult schems; however, there was a Lady

---

[1] It was enacted that 'the most excellent Princess Sophia, Electress and Duchess-Dowager of Hanover, daughter of the most excellent Princess Elizabeth, late Queen of Bohemia, daughter of our late sovereign lord King James the First, of happy memory, be, and is hereby declared to be, the next in succession in the Protestant line to the imperial crown and dignity of the said realms of England, France, and Ireland, with the dominions and territories thereto belonging, after his Majesty and the Princess Anne of Denmark, and in default of issue of the said Princess Anne and of his Majesty respectively.'—12 and 13 Will. III. c. 2. She predeceased Queen Anne, dying 8th June 1713. Her son became King George I.

in the Court, one Mrs. Masham,[1] a new confident of the Queen's, who set about managing them.

The High Treasurer, the E. of Godolphin, was easily displaced, and in consequence of his fall the Duke of Marlebrugh's power in the Army and Interests amongst the Queen's Allies were entirely broken. The French began to exult, and were prompted from England to refuse the same Terms of a peace which formerly they had agreed to.

The Secretary of State, Robt. Harley,[2] was next made use of to carry on the whole project, for under the Title of Earl of Oxford he was made Lord High Treasurer, and as he was an inveterat Ennemy of the Duke of Marlebrugh and Earl of Godolphin, he brought an unexpected change in the Army, for the Duke was at last displaced, and the D. of Ormond[3] was made General in Flanders. A good natured, profuse, innocent man, of little or no experience in military affaires. One Mr. St. John,[4] afterwards Lord Bulinbrook and Secretary of State, *fol.* 95. became the Queen's great favourite next | to the Earl of Oxford. By this Ministry all the Whig ministry was overturn'd, and scarse any thing seem'd to remain but to call in the Pretender.

I was well acquainted with Lord Bulingbroock, he was a smart clever

1 Abigail Hill, cousin of Sarah, Duchess of Marlborough. Having been appointed waiting-maid to the Princess Anne, she acquired great influence, which continued after her mistress ascended the throne. In 1707 she privately married Mr. Masham, who in 1711 was elevated to the Peerage. She combined with Harley, and contributed to the overthrow of Godolphin and Marlborough. Died 1734.

2 Robert Harley, born 1661. He became a Member of Parliament, in 1701 was chosen Speaker, and in 1704 was appointed Secretary of State. On the fall of Godolphin he became Chancellor of the Exchequer, in 1711 was created Earl of Oxford and Mortimer, and appointed Lord High Treasurer. After the accession of George I. he and Bolingbroke were impeached by the Commons, and he was committed to the Tower, but finally acquitted. Died 1724.

3 James, second Duke of Ormonde, born 1665. He distinguished himself at the battle of the Boyne, in 1702 commanded the expedition to Spain, and in 1712 succeeded Marlborough as commander-in-chief in Flanders. In 1715 he was impeached for high treason and retired to France, where he devoted himself to the cause of the Stuarts. Died 1745. His letters relating to the projected rising of 1718-19 are now being published by the Scottish History Society.

4 Henry St. John, born 1678. He became Secretary-at-War in 1704, and in 1710, when Harley succeeded Godolphin, he was appointed Secretary of State. In 1712 he was created Viscount Bolingbroke, but on the accession of George I. he was deprived of his office, and joined the Pretender on the Continent. He afterwards returned to England, where he died 1751.

But whatever success attended these new projectors with regard to themselves, yet it appeared very obvious that they had not as yet prepared the people, and far less the Clergy of England, to cast themselves at the mercy of any Roman Catholick interest, and tho' her Majesty had, I believe, the Hannoverian family and succession in utter abhorrence, yet so wise was she, as to find out that it wou'd be a dangerous step for her to call in her Brother the Pretender, for whatever obligations he might think himself under to her, yet his friends wou'd never be at rest till he was put in the actual possession of the Throne, and the Queen removed. These considerations had terrible effects upon her, for seaing that her Life would be in hazard from the friends of the Pretender and the Roman Catholick Interest, she delayed putting the schems she had agreed to in Execution, and at last, her mind being distracted between hopes and fears, that gave her no rest either night or day, she sickned and died, losing all the Glory and honour that ever she had acquired, 1 Agust 1714.

Her Ministry fell with her, and the Whigs became the only favourites of King George the first. The Jacobites durst not make the least appearance | for their unhappy prince abroad, tho' King George gave them all opportunities; for he came not over for 6 weeks after he was proclaimed in England, during which time the publick affaires were under the management of certain Regents, named by the King in a Writ sent to England before the Queen's death, for her Majesty had a fit of an Apoplexy some time before she died. She recovered, and in this intervale the L[d] Oxford demitted his office of Treasurer, for as he could not go the lengths with some of his own creatures in the Ministry, he could hold his office no longer, and the Earl of Shrewsberry[2] was appointed to succeed him. In the meantime the late shufling impudent Treasurer,

man, a good scholar, and a great Rake.

it is remarkable, however, that even in this jacobite Ministry the friends of the Pretender were so watched by the Whigs and put to it that the Queen her self [was] oblidged to put ...ooo lib. on the head of the Pretender if he should be taken and brought to justice, and the House of Commons to this sum added [1]ooooo lib. ster.[1] this was no small satisfaction to the [county] for the most sanguine jaco- *fol. 96.* bites ... that house many ...hem were of ...d, were oblidged to consent to this Scandalous bargain, tho they imagined they were brought to Scotland to be the Instruments of a new Revolution.

[1] A reward of £100,000 was voted by the first Parliament of George I. to any one who should secure the Pretender upon his attempting to land in Britain. A reward of £5000 had previously been offered by the Tory Ministry of Queen Anne.—Hill Burton's *History*, second ed., vol. viii. p. 263.

[2] Charles Talbot, born 1660. He succeeded his father as twelfth Earl of Shrewsbury in 1668, and in 1694 was created Duke of Shrewsbury. He was Lord High Treasurer of Great Britain from 30th July till 11th October 1714. Died 1718. Swift styled him 'the finest gentleman we have.'

L[d] Oxford, laid claime to King George's favour, because, as he pretended, he had prevented the Tory Ministry in England to go the lengths for the Pretender which they intended. This was indeed true, for the Rogue acted on both sides, having nothing in view but to agrandize himself and his family, but he seemed to forget who broke the whig ministry and encouraged the high flying jacobite party to lay their schems for subverting the Government of his Royal Mistres and the protestant succession. All the 16 peers for Scotland were noted Jacobites, and so were all he employed in the Ministry under him, yea the very Parliament wou'd have gone into his measures, but as he was really a Whig in his heart, he constantly put them off with new delays, till the Queen's death put an end to all these shufling measures.

I was particularly well acquainted with him, for in privat Life he was a kind of Virtuoso, and had a vast collection of Books, Manuscripts, and other curiosities, which were sold about 20 years after his death.[1]

Nature never produced such a man as this prime minister, for it was not in his power to give a direct positive answere to any one Question put to him, so that by this kind of Genius he was enabled, not only to impose upon every mortal, but upon himself, for he knew not often what to wish for, and had but one single thing really in view, which was to retain his dignity and power.

It was my admiration frequently how the People of England bore with this man's Rogueries, for amongst many instances | *fol.* 97. to demonstrat how easily some people will suffer themselves to be imposed on this may serve, that at a time when he wanted a Majority in the House of Peers he got her Majesty to creat twelve new Peers.[2] These men had the confidence, on their

in 1711.

[1] He began to collect in 1705. His miscellaneous curiosities, coins, medals, and portraits were sold by auction in March 1742, and the books, including about 50,000 printed books, 41,000 prints, and 350,000 pamphlets, were sold to Thomas Osborne, the bookseller, for £13,000, much less than the cost of binding. A collection of the scarce pamphlets was printed by Oldys as *The Harleian Miscellany*, 8 vols. 8vo, London 1744-6. The MSS., consisting of 7639 volumes, and 14,236 rolls, charters, etc., were sold to the nation in 1753 for the small sum of £10,000, and form the celebrated Harleian Collection of the British Museum.

[2] In 1711, when the Whigs, by an unprincipled coalition with Nottingham, had secured a majority in the House of Lords, Harley persuaded the queen first to dismiss Marlborough from all his offices, and then to create twelve new Tory Peers. 'Apart from the immediate questions of the day, this creation of Peers has a wide constitutional significance. Just as the deposition of James II. had

ignominious creation, to come to the House of Peers and support their Patron in all his schems. One wou'd wonder how men of tollerable sense and honesty should accept of being made peers on such scandelous Terms, and how the people of England should have suffered themselves to be born down and insulted by such men. But they are fond of Quality, and seem as if they thought the patents of peers were immediately transmitted to them from Heaven. By this bold strock he lost no ground at that time; however, he gave a sufficient profe that he was not to be trusted.

By these and the like methods he was abhored by King George the first, who was a very wise upright prince, and all the favour he cou'd procure was to be saved from the Gallows, which he richly deserved.

And which his own Creatures wou'd have gladly honoured him with.

Amongst those who hated him most were the Jacobites in Britain and Ireland, and indeed they had great reasone, for tho' he cajolled them, yet he never intended to give them the least assistance in their main schem, and so left them in the Lurch at last.

But when his Ministry was acceptable, and nothing expected but a new Revolution in Great Britain, the Jacobites every (*sic*) | managed their affaires with great boldness, and in full assurance that they had the Ball at their foot, and in this confidence I my self and others who had the reputation of being Whigs were treated in Scotland with great neglect and contempt. However, we were resolved to stand our ground, and had the satisfaction to observe that on the Accession of King George, those who had neglected us most were so mean and servile as to be the first who courted our friendship.

fol. 98.

I was in all respects equal with them, for I paid no manner of reguard to them, but treated them as Mordecai did Hamand.[1]

During those confusions in Britain, I continued my former way of living. In the Winter I lived in Town so long as the Court of Exchequer hapned to sit. In the Spring seasons I always lived with my Father at Pennicuik, and continued my plantations on both sides of the Water of Esk. In the

made it evident that if king and parliament pulled different ways it was for the king to give way, so the creation of Peers in 1711 made it evident that if the two Houses pulled different ways, it was for the House of Lords to give way.'—Gardiner's *Student's History of England*, pp. 695-6.

[1] 'Haman saw Mordecai in the king's gate, that he stood not up, nor moved for him.'—*Esther* v. 9.

moneths of June and July, during the Terms of the Exchequer, I lived at my Country house of Cammo, but rode every day to Edin. and attended the Court.

This exercise gave me a great stock of health, especially when joined to my frequent diversions of fowling and fishing, for I constantly attended my Father at the pouting[1] during the summer vacations in the Exchequer.

My plantations at Pennicuik no ways hindered me from improving the Lands and Gardens of Cammo, for I did a great deal about it, all the Plantations except a few Firrs on the East side of the House having been made by me.

But these Exercises never interfered with my studies, for within the House I made a considerable progress in most
fol. 99. studies, | particularly in Greek and Roman Literature. About this time I began to project the writing of A History of the Union of the two Kingdoms in Latine, and to give an account of all the attempts that had been made to unite the Britons under one Head, from the days of Julius Cæsar down to the accomplishment of this great work in 1707.

This I confess was a very arduous attempt, and therefore to accomplish it I not only read over all the Roman Classicks, but made very large Excerpts from them all, particularly from Livy and Salust, whom I was chiefly to imitat in my History.[2]

These studies took up some years, and in the mean time I read over all the Histories and all the Memoirs and Pamflets that related to the affaires of England and Scotland. This gave me a vast deal of work; however, I went through it not without success, and at last began my History.

What I wrote was afterwards copied by my Chaplain, Mr. Ainsley, but was very incorrectly written.

I finished the work at last, but it was so tedious and the success of it so doubtful that I never had the courage nor the time to revise it. Every particular was related with great

---

[1] '*The Pouting*, the sport of shooting young grouse or partridges.'—Jamieson's *Scottish Dictionary*.

[2] Many series of MS. transcripts from Livy and other classical historians are preserved among the Clerk papers. Some are marked in the Baron's handwriting—'which show the vast pains I was at to attain a perfect Knowledge of the Latine Language.'

candour and fidelity, but often the style did not please me, and so from time to time I put off the revising of it in such a way as it might some time or other after my death be published; however, I do not despair | of revising it before I die. *fol.* 100. and if I happen not to do it, I hope it will never be published.[1]

It was not revised in 1725, but on the contrary the original copy by my self was burnt, not from any dislike of what I had done, but because in case it was revised after my death there should be no references to the original Manuscript, as is commonly practised.

About the end of june 1713 I catched cold at the pouting on the moors, and fell into a feaver, which continued with me for 3 weeks. I was brought very low, but by the will of God and the assistance of Dr Clerk[2] and Dr Arthure,[3] two young physitians, I happily recovered. My chief pain and truble lay in my head, which I found vastly eased by the application of a Blister to my back, and a cataplasm of popies to my head. I have made a particular journal of my distemper, so shall say no more here.

In August 1713 it pleased God to incress my Family by another daughter, who was christned Elizabeth,[4] after my mother.

The months subsequent to this were spent as before between my studies and the business of the Exchequer, together with my improvements at Pennicuik and Cammo, till december thereafter, when my children hapned to fall ill of the small-pox. In this distemper it pleased God to remove my third son Hary, whom I burried at Pennicuik Kirk, in the burial place there.

His death was the more afflicting to his Mother and me that he was a very strong healfull (*sic*) Boy as ever I saw in my Life, whereas his elder Brother James was very tender from

---

[1] Three MS. copies of this *History* are preserved among the Clerk papers. One is marked by the Baron:—'*N.B.* This book was very incorrectly copied by my chaplain, Mr. Ainslie, who was not at all acquainted with the Latine orthography. I lokt it over in the year 1746, and altered several things. My own copy, tho' written badly and much interlined, was lost in the troublesome times of the year 1745, when most of my papers were hidden in disorder. However, I make the best of it I can. I have revised it once more in March 1751.'

[2] Dr. John Clerk, eldest son of Dr. Robert Clerk; see note to folio 8.

[3] William Arthur took his degree at Utrecht; received his diploma from the Royal College of Physicians, Edinburgh, 12th March 1707; was licensed to practice 9th February, and was admitted a fellow of the College 1st June of the same year.

[4] She was married to Robert Pringle, afterwards Lord Edgefield, in 1736. See folio 171.

his birth, and continued so till he was 4 or 5 years of Age. My eldest son John was then at Pennicuik.

The following year, 1715, was as remarkable to my Family as it was to the nation.

In January my son James fell ill of the small-pox, for hitherto he had continued free of them. We were in great anxiety about him, because of his weak constitution and bad
fol. 101. habit of body, | but this went over in a few days, and he recovered, not only of this disease, but of several boyls and outbreakings with which he had been trubled. These were plainly oweing to his nurse, whose milk, I am persuaded, was unsound, for most of all her children had the same trubles.

In february my dear Brother and companion Hary fell ill of a Cough, which brought him into a Consumption, of which he died in Aprile after. He was a very ingenious lad, and much given to mathematical and phylosophical studies. When he found himself drawing near his end he wished only to live to see the great Eclipse of the sun,[1] which was to happen on a friday, 2 days before he died, but in this innocent wish he was disappointed, yet submiting to the will of God with great chearfulness. He had a good deal of humure to the last, for when he found he was going off, he called to a friend, Dr Clerk, next his bed, that if he pleased the Glourers might come in, meaning the Gasers and such who rather out of curiosity than sympathy or duty attend the sick till their breath go out.

In May this year I sent my eldest son John to Eton, near Windsor, which was under the direction of one Dr Snap,[2] a very learned man. I did this with the advice and concurrence of the Earl of Galloway and the rest of his Mother's friends. He was exceedingly fit for such improvements as cou'd be acquired at any English school, for he had a very fine genius for learning, and by great application profited accordingly while he staid there. |

---

[1] This eclipse occurred on Friday the 23d April 1715. See *Scots Courant* 27th to 29th April 1715.

[2] Dr. Andrew Snap, chaplain to Queen Anne, and a preacher of considerable reputation, succeeded John Newborough as head master of Eton, resigning in 1719, when he became Provost of King's College, Cambridge. His attack on Bishop Hoadley in 1717 occasioned the celebrated 'Bangorian Controversy.'

I parted with him not without a great deal of uneasiness, *fol.* 102.
but as he was to travel in company with his Unckle, Colonel Stuart, afterwards a Brigadier General in Spain, and had for a school fellow his cousin James Stuart,[1] a son of the Earl of Galloway. I comforted my self in doing what I thought wou'd prove most for his improvement and advantage, for besides a fine opportunity of learning the Greek and Latine, I thought it wou'd be an additional Qualification to him that he understood the English Language, which since the Union wou'd always be necessary for a Scotsman in whatever station of Life he might be in, but especially in any publick character.

But whatever uneasiness I suffered during the first moneths of this year, it was vastly incressed by the publick calamities with which my country was threatened, for a Rebellion broke out, of which I shall give the following short account.

The favourers of the late Royal Family of the Stuarts being vastly disappointed and exasperated at the bad success of their schems by the last Ministry of Great Britain, and the accession of the Elector of Hannover to the Throne, they resolved to trie their fate by an open Rebellion. This was a project chiefly manadged by those who had little or nothing to lose, men of small and desperat Fortunes.

Amongst these the chief Ring-Leader was the Earl of Mar. He was not only my acquaintance but my particular friend. He was at the time of the Union one of the Secretaries of State for Scotland, and so fond of the Union of both Kingdoms | that most of all the privat meetings of the Scotch Commis- *fol.* 103.
sioners for concerting the Articles of the Union were at his House. After the Union took place, he continued in great favour with Queen Ann, and at last joined with the Tory Ministry, which, as I have noticed before, disconcerted all the salutary measures not only of Great Britain, but of all Europe, for he was no mean Instrument in concerting the

[1] Second son of James, fifth Earl of Galloway. He entered the third regiment of foot-guards, and was present at the battle of Fontenoy. In 1752 he became colonel of the thirty-seventh regiment of foot. He was chosen Member of Parliament for the Wigtown burghs in 1734 and 1747, and for the county of Wigtown in 1741 and 1754; and died a lieutenant-general at Calley in 1768.

measures that took place afterwards in the Treaty of Utricht, by which all the advantages were given up to France that had been gained by several years war in Flanders. This Earl came afterwards, in 1711, to be as fond of breaking the Union as ever he had shewn zeal for making it, and I may here notice, by the bye, that at that time the Union had been broke if it had not been for a Resolution taken in Scotland as a condition of breaking the Union, that the succession should be settled to the Kingdom of Scotland on the House of Hannover as firmly as it had been secured by an Article of the Union.

But this bait was so far from taking with the Ministry of England that on the contrary the leading men, who were intent on their jacobite schems, saw it more for the interest of what they had principally in view to continue the Union, for it appeared evident to them that if a Scots parliament should, on the dissolution of the Union, settle the succession as was proposed, it was impossible that the Pretender could have any security on the Throne of England, for that his Ennemies wou'd retire to Scotland, and there be sufficient to form such a *fol. 104.* strong party | as with a little assistance from Hannover and its confederats wou'd be soon in a condition to overturn their new Government. Thus the Union of the two Kingdoms was preserved, and I am persuaded that whatever schem of Government shall prevail in Great Britain, its best and only security must arise from the Union of the Kingdoms.

But to return to the Rebellion, my Friend the Earl of Mar, finding no favour at Court upon the accession of King George, he concerted measures with the jacobites in England, the sum of which was that he should repair to the Highlands of Scotland, and there to draw togither all the friends of the late Royal family, when at the same time some of the leading men of that party should repair to the north of England and raise all the forces they cou'd for King James. Upon this the Scotch and English jacobites should meet on the borders between the two Kingdoms, and after their junction should, with victorious arms, march to London, in order to dispossess King George of the Throne and call home their Master.

Rebellion in 1715.

Such was their main schem, but they failed in the execution of all the most important parts of it.

In the mean time it must be confessed that their Courage and conduct in Scotland far exceeded what was expected, for the Earl of Mar had so much address as to bring to the Town of Perth, the center of all the Enterprise, at least 10,000 men, some have carried the number to 12,000, which I am inclined to believe provided the 1600 men be included that | past the *fol.* 105. Frith of Forth near the Island of May, of which hereafter.

During these convulsions in my native country, I was oblidged to change my course of living and turn a Military Man, for being appointed one of the Liutenants of the Shire of Edin., I was oblidged to act my part in bringing the Militia together. These consisted of a few men, Horse and foot, who never continued 3 days together, and signified nothing in the military way, the Lowland-men being a great deal more unfit for warlike expeditions than the Highlanders who had joined the Earl of Mar. However, with these Militia Troops we sometimes made a show, and perhaps they served to intimidat those who knew nothing about them. They were particularly useful and active when the Highlanders above mentioned past the Forth and were marching to take possession of Edin., for being drawn up on the High way a mile East of Edin., where these Highlanders were to march in order to take possession of the Town, they found themselves oblidged to turn to the right and take possession of the Citadel of Lieth, the ——[1] of October 1715.

That same night, to the great joy of the Inhabitants of Edin., who expected to be plundered by the Highlanders, the Duke of Argyle arrived from Stirling with 200 chosen foot and 300 Dragoons, the foot mounted on country horses for the more Expedition.

Next morning the Deputy Liutenants and all the well affected to the Government of K. George waited on him, and immediately he ordered all his | troops to march down with *fol.* 106. him to the attaque of the Citadel of Lieth.

I waited on his Grace, and we never halted till we were within 300 paces of that place. Here all our men were drawn

---

[1] There is a blank in the MS. here. It was on Friday the 14th of October that the Highlanders seized the citadel of Leith.

up in 2 lines for the attaque. The foot in the center and the Horse on the Wings, our number was as follows.

300 Dragoons, 200 Regular foot, about 200 of the Town Guards of Edin., and about 500 Volunteers, with a Regiment of Militia. These amounting in all to about 1500 men, were drawn up on the Crofts to the Westward of the Citadel. There were likeways 2 Regiments of Militia from the Shires of Merse and Teviotdale, who were drawn up on the Links on the south side of the Town to prevent the Highlanders from escaping.

The Duke called a Council of War, consisting of the principal officers present, in sight of the Ennemy, here it was debated in what manner to attaque the Citadel, for the Duke had never seen it, and the issue was that in regard we had neither Cannon, Bombs, nor Granads, it was impossible to do anything to purpose, for that our Men wou'd be destroied by the fire of the Ennemy before they came near the Ramparts, for altho' these Ramparts and Bastions were ruined ever since the days of Oliver Cromwell, who about the years 1654 and 1655 ordered them to be repaired out of the old fortifications of Leith, yet they were sufficient against such a body of men as we were who came there to attaque them.

fol. 107. On these considerations we were oblidged | to return to the Town in a very disconsolet manner.

The Duke might have been informed of the condition of that place before he marched there, but he thought nothing in Scotland, except Castles, impregnable to his Troops, and we who knew the Citadel never doubted but dismounted Dragoons cou'd force the place sword in hand.

The next thing to be done was to provide artilery from the Castle of Edin., in order to attaque the Citadel next day, but that night the Highlanders, who were under the command of one Brigadier Macintosh,[1] and marched off to Seaton House,[2] where they staid 3 or 4 days.

Here several Detachments were sent out of Edin. to attaque them, but being without cannon we cou'd do nothing.

---

[1] Brigadier MacIntosh of Borlum. He had previously proclaimed James VIII. at Inverness, and seized and garrisoned the Castle there.

[2] The old Seton Castle, the seat of their adherent the Earl of Winton, on the site where Seton House now stands, about eleven miles east of Edinburgh.

At last these Highlanders, by orders from my L[d] Mar, proceeded to join their friends on the English borders, which they did at Kelso and Jedbrugh. There came to them likeways the Earls of Nithsdale[1] and Carnath,[2] the Viscount of Kenmore,[3] and many Gentlemen from the Shires of Dumfrise and Galloway, who, with their servants, made about 100 horse, but they were very unskilled in Military affaires, as were likeways all those who met them as before on the borders between England and Scotland, and, which was still worse, their commander-in-chief, Thomas Foster,[4] was an idle, drunken, senseless man, not good enough to head a company of militia. | Yet they had the confidence to march into England by the *fol.* 108. way of Longtoun, Carlyle, Penrith, Kendal, and at last took their station at Preston, a Town fatal to Scots Highlanders in former times.[5]

Here they were surrounded by some Regular Troops, which consisted only of about 1000 Horse and one company of foot. The Horse made up 4 or 5 weak Regiments of Dragoons under General Carpenter[6] and Wills, and the foot were not above

---

[1] William, fifth Earl of Nithsdale, succeeded his father in 1696. Engaging in the Rebellion of 1715, he was captured at Preston, and sentenced to be executed; but effected his escape through the heroism of his wife, Lady Winifred Herbert, daughter of William, Marquis of Powys. He died at Rome 1744.

[2] Robert, sixth Earl of Carnwath, succeeded to the title in 1703. Engaging in the Rebellion of 1715, he was captured at Preston, and condemned to be executed, but was respited and finally pardoned, and died 1737.

[3] William, sixth Viscount of Kenmure, succeeded his father in 1698. In the Rebellion of 1715 he raised the standard of the Pretender at Lochmaben. He was taken at Preston, and beheaded at Tower Hill, 1716.

[4] A council of war was called by the rebels, but the resolutions arrived at were countermanded next day by Foster, who had not been present at the deliberations, having 'received some little damage in the course of a convivial entertainment, so as to render it necessary that, instead of studying military despatches, he should retire to bed.'—Hill Burton's *History*, second edition, vol. viii. p. 309. 'He was no Soldier: nor was the command given to him as such, but he was the only Protestant who could give credit to the undertaking, being of Note in Northumberland, of an ancient Family, and having for several years been Member of Parliament for that County, and therefore very Popular.'—Rae's *History of the Rebellion*, London, 1717, p. 120.

[5] In 1648 Cromwell routed the Scots royalists, under the Duke of Hamilton, at Preston.

[6] General George Carpenter, born 1657. Having served with distinction in Ireland, Flanders, and Spain, he was, on the outbreak of the Rebellion of 1715,

All their jacobite Friends in Britain were ashamed of their conduct. The account they gave for it was that as there was no Insurrection in England as they expected for their King, they knew that at last they must have succumbed, and therefor they judged it both unsafe and needless for them to fight at Preston, but rather to surrender at discretion in hopes of saving their lives and obtaining Honourable Terms.

300. The Highlanders were about 1000, besides the Lowlanders, which made at least 1200 more. They behaved very poorly, and afterwards, without stroke of sword, surrendered as prisoners of War.

This remarkable event hapned on the 13 Nov. 1715, and the same day the jacobite Army, under the command of the Earl of Mar, was defeated by the Duke of Argyle at the sheriffmoor near Dumblain. Mar's army consisted of more than 12,000 men, whereas that under the Duke of Argyle very little exceeded 3000. The Highlanders made a fire or two in good order, but at last fled in confusion, except a few who remained with the Earl of Mar in what might be called the field of Battle, for they continued there after the Duke marched back to Dumblain.

This seeming Equality of fortune was oweing to the defeat of the Duke of Argyle's left wing, which was not timousely supported, for the jacobite Army which faced the Duke fled near 4 miles, with the Troops who defeated them at their Heels. The Duke fancied that the Route was total, and therefore pursued so far as that he cou'd not return in time to assist his left wing, which fled almost to the bridge of Stirling. |

A gross mistake.

fol. 109.

The above mentioned mistake ruined King Charles the First at a several Engagements, particularly at Edgehill, where Prince Rupert

This oversight was much resented afterwards by King George, and was the chief cause of displacing the Duke after the Rebellion was over; however, I believe this might have befallen any General, for it hapned that one Armstrong, the Duke's Aid-de-Camp, was killed as he was carrying the proper intelligence to the Duke of the Ennemy's disposition.[1] I myself hapned accidentally not to be at that Battle, but heard from

appointed to the supreme command of the forces in the north of England. He prevented the rebels from seizing Newcastle; and, reaching Preston, which General Wills had been ineffectively blockading, he forced them to capitulate, as described above. In the following year he was challenged by Wills, but a duel was prevented by the Dukes of Montagu and Marlborough. In 1719 he was created Lord Carpenter of Killaghy, in the Peerage of Ireland. Died 1732.

[1] This is not mentioned by Hill Burton, but Chambers refers to it. Rae (*History of the Rebellion*, p. 306 and note) states that 'all Communication or Intelligence by Aid-de-Camp or otherwise was interrupted,' for 'Captain Armstrong, one of the Duke's Aids-de-Camp, having received the Orders was killed,' and that, consequently, the left of the King's army, commanded by General Wetham, believing that the right was defeated or surrounded by the rebels, retired towards Dunblane and Stirling.

others that the Moor of Dumblain was so covered with the Ennemies flying that all believed it was a general Route.

in a foolish heat pursued the Wing he had beat for 2 or 3 miles, and on his return found his Master's Troops broke and ruined.

Mar exulted and claimed the honour of the victory because a part of his men remained for some time that night on the field of Battle; however, from that periode and what hapned at Preston, the Rebellion was in some measure at an end, for tho' Mar retired to Perth, and keept his Troops with him for near three Months after, yet he was never able to prosecute his design of marching into England.

In the meantime the poor unhappy pretender, deluded by Mar's letters and the vain hopes of his Friends, embarqued at Dunkirk and landed at Peterhead. He was amused for some days by Mar and his Friends, but coming afterwards to Scoon, near Perth, and understanding better the circumstances in which he was in, he began to dispaire, yet not so avouedly as to discompose his Friends at Perth, for he continued with them till the Duke of Argyle, assisted by near 3000 Dutch Troops, marched to attaque him. He gave orders then to burn Achterarder,[1] in order to disturb the Duke in his march, but this had no other effect than to give the Country people a dislike of him and all his adherents. |

At last he withdrew with his Garisone of Perth to Dundee, *fol.* 110. and from thence to Montrose, where he embarqued in a ship for France. Lord Mar and some others secretly accompanied him. Ld Marishal[2] and other Chiefs who had joined him fled to the north, and dispersed themselves in all the secret corners of the Highlands.

it was much admired that the Pretender did not leave Ld Mar in Scotland to take his fortune with the rest of his Friends whom he had spirited up to their ruine and to the manefest hazard of their Master, for since his Army at Shiriff

The unhappy Pretender did not find his case any way altered for the better, for tho' he escaped the seas and part of the British Fleet with great perril of his Life, yet his misfortunes were but to begin, for as Lewis the 14, King of France, had died some months before, the Duke of Orleanse,[3] who was

[1] Contemporary 'Accounts of the Burning of the Villages of Auchterarder, Muthill,' etc., are printed in the Maitland Club *Miscellany*, vol. iii. p. 441.

[2] George Keith, tenth Earl Marischal, succeeded his father in 1712. He engaged in the Rebellion of 1715, was attainted, and escaped to the Continent. He returned with the Spanish expedition in 1719, and after the defeat at Glenshiel, entered the service of Frederick the Great, who appointed him ambassador to France and to Spain. He was pardoned in 1759, and died at Potsdam 1778.

[3] Philip of Orleans, nephew of Louis XIV., Regent of France 1715-23.

Moor cou'd make nothing of it, tho 10000 against 3000,[1] there was nothing to be expected for the poor unfortunat prince, yet Mar and his party brought him to Scotland when his affaires were in a most desperat condition.

Regent of that Kingdom, was under such difficulties that he neither wou'd nor cou'd give him any assistance. He retired, therefore, to Rome, where I shall leave him.

His Friends at Home, particularly those who surrendered at Preston, were variously distressed. Two hundred of them were carried to London, and after passing through the streets in a most ignominious way, were sent to different prisons. Some made their escape, as the Earls of Nithsdale and Carnwath, but severals were hanged. At Preston and Liverpole more of them suffered than elsewhere, for their number was about 32. A great many were pardoned, and most of them had felt the King's mercy if it had not been for a prevailing party at Court, who wanted to mortify some of those who were principally concerned in the Ministry under the Earl of Oxfoord, and who had shown any satisfaction in the unfortunat Treaty of Peace at Utricht in 1714.[2]

fol. 111. One publick incident I cannot but remember | here, because some of my particular Friends were so unhappy as to be concerned in it, this was in September 1715, just after Mar came to Scotland and had begun the Rebellion, to surprise the Castle of Edin.[3]

There were about 60 or 70 Gentlemen concerned in it, and tho' the attempt was extreemly hazardous, yet they had resolved on it, and at many secreet meetings encouraged one another to persevere in it.

The project was to scale the Castle Wall on the south west

[1] Compare with numbers given at folio 108. Chambers states that the army with which Argyll prepared to attack the rebels amounted, 'by recent accessions from Ireland, to exactly three thousand three hundred men, of whom twelve hundred were cavalry; a force only about a third of that commanded by Mar' (p. 250, ed. 1829); and (p. 253) he estimates the main body brought on the field by Mar as eight thousand, with a *corps de reserve* of about eight hundred.

[2] The Whigs were enraged that, owing to the action of the Tory Ministers, and the removal of Marlborough from command, France, whose Government had always favoured the Jacobites, obtained better terms in the Treaty of Utrecht than would otherwise have been the case.

[3] The attempt upon the Castle was devised by Lord Drummond, who, if it succeeded, was to be made governor. According to Patten (*History of the Late Rebellion*, pp. 159, 160), there were engaged in the attempt 'no less than ninety choice men, picked out for the enterprise, all gentlemen; and each of them was to have £100 sterling, and a commission in the army, if the attempt succeeded.'

side by means of a Ladder of Rops, to be fixed on the Top of the Wall by one Serjeant Ainsley, whom these Don Quixots had corrupted for this purpose. The wall at that time was not above ten or twelve feet high, so that there cou'd be no other difficulty than what they might expect from a numerous Garisone within.

As the appointed time drew near for accomplishing this enterprise, I believe some of the intended conquerors began to discover their want of adequet courage, and therefor, to prevent it, made a secret intimation of it to the justice clerk, then Lord Ormistone,[1] he immediately gave notice of it to the Deputy Governour,[2] who ordered most of his Garrisone to go the round of the Castle Wall. This precaution hapned precisely in time, for just as the Garisone came to that part of the Wall which was to be scaled they found the above Serjeant Ainsley fixing the Laders. He was immediately apprehended, and on the firing of a musket the Heroes below dispersed themselves. Most of them on this discovery fled the country, and the Serjeant was shortly after hanged at the place where he was taken.

This was accounted by the jacobites a very | great misfor- *fol. 112.* tune, but tho' it might have added some reputation to my Lord Mar's Enterprise first, it would have signified at last very little, for nothing appears more a demonstration to me than that the whole schem of the Rebellion was badly timed and miserably executed. At the accession of a new King the subjects who supported him are commonly more zealous than afterwards, for by the Histories of Great Britain it will be found that we are vastly changeable, and seldom fond of any thing for a considerable time. We delight in novelties, and can change Kings and Ministries with no great reluctancy, especially if the Expectations of our selves and friends do not precisely quadrat with the vain or covetous hopes we had conceived.

consider the various fortunes of the Royal families of York and Lancaster.

---

[1] Adam Cockburn of Ormistoun, appointed Lord Justice-Clerk in 1692, and again in 1705, and died in 1735. He was much disliked by the Jacobite party.

[2] Lieutenant-Colonel Stuart. He was deprived of his post and imprisoned in the Tolbooth of Edinburgh for having failed in his duty in connection with this attempt upon the Castle.—Rae's *History of the Late Rebellion*, p. 198.

But to return to my own privat concerns, it pleased God to
1716. [*sic*] make up the loss of my son Hary by the birth of another son, whom I christned George,[1] after the patron of the cause which I had espoused during the Rebellion. He was born 31 octobr 1715.

After the Rebellion was quashed I attended the affaires of the Exchequer and my own Affaires at Cammo and Pennicuik for the remainder of the year 1716.

all the plantations about Pennicuik, except a few at the House, were made by me. The plantations, as usual, at the above places were not neglected.

In february, 5 day 1717, my family was by the providence of God augmented with a Daughter, whom I christned Jean,[2] after my Wife's Aunt, the Lady Grant.[3]

1717. I spent my time this year as usually between the business of the Exchequer, my studies, and my own privat affaires. |
fol. 113. Nothing remarkable hapned till Agust, then I had the curiosity to see Perth, the seat of the last Trubles that affected my Country. Here I catched a severe cold, but on my return I got easily well at Pennicuik by 2 days sport in the moors.

I have many times had occasion to observe that nothing contributes more to my health than exercise, especially a little riding.

I got a Cough again in September following, but it went over in a few days.

On the 24 of Octr. that same year I took a little feaver of cold, which continued with me 3 or 4 days. The symptoms

[1] He was educated at the universities of Edinburgh and Leyden, received from his father the lands of Drumcrieff in Annandale, and married Dorothea, heiress of his uncle, William Clerk-Maxwell (see folio 171 of this MS.), taking her name. He was full of public spirit, a Commissioner of the Customs, King's Remembrancer in the Exchequer, and a Trustee for improving Fisheries and Manufactures in Scotland. At Dumfries he erected a linen manufactory; and he also set on foot various mining schemes for lead and copper, through some of which he suffered great loss. He published several letters on the preparation of wool and on shallow ploughing. On the death of his elder brother, James, in 1782, he succeeded as fourth baronet; and died 29th January 1784.

[2] She married James Smollett of Bonhill. See folio 182.

[3] Jean, third daughter of Sir Patrick Houstoun, first baronet of that Ilk, and his wife Anne, daughter of John Bargany. She was married (1st) to Walter Dundas of that Ilk; (2d) to Richard Lockhart of Lee; (3d) she became the second wife of Colonel Ludovick Grant of that Ilk, who died 1717.—Crawfurd's *Renfrewshire* (Paisley, 1818).

of my desease were very bad for that time, viz., a pain in my back, a pain in my head, a shivering, a louseness and frequent pulse; however, I made use of no medicines.

The year 1718 was transacted with a good many trubles and severe afflictions in my Family, especially after the month of Agust. I went then with my Father to view the Lead works belonging to the Earl of Hopton,[1] for we had then a design of purchessing the lands of Glendorch[2] in the nighbourhood. I went down several of the Lead sinks, and on coming up from one of them the Rope sliped off the Winlase, and I fell down amongst the stones at the bottom; however, as this hapned to me when I was but about 3 fathoms from the ground, I felt no great hurt by it, save that my bones were soar for some days after. | 1718.

We were but badly accomodated at the above place, so that I believe my Father catched cold on his journey, tho' he was otherways a very strong healful man, for on his return to Pennicuik a boile broke out between his shoulders, which in a very few days turn'd to a Mortification. I got him the assistence of the ablest chyrurgeons in Edinburgh, who I believe, under God, saved his life; however, by their severe operations he was so dispirited that for above 6 weeks he differed little from a child. *fol.* 114.

This made a very great impression on me, for as he was a very kind indulgent parent, I suffered more during his illness than I believe he did himself, his wound, by the necessary cuttings and dissections, was inlarged to 9 inches in length, 5 in breadth, and about 3 in deepth, from which the strength of his Body was quite exhausted, for the black and mortified parts required daily to be cut away. He indured all this with great patience, and was happy in one thing, that he never saw

---

[1] Charles Hope, born 1681; created first Earl of Hopetoun 1703; died 1742. The valuable mines of Leadhills, Lanarkshire, had been acquired by the family through the marriage in 1638 of his grandfather, Sir John Hope of Hopetoun, to Anne, only daughter and heiress of Robert Foulis of Leadhills.

[2] Glendorch, in the parish of Crawfordjohn, Lanarkshire, was then the property of the Earl of Hopetoun. About the end of the eighteenth century 'an astonishing and unprecedented width of 18 feet of pure galena' was discovered in the Glendorch mines.—Irving's *Upper Ward of Lanarkshire*, vol. i. p. 63. (Glasgow, 1864.)

the soar, and consequently was never under the Terrors of Death, but still in hopes that he wou'd recover, and indeed about the begining of October he was so well recovered as to ride about again.

Since that time it has been discovered that nothing prevents more... mortification than the Jesuite Bark.

I staid at Pennicuik with him, but not a little valetudinary, for I attended him almost night and day.

I believe the chyrurgeons I emploied did their best; however, they cou'd not help the mortification to spread till nature was in a manner exhausted. |[1]

fol. 115.

On the 5 of Octr I had the happiness, with the recovery of my Father, to have a new augmentation to my Family, for my Wife was safely brought to bed of two sones, whom I christned by the names of Patrick and Hary.[2]

This piece of news was remarkably acceptable to my Father, for my Wife being under much sickness and uneasiness was obliged to remain at Cammo all the time he hapned to be ill at Pennicuik.

During this year I my self keept my health but very indifferently, for in the spring I was ill of a cough, and about the end of October it returned again upon me. I had likeways some distellations of blood from my head, and never wanted a great many scorbutick spots on my breast and back. These prognosticated to me a bad state of health; however, I believe they did me service, for I seldom or never wanted them, especially about the Spring and Autumn seasons.

About the begining of the year 1719 I had the agreable account of my son John's great proficiency at Eton, and to that degree that a noble Duke wrote to me that he did honour to his country. This gratified my vanity very much, for indeed I found that every body spoke of him as the chief Schollar at Eton. He certainly was a prodigious Genius, but nature had ripened him so much that I knew, or at least feared,

Duke of Montrose.

---

[1] A most elaborate account of Sir John's illness is preserved, in a MS. of forty closely written folio pages, among the Clerk papers. It was begun by the Baronet, continued by his son, the Baron, after his father was too ill to write, and finished at length by the convalescent patient. He was attended by two physicians—Dr. Clerk and Sir Edward Isat, and six surgeons—Veitch, Hope, Atkinson, Brown, Lauder, and Hepburn.

[2] See after, folios 189-91 and 222.

that he | cou'd not be long with me, which accordingly hapned *fol.* 116. about 4 years after.

In 1719 I lived much in my former way, sometimes at Pennicuik, bussied about my nurseries and plantations, and sometimes at Cammo, for my Family always was keept there, except when I attended the Court of Exchequer during the months of novembr, January, and february.

I keept my health pretty well, except when I was affected with colds and coughs, which was generally twice or thrice every year, but these went off with Exercise, for during the sessions of the Exchequer in June and July I constantly rode to Town in the mornings and returned at nights.

The scurvy spots which affected my breast and back ever since the year 1710 turn'd to be universal over my whole body for a month or six weeks, but went off without medicines, for I never took any.

I never dealt in Medicines, sickness and health came to me as God sent them.

This year my Father turned very anxious to see my eldest son John, wherefor I brought him home to prosecute his studies at the College of Edin. I had no more to expect from an English education but that he should learn the English Language, for as to his other studies I was sure they cou'd be better acquired at Edin. than at Oxford or Cambridge; besides, I knew there was this bad consequence from an English Education, that Scotsmen bred in that way wou'd always have a stronger inclination for England than for their own Country.

I had many occasions to know that few of our British youth got any benefite at Oxford or Cambridge.

I had the joy to find that my son was vastly improved in his studies, and, which was more, that he delighted in nothing so much as in Books. He excelled particularly in the Greek, and wrote several excellent Poems, both | in that language and *fol.* 117. in Latine. I found likeways that tho' his chief diversions were his studies, yet he was not averse to any Gentlemany Exercises, for he loved Hunting, riding, and fencing.

At the College of Edin. he studied Mathematicks with one Mr Campbell,[1] and had all the other Colleges which were necessary for his improvement.

I keept my health very well all this year, and perhaps so

---

[1] James Gregory, *secundus*, brother and successor of the celebrated David Gregory, was Professor of Mathematics in Edinburgh University at this time; having occupied the chair from 1692 to 1725.

much the better that I was frequently trubled with red scorbutick spots, which continued for a month or two, unless when they hapned to be removed by Moffat Water.[1]

On this account, and for the benefite of Hunting and fishing, I frequented the town of Moffat every year, from the midle of Agust to the midle of septem^r.

1720. This year seemed to have a wonderful effect on the minds of most of the inhabitants of Europe, particularly those of England, France, and Holand. Their Heads ran much on projects, and the main Tendency of these seem'd to be that of cheating, overeaching, and abusing one another by vain and foolish expectations of advantages in the way of Trade. This indeed took with the simple and ignorant, but the wiser sort saw better unto them. However, both the wise and the ignorant went madly into these projects, and many of them brought ruine upon their families, while others exulted in their illgotten wealth.

These projects began in 1718, and were carried on for about 5 years, ending with the ruine of the South Sea company in England anno 1722 and 1723.

The first of these schems was set on foot in France by one John Law,[2] a Scots Gentleman, under the name of the Mesi-
fol. 118. sippi Company. Mesisippi is a vast tract of lands in | America belonging to the French, from whence, as was given out, many

[1] The Moffat Spa was, according to the usual account, discovered in 1633 by Miss Rachel Whiteford, only daughter of Dr. Whiteford, Bishop of Brechin; but Matthew Mackaile, apothecary in Edinburgh, who published his *Fons Moffetensis* in 1659, states that it was discovered in 1658 by a 'valetudinary Rustick.' An enlarged English edition of Mackaile's pamphlet, with the addition of an account of 'the Oyley-Well at St. Catherine's Chappel, in the Paroch of Libberton,' and a character of Mr. Culpepper and his writings, was published in 1664. Among the early notices of the mineral qualities of the well are those by Sir Robert Sibbald in 1683, by George Milligan in 1733, and by Andrew Plummer, M.D., Professor of Medicine, Edinburgh, in 1747. The water was considered a remedy for 'skin complaints and affections of the lungs,' for which the Baron seems to have made use of the Well. Among the Clerk papers is a MS. in the Baron's autograph—'Proposals for the Improvement of Moffat Well, done at the desire of some of the inhabitants,' with an illustrative sketch, a copy of which was sent to the minister of Moffat (the Rev. Robert Wallace) in 1732.

[2] Born in Edinburgh in 1671, the son of a goldsmith and banker, the proprietor of Lauriston. In 1716 he established a bank in Paris, and in 1717 letters-patent were issued incorporating his Mississippi Company. After the ruin of his scheme in 1720, he led a wandering life, and died in poverty at Venice in 1729.

great branches of Trade wou'd furnish vast riches to the undertakers, who were by subscriptions to be joined into one Society. Many, not only in France but in other countries, joined in these subscriptions, and became Adventurers.

The next step taken to give Reputation to this Company was to send several colonies there to build ships and make a vast appearance, as if in reality a prodigious Trade was to be manadged from these Countries.

In the meantime those who were Adventurers made it their chief Trade to sell their shares under the name of actions at immense advantages, even to 3 or 4000 livers for one hundred in the stock of the Company. The parliament of Paris saw very soon into the iniquity and madness of these doings, since it was obvious that the real profits of the Company cou'd never exceed sex p[r] cent at most, even tho' they carried on a very profitable Trade. M[r] Law, the projector, had great shares in this stock, and was not backward in promoting his friends, for by the help of his Credite some of them were entituled to millions in this Company. He imagined it wou'd be for the interest of France to promote this undertaking, which had no solid foundation except what arose from the publick Revenue of France, because the credite of the stock was founded on the interest that was paid on account of the publick debts of France, contracted in the time of the late War. For instance, one to whom the publick owed 1000 livers or Crowns, at perhaps Ten pr cent interest, subscribed this sum into the Mesisippi Stock, and from thence not only drew the Interest from the Treasury of France but all the profits that cou'd arise upon it when manadged by a Company in the way of Trade. | Vast sums of money were thereby brought into France in order to purchess shares in the Company, and amongst the rest the Regent of France, who was then the Duke of Orleans, was a purchaser, and laid hold of this opportunity to raise the value of the species as he thought fit, by doing which he raised vast sums to the Crown of France, and relieved it of most the debts that affected it, but by doing this he broke the Credit of the Company, and so in about the space of two years it went to ruine, and those of the Adventurers who continued longest in the Company sustained all the burden of the loss. However,

N.B. The Parliament of Paris opposed this schem, and made several representations against it, but M[r] Law had the address to [set] down this ... Body as composed of narrow minded ignorant Men in all [matters] of money and Trafeck.

I was particularly acquainted with M[r] Law. He was a Man full of projects, and of a very fertile clear head. He was a Gamster by occupation, and had gained above 100,000 Crowns in this way.

fol. 119.

this publick disaster to France did no ways terrifie the people of England from entering into the very same project in the main, under the Title and designation of the South Sea Company, which chiefly obtained in 1722. It was set on foot by the Ministry at that time,[1] from a vain conceit that as the ruine of the Mesisippi Company had been brought about by the arbitrary power of the Regent and the precarious circumstances of the publick funds in France, so the South Sea Company in Britain wou'd meet with the greater encouragement from the faith and credite of the publick funds there, as secured by Acts of Parliament, which no arbitrary Government cou'd ever affect.

The consequence of these dreams was that the stock of the South Sea Company, established by an Act of Parliament at 5 per cent. interest, was greedily bought up at 120 lib. str. for each 100, and afterwards by degrees it rose to 1000 lib., and to 11 and 1200 lib., according to the notions the Adventurers *fol. 120.* had of the mighty advantages that wou'd | arise to a British Company from the Trade to the South Sea, the priviledges of which Spain had consented to in the late Treaty of Utricht,[2] and some other Treaties of commerce with that country.

But at last people's eyes were opened, and they discovered that all this Trade cou'd produce really not above 5 or 6 pr. cent., which, with the 5 pr. cent. interest paid by the Government on the original stock, might give the stock so much real value as that 200 lib. originally subscribed into the Company might be worth 200 lib., and no more; from this discovery. Men who were esteemed worth 100,000 lib. in this Company tumbled of a sudden down to 7 or 8000, but this was not the worst of it, for as the 100,000 lib. was purchased when the stock sold at 5 or 600, and all the purchess money borrowed

[1] When the company came into operation in 1711, Lord Oxford was its governor, and St. John and Benson, the Chancellor of the Exchequer, were among its directors.

[2] 'On the 26th of March 1713, by a separate treaty of forty-two clauses, France resigned the Assiento' (the 'privilege or monopoly for supplying the Spanish colonies in the western hemisphere with negro slaves') 'and Spain conveyed it to Britain for thirty years, with, at the end of this period, possession for three years for the purpose of winding up the affairs of the traffic. The obligation on the part of Great Britain was to supply 4800 negroes annually.'—Hill Burton's *Reign of Queen Anne*, vol. iii. p. 223.

at an Interest of 5 pr. cent., the proprietor of the 100,000 lib., instead of finding himself immensely rich, found he owed 40 or 50,000 lib., without any real fund to pay it except the original stock, which was perhaps not worth above 7 or 8000 lib.

Many Bankrupcies hapned at last, and in a manner the whole nation was bankrupt, only that by good fortune we were Debtors to one another, so that what one man lost another gained. Yet, in general, it may be said that there was an immense national loss, for as the most pragmatick Heads in the nation were chiefly the loosers, the nation was deprived of these Heads and hands who contributed most to enrich it in the way of Trade.

By the Example of the South Sea Company | many other *fol.* 121. Companies and Societies were erected both in England and Holand, but all of them came to ruine in the same way.[1]

I must not here forget to mention that tho' I saw very early into the folly of the South Sea schem, yet I was an Adventurer for 200 lib. ster. of the capital stock, and lost thereby about 400 lib. ster. However, I reckoned it no small happiness to my Family that I got so well off, for some of my particular friends and Acquaintances in Scotland were quite ruined by it, their all was at stake, and all indeed they had saved lay at the mercy of those from whom they had purchessed. Some of them met with compassion from those, after a great many solicitations, some had publick reliefs from the bounty of the Crown, but none of them recovered intirely their losses.

Those who had chiefly gained were those who were in the Ministry, and who were let into the misteries of the same; but

---

[1] By an order of the Lord Justices, dated 12th July 1720, eighteen petitions for letters-patent to found companies were dismissed, and eighty-six other companies were declared illegal, and abolished accordingly. The objects of the companies were in many cases of a most extraordinary character,—'For a wheel for perpetual motion, capital, one million;' 'For the transmutation of quicksilver into a malleable fine metal,' etc., etc.: but the most marvellous of all was 'A company for carrying on an undertaking of great advantage, but nobody to know what it is.' The prospectus merely stated that the capital was half a million in 5000 shares of £100 each, deposit £2 per share. Each subscriber on depositing was to be entitled to £100 per annum per share. Full particulars were to be announced in a month, when the remaining £98 per share would be called up. The projector opened his office in Cornhill; and, before he shut and decamped at three o'clock, had secured £2000 in deposits!

had men been willing to be undeceived they might soon have discovered that the whole schem was a meer buble and imposition upon men who are often but too willing to flatter their vain hopes and extravagant avarice. It was a meer Game of Fortune, where such only cou'd gain who had the sense to come soonest out of this Company.

Many of my Acquaintance might have come off with considerable sums if they had drawen in time, but in daily expec-
fol. 122. tation | that the valow of the stock wou'd still rise, they continued on till it rose to 11 or 1200, and then it tumbled down all at once to its original and intrinsick valow, which arose only from the Interest which the Government annually paid to the Company, which was 5 pr. cent.

The occasion of this suddain downfall was when the great Men concern'd in the secrets of Affaires had satisfied their avarice, and knew they cou'd conceal no longer from the publick that the Trade of the company was a meer jest, and that nothing was to be expected from it, then they began to sell out much under the current valow of the stock, that is, when that stock was commonly sold on the Exchange Aley at 11 or 1200 for one, they sold out at 1000, or under. Upon this piece of knowledge all the Rouguery was discovered, and in 2 or 3 days these stocks bore no price at all, for nobody wou'd any more deal in them. Thus all of a suddain Rich Men, or at least those who placed their confidence on their imaginary riches, fell into contempt with all sorts of people, their Gilded Coaches and fine furniture were sold off to pay a part of their debts, and they dwindled down to their primitive nothing.

Some concerned in this Company had from 100000 lib. to 700000 and upwards, who were not worth a groat at first, and worth less than nothing at last. This strange turn of Fortune made some of them destroy themselves, and many to have refuge in bedlam.

There were in the mean time some of the Ministry and their Friends who made vast sums, but as they were ashamed of their ill gotten wealth, the greatest pains imaginable were taken to conceal it.

But to return to my own privat affaires: During the year 1720 I lived as formerly, and went through the same circle of studies and occupations.

I keept my health very well till about the month of Septembr, when I fell into a fainting fit, a Deliquium Animæ, that
fol. 123. continued about a minute or two. | The occasion was my eating something which it seems disagreed with my stomach,

for I first fell asleep in a chair in my own Room, then grew very ill, vomited, and fainted. My Wife and family were terribly alarmed, but I recovered, and, blessed be God who preserved me, was as well in an houer after as ever I was in my life.

The same thing once befell me before in the year 1715, and my recovery was as suddain. I discovered from this incident, and many others of a different kind, that I had but a very weak stomach, and that the least excess put me in great disorders; in the meantime, this excess was never very criminal in me, for I never exceeded in drink, but often in plain meats, and in quantities which others wou'd have thought only necessary for supporting of nature, but amongst sober men what only suffices nature in some, is excess with them.

The above accidents became sufficient warnings to me of my own frailty and mortality. I wish only to die with the same quietness and serenity of mind which I was in when I had these two fainting fits, to die wou'd then be rather a pleasure than a pain.

This same year, about the end of October, I carried my son John to visite his Aunt, the Countess of Glencairn, at Finliston, in the shire of Renfrew.

We parted from Cammo on the 28, and lay that night at Kilsyth. Next day we got to Finliston, crossing Clyde at the village of Kilpatrick.

We were very affectionately entertained, but staid there only 4 days. |

We returned by the way of Houston, and lodged there with *fol.* 124.
my Wife's unckle, Sir John Houston. Next day we came to Glasgow, where I visited my old friends and acquaintances when I was at the College there. The Earl of Glencairn accompanied us to this place. I return'd home the 6 of Novembr, and waited afterwards on the Court of Exchequer.

In the month of Decembr thereafter I lost a very good friend, the Lady Ormistone,[1] my Wife's mother. I entertained,

[1] Anne, second daughter of Sir Patrick Houstoun, first Baronet of that Ilk. She was married (1st) to Sir John Inglis, first Baronet of Cramond; (2nd) to Sir William Hamilton of Whitelaw, a Senator of the College of Justice; and (3d) to Adam Cockburn of Ormistoun, Lord Justice-Clerk.—Crawfurd's *Renfrewshire* (Paisley, 1818).

as was my duty, a very great respect for her. She was very much regretted by all her friends, as well as by her children and my self. My Wife by her Mother's death sustained a very great loss, for she had been a very affectionate Mother to her, and had taken great care of her Education. My Mother-in-law's name was Ann Houston, Daughter of Sr Patrick Houston and Jean Hamilton,[1] daughter of the Lord Bargeny.

1721. After her Death at Edin., I returned with my Wife to Cammo, and in January 1721 I return'd to Edin. and waited on the Exchequer. In my leisure Houres I applied much to the reading of the Classicks, for I was resolved to write a History of the Union in Latine.

N.B. this good design answered the end.

My son John continued at the College of Edin., and the rest of my children remained with their mother and me at Cammo. In the Spring seasone, for the month of March, I went to Pennicuik, and carried on the plantations.|

N.B. These plantations were only finished in 1754 there.

fol. 125. Being very intent on these things I got cold, and felt a feavourish disposition with a soar throat, but these symptoms soon went over, and a Cough succeeded, which continued with me near three months after, tho' in a very moderat way.

In Aprile, about the end thereof, my son John fell ill of a Cough, and was very Hectique. His danger had not been discovered to me, for he was then at Edin. and I in the Country; however, he grew better, and both upon his account and my own we went to drink the Goat whey near the Loch of Monteeth. My Wife, and three other friends, with two of my Daughters, were with us. The place is the most agreeable in the world, and we were lodged in the Minister's House.[2] I staid there during the month of May, and returned to the Exchequer in June. All of us were a great deal better by this journey, and my son grew perfectly well.

In the vacation of the Exceqr., between 22 June and 7 July, I waited on my Father to Crauford moor to the pouting. We lodged at Elvand foot,[3] where we staid only two days, for

[1] Douglas, in his *Baronage* and *Peerage*, calls her *Anne*, daughter of Lord Bargeny.

[2] The minister of the Port of Monteith at the time was the Rev. Arthur Forbes, called and ordained 1696, died 1724.

[3] Elvanfoot, in Lanarkshire.

my Father grew very ill of the Gout, and was forced to return home in a weak condition.

On the 1 of Agust, being much importuned by the Earl of Galloway to visite him, and to bring my son, his nephew, with me, I accordingly set out, and lay at Daufington that night. As the master of the House was my Cousin German,[1] I carried Mr. Broun.
him with me. We lodged next night at a publick House near Drumlanrig, and next day, by way of Penpunt[2] and the Auld Claughan, we came to Sorbie, the House of my Brother in fol. 126.
Law, Colonel John Stuart, to whom we were very acceptable. From there we went next day to Glasertoun, the seat of the Earl of Galloway. We were all very well and most affectionatly used. I intended to have staid there only two or three days, but as I was threatned with a kind of Aguish distemper, I shortned my visite, and returned homewards by Clery, the seat of the Lord Garlies,[3] eldest son of my Friend the Earl. We staid here one night, and returned home by the way we came.

The Autumn and Winter were spent by me in the usual manner, and, saving some of my ordinary scurvy spots, I kept my Health very well.

Now follows the year 1722, a year full of sorrow and truble to me, as will appear from what follows.

My son John having got Cold at the burial of his cousin the Lord Carnegy,[4] son of the Earl of Southesk and Lady Mar-

---

[1] Mary Clerk, eldest daughter (not third, as stated by Douglas in his *Baronage*), became the wife of Andrew Brown of Dolphington. She was born 13th April 1648, and died 9th March 1690; see MS. Family Register, from which it appears that Margaret, referred to above (folio 38, note 3), on the authority of Douglas, as the eldest daughter, was actually the second, having been born 1st December 1650.

[2] Penpont, in Dumfriesshire.

[3] Alexander, Master of Garlies, succeeded his father, as sixth Earl of Galloway, in 1746, married Lady Anne Keith, daughter of William, ninth Earl Marischal, and died 1773.

[4] Only son of James, the (attainted) fifth Earl of Southesk. Douglas in his *Peerage* does not state his name, but simply mentions that he and his sister 'both died young.' His mother was eldest daughter of James, fifth Earl of Galloway, whose aunt, Lady Margaret (eldest daughter of Alexander, third Earl of Galloway), was Clerk's first wife. Allan Ramsay wrote an Elegy on his death; see his *Poems*, vol. i. p. 180 (London, 1800).

garet Stuart, he relapsed into his last year's Hectique distemper, and from the middle of March continued worse and worse. I used all the Advice and Remedies that cou'd be thought on, but to no purpose.

In the mean time my Honest Father fell ill at Edin., on the 7 of the same month, but, recovering a little, got home to Pennicuik, and languished for several days after. I came accidentally there to visite him, for no body suspected him to be in any danger, nor had he any bad opinion of his own case, save that he was growing daily weeker, and complain'd a little
fol. 127. of a lousness; however, he was present at the Marriage | of my sister Mary with Mr. Moncrief of Culfargy,[1] tho' by no means he approved of it. This gentleman had an Estate of about 5000 merks yearly, and was Minister at Abernethy. My Father, as he paid a great respect to ministers, did not oppose the marriage, nor did I medle in it, since my sister, whom I exceedingly loved, gave way to it.

My father never keept his bed, but was at dinner with us and the young married folks that day he died. He was at family worship with us in the evening, and about nine went to bed. We thought him tollerably well, and no body in the least suspected that he was near his end, for he spent some time reading in bed, as was his usual manner, and in this position fell into a fainting fit, and died without the least groan.

My Mother in Law and sisters, seeing his candle burning, and suspecting nothing of what had befallen him, continued going in and out of the Room, but when my Mother thought of going to bed to him, and receiving no answere from him to something she said, she had the great and surprising affliction to find him not only dead, but that he had been so for some time before, he being cold and stiff. All the family were much alarmed. We tried to bleed him, but found all in vain, he was gone without any possibility of Assistence, and left us all in the outmost Grief and affliction for him.

We found that he had been reading on a book of sermons published by one Mr. John Williamsone,[2] minister at Enneresk.

---

[1] See folio 6, note 1; also Additional Note L,—Culfargie.

[2] Son of the celebrated David Williamson, minister of St. Cuthbert's, Edinburgh. He was called to Inveresk in 1702; took part in the famous 'Marrow Controversy,' and was author of various pamphlets and sermons; and died 1740.

Thus it pleased God to remove my Worthy Religious Father on the 10th of March 1722, being 72 years of Age, 10 months, and 3 days. He was a very kind, provident, and indulgent parent to me, particularly, very exact and | diligent in all his *fol.* 128.
affaires. His charity was no less remarkable, so that he died much beloved and honoured by all good men. His piety, knowledge, and assiduity appear from a great multitude of his journals, writings, papers, and Memorials, many of which are in the charter Room at Pennicuik, and many of them in a Cedar chist in the Library, which chist he, it seems, once designed for his coffin. All these papers were chiefly written for his own diversion, and without the least view either to publish them in print, or to spreed them amongst his friends, wherefor they lie there as they were intended, only for the use of his children and nearest relations.

After his death, I caused seal up his closets and cabinets, and delivered the kies of them to Mr. William Macgeorge,[1] Minister at Pennicuik, for tho' he himself had informed me that he had setled all his Estate upon me, and left me his Executor as well as his Heir, yet because I had many Brothers and Sisters who had very just pretensions to enquire how our Father had setled his Affaires, therefor I was desirous that every thing should be lookt into, at such a time as other friends cou'd be present and Witnesses to all the papers left behind him in their or my Favours.

I knew that my Father had left directions for his burial, but because these were in one of his closets which were under seal, I cou'd not have the opportunity to read them, but proceeded to follow such directions as I thought were probably agreeable to the orders he had left. I wrote therefor burial letters to a few select friends and nighbours, | who, with a Herse and six *fol.* 129.
Coaches, deposited his Corpse in the Burrial place at Pennicuik.

After I had performed this last duty to my Father, I return'd to Pennicuik House, and in presence of my Cousin, Mr. John

---

[1] The Rev. William M'George, A.M., son of William M'George, minister of Heriot, studied at the University of Edinburgh, where he received a bursary on Johnston's foundation in 1683. He was ordained minister of Penicuik 1695, and died 1745, in his seventy-seventh year.

Forbes,[1] one of the Deputy Shiriffs of this shire of Edinburgh, I opened the above mentioned closets and cabinets that had been sealed up.

Several of my Brothers and other Friends were present, and we found that by my Father's Testament I was nominated his Executor and universal Legatee, with such provisions for my Brothers and Sisters as were contained in separat and distinct Bonds to each of them.

Amongst other papers we found my Father's directions for his burrial, which were singular in two particulars. The first was that his body should be put in the Cedar chist, which he had provided for his coffin above 25 years before. The other was that no mournings should be used by his children, both which particulars were not followed, and I believe tho' they had been known in due time, neither his Lady nor his children had consented to them. He left them, I believe, rather as Tockens of his Humility and self denial than that they should be obeyed.

By the loss of my Father I found my cares vastly incressed, for instead of one great Family of my own I had now two, but still I must with thankfulness remember the provident care which Almighty God and my kind Father had taken of them
fol. 130. both, for there was | enough for us all, and a great deal more than any of us deserved. In the mean time I cannot but bless the same almighty power that as He has bestowed a competent stock of worldly means upon me, so he has given me a Heart to part with some of it to those who deserve better than my self.

In the course of my management I thought it particularly my duty to use my Mother in Law well, not only because she had always behaved her self towards me with the greatest affection and civility, but because she had been a very dutiful and verteous Wife to my Father. I made her therefor wel-

---

[1] John Forbes, son of Sir David Forbes of Newhall, admitted an advocate 20th June 1713. He was a great friend of Allan Ramsay, the poet, who, in 1721, addressed him in an ode (see *The Gentle Shepherd . . . Landscape Illustrations*, Edinburgh 1814, vol. i. p. 55), and in 1728 wrote an Elegy on the death of his wife. His cousin, Duncan Forbes of Culloden, when he became Lord Advocate in 1725, appointed Forbes one of his Advocate Deputes. His mother was Catherine, youngest daughter of John Clerk, first owner of Penicuik.

come to live in the House of Pennicuik for several months after my Father's decease, and as a farther evidence of my regard to her, I submitted a difference between her and me to her nearest Relatione, one Mr. Roger,[1] a minister, to be determined as he thought fit, tho' I thought I had a great deal of the right on my side, Question being about certain things that were actually amongst the paraphernalia of my Mother. The above Gentleman determined the matter in a way agreeable to us both, so that till her death, which was many years after, we lived in the greatest Friendship.

I did likeways all I cou'd to make her children easy. I paid my sister Mary's portion of 10,000 merks Scots before she left Pennicuik House, agreable to a clause in her Contract of Marriage with Mr. Moncrief to that effect, and tho' my Brother James had spent his portion of 15,000 merks, which his Father left him by a bond of provision, yet I paid it to him | again, tho' his discharges to his Father for it were actu- *fol.* 131.
ally in my Custody.

After I had reviewed my Father's Affaires at Pennicuik, I returned to Cammo, where I had left my wife and family, and there lived for the space of 14 Months.

In the mean time my dear son John grew daily worse, tho' I carried him again to the Goat Whey at the Port of Monteeth. His disease went on in spight of all his physitians, who prescribed everything proper in his case. He continued to languish all the months of June and July, tho' he was able to ride about, and frequently 15 or 20 miles, without any uneasiness. Towards the beginning of Agust he turned very weak, and I began entirely to dispaire of his Recovery.

On the 9 of that month I went over to Pennicuik to visite my Mother in Law, and on the 10th my son came to us in a chariote, and returned to Cammo next day, for he found not that relief in the Aire of Pennicuik which he expected. As he was very fond of books, he had the satisfaction to be carried up to the Library, where he had many books of his own, but tarried there a very short time, being extreamly Asthmatick

[1] Probably the Rev. Andrew Rogers, minister of Galston, in the Presbytery of Ayr, from 1692 till his death in 1735.

and uneasy. When he return'd to Cammo he fell very ill in the night-time, and wanted much to see me. An express was sent to Pennicuik, and I went over immediately to Cammo, but before I came it pleased God to remove him, to my unspeakable Grief, being then 21 years of Age, 8 months, and a few days.[1]

fol. 132. I had a great many reasons at that | time to be vastly afflicted for him, since he was not only a very singular lad for all manner of good qualities, but was the only child of his mother, he was tall, handsome, good natured, and well disposed. He had a great sense of Religion, and was an excellent schollar. He was likeways a fine mathematician, and had a very fine taste in every thing to which he applied himself. He was very sober and temperat, and what endeared him most to my Wife and me, he was an exceeding kind and dutiful son. I burried him at Pennicuik by his Grandfather, who doated much upon him, and was so far happy as to die before him. His Books were, according to his desire, carried to Pennicuik, and placed by themselves, where there are likeways some of his Writings, which gave evidence of a very extraordinary Genius in so young a lad.

After this second affliction I returned back to my Family at Cammo.

Here I had time to reflect on the goodness of God, that tho' he had lately deprived me of my Eldest sone, yet I had reasone still to be very thankfull for the Children he had left me, for I had no fewer than 5 sones and 4 Daughters. However, at that time I was tempted to think that the son I had lost was worth them all, since they were so young, that, considering my own

---

[1] Allan Ramsay's memorial verses, addressed to Sir John Clerk on the death of his son, were printed at the time on a folio leaflet, a copy of which is placed in the present MS. volume. The poet refers to the previous death of Lord Carnegy, mentioned above (folio 126) :—

> 'Bravely resign'd, obeying Fate's command,
> He fixed his Eyes on the immortal Land,
> Where crowding Seraphs reach'd him out the Hand.
>
> Southeska's smiling Cherub first appear'd,
> With Garlies' consort, who vast pleasure shared,
> Conducting him where Virtue finds Reward.'

The verses are reprinted in Ramsay's *Poems* (see vol. i. p. 186).

weak constitution, I cou'd not promise my self so long a Life as to see them good for any thing.

About the end of this summer I went over to Culfargy, near the Bridge of Earn, to visite my sister Mary and my new Brother in Law. She seemed to be very content and easy in her circumstances, for Culfargy was a very sober good man, except he should carry his very Religious whims so far as to be very uneasy to every Body about him, as indeed hapned not long after. |[1]

In October I carried my wife and some of my children to Pennicuik House, where we staid for a Month, and afterwards came to Edin. to attend the Court of Exchequer. About Martinmass thereafter, my Mother in Law left the House of Pennicuik, and removed her Family to Edin. for the Education of her children. Tho' she had lived at Pennicuik since my Father's death to that time, yet I had maintained her Family and paid up her joynture to that Terme without deducting anything. I likeways paid to all my Brothers and sisters the annual rent of their portions left by my Father, with the expenses of their mournings.

The number of the children my Father left by my Mother in Law were James, Robert, *fol.* 133. Hugh, David, and Alexander, being 5 sones and 4 daughters, Mary, Catharine, Christina, and Margaret. Besides myself and my Brother William, Elizabeth, Barbara, Sophia, in all 13 children.[2]

This Winter, while I staid at Edin., I came to a Resolution to sell Cammo, since I found it inconvenient to live at it when the Bulk of any Estate I had lay on the South side of pentland hills, to wit the two Baronies of Pennicuik and Laswade, with the lands of Utershill,[3] all which had been in the possession of my Father. I was likeways the more induced to do this that my father wisht and expected that I should for the most part take up my residence at Pennicuik, where I had already made a good many plantations and other improvements.

I was likeways resolved to build a small house at Mavisbank, under the Town of Lonhead, which my Father inclined frequently to have done, because his Coal works there, with a

---

[1] See Additional Note L.

[2] The number here has been altered, but *fourteen* children are enumerated. Douglas in his *Baronage* makes fourteen children in all, including Henry, who was born 6th June 1678, and died 19th April 1715 (see folio 101), but omitting David, who was born 25th January 1708, and died of fever at the age of seventeen.

[3] The ruins of Uttershill Castle are on the right bank of the Esk, a mile and a quarter east of Penicuik House.

multitude of Feuers and Tenants, required his frequent attendance. He had carried the matter so far as to make several designs for this House with his own hands, but at last thought himself too old to begin to build Houses. |

fol. 134. In the mean time, when I was thinking of these projects, I
1723. received a new cheque to them, for my youngest son William, a very hopeful Boy of a year old, sickned in novembr 1722, and died 3 january 1723. His desease was a suddain truble in his Head, to which we cou'd find no name, and a little after my youngest Daughter Mary, who was born 28 Agust 1720, died on the 2 of March. Both these children I burried at Pennicuik. These had been very heavy afflictions to me, if the loss of my eldest son had not in a great measure defaced all the sense of losses I cou'd sustain. Thus, in less than a year, I lost my Father and three children, and saw at the same time a new misfortune approaching, for my only Brother William seemed to be in as dangerous a condition as a Hectique disposition cou'd bring him to.

I was likeways threatned with the greatest loss of all, for my wife sickned at Edin., and was reduced to a meer shadow; however, it pleased God to recover her again in the months of March and Aprile, when we least expected this happiness.

I carried my Family to Pennicuik in Aprile, where my wife was perfectly restored to her health, but my Brother William,[1] who came with us, grew daily worse, and died, aged 40 years. He was an Advocat, and was married to Agnes Maxwell, daughter and Heiress to John Maxwell of Midlebee, in Anandale. He left behind him only a daughter, Dorothea Clerk, who fell under the Tutory of her Mother, a very verteous woman, and me, of whom hereafter.[2]

In May 1723 I not only finished my design for the House of

---

[1] William Clerk, third son of the first baronet of Penicuik, was born, according to the MS. Family Register, on the 12th July 1681. He was admitted an advocate 20th January 1705. His poetical correspondence with Dr. Alexander Pennecuik will be found in *The Gentle Shepherd. . . . Illustrations of the Scenery* (2d ed., Edin. 1814), vol. ii. pp. 640-42. 'From his liking to visit, and shift about, from house to house, among his companions, he got the name of Wandering Willie.'—*Id.* Note, p. 640.

[2] See folios 151 and 171.

IX

MAVISBANK HOUSE

Mavisbank,[1] under the correction of one Mr. Adams,[2] a skilful | Architect, but laid the foundation of the House about 300 *fol.* 137 [*sic*]. yards west from a little Farm House, which I believe for some generations past went under the same name. All the fine stone in the front and Cornice was brought from a Quary at the Linn of Roslin, and the coarser sort of large stones were brought from the Birrit [?] foord, near Pennicuik Town. What encouraged me to this expensive carriage was that some of the Tenants in Laswade were oueing me 2 or 3 years rent, and were under no condition to pay me any other way than by their Horses and carts.

In the building of this House my Architect contended about making it a story higher, in which if I had complied, the fabrick wou'd have lookt like a Touer, and been quite spoiled, but however the Architecture may please or displease, it is oueing chiefly to my self.

This year I began likeways another expensive and laborious 1723. work, which, however, I am persuaded will be of great benefite to my self and Family. For as the Coal works in Lonhead were now carried on in the Farm of Edgefield,[3] near Ld Ross's[4] Baronie of Melvile, I forsaw that in less than 10 years they wou'd be at an end, unless I carried up a new level 500 fathoms at least east from the Level mouth in Buldsdean Burn,[5] under the Farm of Brughlee. Therefor having taken proper measures of the descent, and considered what coal was to gain by bringing up a Level about 150 fathoms from the new House of Mavisbank, on the Brae | east of what I designed for a *fol.* 138. Garden, I began the work this summer. My purpose was to cut the coal seams neer the Town of Lonhead, tho' I knew that

---

[1] Mavisbank House. *See* Illustration No. IX. and Additional Note M.

[2] William Adam of Maryburgh, architect and 'King's Mason in Edinburgh,' designed Hopetoun House and the old Royal Infirmary, Edinburgh. He died 1748. Robert Adam, the celebrated architect, was one of his sons. John Clerk of Eldin, author of the *Essay on Naval Tactics*, seventh son of Baron Sir John Clerk, married Susan, William Adam's seventh daughter; and their son was Lord Eldin, the judge.

[3] Edgefield, half a mile north of Loanhead.

[4] William, twelfth Lord Ross, born 1656, succeeded his father, 1682. He was a commissioner for the Union and one of the lords of the Treasury. Died 1738.

[5] Bilston Burn, which joins the Esk about half a mile south of Loanhead, at Burghlee Farm.

the distance was neer 300 fathoms. I forsaw likeways the expence, that being a work of 8 or 10 years labour it wou'd cost me not much down of 1000 lib. str., but at the same time I knew that, after meeting with the coal, I wou'd make one year with another by it at least 300 lib. str. for 30 or 40 years after. About the end of Octr I stopt my masons upon their having finished the first story of the House of Mavisbank, with a design to begin again in March or Aprile thereafter. I keept my Health very well this Winter, except that now and then I was trubled with a Cough.

This calculation proved just.

1724. In May 1724 I sent to the Highlands and purchessed a score of Goats, which I keept at Brunstane and Achencorth.[1] They served the end I intended to very good purpose, for by using their Milck or Whey my wife was entirely recovered from her indispositions. This summer I concluded the sale of Cammo with one Mr. Hog for 4200 lib. ster., or thereby, and by this bargain recovered more than I had laid out upon it while I possessed it, for it cost me but about 2800 lib. ster. I had lived very agreably there for the space of 13 years.

'tis now found that Ewe milck or whey is very little inferior to that of Goats.

All this summer I continued to carry on the House of Mavisbank and brought it up to the Roof.

In October, as usual, I got a great cold, and by a Rheum and truble in my head all my Teeth loosed and seemed ready
fol. 139. to drop out, | but by keeping warm for a few days and a little Exercise I grew as well in november, tho' in the Aire of Edin., as ever I was in my Life. This was the first time I found that by the louseness of my Teeth old age was begining with me, and that the pins of my Earthly Tabernacle were dissolving, but the weakness of my constitution prepared me for these things, for I may say with Cæsar that *emori nolo sed me mortuum esse nihil curo*.

On the 10 of March this year my Family was incressed by another Daughter, who was christned Joanna, after my deceased son. About the end of Aprile I took a journey into the north of England in order to observe the Coal works at Newcastle and all along the River Tyne. I had likeways a

[1] Brunston, a farm about a mile south-west of Penicuik House, containing the ruins of the castle of the Crichtons of Brunston. Auchencorth lies half a mile south of Brunston, to the north-west of Auchencorth Moss.

very great desire to see the famous Roman Wall in England, which was at first carried on by way of a vallum and earthen Bank by the Emperor Hadrianus, and afterwards fortified by a stone wall under the Emperor Severus.

I carried in my company a great lover of Antiquities, one Mr. Alex. Gordon,[1] who had been bred up for many years in Italy, my cousin, Mr. Brown of Daufington, and my son James, being then about 15 years of Age.

We lay at Kelso the first night, and at Morpeth the night after. From thence we rode to Newcastle, where I staid for three days, of which one was spent going down the River Tyn to Tinmouth Shiels. I was attended by one of the Aldermen of the Town, to whom I had been recommended. | Upon a *fol. 140.*
Sunday which interveened I went with my company to Dur-

---

[1] Alexander Gordon, antiquary, was born at Aberdeen about 1692, and took his degree of M.A. in the university of that city. He studied music in Italy, and on his return taught languages and music, and painted portraits in oil. He devoted himself to investigating the Roman remains in Scotland and the North of England, and in 1726 published his *Itinerarium Septentrionale; or a Journey thro' most of the Counties of Scotland and those in the North of England*, a work of much research. It will be remembered that this is the volume which Scott introduces in the opening of *The Antiquary* as in the possession of Oldbuck. At the same time Gordon announced *A Compleat View of the Roman Walls in Britain*, but this never appeared. He was afterwards a partner with John Wilcox, a bookseller in the Strand. He published *The Lives of Pope Alexander VI. and his Son Cæsar Borgia*, London, 1729; *Lupone, or the Inquisitor: a Comedy*, London, 1731, and a translation of Maffei's *De Amphitheatro*, London, 1730. In 1736 he became secretary of the Society for the Encouragement of Learning, and succeeded Stuckeley as secretary to the Society of Antiquaries; and he was also appointed secretary to the Egyptian Society, and published *An Essay towards explaining the Hieroglyphical Figures on the Coffin of the Ancient Mummy belonging to Capt. William Lethieallier*, London, 1737. In 1741 he sailed for South Carolina as secretary to James Glen, F.S.A., the governor, and he died at Charleston in 1755. Clerk was a warm friend and patron of Gordon, who was a frequent visitor at Penicuik; and the Baron maintained a correspondence with him after he had settled in America. Sir John was the most liberal of the subscribers to the *Itinerarium*, for his name appears for no fewer than 'five Books' or copies. In the preface, Gordon refers to his friend in very laudatory terms:—'Neither can I, in Gratitude, omit, in a particular manner, to acknowledge my many and repeated obligations to Sir John Clerk, Baron of the Exchequer in Scotland, who is not only a Treasure of Learning and good Taste, but now one of its chief Supports in that country.' Gordon's account of the route traversed by the Baron and himself will be found in pp. 71-82 of the *Itinerarium*.

ham,[1] where we heard divine service perform'd with all the Musick and solemnities of the church of England. We were most civilly entertain'd here by the Clergy. Next day I viewed all the coalworks near Newcastle, and considered all the methods and Machinery used there for working or raising the Coal.

We proceeded then to view the Roman Wall or prætentura, which began to appear near a villa called Benwell,[2] where we were kindly entertained by the Master of the House, one Mr. Shaftoe;[3] from thence by the said Roman Wall and several Roman Camps and buildings we came to Hexham, where we lodged all night.

Next day we struck again into the course of the Wall, and proceeded to House Steeds, where I found near 40 Sculptures and other considerable Remains of a Roman station there, which was called Præcolitium.[4] We came from thence to Thirlewall Castle,[5] one of the Remains of that great Roman work. We

[1] Clerk seems to have formed some friendships in Durham, for in the Library of the Royal College of Physicians, Edinburgh, is a volume, *Durham Cathedral as it was before the Dissolution of the Monasteries* . . . Durham, 1733, which bears an autograph inscription, 'To the Honble Sir John Clerk, Baron of His Maj^ties^ Exchequer in Scotland, this grateful Acknowledgm^t^ is offered in Return for many singular Favours by his obed^t^ Servt., Chris. Hunter. Durham, Aug. 6th, 1733.'

[2] Near the village of Benwell is Condercum, the third stationary camp on the Roman Wall; further west is Vindobala; and then, near Halton Castle, Hunnum, the fifth station, is reached.

[3] Robert Shaftoe of Benwell Tower, succeeded his father, Robert Shaftoe, Alderman of Newcastle, in 1714; was High Sheriff of Northumberland in 1718; and died 1735. Gordon describes a Roman altar in his possession.—*Itinerarium*, p. 49.

[4] Procolitia is the seventh stationary camp on the line. Further west, at Housesteads, is the famous camp of Borcovicus, pronounced by Gordon to be 'unquestionably the most remarkable and magnificent station in the whole island.' Many of the altars and figures formerly here are now in the Museum of the Society of Antiquaries, Newcastle-on-Tyne. 'When I had the honour to traverse this ground, for the first time, with Sir John Clerk, Baron of the Exchequer, we caused the place to be dug where we were then sitting, amidst the ruinous streets of this famous *Oppidum*, and found another small statue of a Soldier, accoutered in the Roman Habit . . .'—Gordon's *Itinerarium*, p. 77. This figure, with three altars and a bas-relief from Housesteads, and other classical remains, were presented to the Society of Antiquaries of Scotland by the Right. Hon. Sir George Clerk, in 1857. See their *Proceedings*, vol. iii. p. 37.

[5] Thirlwall Castle, on the Tipalt, near the camps of Magna and Amboglanna, is a mediæval fortress, now in ruins, containing stones taken from the Roman Wall.

lay again at a Villa of the Earl of Carlyle,[1] called Norham Castle, from thence, still keeping along the Wall, we came to Corby Castle, where the proprietor, one Mr. Howard,[2] made us stay to dine with him. In the afternoon we visited Seelby Castle where there are a good many Roman Antiquities. The owner Mr. Gilpin[3] was very civil to us, and as he was Recorder of Carlyle he wou'd needs wait on us to that Town. Here we staid all night, and next day, tho' I inclined to have been incognito, the Recorder brought the Lord | Maier and Aldermen to *fol.* 141. wait on me. They were very civil in their compliments as what they thought was their duty to one of his Majesty's judges. However, as I was not there in the Equipage of a judge I cou'd easily have dispensed with the Honour they did me. Mr. Gilpin carried me every where, and as he was himself an excellent Schollar and Antiquarian, I had all the pleasure imaginable in his Company.

N.B.—This gentleman, dying a few years after, left me his staff with a silver head, wherein is an Inscription that it was made of a piece of oake which was taken out of the foundation of the above-mentioned wall. I lookt particularly to Severus' stone wall as it passed through a moss near Seelby Castle, and found it was built on great oak Trees

I have written a particular journal of this little Trip to England and therefor shall say no more of it here.

From Carlyle I returned by the way of Moffet to Pennicuik, exceedingly well satisfied with what I had seen.

This summer I put on the Roof of Mavisbank, and built the Garden Walls there.

In the winter I went with my Family to Edin. and attended the business of the Exchequer.

In the Spring of the year 1725 I went to Pennicuik, and carried on my Plantations and other improvements there.

I continued likeways as formerly to give a constant applica-

[1] Charles Howard, third Earl of Carlisle. Born 1674; First Lord of the Treasury, 1701 and 1715; died 1738.

[2] William Howard, third son of Sir Francis Howard, Knight, of Corby Castle, succeeded his brother in 1702, and died in 1739. Gordon describes and figures an altar in his collection.—*Itinerarium*, p. 96.

[3] William Gilpin, of Sealesby Castle, was born 1657, the eldest son of Richard Gilpin, M.D., the celebrated Nonconformist divine and physician. He became recorder of Carlisle, 1718, and was noted for his antiquarian and artistic tastes. He died, 'not a few years after' 1724, but in the end of that year, and was buried on the 14th of December. See *Dict. of Nat. Biography*, vol. xxi. p. 382. Various altars, urns, an intaglio, etc., in the collection of Mr. Gilpin, are described and figured in Gordon's *Itinerarium*, see p. 95. 'This Gentleman's death was a fatal stroke to learning in that country, he being an indefatigable Collector of Antiquities; nor did I converse with any Person there who understood them better.' See also p. 81.

placed across the foundation, which were black but entire, tho they had leyn there about 1500 years.[1]

tion to my studies at all times of the day, having seldom given myself much truble with any company that came to see me. I never cou'd drink, so that no body found themselves disappointed.

On the 17 octobr. the same year my Family was incressed
fol. 142. by another Daughter | called Barbara, after a sister of mine, the Lady Cairnmoor.[2]

Towards the end of this month I fell suddainly ill on a Sabath day, fainted and was extreamly sick, was very feaverish for 3 days, and at last my desease appeared to be the Rose or St. Anthony's fire on my left Leg. I was very uneasy afterwards for several days, and keept my Bed near 3 weeks before I was able to walk again. My Weakness even continued for 6 weeks after, but it pleased God at last to recover me perfectly, and I reckon it no small happiness that I am now and then treysted with slight afflictions. My prosperity should otherways make me forget the Almighty power to whom I owe all my enjoyments.

In january 1726 I returned with my Family to Edin. and attended the Court of Exchequer.

In Aprile a coal was discovered at the Damhead of Pennicuik, about 4 feet thick. I wrought it a while until it run under the Water at the upper call of the Damhead. I mention this circumstance cheefly on account of the following observation that tho' my Father and Grandfather had spent a good deal of money on discovering a coal at the Mill of Pennicuik near the great Bridge, yet to me it was discovered by so insignificant an Animal as a Mole, which, upon the croft [?] of it, threw up some of the Coal, and shewed that often great things are unexpectedly brought about by very mean instruments. However, this coal did not produce much, for runing under the

---

1 'In cutting the canal from Carlisle to the Solway Firth, in 1823, a prostrate forest of oaks was discovered. The engineer of the canal says, ". . . Although the precise period when this forest fell is not ascertainable, there is positive proof that it must have been long prior to the building of the Wall, because the foundations of the Wall passed obliquely over it, and lay three or four feet above the level of the trees."'—Bruce's *Roman Wall*, pp. 310-311.

2 Barbara Clerk, second daughter of the first Baronet of Penicuik, was born 2d December 1679. She married (1st) John Lawson of Cairnmuir, and (2d) Dr. William Arthur; and died aged fifty-five.

Croft land of Pennicuik it was in | (danger?) of doing more *fol.* 143. mischief than it did good. It is still to be found on the south side of the Damhead, at the foot of the Brae, on the north side of Easter Ravensnook,[1] from whence no doubt it takes its course westward to the Moor of Pennicuik, where I believe all the coal-seams of the shire of Lothian terminat.

This year I attempted a poem in Milton's way under the Title of the Country Seat,[2] but tired upon the revising and correcting the style of it as I ought, which I did purposely to prevent its being ever published.

About this time I was invited to correspond with two 1726. learned Gentlemen in England upon Greek and Latine Literature, and particularly upon Antiquities. These Gentlemen were Roger Gale, Esq.,[3] a commissioner of the Excise in

[1] The ruins of Ravensneuk Castle are about half a mile, and the farm about a mile, east of Penicuik House.

[2] A copy of this poem (which extends to over 1300 lines of blank verse, each stanza ending with a rhymed couplet) in the Baron's autograph, is preserved among the Clerk papers. It is dated 1727, and bears a note that 'according to Horace's maxim' it is to be revised in nine years, followed by the entry,—'I have accordingly revised the above poem, and, in the main, find it either right, or at least agreeable to my own sentiments. I speak as to the subjects treated of; but as to the dress, if I had Leisure, I cou'd find in my heart to help several things, tho' not very material. Pennycuik, 18 December 1736, John Clerk.' The poetical value of the work is small, but it contains much excellent advice as to the planning of a country-seat in the taste of the period. The author seems to have been less peremptory as to the non-publication of this poem than he was in the case of his *Memoirs of my Life* and his *Travels*. Its preface begins:—''Tho I have no design to publish the following poetical Essay, nor will ever acknowledge myself the Author of it in print, yet because it may some time or other fall into the hands of those who may publish it, I shall say a few things to the Reader.' In a passage further on he would appear to anticipate its anonymous publication,—'As to the Rules and Directions given in this poem, let my reader think the more of them that they are tendered by a person in a Mask. They may be recommended to him, as is the custom of Mountebank Doctors to recommend their medicines,—from study, travel, and experience, but they are left to speak for themselves.'

[3] Roger Gale of Scruton, Yorkshire, was born in 1672, and educated at St. Paul's School and Trinity College, Cambridge. He represented Northallerton in Parliament in 1705, 1707, 1708, 1710; in 1715 was appointed a commissioner of stamp-duties; and in 1714 a commissioner of excise, but he was displaced in 1735 by Sir Robert Walpole. He was first vice-president of the Society of Antiquaries, and treasurer of the Royal Society. In 1709 he edited with notes the *Antonini Iter Britanniarum* of his father, Thomas Gale, Dean of York; translated Jobert on *The Knowledge of Medals*, 1697; and contributed

England, and one Doctor Stuckley,[1] first a physitian and then a clergyman. Both were the Authors of several good things, particularly the last, tho' not so learned and judicious a Man as the first. I entered likeways into a Correspondence with the Earl of Pembroke,[2] who was Plenipotentiary at the Treaty of Reyswick when I was in Holand in 1698.

This Correspondence[3] procured me the Credite to be made a member of the Antiquarian Society in London, of which the Earl of Hartfoord,[4] Eldest son of the Duke of Buckingham,
fol. 144. was president. Both these Lords | shewed me afterwards many

---

to the *Philosophical Transactions*, the *Gentleman's Magazine*, and *Britannia Romana*. Nichol's *Bibliotheca Topographica Britannica*, vol. iii. (*Reliquiæ Galeanæ*), contains various of his papers, and his correspondence with Clerk and other antiquaries. He died at Scruton in 1744.

[1] William Stukeley, a celebrated antiquary, was born at Holbech, Lincolnshire, in 1687. He studied at Cambridge, and, under Dr. Mead, at St. Thomas's Hospital, and took his degree of M.D. in 1719. In 1726 he settled as a physican at Grantham; but, turning his attention to the church, he was ordained in 1729, and became Rector of All Saints, Stamford; and in 1747 was presented to the rectory of St. George, Queen Square, London. He was a member of the Royal Society, and one of the first of those who, about 1717, revived the Society of Antiquaries, of which he was its secretary for many years. In 1741 he was one of the founders of the Egyptian Society; and he was author of many works on medical and antiquarian subjects, of which the most important is his *Itinerarium Curiosum*, published in 1724. He died in 1765.

[2] Thomas Herbert, born 1656, succeeded his elder brother as eighth Earl of Pembroke in 1683; in 1690 was appointed First Lord of the Admiralty; in 1692 Lord Privy Seal; and in 1697 first plenipotentiary at the Treaty of Ryswick. He was an eminent collector and patron of art and literature, and president of the Royal Society 1689-1690. In 1690 Locke dedicated his *Essay on Human Understanding* to him, and Berkeley his *Principles of Human Knowledge*, in 1710. He died in 1733. Allan Ramsay refers to him in his 'Ode to the Earl of Hartford, etc.';—

> 'Pembroke's a name to Britain dear
> For learning and brave deeds of weir (war);
> The genius still continues clear
>   In him whose art
> In you rare fellowship can bear
>   So great a part.'

[3] Copies of some of the Baron's letters to these personages are preserved among the Clerk papers.

[4] Algernon Seymour, born 1684, styled Earl of Hertford till 1748, when he succeeded his father as seventh Duke of Somerset (not *Buckingham*, as stated by Clerk). He became a fellow of the Society of Antiquaries 16th January 1724; was created Earl of Northumberland and Earl of Egremont in 1749; and died 1750. In 1728 Allan Ramsay addressed 'An Ode to the Earl of

civilities, of which hereafter, and the Earl of Pembroke sent me his picture,[1] which is now one of the ornaments of Mavisbank.

My Correspondence with those Lords and Gentlemen went on in a very friendly manner, and I was induced by their invitation to undertake a journey to London the year after.

I spent the months of november and december at Edin. attending the Court of Exchequer, save about Christmass that I and all my Family were always at Pennicuik for 3 or 4 weeks.

I returned to Edin. the 23 of january 1727, staid there till the begining of March, and on the 16 of that Month set out in company of a very agreable Gentleman, Mr. Spithel of Louchat,[2] for London. 1727.

We arrived there about the begining of Aprile, and staid

Hartford and the rest of the members of the Society of British Antiquaries' (see *Poems*, vol. i. p. 138, London edition of 1800):—

'To Hartford and his learnèd friends,
Whose fame for science far extends,
A Scottish muse her duty sends,
From Pictish towers:
Health, length of days, and happy ends,
Be ever yours.

. . . .

'Among all those of the first rate,
Our learnèd Clerk, blest with the fate
Of thinking right, can best relate
These beauties all,
Which bear the marks of ancient date,
Be-north the wall:

'The wall which Hadrian first begun,
And bold Severus carried on
From rising to the setting sun,
On Britain's coast,
Our ancestors' fierce arms to shun
Which galled them most.'

[1] This portrait is still in the possession of the head of the Clerk family. It is a three-quarters length, representing the Earl in armour, as Lord High Admiral of Great Britain and Ireland, a post to which he was appointed in 1701, and again in 1708. The figure is painted by William Wissing, and the background of sea and ships by William Vandevelde, the younger.

[2] James Spittal of Leuchat and Blair Logan was born about 1663, son of Alexander Spittal of Leuchat. Though a Whig and a Presbyterian he went to Rome, and obtained a dispensation from the Pope to marry his deceased wife's sister, who was a daughter of Sir James Holburne of Menstrie. After her death he travelled much in Italy, Germany, and France; and on his return,

above 7 weeks. During this time I was very civilly used by every body and particularly by the above mentioned Lords and Gentlemen. I was frequently entertained at their Houses, and carried about by them to see every thing that was valouable either in London or near it. I was frequently at Court, and saw the Royal Family on several occasions. I never gave his Majesty King George the first the truble of receiving me with a kiss of his hands, but was introduced to the Prince[1] by the Earl of Pembroke who never failed to do me all the Honours in his power. I was by him made acquainted with the Duke of Devonshire,[2] the Earl of Burlington,[3] the Lord[s] Carteret[4] and

in 1700, his society was greatly sought, and he was regarded 'as a man of fashion who had studied books and men to excellent purpose.' He was Provost of Inverkeithing, 1696-1704; and represented the burgh of Inverkeithing in Parliament, 1696 to 1707. He was the last surviving member of the Union Parliament, and 'used to give precious anecdotes of the people who made a figure in the tempestuous debates which took place while the Union was under agitation.' Ramsay of Ochtertyre relates that once while visiting at Tullibole in 1756 or 1757, 'At the company's breaking up after supper, he took me to his bedroom, where he sat till three in the morning talking over his travels, and of people who had made a great figure at home and abroad. I admired the shrewdness and *naïveté* of the remarks of a man past ninety whose faculties were entire. . . . He spoke the most elegant Scots I ever heard, probably the language spoken at the Union Parliament, which was composed of people of fashion.' See *Scotland and Scotsmen of the Eighteenth Century from the MS. of John Ramsay of Ochtertyre*, vol. ii. pp. 290-94, where many of Spittal's quaint sayings are preserved.

[1] George Augustus, Prince of Wales, succeeded his father as George II., and was crowned 11th October 1727.

[2] William Cavendish, born about 1673, succeeded his father as second Duke of Devonshire 1707; was appointed Lord President of the Council in 1716, and again in 1726. He married Rachel, elder daughter of William, Lord Russell, and died in 1729.

[3] Richard Boyle, succeeded his father as third Earl of Burlington, 1704; was invested a K.G. 1730; died, 1753. Pope inscribed to him the Fourth Epistle —'Of Taste'—of his *Moral Essays*:—

> 'But you, proceed! make falling arts your care,
> Greet new wonders, and the old repair;
> Jones and Palladio to themselves restore,
> And be whate're Vitruvius was before.'

[4] The great rival of Walpole, John Carteret, second Baron Carteret, born 1690, succeeded his mother in 1744 as Earl Granville. In 1719 he was Ambassador-Extraordinary to the Court of Sweden; in 1721 Principal Secretary of State; and in 1724 he was constituted Lord-Lieutenant of Ireland. Died 1763. According to Swift he possessed 'more Greek, Latin, and philosophy than properly became a person of his rank.'

Malpas.[1] | I was frequently in Company and at dinner with my old friend and acquaintance Mr. Compton,[2] speaker of the House of Commons. My Lord Burlington invited me to his fine Country seat at Chisewick,[3] and was extreamely civil and complaisant to me. Likeways one Mr. Johnstone of Twickenham,[4] who had been one of King William's secretary of state, had me at his Country seat, and amongst other things regalled me with a sight of all his great improvements in Gardening. Mr. Gale was never from me, and there was one Smart Lethalier, who had been my eldest son's school fellow at Eton, who never was out of my company, such was the affectionat remembrance he had for his deceased companion, $\overset{22}{10}$ years after their first acquaintance. I was every friday at the meeting of the

fol. 145.

Afterwards Lord Wilmington.

---

[1] George, Viscount Malpas, K.B., born 1703, succeeded his father as third Earl of Cholmondeley in 1733. He was Keeper of the Privy Seal in 1743; and in 1745 he raised a regiment of foot for the royal service. He married Mary, daughter of Sir Robert Walpole, first Earl of Orford. Died 1770.

[2] The Right Hon. Sir Spencer Compton, third son of James, third Earl of Northampton, was Speaker of the House of Commons from 21st March 1714 till 7th August 1727; was raised to the peerage as Baron Wilmington in 1728; and in 1730 appointed Lord Privy Seal and created Earl of Wilmington. In 1733 he became Lord President of the Council, and was invested a K.G. Died 1743.

[3] Chiswick House, Lord Burlington's seat, on the Thames, celebrated for its associations with Pope, and afterwards with Fox, Canning, and Garrick. It is referred to in *London and its Environs Described*, 1761, as 'a villa which for elegance of taste surpasses everything of its kind in England.'

[4] 'Secretary Johnston,' James Johnston, a younger son of Sir Archibald Johnston, Lord Warriston, was born about 1643. After his father's execution, in 1663, he fled to Holland, where he studied law. He was introduced by his cousin, afterwards Bishop Burnet, to Lord Romney; and was engaged in negotiations in favour of William of Orange, after whose accession he was appointed, in 1692, on the resignation of Lord Melville, joint-Secretary for Scotland with Sir John Dalrymple. In 1695 he was a chief instigator of the inquiry into the Massacre of Glencoe; and in the following year he was dismissed by the king for promoting the bill for establishing an African Company. In 1702 he settled at Orleans House, Twickenham, and devoted himself to gardening and planting. Mackay in his *Tour through England* (2d ed., vol. i. pp. 63-64) mentions that 'He has the best collection of fruit of all sorts of most gentlemen in England. His slopes for his vines, of which he makes some hogsheads a year, are very particular, and Dr. Bradley, of the Royal Society, who hath wrote so much upon gardening, ranks him among the first-rate gardeners in England.' He died at Bath in 1737. The contemporary estimates of his character are very various. Swift styles him 'one of the greatest knaves, even in Scotland.'

Antiquarian Society, where I found every member doing their outmost to advance learning and improve one another by a learned, frank, and easy Conversation. All our new discoveries were mentioned here, and such medals, Inscriptions, and other remains of Antiquity produced as gave us all mutual satisfaction.

When I was in London I waited on Sir Hans Sloan,[1] President of the Royal Society, and saw at his House a greater Treasure of Valouable Antiquities, jewels, and medals, and Gold, silver, and copper than I had ever seen in the greatest Cabinets abroad. There was likeways such an Infinity of natural

fol. 146. Curiosities as wou'd | require volumns to describe, for it is computed that Sir Hans had in his Custody of such things as I have mentioned to the valou of 200,000 lib. str.

I was afterwards introduced by Mr. Gale into the Royal Society, and saw Mr. Desaguiliers[2] make some Phylosophical Experiments amongst them.

When I visited the Duke of Devonshire, being introduced by the Earl of Pembroke, his Grace treated me with much civility, and shewed me a most valuable Treasure of Books, Antiquities, Medals, and other Curiosities.

Earl of Pembroke.

In the possession of the Earl himself, at his House in London, I saw many fine Books and Pictures of the best

---

[1] Sir Hans Sloane, Bart., born at Killileagh, co. Down, 1660. About 1687 he became physician to the Duke of Albemarle, governor of Jamaica, and while there brought together a valuable botanical collection. On his return, in 1689, he settled in London, where in 1694 he was appointed physician to Christ's Hospital; in 1716 was created a Baronet; and in 1727 became physician-in-ordinary to George II., and was elected to succeed Newton as president of the Royal Society. He bequeathed his vast collections, including books and MSS., to the nation, for £20,000 to be paid to his family; and they formed, with the Harleian and the Cottonian MSS. the foundations of the British Museum. He died 1753.

[2] Jean Théophile Des Aguliers, natural philosopher, was born at La Rochelle in 1683. He studied at Oxford, and, in 1710, became successor to Dr. Keil as lecturer on experimental philosophy in Hart Hall. In 1714 he was elected fellow of the Royal Society, and invited to become their demonstrator and curator, and in 1742 he received from them the Copley medal for his successful experiments. He was inventor of the planetarium for determining the exact distances of the heavenly bodies, and author of many works and articles on scientific subjects. Died 1744.

Italian Masters. Amongst other choise books I saw the *Speculum salutis*,[1] which is thought the first book that was ever printed. The Earl has it both in Dutch and Latine, but the cuts in it are the same, being done very coarsely from Wooden plats. The leaves are not printed on both sides but pasted together, for so far only printing was carried in its infancy.

I was likeways made acquainted with Doctor Woodward,[2] who has a vast collection of natural Curiosities, as he himself, in my opinion, was the greatest Curiosity on earth, being a vain, foolish, affected Man. His natural History, however, is a book that deserves to be read, as it treats very well on Minerals and fossils.

My Ld Pembroke had recommended to me to see his House, Statues, and pictures at Wilton,[3] in Wiltshire, near Salisbury. I went accordingly there, and saw the greatest collection of

---

[1] The *Speculum Humanæ Salvationis*, though not the first printed book, and of uncertain date, belongs to the infancy of the press, and marks in a curious manner the transition from block printing to printing from movable types, presenting as it does an example of both processes simultaneously in one volume and on one page. It is a picture-book of sacred history, in which the cuts and a few words are engraved on wood, while the text below is for the most part from metal types. The four earliest editions, without date, are of Dutch origin; two (the 1st and 3d) are in the Dutch language, and the others (2d and 4th) in Latin. Of none of these editions are there a dozen copies now known. The copies in possession of Lord Pembroke were the first Latin edition (containing sixty-three leaves, twenty of which are engraved on wood) and the second Dutch. According to Ebert (*Bibliogr. Dict.*) the two copies acquired by Lord Spencer were also of these same editions. A full account of the work will be found in the facsimile reproduction by J. P. Berjeau: *Speculum Humanæ Salvationis, le plus ancien monument de la Xylographie et la Typographie reunies, avec Introduction*, etc. —L.

[2] John Woodward, M.D., naturalist and antiquary, was born in Derbyshire in 1665. He was elected to the medical professorship of Gresham College in 1692; published in 1695 his *Essay towards a Natural History of the Earth and Terrestrial Bodies*; and in 1693 was elected a fellow of the Royal Society. He wrote also on medical and antiquarian subjects. He died 1728, and his valuable collections were bequeathed to the University of Cambridge, with a fund for the endowment of an annual lectureship.

[3] An account of the works of art at Wilton, almost contemporary with the Baron's visit, will be found in the *Description of the Earl of Pembroke's Pictures*, by C. Gambarini of Lucca, published in 8vo at Westminster in 1731. *See* also *A Description of the Pictures, Statues, Bustos, &c., at the Earl of Pembroke's House at Wilton*, by Richard Cowdry, 1751 and 1752; and *A Description of the Antiquities at Wilton House*, by James Kennedy, of which editions were pub-

Greek and Roman statues that ever I saw in any palace abroad; besides, there are several capital pictures there of Raphael, Guido, Hanibal, Caraci, Rubens, and others, but I think one of
fol. 147. the finest pictures | in Europe is that of the Pembroke Family by Vandyke, nothing but Life itself can equal the beuties of 5 or 6 of the Figures. The picture will be near 25 feet in length, and 18 or 20 in height. It takes up the whole end of the great Hall.[1]

The House was formerly an Abacy and was afterwards beautified and enlarged by the Famouse Architect Inigo Jones.[2]

I staid at Salisbury all night and with great satisfaction saw the Cathedral. Here our Country man, Doctor Burnet, the Bishop, had for many years officiated.[3]

In returning to London I went through Salisbury plain, and saw the famous old British Monument called Stonehenge. This consists of several circles of stones, many of which are 26 foot high and 4 or 5 broad, above are some vast stones lying across from one to another. Some have thought it Roman, but I cannot come into that opinion. Inigo Jones has left us a description of it,[4] but the best description is at present under the hand of my Friend, Doctor Stuckley.[5]

---

lished in 1758, 1759, 1771, and 1774. Writing to Clerk in 1726 Roger Gale characterises the antiquities at Wilton as 'without doubt not to be paralleled on this side the Alps;' but the collection of sculpture has not maintained the great reputation which it then enjoyed.

[1] The work of Vandyck referred to is the great full-length group of Philip Herbert, fourth Earl of Pembroke and his family, of which Horace Walpole remarks that 'though damaged, it would serve alone as a school of this master.' It was engraved by Baron in 1740.

[2] In 1633 the fourth Earl of Pembroke rebuilt the front of Wilton House in a magnificent manner. Charles I. recommended that he should employ Inigo Jones, who, however, was too much occupied to accept the commission; but Solomon de Caus, who carried out the work, received many suggestions from him. In 1647 the south side of the house was destroyed by fire, and it was rebuilt 'with the advice of Inigo Jones; but he being then very old, could not be there in person, but left it to Mr. Webb.' See Aubrey's *Natural History of Wiltshire*. Jones built a grotto and the stables at Wilton, the drawings for which are preserved at Worcester College and Chatsworth.

[3] Dr. Gilbert Burnet was Bishop of Salisbury from 1689 till 1715.

[4] *The most Notable Antiquity of Great Britain, vulgarly called Stone-heng, on Salisbury Plain, restored by Inigo Jones*, folio, London, 1655.

[5] *Stonehenge, a Temple restor'd to the British Druids by William Stukely, M.D., Rector of All Saints in Stamford*, folio, London, 1740.

I saw likeways on my return Old Sarum, being a very antient British fortification, rising in several storys like a Piramidical Mount. It has not as much as one house in it, and yet has the privilege of sending two members of parliament. Near it is Amsberry,[1] a very fine little House, built by Inigo Jones, and belonging now to the Duke of Queensberry.

Upon my return to London I was closely examined by the Earl of Pembroke as to what I had seen at his seat of Wilton, but was on my guard to give him satisfaction.

One day I went from London to Hampton Court to visite the famous Cartoons by Raphael.[2] I found them painted on paper | as paterns for Tapestry, which was afterwards made at *fol.* 148. Antwerp and carried back to Rome, but the Cartoons were bought up by King Charles the First, and upon being repaired by order of the late King William and Queen Mary, are now become not only the greatest ornaments in Hampton Court, but of all England. The true spirit of the great Master Raphael is more to be discovered in them than in any of his best picturs.

I visited most of the fine Seats about London, and am of opinion that there are more fine Houses in England than in Italy, tho' all of them not so well ornamented.

Amongst those I visited in London was Doctor Mead,[3] who is a Man of Learning, and has a vast collection of Books, picturs, prints, Medals, Antiquities, and other valouable things.

---

[1] Amesbury House, Wiltshire, was erected, from the designs of Inigo Jones, by his nephew John Webb.

[2] The cartoons commissioned by Leo x. for the decoration of the Sixtine Chapel, and painted, from Raphael's designs, by himself and his pupils in 1515-1516, were ten in number; and the tapestries executed from them by Pieter Van Aelst at Brussels are now in the Vatican. Seven of the original cartoons were purchased for Charles I., and remained at Hampton Court till a few years ago, when they were transferred to the South Kensington Museum.

[3] Dr. Richard Mead, Vice-President of the Royal Society, and physician-in-ordinary to George II.; born in 1673, and trained under Graevius of Utrecht. He travelled in Italy in 1695-1696, and laid the foundation of his collection of antiques, of which the crown was the bronze head of 'Homer' (Sophokles), formerly in the collection of Thomas Howard, Earl of Arundel, and introduced in the portrait of himself and his Countess, by Vandyck, at Arundel Castle. Mead died in 1753, and the greater part of his collection was sold by auction in 1755, when the bronze head was purchased for 130 gs. by the Earl of Exeter, who bequeathed it to the British Museum.

Amongst other things, he has a head of Homer found amongst the rubish of Justinian's Palace at Constantinople, and very probably the head of that famous Statue of Homer so much commended by Cedrenus,[1] which he says was destroied by the burning of the above mentioned palace.

Cedrenus, a Bysantine Writer.

My Country Men at London were all very civil to me, particularly the Dukes of Hamiltone[2] and Argyle, Queensberry,[3] Roxburgh, and Montrose; the Earls of Illay, Aberdeen,[4] and others.

I keept a diary of all I saw or met with in England, which will be found amongst my Manuscripts.

I returned to Scotland by the way of York about the end of May in company with two good friends, Mr. Pringle of Haining[5] and Colonel Douglass,[6] who were Members of Parliament.

This summer, 1727, I bought the lands of Drumcrief,[7] near Moffat, from the Duke of Queensberry. This Duke treated me with the same friendship and civility his Father did, for about a year before he had made me one of his Trustees in the management of his affaires in Scotland. |

---

[1] George Cedrenus, a Greek monk of the eleventh century, who wrote chronicles, beginning with the Creation, and ending with the year 1059.—L.

[2] James, fifth Duke of Hamilton and second Duke of Brandon, succeeded his father 1712, and died 1743.

[3] Charles, third Duke of Queensberry and second Duke of Dover, born 1698, succeeded his father in 1711. He was appointed Keeper of the Great Seal of Scotland, 1761, and Lord-Justice General, 1763. Died 1778. His portrait and that of his Duchess, Lady Catherine Hyde, daughter of Henry, Earl of Clarendon and Rochester, celebrated in the verse of Pope, Swift, Prior, and Gay, are still in the possession of the Clerk family. The former is painted by Miss Ann Forbes, the latter by William Aikman.

[4] William, second Earl of Aberdeen, was Member of Parliament for the county of Aberdeen in 1708; succeeded his father in 1720; died 1746.

[5] John Pringle of Haining, passed advocate in 1698; represented the county of Selkirk in the Scottish Parliament from 1703 till the Union; and was a member of the British Parliament till his elevation to the bench, as Lord Haining, in 1729. He died in 1754.

[6] Fifth son of James, tenth Earl of Morton. He was member for the Linlithgow Burghs 1708-10, 1710-13, 1715-22; for Orkney and Shetlandshire 1713-15, 1722-27. He succeeded his brother as fifteenth Earl of Morton, 1730, and died 1738.

[7] See Additional Note N,—Dumcrieff and Craigieburn.

The Duke of Douglass[1] did me the same honour, but he having in a Frantick fit murdered his own Cousin German, Captain Ker,[2] I gave up medling in his Affaires, since there were neither Reward nor thanks to be got by serving him. I had indeed no salary or reward from the Duke of Queensberry, but having received very great favours from his deceased Father, I cou'd do no less than serve him and his family to the outmost of my power, and besides, I was by promise to him on his death bed solemnly engaged to assist his son in all his affaires.

fol. 149. *N.B.*—This Duke in cold blood murdered his Cousin while sleeping in his bed, by shooting him through the head. He committed this barbarous and cowardly Action tho' he was a man of great Courage, and

[1] Archibald, third Marquis of Douglas, born 1694; succeeded his father in 1700; and was created Duke of Douglas in 1703. He was active in the royal interest during the Rebellion of 1715, and fought at Sheriffmuir. The celebrated 'Douglas Cause' followed his death in 1761, when the ducal title became extinct.

[2] 'In 1725 a tragedy occurred which considerably overshadowed the remainder of the Duke's life. This was the death of Captain John Ker, a natural son of Lord Mark Ker [the Duke's brother-in-law], a young man of whom his Grace was very fond, and who was then staying at Douglas Castle. The particulars of the tragedy have been so variously related that it is impossible to ascertain the exact details, but there seems no doubt that the young man fell by the Duke's own hand, while they were fencing or otherwise. A few days afterwards the Duke went to Edinburgh, and sailed for Holland.'—Fraser's *Douglas Book*, vol. ii. p. 467 (Edin. 1885).

'In the end of this moneth [May 1725] the unhappy Duke of Douglas killed, in his own house, his cousin-german, Lord John Ker's only son and heir. The occasion of it they that are favourable to him give thus. A debauched fellou in the neighbourhood had born himself in upon the poor Duke, who for many years had been crazed in his brain, and the Duke keeped too much company with him, who was every ways below the Duke. Mr. Ker, at the Duke's desire, had come to the Castle of Douglas, and stayed some days with the Duke. He was a young gentleman in a Captain's post, I think, and the Duke was very fond of him. He took the freedom to tell the Duke the above-said insignificant fellou was admitted to too much familiarity with his Grace; that though he was every way below the Duke of Douglas, yet he, the Captain, would be ashamed to keep company with him! The Duke seemed not displeased with his cusin for his freedom, but was so weak as, next time the fellou came to him, to tell him what the Captain had said. The villan fleu out in a passion, and said the Captain had maltreated the Duke, and presumed too much in chusing his company for him, adding, wer he Duke of Douglas, he would pistole him for what he had presumed to do! It seems this divilish advice took with the poor man, yet he caryed himself most civilly to his cousin all that day, and they supped together, and parted as they used to doe. However, after Mr. Ker was in bed and asleep, the Duke, without letting anybody knou, came softly into the room, shot Mr. Ker through the head, and stobbed him in two places in the breast; and when some servants with the noise were awakned, the Duke was in his room, and confessed, with seeming sorrow, that he had killed his cousin. In a few dayes the Duke went in to Edinburgh, and gote into a ship, and went to Holland. This is the common report of this lamentable affair.'—Woodrow's *Analecta*, vol. iii. p. 208.

never cou'd give any account of the cause. He was advised afterwards to fly [from] the House of Douglass, which he did for a [year] or two, but [the] King, understanding that this base action was oweing to mad ness, he has hitherto suffered him to live at the Castle of Douglass without any molestation. Anno 1754, this Duke lives still at Home.

This Summer I bought likeways the Lands of Lauhead and Marchwell[1] from Mr. Bothwell of Glencross,[2] because my Father once intended to have purchessed them, being contiguous to the Lands and Barony of Pennicuik.

The superiority of these Lands is included in the Tailzy[3] of Glencross, but it is disponed to me, and I think my right to the Superiority is as good as what I have to the Lands, since the Tailzy of Glencross was never Registrated in the Register of Tailzies, and since the Tailzy itself is very defective in many particulars.

I had before furnished up some Rooms at Mavisbank, wherefor I went and lived there with my Wife and part of my Family for the months of June and July when the Court of Exchequer was siting, and from thence rode every morning to Edin., which I found contributed greatly to my health. |

fol. 150. In this year, 1727, I was by a Commission under the great Seal constituted a Trustee for our Manufactures in Scotland.[4]

---

[1] Marchwell is about a mile and a half north-west of the town of Penicuik; and Lawhead is about half a mile south-west of Marchwell.

[2] Alexander Bothwell of Glencorse. See note [1], p. 141.

[3] Entail.

[4] By the fifteenth article of the Treaty of Union, it was enacted that £2000 per annum should, for some years, be applied towards the encouragement and promotion of fisheries, manufactures, and improvements in Scotland, as an equivalent for the increase of duties of Customs and Excise. In 1718 this sum was made payable for ever out of the Customs and Excise in Scotland; and in 1725 an Act was passed which provided that, when the produce of three pence per bushel of duty on malt should exceed £20,000 per annum, such surplus should be added to the above-named £2000. In 1727, 'on a representation from certain public-spirited gentlemen in Scotland (Duncan Forbes, King's Advocate; Charles Areskine, King's Solicitor; Baron Sir John Clerk; Lord Royston; Lord Milton, and others), seconded by an application from the Convention of the Royal Boroughs of the Kingdom, his Majesty King George I. issued letters-patent for the appointment of a Board of (twenty-one) Trustees, with power to administer the fund. By means of premiums, and in other ways, much was done for the encouragement of the linen manufactures; weavers were brought over from France, and established on the site of the present Picardy Place; and in 1766 a hall for the sale of linen was opened in Edinburgh. In 1809 the number of Trustees was increased to twenty-eight, and seven of them were appointed Commissioners for the Herring Fishery. A new Fishery Board was constituted by Act of Parliament in 1882. In 1828 new letters-patent were issued, giving the trustees extended powers; and in 1847 an Act was passed enabling the Treasury to appropriate the funds towards the purposes of education in the fine arts generally. In 1760 the Board founded a school of design, com-

The Trustees were 21 in number, who were likeways to encourage the Cod and Herring Fishing on our Coasts. This was done in perseuance of an Act of parliament in the last session under King George the first, but it hapned that this good and wise King died at Osnabruck in his way to Hannover in june last.

On the 10th of Agust this year it pleased God to incress my Family by another Daughter, who, after my Wife, was christned Jennet. About the 10 of Agust, after the Exchequer Affaires were over, I returned to Pennicuik, and about the 20 of the same month I and a part of my Family went to Moffat, for at that time I had but little accomodation at Drumcrief, which I had bought. However, I began to do some things there in order to live there once a year for a month, for the benefite of Moffat water, and for the diversions of shooting and fishing, which were there in greater perfection than any other place I kneu.

In novemb^{r} the same year and in january 1728, I carried 1728.
part of my Family to Edin., and attended the Court of Exchequer and the Manufactories and fisheries which were intrusted to me and others as above. From this time I always officiated as chief Baron, for upon the death of our Lord Chief Baron Smith, one of my Brothers in this Court, Baron Lant was, by the interest of his Friends in England, made Chief Baron,[1] but never attended except for 3 or 4 weeks in summer. |
In March 1728 I returned from Edin. to Pennicuik, and *fol.* 151.
attended closely to my studies and plantations.

This seasone I began my new way on the South side of the

monly known as 'The Trustees' Academy,' the first institution of the kind in the United Kingdom established at public expense; and here most of the eminent Scottish painters have received instruction. In 1828 this school was affiliated with the South Kensington Department. An excellent gallery of casts from the antique was also purchased. The National Gallery of Scotland and the Scottish National Portrait Gallery were placed under the control of the Board when they were founded in 1850 and 1883; and, when the Museum of the Society of Antiquaries was made over to the nation in 1851, this also was committed to the direction of the Board.

[1] See note [1], page 73. Lant was succeeded as Chief Baron by John Idle, ('the weakest of men,' Ramsay of Ochtertyre twice styles him, *Scotland and Scotsmen*, vol. i. pp. 78, 134, notes) on 2d November 1741. *Register of the Great Seal* (*Paper Register*), Book VIII. No. 159. See also folio 193, where the date is given wrongly by about two years.

Knights Law,[1] for before there was no other Road to the House of Pennicuik than by the north side of the Knights Law, and in this project I was oblidged to build a Bridge over the East burn which was founded this summer. This wou'd have been an expensive job to me if it had not been that I bestowed 8 years upon it, and finished it with my own Men and carts, except what related to the Lyme and Mason Work, which came altogether to no great sum. However, as it gave an easier, better, and shorter access to the House, there was nothing that I ever did which cost me less truble or gave me more satisfaction.

In March 1728 my brother William's Relict, Agnes Maxwell, who had been married to Major Le Blanc, died, and left only a daughter, Dorothea Clerk, who became my charge. The Major died some time before his Wife, and left my niece, the s^{d} Dorothea, a good dale of money by way of Legacy, and the rest of what he had, being in all about 40,000 merks, was left to his Wife and some other friends.

The girle was about 7 or 8 years of Age, and her Mother left it upon her to marry my son George. She was left Heiress of Midlebee by the death of her Grandfather and Mother, but this came not to exceed 100 lib. str. yearly, because of some debts which affected it, but by what was left by her mother
fol. 152. and Major Le Blanc she might be worth at least | 2500 lib. str., all debts paied.

In summer this year I began to build the north pavilion of Mavisbank, having already built the south pavilion for the benefite of my stabling and coach house. I began likeways to enclose several pieces of ground in the moor of Louhead, which, being covered with whins, yealded nothing.

I was at Drumlanrig[2] this year for 10 days, and applied very closely to the Duke of Queensberry's Affaires.

---

[1] This forms the chief approach to the present Penicuik House.

[2] The lands of Drumlanrig have been possessed by the family of Douglas since the fourteenth century; and they were confirmed to the ancestor of the Earls of Queensberry, Sir William Douglas, son of the second Earl of Douglas and Mar, the hero of Otterburn, by a charter, written with his own hand, by James I., in 1412, when he was in captivity in England. See Fraser's *Book of Douglas*. The present Drumlanrig Castle was erected, on the site of an older structure, between 1675 and 1689, by William, first Duke of Queensberry, grandfather of the nobleman mentioned above.

In november this year I was with my Family at Edin., and bought the half of the Lands of Craigyburn[1] from Mr. Johnstone of Girthead; the other half was in the hands of Mr. Tod,[2] Minister at Duresdeer, which I intended likeways to have bought, but cou'd never make a bargain with him. However, as the lands of Craigyburn were undivided, we made an exchange, and my half was laid contiguous to my Lands of Drumcrief.

In December this year it pleased God to give my Family another incress by the birth of a son, who was christned John,[3] after my deceased son.

In February 1729 I again was at Edin. with my family on the business of the Exchequer, and in the spring I attended the Duke of Queensberry's Affaires for 10 days at Drumlanrig. 1729.

In the months of june and july I lived with my family at Mavisbank, and from thence every day I attended the Court of Exchequer.

In Agust I was at Drumcrief for some weeks. My Wife and two of my Daughters were with me, but on her return, when she was paying a visite from Daufington to the Minister's Wife at Dunsire, one Mrs. Bredfoot,[4] the coach was

---

[1] See Additional Note N,—Dumcrieff and Craigieburn.

[2] 'Thomas Tod, M.A., had his degree at the University of Edinburgh, 11th July 1687, and was licenced by the Presbytery of Selkirk 27th May 1696, his licence having been postponed from 23d Oct. preceding, as he demurred to take the oaths of allegiance and assurance. An extract of his licence was refused 31st Dec. 1696, as he scrupled to acknowledge King William as the lawful magistrate of the kingdom, but it was allowed in common form 16th March 1699, he having promised all due obedience to the civil magistrate, and is called [to Durisdeer] 8th May, and ordained 5th Sept. 1700. He threatened separating from the Church in 1712, on account of the Oath of Abjuration, but did not; got the church rebuilt in 1720, and died 28th June 1742, in his eighty-fifth year. . . .'—Scott's *Fasti*.

[3] John Clerk of Eldin, F.R.S., born 20th December 1728. He was author of the celebrated *Essay on Naval Tactics*, 1782, and his curious series of *Etchings* was published by the Bannatyne Club in 1825 and in 1855. He died in 1812. See note [3] to page 115.

[4] The Rev. James Bradfute, son of the Rev. John Bradfute, minister of Pettinain, was at this time minister of Dunsyre, Lanarkshire. He was called in 1712, and died in 1758. He married, in 1717, Jean, daughter of James Mure of Rhoddens, who died in 1763. His son John succeeded in the cure, and was an intimate friend of Sir James Clerk, the Baron's son, and frequently his companion in his pleasure tours through England and Scotland.' See *The Gentle Shepherd*

fol. 153. unfortunatly overturned, and she very much | bruised. By this accident she was oblidged to continue in the Minister's house for 3 days, and was afterwards carried to Pennicuik in a chaire. It was a great happiness to me and my Family that she was not killed, for she was in great danger, and continued very ill for near two months after. She recovered at last by the assistance of 3 chyrurgeons and many applications.

In novemb^r and part of Decemb^r as usual I attended the Court of Exchequer, and still was oblidged to officiat for Lord Chief Baron. About this time I was informed by a letter from Roger Gale, my good English friend and constant correspondent, that I was chosen a Member of the Royal Society.

I was made a Member of the Royal Society, an Honour I valow much.

Thus I have brought this History of my Life to the year
1730. 1730, when I grow old and grey headed, but have reasone to bless God that for a long time I have continued in a state of perfect health, which I attribute to nothing more than Exercise and Riding. I am free from the Gout and Gravel, deseases which afflicted both my Grandfather and Father about my time of Life.

As to my worldly circumstances, I have rather incressed them than diminished them; at least by my Improvements I haue made the Estate my Father left me of much greater valou and extent; and amongst other things I am persuaded I have, within these 30 years, planted more than 300,000 Trees, which in time may be of considerable valow.

N.B.—The Lands of Pennicuik

About this time I got my Tenants at Pennicuik to divide their Lands, for till now all of them were in Run-Rig.[1] This I

. . . *Illustrations of the Scenery* (vol. i. p. 94), where (vol. ii. p. 659) his poem, 'A Morning Walk,' is quoted from his description of the parish of Dunsyre in the first edition of the *Statistical Account of Scotland*. He also wrote an *Essay on the Fisheries* published in the *Transactions of the Highland Society*.

[1] Run-rig lands, strictly speaking, are those in which the alternate ridges of the fields belong to different proprietors. Such a division 'marks,' says Professor Rankine, 'the epoch at which the strict rule of a community of immovables began to yield to the convenience of absolute ownership.' In 1695 an Act was passed by the Scots Parliament for dividing such lands, with the exception of acres belonging to boroughs or incorporations. In interpreting this statute the Court have not confined its provisions to run-rig lands in a strict sense of the word,—but extended them, to quote Erskine, 'to cases where the properties of the several heritors are broken off, not by single ridges but perhaps by roods or acres;' and he adds, 'without this extension the statute would have contri-

found a very difficult matter, for that few Tenants cou'd be induced to alter their bad methods of Agriculture. | Toun were in 27 different parts, tho in the *fol.* 154. hands of 3 Tenants, and none of these parts inclosed.

Amongst my Improvements at Pennicuik, I took in a Garden at the Damhead, and built a small House,[1] which I called Eskfield, and let it to a Gardiner. This summer I bought from Mr. Sinclare of Roslin the superiority of the Lands of Carnhill,[2] Easter and wester Ravensnook all which are parts of the Barony of Pennicuik.

At Mavisbank I went on with my Gardens and inclosures, and I altered the face of the Moor of Louhead by inclosures with Hedges and ditches, whereas before nothing grew here but Whins and Hether, nor did it pay any rent at all.

These are the Gifts of God, and I commit them to his care:

Θεοῦ διδόντος οὐδὲν ἰσχύει φθόνος.

sed cum Horatio, lib. 2, ode 14:

Linquenda tellus, et domus, et placens
Uxor: neque harum, quas colis, arborum
Te, præter invisas cupressos,
Ulla brevem Dominum sequetur.

Haveing keept our Christmess at Pennicuik, I went to Town on the 23d january, as usually I did, to attend the business of the Exchequer. 1730.

In Aprile I was for 10 days at Drumlanrig, on the Duke of Queensberry's affaires.

In june and jully I was with my Family at Mavisbank, and every day at Edin.

This summer I began to carry on the large square pond on the north-west side of the House of Pennicuik. It was always in my time a Bog, and some part of it a Peat moss. This square pond now, in the year 175[1], is the greatest ornament of the House of Pennycuik.[3] I have in it at this

buted little either to the beauty of the country or to the improvement of agriculture.'—*Institutes* III. 3, 59. The term 'run dale' was applied to the larger intermixed portions. The Court have refused to apply the Act to pieces of ground where the area exceeded four acres. A lengthy and learned disquisition upon the division of 'run rig' and 'run dale' lands will be found in the judgment of Lord Deas delivered in the case of the Baroness Gray, and reported in III. *Rettie's Court of Session Reports*, 1043.—M.

[1] This house and the quiet, sheltered, old-fashioned garden still exist; but the large new gardens are on the higher ground at the north of Penicuik House.

[2] Cairnhill, to the north of the Penicuik policies.

[3] This pond is still 'the greatest ornament of the House of Pennycuik,' with its richly wooded banks and island, and the fine glimpse, above the tree-tops to

time both Carps and Tinches, besides perch and Trouts.

In the month of Agust I was with my Wife and some of my Family at Drumcrief. We made use of Moffat Water, each of us a Bottle at a time, and found great benefite by it, for this water contributes much to sweaten the blood, and conse-
fol. 155. quently to prevent many | deseases. Formerly all who came to Moffat used to drink 4 or 5 bottles of it daily, but by experience it was found that one Bottle did a great deal better.

1731. About this time the fine pieces of Antiquity now at Pennicuik [were] found near the Roman [cam]p at Midlebee. They consist of a statue of the Godess Brigantia ... 2 altars inscribed to Mercury. These stood in a little [te]mple which, by age, had fallen down and become a Ruinous kind of heap.

This year, upon hearing much said of the reputation of the School of Louder,[1] 3 or 4 miles south of Penrith, in England, under the direction of one Mr. Wilkinsone, I sent my son George there, and boarded him with the Master.

In the begining of this year, my Wife had a very unlucky accident, for she slipt upon a piece of ice, and broke her Arm belou the Elbow, at least one of the Bones was dislocated and the other Broken. I my self instantly reponed the Bone which was dislocated, for I observed that dislocations at the wrest, if not immediately set right, will never after be reponed. I sent in the mean time for a chyrurgeon to take care of the fracture. She recovered very well of both, but not till several weeks after.

[1732.] These Ruines were in the grounds of a poor Lady. She caused some of the

In Aprile I went to Drumlanrig for 10 days, and in june and july was at Mavisbank for the better exercise and giving my attendance on the Court of Exchequer, riding every day from thence to Town. About this time my eldest son James began his Travels. He went first into England in company of

---

the north, of the peaks of the Pentland Hills. Among the Clerk papers is a MS. in the Baron's handwriting, dated January 2, 1745, and docketed 'Memorandums in relation to the great square Pond on the West side of Pennicuik House which will sometimes deserve to be read for the better keeping of it in proper order.' It contains two plans of the lake and its surroundings, and remarks on its soil, water, islands, plantations, fish, etc. 'I made it in 1733 at no great Expense, for it had served for a peat Moss to the Family several years before in my Father's and grandfather's time.'

[1] Lowther. 'The Baron's precepts to his son George when at school in Cumberland are worthy of Polonius. He advises him to be kind to his companions, as he could not tell what they might be able to do for him thereafter, and to be sure to take the opportunity of "learning the English language," in which the Baron himself regrets his own deficiency. "You have nothing else to depend on but your being a scholar and behaving well." He (the Baron) is described in the autumn of his days as "humming along and stuffing his pipe in order to whiff it away for half an hour."—Campbell and Garnett's *Life of James Clerk Maxwell*, p. 17.

his Unckle, Mr. Robert Clerk, Advocate,[1] and after staying about London till the begining of Oct^{r}, he was then to go over to Holand, and to study the Law at Leyden.

In Agust I went to Drumcrief, and from thence into Westmorland to see my son George at Louder. I staid there and at Penrith 3 days, and found all going | very well with him. *fol. 156.* His master, Mr. Wilkinsone, seem'd to answere the charecter I had got of him, for he was indeed a learned, honest, diligent, careful man.

After my return I staid at Home till novemb^{r}, that I went to attend the Court of Exchequer. I did the same in january and february 1732, still officiating for the Chief Baron in the absence of Mr. Lant.

On the 15 March my Wife was delivered of a son, whom I christned Mathew,[2] after our Chief Baron, who was sensible and grateful for supplying his place in his absence, so that no body had any occasion to complain of him. I have now, blessed be God, six sones and as many Daughters, who are all very promising children.

I have not means to support and provide for them as I hope they will all deserve, but I trust in the providence of God, and have had many Experiences which oblidge me to believe that he never increases Families or Mankind in General but for his

stones to be made use of for building a little Stable. [When] I chanced to pass the way, I discovered the stones, and gave the poor Lady a guineas for them. I consider these Antiquities as the chief of the kind now in Britain, and therefor I wrote a Latine dissertation[3] upon them, that at least posterity may not despise and destroy them. The above remains of Antiquity I still valow exceedingly after they have been now in my possession since 1731 to 1751, and I doubt not but some great

---

[1] Robert Clerk, fifth son of Sir John Clerk, first Baronet of Penicuik, born 20th October 1702; and passed advocate 4th December 1725. He became one of the Commissaries of Edinburgh; married Susan, daughter of William Douglas of Lympandoun; and purchased the mains of Collington in Mid-Lothian, in which he was succeeded by his eldest son, John, an East India merchant.

[2] See folios 249 and 250. 'Died abroad in the service of his country.'—Douglas's *Baronage.*

[3] In 1732 Gordon published, in the *Additions and Corrections by Way of Supplement* to his *Itinerarium*, an account by Clerk of these Roman remains, much to the Baron's annoyance, as appears from his letter to Gale, 13th March 1732: but the 'Latine dissertation' was not written till 1743 (see folio 193), and not printed till 1750;—*Dissertatio de Monumentis quibusdam Romanis in boreali Magnæ Britanniæ parte detectis anno MDCCXXXI.* (*Edinburgi: apud T. et W. Ruddimannos,* MDCCL.) 4to. The statue of Brigantia and the two altars, along with the head of a female statue and an inscribed stone from Middleby, and other classical remains, were presented to the Society of Antiquaries of Scotland by the Right Hon. Sir George Clerk in 1859. See their *Proceedings*, vol. iii. p. 37.

men in England who are Lovers of Antiquity have so far rever[enced] the Heathen Reli[gion] as to have built a [tem]ple for the sake [of] this statue. It is] certain, as Tacitus writes in his Agricola, that the Brigantes were 1733. the [most] powerful nation [in] Britain, and that [with] probability this *fol.* 157. statue was like another Diana of Ephesus.

unsearchable purposes, and that he never gives mouths without giving meat to them, if they deserve it.

In Aprile I went to Drumlanrig for 10 days, and return'd by Drumcrief, having a little repaired the House and put the Garden in better order.

In june and july I lived as formerly at Mavisbank, and in Agust returned to Pennicuik. In november and December I attended the business of the Excheqr. as formerly.

In Aprile and May 1733 I was invited to London to wait on some of my English friends at Court, for tho' there was nothing there which I had to ask, yet it was thought advisable that once in 6 or 7 years I should endeavour to keep up an Acquaintance and correspondence with some of the King's Ministry. |

I thought these reasons tollerably good, but I had likeways another motive, which had more effect on me than any thing else. I had a cousin, one Laurence Chartres, who lived at that time with Mr. Horace Walpole, Brother to Sir Robert Walpole, the prime Minister, and who was much intrusted with the Country affaires of both these Brothers. He lived at Woolerton in Norfolk, the House of Mr. Horace Walpole,[1] and had the charge of a great number of Masons and Wrights who were emploied in building this House. He had but little knowledge in these matters, and as I heard he had begun of late to drink and squander away his Money, I thought a visite from me might be of service to him, as I knew he both put confidence in me, and thought himself under some kind of ties to follow my advices. I had likeways some distant views that as I had six sones, some of them wou'd want the assistance of my best English Friends to be put in a way of living.

With these projects in my mind I set out for London,

[1] Horatio, Lord Walpole, second surviving son of Robert Walpole, and younger brother of Sir Robert Walpole, first Earl of Orford, was born at Haughton, in 1678. In the time of George I. he was Under-Secretary of State, Secretary to the Treasury, and Envoy to the Hague. From 1723 to 1730 he was Ambassador in Paris, and from 1733 to 1739 Ambassador to the States-General. He was created Baron Walpole of Wolterton in 1756; and died in 1757. An account of his seat of Wolterton—'of my own building'—will be found in a letter of his, dated 29th May 1745, to the Rev. Mr. Milling, given in Noble's *Memoirs of Horatio, Lord Walpole*, p. 287.

carrying in my company one Mr. Bothwel,[1] the eldest son of my neighbour Mr. Henry Bothwel of Glencross, with two servants.

This Henry Bothwell took afterwards upon him the Title of Lord Holyroodhouse, from whom his Family was thought to have descended.

We went by the way of Moffat, Carlyle, Pynrith, Appleby, Stanmore, Borroubridge, and so on to Duncaster; from thence I turned off the London Road and went directly to Lincoln, and from thence to Lyn Regis, for I was resolved to see Houghton hall,[2] the seat of S^r^. Robert Walpole, in my way to Woolerton, the House of Mr. Horace Walpole, where my friend Laurence Chartres lived. I was astonished at the magnificence | of 'Houghton hall, and especially the furni- *fol.* 158.
ture, for amongst other things of vast valow I observed a prodigious collection of fine pictures by the best Masters. I have written a journal of what I saw in this trip, and therefor shall say nothing here about it, only that I staid with my friend Mr. Chartres at Woolerton two days, and back with him to Houton hall, where we bestowed a day more; from thence I went to the Viscount of Townsend's House,[3] about 6

[1] 'It was moved in Parliament, 11th July 1704, that Alexander Bothwell, now served and retoured heir to the last Lord Holyroodhouse may be marked on the rolls of Parliament, conform to his precedency;' and it was ordered that the writs for instructing thereof may lie in the clerk's hands, that the members may have inspection thereof.' On the death of Alexander Bothwell, his son, Henry, petitioned the king, 8th February 1734, to have his right and title to the honour and dignity of Lord Holyroodhouse established. 'This petition was by his Majesty's commands laid before the House of Lords, 20th March 1734, but no determination was ever come to respecting it.'—Douglas's *Peerage*. His eldest son, Alexander, the Baron's companion mentioned above, married, in 1735, Lady Margaret, eldest daughter of Charles, sixth Earl of Home, and died without issue.

[2] Houghton Hall, now the property of the Marquis of Cholmondeley, was erected by Sir Robert Walpole in 1722, Thomas Ripley, its architect, working from the designs of Colin Campbell. The noble collection of pictures were catalogued by Horace Walpole in his *Ædes Walpolianæ*, London, 1747; and the finest of them were sold in 1779 by George, Earl of Orford, to Catherine, Empress of Russia, for £40,555. A series of engravings from the pictures was published by Boydell in 1788.

[3] Charles, second Viscount Townshend, succeeded his father, 1687; was a commissioner for the Union, 1706; along with Marlborough a plenipotentiary to treat with France, 1709; and President of the Council, 1720. He married (1st) Elizabeth, sister of Thomas Pelham-Holles, Duke of Newcastle; and (2nd) Dorothy, sister of Sir Robert Walpole, first Earl of Orford; and died 1738. His Norfolk seat was Raynham Hall.

miles from it. This Lord had been my Acquaintance in Leyden, having studied the Civil Law with him under professor Vitriarius.

Here I was very kindly entertained, as I was likeways at Houghton Hall and Woolerton, by Mr. Horace Walpole's orders. I parted there with my Friend Chartres, after I had given him such advices as I thought proper. He returned back to the place he came from, and I went forwards to London.

There I visited all my old acquaintances, particularly Mr. Horace Walpole, who introduced me to his Brother, Sir Robert. He was very civil, and entertained me with what he had done, or was to do, about Houton hall.

I visited likeways all my friends about London, and was frequently with the Earles of Burlington and Wilmington. The last was at my first acquaintance with him, above 30 years before, only an Esquire of the Family of Northampton;[1] then he was speaker of the House of Commons for two Parliaments, each of which continued 7 years as by Law appointed, and upon his growing very rich, and being weary with the fatigues of his great station, he withdrew, and was made an Earl. |

fol. 159. I was at Court several times, and at last, having made all the Interest I cou'd with my English Friends and acquaintances, I returned Home about the end of May.[2]

---

[1] See note [2] to page 125.

[2] Among the Clerk papers there is a copy of a letter from the Baron to Roger Gale, dated 11th June 1733. 'Being come home I think it my duty to return you my kind acknowledgements for all your civilities to me in London. Would to God you would give me an opportunity to acknowledge them in another Way, by your coming into this country, or send your son to me. It would be only an affair of two Weeks trouble to yourself, and as for your sone I must begg leave to insist on his comeing, as a Necessary piece of Travels, for we [viz., the two countries of England and Scotland] shall unite the better both on Church and State if our young people be better acquainted with one another. The old saying, *Turpe est peregrinari domi*, will I hope hold good as to Scotland as well as England, since our Interests as well as our territorie are inseparable. I shall trouble you with a rout which you or your son may distinctly know the Way, and where to Lodge in Edinburgh till I see you. [See Additional Note O.]

'After I left you I dined at Stiltoun and lay at Stamford. I came to the last place about 7 in the afternoon, and after puting up at the Bull I went directly to Dr. Stukeley. He was very kind and look'd very smug and canonical. He

I went through the circle of my occupations this year as 1734.
formerly, and amongst other things rejoiced that as a trustee for the Manufactories I had the happiness to observe annually some success, particularly in the Linen, for from 2,200,000 yards stamped, there was now between 4 and 5 millions of yards.[1]

The coarse wool manufactories did not succeed so well, yet I found that all the coarse Wool of Scotland was some way or other manufactured, which was the best success we cou'd expect.

The Fisheries, notwithstanding all our care, never advanced, and when manadged by the force of premiums I imagined they did no more service to the country than other Improvements which cost more than they are worth.

In Agust this year I was with my Wife, my eldest Daughter, Ann, and my sones George and Patrick, at Drumcrief, and from thence all of us made a trip into England the length of Carlyle. The ladies had the satisfaction to see a little of the north of England, for they saw the first seat there, Corby Castle, mentioned before, which belongs to Esquire Howard; they likeways had the pleasure to see a Cathedral at Carlyle, and to hear the Church Musick there, which was all they wanted.

George was at that time brought from Louder school.

We staid in England only 3 or 4 days, and returned back to Drumcrief. |

In january and february 1735 I attended the business of the fol. 160.
Court as formerly, and as I had done in november. and 1735.
december before.

About this time, my friend Laurence Chartres at Woolerton

---

suped with me that night, and next morning I breakfasted with him.' The letter then describes the Roman coins shown him by Stukeley, and some in his own collection; and concludes, 'I had a letter from my son [James] upon my return, dated at Rome in Aprile last, where he tells me that the modern Architecture is now turned into the gothick manner of the most polite taste. I hope when he returns to London you will find him a greater virtuoso than his father.'

[1] The books of the Board of Manufactures (*Accompts of Linen Cloth stamped in Scotland*) show that, in the year ending 1st November 1728, 2,183,978 yards of linen, valued at £1,033,312, 9s. 3d., were stamped by the Board; while in the year ending 1st November 1734 the number of yards stamped was 4,893,499, valued at £185,224, 3s. 11d.

turn'd delirious upon drinking too much and prosecuting some Love projects, wherefor his patron, Horace Walpole, carried him to London, but upon this disgrace, being a man of great spirit, he poisoned himself, deliberately as was supposed, with too much Laudanum, for after sleaping very high (*sic*) for about 40 houres, his bedchamber was broken open and he was found dead, and the glass which had contained the Laudanum standing by him. By his Death I lost all the interest I cou'd propose in the Walpole family. However, I have as much experience in the Affaires of this World as to put my trust in no persone or thing, all that passes here below is by the wise direction and providence of Almighty God, and the Man is happy, very happy, who can subdue his passions and inclinations, calmly submitting to his fate, yet at the same time to neglect no means that can with honour and honesty contribute to the advancement of his Interest.

In Aprile this year I was at Drumlanrig for 10 days, as usual, upon the Duke of Queensberry's affaires, and when these were over I made a Trip to Galloway to visite my distressed friends, My Lord and Lady Galloway, for a little before this, by My Lady's own negligence in a Garret, their House of Glasertoun was burnt down to the ground. The Earl and his Lady were retired, at that time, to the | Town of Whithern,[1] where they had taken a House. I staid with them two days, and came afterwards to Sorbie, where I visited my good old friend the Brigadier, Brother to the Earl, and from thence I came to Pouton,[2] where I got the Custom house boat to Kirkcubright. Next day I came to Drumfrise, and from thence by the way of Drumcrief to Pennicuik.

The principal seat of the Family of Galloway.

fol. 171 (sic).

This year my son George privately married my deceased Brother William's Daughter, Dorothea Clerk.[3] I had no hand or concern in the Match, but I hope it will prove a happy Marriage to both. I never recommended her to George, since I was her Tutor, but she had this advantage, that

[1] Whithorn.

[2] Powton, about 9 miles south-east of Wigtown. Near it was erected Galloway House, the seat of the Earls of the name. See folio 202.

[3] See before, page 134. See also Additional Note P,—The Estate of Middlebie.

her Mother, before she died, frequently recommended George to her.

As my s^{d}. son seemed very intent to study the Law in Leyden, and his Wife and he being too young to live together,[1]
I sent him to Holand in January 1736, where he had the 1736.
advantage of staying with his eldest Brother James.

My son Patrick, tho' a very good Schollar and a fine Mathematician, seemed fond of the Army, and therefor an Ensign's Commission was bespoken for him in one Colonel Handyside's Regiment of foot, at that time in Ireland, for which I was to pay 400 lib. ster.

His Twin brother Hary had long before chosen the sea man Trade for his occupation, and was at that time in Jamaica in one of the King's ships, commanded by an excellent officer, Captain Oliphant, who was very kind to him.[2] |

About the begining of this year my second Daughter, Bettie, *fol.* 172.
was married to Mr. Robt. Pringle, Advocat, of the family of Stitchel.[3] My consent was not given to this Marriage, from the notion I had that there was not a sufficiency between them to make the Marriage state any way easy to them, but the young Gentleman being a persone of great Honour and diligence in his business, I am hopeful that they may do well enough. Riches seldom or never give the expected contentment, those are only rich and happy who can live with contented minds. One who lives within his Incomes is always richer than he that lives beyond them, let his Quality and incomes be never so great.

This Winter went over with me as others have done, without any singular incidents.

In Aprile 1737 I was at Drumlanrig for 10 days, where 1737.
open Table was keept for all the Gentlemen of the Country, as usual. My L^{d}. Duke was always in London, and only Mr.

---

[1] George Clerk was then aged twenty, and his bride was about seventeen.

[2] See Additional Note Q,—Letter from the Baron when sending Patrick and Henry to school.

[3] The marriage was in February, see MS. Family Register. Robert Pringle, son of Thomas Pringle, W.S., and grandson of Sir Robert Pringle, first baronet of Stitchell, passed advocate in 1724; in 1748 was appointed sheriff-depute of Banffshire; and in 1754 was raised to the bench as Lord Edgefield. He died in 1764.

Boyle,[1] Brother of the Earl of Glasgow, assisted me as one of the Commissioners. There were 3 or 4 others who never attended.

I found the Duke's Tenants as formerly very poor and not very honest, tho' great pretenders to Religion of that kind which, amongst the people of that Country, passes for the strictest kind, tho' generally it consists in no more than hearing of long sermons and prayers, and idleing away their Time on the sides of Hills, reading on books of Controversy and Acts of the General Assemblies.

In May this year it pleased God to give my Wife and me a Son in our old Age, for I was entering into the 62 year of my
fol. 173. Age, and my Wife about 51. We christned | the Child by the name of Adam,[2] after a worthy Friend of ours, Adam Cockburn of Ormiston, Lord Justice Clerk. The boy seem'd to be one of the strongest and liveliest of our Children at his age.

My son George returned this year from abroad, but my son James was so earnest to continue for some time in Holand, that I was oblidged to consent to his request, tho' with much reluctancy, and I feared it wou'd be attended with great expence to my family, as well as loss of time to himself.

The Month of Agust this year was so far lucky to me that I brought up the Coal-level at Mavisbank to the Town of Lonhead, from whence I and my Successors have reasone to expect considerable profits if the coal be manadged as it ought to be. There are leveled by it at least 14 seams of workable coal from Buldsden Park[3] to the Marches between the Baronies of Laswade and Melvile, but as to these matters, I keep a journal at Mavisbank, which ought to be diligently considered.

This summer went over as usual, sometimes at Mavisbank and Edin., and sometimes at Pennicuik and Drumcrief. In December I fell into a kind of bloody Flux, which alarmed me, but upon coming out to Pennicuik I grew immediately well.

1738. On my return to Town in Jan. 1738, the same disease recurr'd, whereby I discovered that the true cause of it was the eating of oysters raw and drinking up the juice within the shels, which is nothing but sea water. On this discovery I forbore this practise, and my desease evanished in 3 days.

If I had consulted physitians they might have done me mischief, for they

[1] The Hon. Patrick Boyle, of Shewalton, second son of David, first Earl of Glasgow. He passed advocate in 1712; was raised to the bench as Lord Shewalton in 1746; and died unmarried at Drumlanrig in 1761.

[2] 'Died abroad in the service of his country.'—Douglas's *Baronage*.

[3] Bilston Park.

cou'd not have discovered the true cause of my malady.

On the 8 of Feb. I entered into the 63 year of my Age, and because this is commonly thought a fatal year, I began to reflect on the state both of my mind and of my Body.

This year I burnt and destroied several Poems, both in English and Latine, of my composition, and likeways several Essays, particularly some political observations on the prim[e] Ministry of Joseph in the Reign of P[ha]raoh, King of Egypt.[1] Some of these I thought not so fit for the times and I desired to spend the rest of my days in p[eace] and quietness, as f[ar] removed from sche[mes] of politicks as I thought became o[ne] in the peaceable station of a judge.

I have not altogether so tenacious a | memory as I used to *fol. 174.* have about my Age of 20 or 25, but cannot at all complain of it, few people have a better. I can read, write, and think whole days with pleasure, but am usually more critical and nice, both as to my own performances and those of others, than I used to be, and for that reasone read nothing that entirely pleases me. I have therefor carried things to so great a height that I dayly burn a good many things that wou'd please others, and I should be inclined to burn every thing I ever wrote, if it was not that I shun to read them over. A Latine History I have written, *de Rebus Britannicis*, is of this kind, but because I am still in hopes to take so much time and patience as to correct it, therefor it remains still undistroied.[2]

As to the Health of my body I can noways complain, for I am seldom or never trubled with any deseases, except little slight feavers and colds in the Winter seasone, but which are so moderat that they never confine me to the House above a day.

My Legs continue as firm under me as ever since I broke one of them in my young days, as above. I ride commonly at the shooting, but can walk two or 3 miles when incited by the Game.

My Eyes began to fail at 48 years of Age, and then I scrupled not to make use of spectacles, the good effects of which are, that I think my Eyes are now as good as then, and that in day light I can read as well without them as with them.

In my fits of cold I have sometimes | a difficulty of breath- *fol. 175.* ing, and a stoping or Ratling in my Lungs, but these symptoms go off. The greatest sensible decay I find about me is in my Teeth, for I begin to lose some of them every year by a kind of scorbutick disposition in my Gums, for they fall out perfectly white and entire.

---

[1] That the 'Observations on the Prime-Ministry of Joseph in the Reign of Pharaoh King of Egypt' may have been a political satire seems to be suggested by the reasons he assigns for destroying it.

[2] See page 84, and note [1] to page 85.

I was in Aprile at Drumlanrig, and in june and july at Mavisbank as formerly.

About the seasone of planting I made the Avenue which runs Southward from the House through the park of Coldshoulders;[1] if the planting grow, and the Avenue terminat on any object, as a porch or ruine, it will make, in time, a very good figure from the House, for 'tis to be observed that since the House of Pennicuik is situated on a high, cold, wild ground, it can no way be so much improven as by planting, and some Houses to take off the dismal prospect of the moors.

In Agust I took a journey into Yorkshire to visite my friend Roger Gale at his House of Scruton. A friend of my Wife's, Sir James Holborn,[2] and my son Patrick, were with me. We set out by the way of Kelso and Wooler Houghhead,[3] Morpeth and Newcastle, and came to Durham, where we staid and heard divine service at the Cathedral on a Sunday. From thence, on the Munday, we went to Percebridge,[4] and from thence to Scruton. My good friend and his son made us very welcome, *fol. 176.* and next day he accom|panied me to the famous Studley park near Rippon, belonging to one Mr. Aiselbee,[5] who had bestowed vast expenses on its embellishments, but this was all the return

[1] This fine avenue, extending southwards from Penicuik House to above the Esk, still exists.

[2] Sir James Holburne of Menstrie, father of Admiral Francis Holburne, was created a baronet of Nova Scotia in 1706, and died in 1760. His father, James Holburne of Menstrie, married Janet, daughter of John Inglis of Cramond, and aunt of Lady Clerk, the Baron's second wife.

[3] Wooler, in Northumberland, on the declivity of the Cheviots, 46 miles north-west of Newcastle-on-Tyne. The Haughead lies a little south of the town.

[4] Pierce Bridge, about three miles north-west of Darlington.

[5] John Aislabie, born 1670; fourth son of the registrar of the archi-episcopal court of York. In 1695 he was elected member of parliament for Ripon; he represented Northallerton from 1702 till 1705; and was again member for Ripon, 1705 till 1721. In 1714 he was appointed treasurer of the navy. On March 8th, 1721, he was pronounced guilty of 'most notorious, dangerous, and infamous corruption,' in that he 'had encouraged and promoted the Dangerous and Destructive execution of the South Sea scheme with a view to his own Exhorbitant Profit,' and was expelled from the House, and next day he was committed to the Tower. He was permitted to retain the property of which he had been possessed on and before 20th Oct. 1718; and on his release he retired to Studley Royal, and occupied himself in improving his estates. He died 1742.

he made the publick by his ruinous conduct of the South Sea schem when he was a Lord of the Treasury in 1722.

Here I saw a perfect superfluity of Temples, Grotos, Parterrs, canals, and all other Embelishments, which seemed to become a prince more than a privat Man. We dined at Rippon and at night returned to Scruton.

I staid 3 days with my friend, and at last took journey homewards by the way of Richmond, Gratebridge,[1] Brust,[2] Penrith, and Carlyle. I visited near this last place Corby Castle, which I found my Acquaintance Esquire Howard had vastly improven.

From Carlyle I came to Drumcrief, where I staid some days with my son George and his wife, to whom I made over this little Estate.

In Harvest I was at Pennicuik, and in nov. and December *ut supra*.

The Great Frost in 1739.

I was at Edin. in january and february 1739, in these two Moneths and December before there was the most severe frost in this country that perhaps was ever felt.[3] All the grass was covered with a vast load of snow for 6 weeks at least, and all the springs and Rivers were frozen up. The consequence of all which was that much of our Wild Fowl and Birds died for cold and want of meat, particularly we lost all our Duke and Drake, all our Snipes, Woodcocks, Mavises, etc. I have seen in my time Duke and Drake in every Loch and pool, | and in *fol.* 177.
every bog 3 or 4 dussan of Snipes, the Woods, particularly

---

[1] Greeta Bridge, four miles south-west of Barnard Castle.

[2] Brough.

[3] The celebrated frost of the years 1739-40 N.S., see Arnot's *History of Edinburgh*, pp. 210, 211. 'In the beginning of this year (1740) the weather was remarkably severe. The cold was so intense, that above Alloa the Forth was entirely frozen over; nay, there was even a crust of ice at the Queen's-ferry. By the mills being stopped, a great dearth was occasioned; by the vast quantities of snow upon the ground, coals were brought into the town with difficulty, and several persons perished with cold.' For an account of the effects of the frost in London, commemorated in several contemporary engravings, see Andrew's *Famous Frosts* (London, 1887), pp. 44-51. A fair was held on the frozen Thames, an ox being roasted whole on the ice, and a printing-press kept in active operation. It was in 1740 that the Empress Anne of Russia erected her famous ice-palace on the banks of the Neva.

N.B. This loss was not recovered at revising this paragraft in 1745.

that at Mavisbank, had in it hundreds of Mavises, and in the Winter time plenty of Woodcocks, now all these poor creatures were destroied, and found by dussans in several places.[1]

On the 13 of this Month of January 1739 a very memorable Hurricane[2] hapned in a stream of Wind from the South West which spread about 10 or 12 miles in breadth from sea to sea.

I was then at Pennicuik with my Family, and never doubted but to be burried in the ruins of my house. It began about eleven of the night, and continued till about one next morning. Most of all my old Trees were quite destroied, some broken by the middle parts, and some blowen out of the ground. In a word I lost 1400 Trees, for I caused the computation to be made, and, which was exceedingly odd, some Trees were blowen down in the middle of some left standing.

It is certain that nothing like it ever hapned in Scotland for 200 years past, for as I had a plantation of that Age about the House of Brunstane, they had all stood in their rowes since their first plantation till this unhappy day, whereas, if any such hurricane had hapned, as above, the defects had easily been discovered in their several roues.

One thing I admired extreamly that amongst other Trees standing pretty thick I had one Ash Tree of my Father's planting about 60 years ago, which was about 18 inches in diameter, sound and high. This Tree was twisted in the middle and broken, which I do not believe that 100 Men with all their strength cou'd have done. |

fol. 178. How the Roof of the House of Pennicuik hapned then to resist this storm is more than I can account for; however, many other Houses and chimnies were blowen down, and for

---

[1] Ornithology was one of the many subjects in which the Baron was interested. See his letter to Gale, 13th April 1730; his 'Observations upon the Flight and Passage of Fowls' in a letter to Gale, January 30, 1730-1; 'Remarks' on the same by John Machin, Secretary of the Royal Society; and 'Observations on the Remarks' by Clerk, and his letter on the same subject, 31st March 1731. Nichols' *Bibliotheca Topographica Britannica: Reliquiæ Galeanæ*, vol. iii. pp. 260-82.

[2] An account of this storm—'the most violent hurricane (with lightning) ever felt' in Edinburgh—will be found in the *Scots Magazine*, vol. i. It followed on an eclipse of the moon, and raged from one to four on the morning of the 14th of January 1739.

the most part all the Houses in the stream of the Wind were uncovered.

I cannot but here mention another memorable thing, viz., that all the fine shrubs in this country, particularly the Rosemary, were, by the hardness of the Winter, quite destroied. 'Till then Rosemary grew on all the south braes of Mavisbank like Broom, and the Bees fed plentifully on it, but in the great frost I had not one single stalk preserved of it, nor had they any in all Scotland that I cou'd hear of, except a small bush which grew on the outside of the kitchen wall at Edmiston, within 2 miles of Edin. We were then all oblidged to get Rosmary seed from Spain, and I got a stalk or two of what grew at Edmiston,[1] and brought up a stock from the seed.

In May this year I took a resolution to see the northern parts of this Country, where I had never been, and for that end I set out with my son George and one of my neighbours, Mr. Dewer of Vogrie,[2] to Inverness.

We lay a night at Perth, and from thence by the way of Dunkel came to General Wade's high road, which I pursued to Ruthven in Badenoch, where it ended. This Road leads by the Blair of Athole through the middle of the Highlands, and was made only 2 or 3 years before. I traveled it in a chaise, and found all the parts of this useful way exceedingly good.

I staid at Inverness 2 or 3 days, and was very civilly entertained by Duncan Forbes of Colloden,[3] president of the session, at his seat there. | From thence I took journey homewards by *fol. 179.* the Coast way, where I saw Nairn, Forress, Elgine, Bamff, Fochabrs, Gordon Castle, and the fine new House building for the Irish Lord or Scotish Laird of Bracoe.[4]

---

[1] Edmonstone, near Liberton, a seat of the Don-Wauchopes.

[2] Vogrie, in the parish of Borthwick, Midlothian, acquired by the family of Borthwick about the beginning of the eighteenth century.

[3] Duncan Forbes of Culloden. Born 1685. He rendered important service to the Government during the rebellions of 1715 and 1745; was appointed Lord-Advocate in 1725, and Lord President of the Court of Session in 1737; died 1747. His uncle, Sir David Forbes of Newhall, had married the Baron's aunt. See page 110, note [1].

[4] William Duff of Braco and Dipple; born 1697. In 1735 he was created Baron Braco of Kilbride, in the county of Cavan, Ireland, and in 1759 Viscount Macduff and Earl Fife in the peerage of Ireland. Died 1763. Duff House was completed in 1745 at a cost of £70,000.

I visited in my way to Aberdeen my good old Friend the Earl of Aberdeen, with whom I dined.

At Aberdeen I staid two days, and was very kindly entertained by the Magistrates and Professors of the two Colleges there. From Inverness to Aberdeen the different Tempers of the Inhabitants were very remarkable to me, for till I came to the confines of Aberdeenshire I found all the people idle, and no other business going on but that of smugling and drinking, except in Strathspey, where there is a vast deal of yarn spun by some verteous people who are Tenants to the Family of Grant in Aberdeen, and all the shire over every body from 5 years of age, male and female, was emploied in kniting of stockings, of which they drive a considerable Trade.

The salmon and other fishes yeald, indeed, a considerable employment to some all along the northern coast, but this branch of Trade does not employ the 40th part of the Inhabitants.

At Kinard, the seat of the Family of Southesk before the Rebellion, I saw a very fine picture[1] of the Ld Maitland, by Carolo Moratti.

From Aberdeen I returned to Edin. by the way of Brichen, Kinaird, Panmore, and Dundee, very well satisfied with what I had seen, and from thence observed that no man can employ a little of his time to better purpose than in making himself acquainted with his own Country, for he can either lairn from those he meets with, | or do service by endeavouring to instruct them. *fol.* 180.

In june and july I attended the Exchequer as usually, and in the meantime lived with most of my Family at Mavisbank.

In Agust my learned friend Roger Gale of Scruton,[2] and one Doctor Knight,[3] one of the king's chaplains, came to Scotland to see the country and make me a visite.

---

[1] This picture cannot now be identified. There is a portrait of the Duke of Lauderdale at Kinnaird Castle; but Lord Southesk informs me that this is believed to be a copy from an original presented by his grandfather or great-grandfather to the Lauderdale family.

[2] See Additional Note O,—Baron Clerk and the Restoration of Rosslyn Chapel: Date of its Foundation.

[3] Samuel Knight, D.D.; born 1675; studied at Trinity College, Cambridge; was presented to the vicarage of Chippenham, Cambridge, 1770, and to the rectory of Bluntisham, Huntingdonshire, 1717; was appointed chaplain to George II. in 1731, and became a prebend of Lincoln, 1742. About 1717 he was one of the refounders of the Society of Antiquaries; and he was author of a *Life of Dr. John Colet, Dean of St. Paul's*, 1724, and a *Life of Erasmus*, 1726. Died 1746.

They staid with me some days, both at Pennicuik and Mavisbank, and I waited on them back to Carlyle in their way homewards. From this place I thought it might be useful to me to go to Whitehaven, about 30 miles westward, to visite the Coal works of Sr James Louder[1] there. I made this trip with great satisfaction, but the way to the place being for many miles through a good but uncultivated country, I cou'd not but reflect that it was the hight of folly to send away numerous Colonies of Men and Women to the West Indies when even England produced vast tracts of Ground which go under the name of Commons, where nothing of Culture or good management appears.

At Whitehaven I took notice that Sir Ja. Louder, by the meer force of money, was working a field of Coal under the sea, which neither he nor any man else had ever attempted but from ignorance and a vast stock of Richess, for no man but he who is reckoned the Richest Commoner in England cou'd ever have imagined that a field of 2 or 3 miles square of coal cou'd be wrought under the sea, where the least crevise, sit(?), or break in the strata above wou'd drown all his men and his coal in a few minutes. | It is very rare to find strata of that solidity *fol. 181.* and consistency as to keep togither for 5 or 10 yards. I told S^ir James so much, and I found that he made of these coal works 5000 lib. clear money yearly, tho' they were all wrought at a vast expense by fire Engines and other Machines, for tho' he had none of the sea water coming down upon him, yet he had a great abundance of other water from springs and old Wasts. I observed likeways at Whitehaven that they had several seams of Coal besides what was wrought under the sea, and saw evidently that these were the very same with the Newcastle seams or strata which, with some interruptions, run from thence to the West sea. I refer the rest to a particular account I wrote of this Trip, which I found had been useful to me.[2]

---

[1] Sir James Lowther, fourth and last baronet of Whitehaven; M.P. for Cumberland 1708 to 1722, and 1727 till his death in 1755.

[2] The Baron wrote a more particular account of his visit to Whitehaven and of the coal-works there to Roger Gale. The letter, dated from Penicuik, 19th August 1739, will be found in Nichols' *Bibliotheca Topographica Britannica:*

I and my son George, and my companion, S[ir] James Holborn,[1] returned homewards by the way of Bulness, which some take to be the antient Blattum Bulgium.[2] I saw here with great pleasure very considerable remains of the Antient Roman stone Wall built by the Emperor Severus, which comes all along west from Newcastle, as I have noticed above.

We crossed over Solway frith at this place when it was low water, and found no difficulty in our passage, tho' always dangerous except in summer.

From thence we came to Anan, and from thence to Drumfrise, where my son George and his wife had taken up their residence.

fol. 182. On my return to Pennicuik I lived as formerly, | and in october thereafter it pleased God to return to us my eldest son James. This incident gave his Mother and me very much satisfaction, and the more that he did not return the worse for his Travels like several of our young Gentlemen. All they lairn abroad is to know how to spend what they have with more profusion and to have an invincible aversion to their Country.

The Expence of Mavisbank and all my other improvements

This summer, 1739, I put the finishing hand to Mavisbank.

Reliquiæ Galeanæ, vol. iii. pp. 326-33. 'I staid all Saturday in this town [Whitehaven], and saw everything that deserves to be seen: the greatest curiosity is Sir James Lowther himself. Whenever his death happens, it will be much felt by the people of this place; for when the money comes to be divided, the coal will be set in farm and consequently brought to the verge of ruin.'

[1] This is the first mention of these companions having accompanied him on this expedition to the south.

[2] Gordon writes that, having visited Kirkland and Fesa-Cross, 'After this I found another Watch-Tower 66 Foot square; 365 Paces beyond that, the Wall measures 8 Foot of a perpendicular Height: and thus both the Wall and the Ditch, continuing distinct and plain, run a little more Westerly to *Bulness*, or *Blatumbulgium*, at which Place the last Fort upon the Wall is to be seen where it ends. And thus I finished my Survey, from three Miles beyond *Newcastle*, on the *German* Ocean, to this Place of *Bulness*, on the *Solway* Frith, or *Irish* Sea.'—*Itinerarium*, p. 82. Among the Clerk papers is a MS. of fourteen folio pages, with sketches of inscriptions, etc., titled 'Ane Account of Some Roman Antiquities observed at Bulness upon Solway Frith in Cumberland, with some remarks on the Roman Wall to be seen there.' Its prefatory remarks indicate that it was prepared by the Baron as a communication to a learned society, probably the Society for the Improvement of Learning and Philosophy, mentioned at folio 192.

It has cost me first and last a good deal of money, but as it was finished by degrees from the year 1723 I never much felt the weight of it.

In november and decemb^r I attended the business of the Exchequer as formerly. In january 1740 my Daughter Jean was married, I hope happily, to Mr. Ja. Smollet of Bonhill, Advocate, son of Commisar Smollet.[1]

About the time the publick disorders and Animosities in Great Britain came to a very great height. S^ir Robt. Walpole, who had been first minister to King George the first ever since the year 1722, continued in the same degree of favour with King George the 2^d, and this constancy to one man begot a great many Ennemies, who publickly professed themselves to be patriots, but inwardly were such only who, fretted with envy at S^ir Robert, pretended all was in disorder, because they and their Friends had been for so many years excluded from those favours which are always engrossed by those who best can support the | dignity and authority of the prime Minister.

was defraied by the Crown, for I may honestly averr that I never spent one farthing of my pr[ivate] Estate this way. [My] Salary as a Baron of the Exchequer did much more than answere all the Expence of my building and other embellishments either at Pennycuik, Mavisbank, or elsewhere, and I had a fixed principle that what I got from the pub[lick] behoved in justice to be laid out in the maintenance of the poor of my country.

The clamours of these patriots rose so high that at last the *fol.* 183.
Country began to think them in earnest, and this produced an alteration of measures upon the Elections for a new parliament in 1741. In a word, tho' the king had a very great regard to S^ir Robert, yet being at that time engaged in a War with Spain, he was forced, like many former British kings, to take himself to that party that cou'd best support him in the War. For tho' it is a prerogative of the Crown to make War as well as peace, yet it is of no significancy when it is in the option of

---

[1] James Smollett, son of George Smollett, styled of Inglestone, in the county of Edinburgh, commissary of Edinburgh, and provost of Dumbarton, and his wife Katherine, a daughter of Sir Hugh Cunningham of Bonnington, provost of Edinburgh; and grandson of Sir James Smollett of Bonhill. He was admitted an advocate in 1733, and was a commissary of Edinburgh and sheriff-depute of Dumbartonshire. He succeeded his cousin in the estate of Bonhill in 1738; and in 1763 purchased the estate of Cameron from Colonel Charteris of Amisfield, and was there visited by Tobias Smollett, the novelist, his cousin, in 1766, a visit commemorated in *Humphrey Clinker*, and by Dr. Johnson in 1773, as recorded in Boswell's *Life*. He died, without issue, in 1776, and bequeathed his books to aid in founding a parochial library for the use of the parishes of Bonhill, Dumbarton, and Cardross. See Irving's *Book of Dumbartonshire*, vol. ii. p. 186.

the House of Commons of Great Britain to support a War or not by giving or denying the necessary subsides.

Sir Robert, on the siting down of this new parliament, saw it wou'd be in vain to strugle against the Tyde by some Essays he had made of the strength of his own Friends at some of the principal Elections, and therefor fairly told his Majesty that now he could serve him no more. To avoide, then, the noise, clamour, and danger that he saw he wou'd meet with if he continued in the House of Commons, he easily procured a patent from his Majesty creating him Earl of Orfoord. Thus he went up to the House of Peers, and that he might the better *fol.* 184. ballance the loss which his | Royal Master might sustain in the House of Commons, he carried with him one Mr. Poltney,[2] the head of the patriot party, who was created Earl of Bath.

Particularly that of Chipinham, tho he had both the Law and common justice on his side.[1]

---

[1] 'A question on the Chippenham election was carried against the minister by a majority of one, 237 against 236, and the party gained so considerable an accession, by the desertion or absence of several members of the Court party, that the final decision of the Chippenham election was carried against the minister (2d February 1741-2), by a majority of 16, 241 against 225. Walpole seemed to have anticipated this event, and met it with his usual fortitude and cheerfulness. While the tellers were performing their office, he beckoned Sir Edward Bayntun, the member whose return was supported by opposition, to sit near him, spoke to him with great complacency, animadverted on the ingratitude of several individuals who were voting against him, on whom he had conferred great favours, and declared that he should never again sit in that House. On the 3d of February the House adjourned at the king's command, signified by the Chancellor, to the 18th. On the 9th, Sir Robert Walpole was created Earl of Orford, and on the 11th he resigned.'—Coxe's *Walpole*, vol. i. p. 695.

[2] William Pulteney, born 1682; Secretary at War, 1714-17; created Earl of Bath, 13th July 1742; died 1758. A main aim of Walpole at this time was 'to detach Pulteney, who then headed the Whigs in opposition, from the Tories.' He accordingly 'advised the king to form a Whig administration, and suggested the propriety of applying to Pulteney. One of the greatest difficulties under which he laboured in the course of this political transaction, was to conquer the king's repugnance to Pulteney, which at this time seemed almost insuperable, and to persuade his Majesty to commence the negotiation, and acquiesce in Pulteney's expected demand of a peerage. Having at length overcome the king's pertinacious inveteracy, he said to his son Horace, "I have set the king upon him," and at another time, in the further progress of the king's compliance, he triumphantly said, making at the same time a motion with his hand as if he were locking a door, "I have turned the key of the closet upon him." After various negotiations, Pulteney named the Earl of Wilmington, First Lord of the Treasury; Sandys, Chancellor of the Exchequer; Carteret, Secretary of State; Sir John Rushout, Gibbon, and Waller, Lords of the Treasury; a new Board of Admiralty, including Sir John Hynde Cotton;

He was succeeded in his prime Ministry by one Lord Carteret, who, tho' a man of great parts, has not those personal regards paid to him which S[ir] Robert Walpole had.

But Lord Carteret was a persone much moreacquainted with forreign Affaires, and in strictness a fitter persone, than Sir Robert for a publick Minister, but both of the[m] were such Machiavelian politicians as to make a je[st] of solemn contr[acts] and engagements publick or privat, from thence spr[ang] the phrase which obtained much at the time that Man was wrong [indeed?] who dealt in honour and conscience, and from the[nce] a general contempt of all but Party.

I had the fortune of a very long acquaintance with S[ir] Robert, having been a Member of Parliament with him in 1708, immediatly after the Union.[1]

He was a good-natured agreable man as ever I knew in my Life, and for his acquired parts no body cou'd go beyond him. He was bred a Lawer, and as he came into parliament very early, some years before I knew him, he laid himself out to understand the general constitution of his Country, the forms of parliament, and circumstances of the publick Revenue in all its branches, above any Man in England. He was likeways naturally very Eloquent, and spoke with a freedom and dignity which no Man had in so great a perfection as himself. With these qualifications and a natural Talent of Application, he brought about these great Events which afterwards hapned, for he not only brought himself into favour with King George the first but was deemed the greatest supporter of the Royal Dignity that was to be found amongst all the King's subjects. His great Talents of Eloquence and Knowledge of all the affaires belonging to the Treasury and House of Commons brought him up to be prime Minister under the Title of Chancellor of the Exchequer, | and to this dignity was added that of being *fol.* 185. created a Knight of the Garter tho' a Commoner. In this station he continued to the periode above mentioned, and in the mean time greatly enriched himself, family, and friends.

His chief maxim of state was to propagate peace at anyrate with all the nighbouring kingdoms, well knowing that it wou'd not be in his power to support a War by reasone of his Adversaries in Parliament. This accordingly hapned, for when a War was entered into against Spain in 1739, and which was

and the Marquis of Tweedale, Secretary of State for Scotland. For himself he demanded only a peerage and a seat in the Cabinet.'—Coxe's *Walpole*, vol. i. pp. 698-99, and 702.

[1] On the death of his father, Walpole was elected member for Castle Rising, which he represented in the two last Parliaments of King William. In the first Parliament of Queen Anne he was returned for Lynn Regis, which he represented till he was created Earl of Orford. In 1708, the date mentioned above, he was appointed by Marlborough Secretary at War.

undertaken much against his Inclinations,[1] his power from that time began to decline, as the patriots took every day fresh occasions to complain, for, as they pretended that either the publick money was not manadged to purpose or the War with Spain neglected, still the clamour against Sr Robert continued. Thus fell this Great Man, but he fell without any disgrace, for the same men who envied and hated him on account of his prime ministry had a very great regard to his personal merits and other excellent qualifications.

But at the same time the Ministry was changed the credite of Patriotism fell, for a great many of those who had exclaimed against S^ir^ Robt. Walpole's measures, and declared themselves for Triennial Parliaments, and against standing Armies, came into all the measures of the Court, and, upon coming into Offices, seemed by their conduct to approve of the same things against which they had formerly exclaimed.

But to return to my own privat affaires, I spent the Spring
seasone of the year 1640[2] as before, and my Wife and I went
fol. 186. to pay a visite in Agust to our son George and | his Wife
at Drumcrief, and that same month I went to look after some
of the D. of Queensberry's affaires at Drumlanrig.

In the Month of September my son Patrick was kindly but unfortunately invited by my Lord Cathcart[3] to go to the West Indies with him upon an Expedition which his Ldp. was to command.

Patrick had a very great genius for the Ingeneering business. I had bred him abroad in Flandrs, and as he was naturally very industrious, he made drawings of all or most part of the frontier Towns. By so doing he made himself very acceptable to the officers of the Army, particularly the great Duke of Argyle and Lord Cathcart. He imbarqued with his Ldp. at the Isle of Wight, and sailed as one of his Aids de Camp and Chief Engeneers on the 24 Octr. 1740.

Sr Robert after his fall was not, like other Ministers, in disgrace with his Master the King, for he continued loved and honoured by all the Royal Family, and tho' he sometimes retired to his ... in Norfolk, yet he was consulted in all important affaires, and even by his successor, the Lord Carteret.

It wou'd be happy for all the people of Great Britain if henceforth they wou'd believe what publick British Patriotism is, for 'tis nothing but a Cant word, which signifies self-interest and Rou[g]ery.

N.B. This summer I caused build the little Hut at the head of Dyknook Rig in the moor of Pennicuik, for the preservation of the Game, and gave it the name of the Spy. Here I and the Ladies

---

[1] He is reported to have said, when the church bells were pealing to celebrate the tidings that war had been declared, 'They may ring the bells now, before long they will be wringing their hands.'

[2] Evidently a slip of the pen for 1740.

[3] Charles, eighth Lord Cathcart, born about 1686, distinguished himself at Sheriffmuir by a cavalry charge which routed the left wing of Mar's army. He

At the same time his Twin Brother, Henry, bred to the sea, was made a Liutenant in a 70 Gun ship called the Prince of Orange. This ship set out with the rest of the Fleet under the Lord Cathcart, but by a violent storm was blowen in to Lisbon. Thus the two Twin Brothers, of whom I had great hopes, were divided, and never saw one another more.

In november and december I attended the Exchequer at Edin., and about this time began a very great Dearth of provisions as was ever known in Scotland for above 40 years past.

The Magistrats of all the Towns in Scotland did all they cou'd for the support of their poor, and the Country Gentlemen contributed very great sums for their relief, particularly in the shire of Edin.; but I found that when a plentiful Harvest succeeded, we were so far from receiving thanks from the Country people whose Lives we had supported, that they were either insensible or ungrateful for the favours we had done them, | and, which was a strange delusion, tho' we had brought from England and Holand many thousands of bolls to support them, yet they asserted that all was done for our own private advantages, not believing it possible that we had bought Victuel for them at a 3[d] or a 4th dearer than we sold it to them, and yet this methode of providing for them cost the gentlemen of this shire above 2000 lib. ster.[2]

of Pennicuik dine once or twice every year at the Pouting.[1] I was consulted and intreated by Patrick to give my consent to his going on this Expedition, and never consented to it, but on the contrary protested against it. *N.B.* At the above hunting Hut at the head of the Dykenook Rig, I, with my ... and two three Ladies ... some other friends, dined on the 16 july 1754. We saw 2 or 3 *fol.* 187. cov[ies] of Pouts and catched a few.

This year I began to inclose the Grounds on the north side of Pennicuik called the Glaskils,[3] but hitherto I have found that our Scotch Tenants are so far from understanding or encouraging Inclosures that they take all the pains in the world to destroy them.

This year I likeways finished at my own charges the steeple of the Kirk of Pennicuik,[4] which had been begun 7 years before,

was appointed commander-in-chief of the expedition against the American dominions of Spain, but died at sea, 20th December 1740.

[1] This summer-house still exists in a good state of preservation.

[2] The dearth led to riots in Edinburgh, Leith, Musselburgh, Prestonpans, etc. See *Scots Magazine*, vol. ii. pp. 482-84, and 577; and vol. iii. pp. 45-6, and 142-43.

[3] Gaskhill, north-west of the town of Penicuik.

[4] In 1743 the Baron addressed a memorandum to the Kirk-Session regarding the allocation of church-seats, in which he claimed two-thirds of the entire space,

and I carried on some part of the Bridge within my inclosures at a place which has got the name of Montesina's cave.

1741. In january this year I continued my improvements at Pennicuik house, as I have done constantly above 30 years, and for that end had 7 or 8 men always imploied to drain, ditch, or hedge, especially in the spring seasons.[1]

The business of the Exchequer went on as formerly, but our Chief Baron was still absent. This year I lookt at a Manuscript History I had written in Latine, de Imperio Britannico but found it such an unlickt cub that I had no heart and no time to revise it with that accurracy which it wou'd have required, but still I hope to live to do it and make it useful to posterity, there being no facts represented in it but what I believe to be true. |[2]

fol. 188. Some [*sic*] of june 1741. This year the new parliament, as before mentioned, being met, the ministry were changed, and amongst other new Ministers the Marquise of Twedale[3] was made Secretary of State for Scotland, an office which no body had enjoied for about 14 years before, when it was held by the Duke of Roxbrugh.[4] But I must go a little back to notice that the Duke of Queensberry and the Dutchess attended the new Elections in Drumfrise shire, and were violent against the ministry, but as I cou'd not by law be chosen a member of parliament, so I thought it no ways my business to join in a party or bussy

She was an active Lady, and a great Ennemy to the late Ministry.

stating that in 1733 he had built an aisle to the church; that the whole steeple was built by him at considerable charge, and it was from the church only he could have access to it; and that the bell was a gift by his grand-uncle. He also mentions that the under part of the steeple had hitherto been used as a temporary prison for rogues and thieves. See Wilson's *Annals of Penicuik*, pp. 77-8, where a view of the old church and steeple, or rather tower, is given; also *A List of Improvements*, printed at the end of the present MS.

[1] See Additional Note R,—Scheme for Improvement of the Barony of Penicuik.

[2] See pages 84 and 147; also page 85, note [1].

[3] John, fourth Marquis of Tweeddale, succeeded his father 1715. He became principal Secretary of State for Scotland in February 1742, on the resignation of Sir Robert Walpole, and resigned in January 1746, when the office was abolished. He died 1762.

[4] 'He joined Lords Carteret and Cadogan in attempting to remove Sir Robert Walpole and Lord Townshend, for which he was dismissed from his place of Secretary of State, 25th August 1725.—Douglas's *Peerage*. According to Haydn (*Book of Dignities*), Charles, Earl of Selkirk, was Secretary of State for Scotland in 1731.

my self about Elections.[1] However, both the Duke and Dutchess,[2] when they came to Edin., were twice at my House of Pennicuik and Mavisbank.

About this time I was anxiously concerned for my two sons, Patrick and Henry, and at last got letters from them. The first, after regreting his misfortune, acquainted me with the Death of the good Lord Cathcart, who, if he had lived, might have prevented the disputes which afterwards fell out between Admiral Vernon[3] who commanded the Fleet, and General Wentworth[4] who commanded the Troops, at the siege of Carthagena.

Hary acquainted me in his letter of the disaster that had befallen the Prince of Orange Man of War, in which he was, at Lisbon, and that he had almost been killed by the fall of the main mast in a storm.

I had a letter soon after from Patrick at Jamaica, wherein he acquainted me of his having been very ill, but that he was

---

[1] A proof, however, of the care with which the Baron watched the political events of his time is furnished by a MS., preserved among the Clerk papers, partly in his autograph, partly in the hand of an amanuensis, written in the character of 'A Gentleman of Holland,' and defending the Excise Bill of 1733, and other measures of Walpole's Administration.

[2] 'Kitty beautiful and young
And wild as colt untam'd.'

See note [3], page 130.

[3] Edward Vernon, whose father was a Secretary of State under William and Mary, was born in 1684. In 1702 he served under Hopson in the engagement with the French at Vigo, and under Rooke in the fight off Malaga, 1704. In 1739 he was appointed vice-admiral of the blue, and commander of the squadron despatched to the West Indies against the Spaniards. He sailed from Spithead, 23d July; and attacked and captured Porto Bello, 20th November. In the spring of 1741 he made an unsuccessful attempt on Carthagena, of which Smollett, who accompanied the expedition, has given a graphic account in *Roderick Random*. During the Rebellion of 1745 Vernon guarded the coasts of Kent and Sussex. Soon after, his name was struck off the list of admirals, for his appointment of a gunner in opposition to one recommended by the Lords of the Admiralty. He was chosen member for Penryn, Cornwall, in 1727; and for Ipswich, Sussex, 1741, 1747, and 1757; and died in 1757.

[4] Brigadier-General Thomas Wentworth. He was promoted Lieutenant-General in 1745, and in the same year was appointed colonel of the Horse, late Field-Marshal Lord Viscount Cobham's. In 1746 he was president of the court-martial which tried and acquitted Colonel Durand in connection with the surrender of Carlisle to the rebels; and he died 'at the Court of Turin' in 1747.

then very well recovered, and going with the rest of the Troops to the Siege of Carthagena.

fol. 189. I expected with impatience to hear of the good success of this Enterprise and of Patrick's perfect health, but instead of that, had the melancolly account from one Captain Lin, whose comrade my son was, that he died in his arms of the sickness he formerly contracted at Jamaica, and that the little recovery of his health, which he pretended to when he left Jamaica, was only to be allowed the liberty of accompanying the General in the intended Expedition.

On this sad news, not only my Wife and I, but all the Family, abandoned our selves to the greatest grief and truble imaginable, for we had always lookt upon him as the rising hope of our family, or at least with no small pleasure and vanity, for besides the great parts and Genius he was possessed of, he was otherways a very proper, handsome young Man as one cou'd see. I continued to mourn many days for him, and cou'd not help frequently crying with King David when he lost his son Absalom, O my son, my son Peter, wou'd to God I had died for thee!

He resembled very much my eldest son John, in all his manner as well as his persone, and died much of the same Age, being 22 years and 8 months old.

I have reasone in the mean time to be thankful to God that he died much honoured, respected and regretted by all the military Men who were acquainted with him, for many children die who are a disgrace to their parents. By the favour of his Colonel, Col. Handyside, he keept his Ensigncy in England, and in the above-mentioned Expedition he served as one of the chief Engineers. |

fol. 190. As to the Expedition itself, it was altogether a foolish, mad project, for tho' we had gained the Town of Carthagena, all our Men must have died in keeping of it, for tho' the constitution of a Spaniard may bear with such a warm climat, yet the people of Great Britain cou'd have keept it no longer than to burry one another. I am thankful of one thing, that when Patrick wou'd have advised me by a letter to suffer him to go to America with my L[d]. Cathcart, I absolutely refused my consent at first, and at last, upon his reiterated requests, I wrote to him that tho' I cou'd not consent, yet I wou'd not hinder him to do in it as he thought fit.

After this unfortunat Expedition, the British Fleet returned to Jamaica; and upon some differences that fell out between the Admiral and the General, both were recalled, while at least 4 or 5000 men died under their conduct, for by the bye, the General was a raw, unexperienced officer, and the Admiral was a forward, interprising kind of Mad Man, very fit to command a small squadron on a dangerous expedition, but no ways cut out to command the British fleet.

This same year, but before I had the account of the Death of my son Patrick, my son James desired liberty to go to London to improve himself the best way he cou'd, but he staid not long there when he importuned me for liberty to go over and see the solemnities at Francfort, for choising a new Emperor on the Death of Charles the 6th, who had succeeded his Father Leopold, and afterwards his Brother Joseph, in the Empire of Germany.[1] |

I consented, tho' very unwillingly, but I saw I cou'd not *fol.* 191
help it.

About the end of summer I received a letter from my son Hary at Jamaica, confirming his Brother's Death, and he sent me a journal left amongst his papers, containing an account of all that was done at the siege of Carthagena, 'till two days before he died.

I received afterwards from my son Henry, one of Peter's drawings of the Town and fortifications of Lyle[2] in Flanders,

---

[1] 'At the decease of the Emperor Charles VI. in 1740, his hereditary dominions devolved of right (by the Pragmatic Sanction) upon his only daughter and heiress the Archduchess Maria-Theresa, but were claimed by the husband of his niece (Maria-Amelia, daughter of Joseph I.), Charles [Albert], Elector of Bavaria, who was declared king of Bohemia in 1741, and crowned Emperor of Germany at Frankfort the following year, as Charles VII. This dispute disturbed the tranquillity of Europe, and occasioned a war in which all the great European powers were involved, and which did not terminate until three years after the death of Charles VII., when Maria-Theresa had her patrimonial dominions guaranteed to her by the treaty of Aix-la-Chapelle in 1748.'—Haydn's *Book of Dignities*, p. 21 (edition of 1851).

[2] Lille. Captured by Louis XIV. from the Spaniards in 1667; surrendered in 1708 to the Duke of Marlborough and Prince Eugene; and restored to France at the Peace of Utrecht in 1713.

which is exceeding fine, with another copy by a different scale; these he did about a year before, when he studied Fortification in that city.

I had likeways sent me several other drawings by him, all which I keep in a long white-iron case in the Charter Room of Pennicuik.

During the remainder of this year I lived at Pennicuik and Edinburgh, as formerly.

1742. In january and February 1742 I lived much in the same way, and took many observations upon a comet which appeared first in the constellation of Lucida Lyræ; from thence it took its course Westward within 5 degrees of the Pole Star, its Tail after its perihelion was in length about 10 degrees, and at last it vanished out of sight in the Month of March.[1]

The Cave of Hurley. This is on several accounts remarkable, particularly that about the begining of

This year I made the antique Cave at Hurley where I had made a large pond, and stocked it with Carp and Tench brought from Corby Castle near Carlyle. I caused this pond *fol. 192.* to be inclosed, | and the little Hill in the middle got the name of Clermount. This is a Rural Scheme which, in my opinion, adds a good deal of Beuty to the Enclosures of

[1] 'P. S. Coll. of Edinburgh, March 9 (1742).—We got the first account of the comet that now appears from some carriers from the West Country. They saw it in the east on the 19th of February, in the morning. It has been observed at London since the 23d, and here since the 25th. Its course has been from South to North nearly, with a little inclination East—from the tail of Aquila through Lyra, Cygnus, and Draco to Cepheus. It moved at first between 5 and 6 degrees in a day; but moves now more slowly, describing between 2 and 3 degrees in a day only. The tail was 6 degrees long on the 23d, but last Thursday morning, after the moon was set, the tail appeared considerably longer. The comet was very near to ϵ in Draco on Friday night, and to χ in Cepheus last night. It appears under the pole in the evening, within 13 degrees of it, and will probably come within 7 degrees of the pole-star in some days.'—*Scots Magazine*, vol. iv. p. 94. Under dates 22d March 1741-2, and 8th April 1742, the Baron writes to Roger Gale regarding this comet:—'Its tail, even according to Sir Isaac Newton's notions, diffuses vapours through the planetary world, and consequently must affect mankind in some degree or other. I defy any historian to show us so many alterations as have been in the affairs of Europe since its first coming into our latitude. I know not what diseases of the body it may bring along with it, but it is pretty odd that about two weeks ago all our forces fell ill of the cold in the space of 24 hours, both in Edenborough and in the country.' 'The path of it has been exactly observed by Mr. MacLaurin, our mathematician in Edenborough.'—Nichols' *Bibliotheca Topographica*, No. II. part I., pp. 351 and 352.

[2] This cave and pond still exist on the Penicuik estate.

Pennicuik house, as it resembles the Grotto of Pausilipo at Naples.[1]

November the sun shines quite through it to the Haugh on the opposite sde. about 20 minutes after 9 in the forenoon.

About this time, likeways, I went on with the Enclosure of Hurley towards the moor, where to civilize the prospect I built two little Houses, and gave each a Garden, which was planted round with barren Trees and thorns.

The whole farm of Hurley paid me but 200 merks, so I thought it very easy to improve it by degrees.

In May this year I carried my Wife and two of my Daughters to Dalguse,[2] to drink Goat whey, on the side of Tay, 4 miles above Dunkell, but here I left them, and returned to Edin. at the siting down of the Court of Exchequer.

This summer I diverted my self by writing an Essay on the Antient Languages of Great Britain,[3] and when finished, gave it to the Society for the improvement of learning and phylosophy, of which I was a member.[4]

I had given this Society several other papers before.

From the begining of the year 1743 I lived as formerly, sometimes in Town and sometimes in the Country.

In Aprile I attended the Duke of Queensberry's Affaires at Drumlanrig, and particularly I made a narrow scrutiny into the state of his Lead mines at Wanlockhead.

---

[1] The Grotto of Pausilippo, south-west of Naples, described by Seneca and Petronius, and in the Middle Ages believed to have been the work of Virgil, whose 'Tomb' is near.

[2] Dalguise, in the parish of Little Dunkeld. For an interesting account of this expedition to the Highlands see the Baron's letter to Gale in Nichols' *Bibiotheca Topographica*, No. II. part I., p. 357.

[3] A MS. copy of this essay, signed 'J. C., 1742,' is preserved among the Clerk papers. It was published in Nichols' *Bib. Topog.*, No. II. part I., pp. 362-84.

[4] The Philosophical Society of Edinburgh, the precursor of the Royal Society of Edinburgh. In 1731 a Society had been started for collecting and publishing papers on medicine and surgery; and in 1739, its scope having extended, at the suggestion of Professor Colin Maclaurin, so as to embrace the subjects of philosophy and literature, it took the title of The Society for Improving Arts and Sciences, or The Philosophical Society of Edinburgh. Its President was James, fourteenth Earl of Morton, afterwards President of the Royal Society, London; its Vice-Presidents Baron Sir John Clerk, and Dr. John Clerk (see note [1], page 11), and its Secretaries Professor Maclaurin and Dr. Plummer. Its meetings having been interrupted, the Society was revived by its new Secretaries David Hume and Dr. Alexander Monro, and volumes of Transactions were published in 1754, 1756, and 1771. In 1782 Principal Robertson proposed a scheme for further extending the scope of the Society, so as to embrace every branch of science, erudition, and taste; and the Royal Society of Edinburgh, including all the members of the Philosophical Society, was formed, and incorporated by royal charter in 1783. See Tytler's *Memoirs of Lord Kames*, vol. i. p. 184 and note.

In May I carried my Wife and some of my Lasses to the Goat whey at Wooler Haughhead. We staid about 4 weeks; from thence I carried them to Morpeth, Newcastle, and Durham. In this last place, being the 29 of May, they heard the church Musick perform'd on the top of the steeple, this being a High Church form observed there for the celebration of the Birth and Restoration of King Charles the 2d, or as some of the clergy pretend, for the Restoration of Monarchy, which for some years before Oliver Cromwell and his party

fol. 193 had ruined. | Some pretend to say that this solemn church Worship is in order to introduce another Restoration, but the truth is, I believe, it is a custom begun in 1660, which the High Church party is not willing to abolish, nor are the common people willing to want this accustomed diversion.

A Latine (Treatise written by me on the statue of Brigantia and the Two other large stones with Inscriptions at Penycuik, and which were found in Anandale on the side of the Antient Roman Camp at Midlebee. This I did chiefly that these valouable Monuments may be preserved.

This summer was spent as formerly, but I wrote a Latine dissertation on the Roman Monuments at Pennicuik House, which is likeways design'd as a present to the Society above named for the encouragement of Learning.[1]

I cannot omit here to take notice of a considerable alteration in our Court of Exchequer, for towards the end of the year Mathew Lant, our Lord Chief Baron, died, and was succeeded in office by Councellor Idle.[2]

The late chief Baron was a poor, Harmless, timorous Man. I had done him considerable services by supplying his place in his absence at London for many years, and had great returns of Civility from him and his friends.

I was spoken of to succeed him, but those who have friends in any great offices in England will always be preferred to any Scotsman.

The Comet.

About the end of the year 1743 and begining of the year 1744, we had again the great pleasure of seeing a new Comet[3]

[1] See page 139, and note [1] there; and marginal note to folio 241.

[2] See note [1] to page 73; and note [1] to page 133.

[3] 'College of Edinburgh, Jan. 9, 1744. A comet has appeared for some time near the head of Andromeda, equal to a star of the second magnitude. It was observed at London, Paris, and in several parts of Scotland on Friday, the 23d of last month; but was seen before that time in Switzerland. It moves slowly. About Dec 29th it changed its right ascension by its daily motion Westwards, two minutes of time daily, and its declination by moving Southwards about nine minutes of space.'—*Scots Magazine*, vol. v. p. 573.

as it moved with great swiftness in a parabolical curve inclined to our Earth. We saw it for many days. It began to be visible in the Constellation of Andromeda. In its motion towards the sun, its velocity was much accelerated, and it came to its perihelion about the 21 feb. 1744. Its Tail, as it approached the sun, was in appearance 25 degrees | in length, *fol.* 194. which, considering its vast distance from us, being above 50 millions of miles, cou'd not be under many millions of miles in length. It made its perihelion, or circle about the sun, from within the orbite of Mercury, which is commonly reckoned to be about 30 millions of miles distant from the sun, its bulk or diameter was near to that of Venus.

After its perihelion on the said 21 of feb., I saw it no more, for by its swift, parabolical course, it took its way almost opposite to this part of the World, tho' it might have been seen by the Inhabitants of Hispaniola and Jamaica some few days after.

This year, about the 19 or 20 of feb., I came out to Pennicuik and in a clear fine morning, half an houer befor the sun rose, I saw the beutifullest schene in the Heavens that perhaps, ever was seen by any body at one time, for by the assistence of a Reflecting Telescope I saw first the Comet with its Tail in the greatest glory it had ever appeared, being at that time within a day or two of its perihelion. Next I saw the planet of Venus in great beuty, and towards the west the planets of Saturn and Jupiter with their satellites; but what made the finest appearance of all, was the moon near her last quarter, just going down upon the Top of the black hill north west of Pennicuik House. Next the sun rose in great splendour, which yet for half an houer did not obscure the Comet, for both it and its Tail appeared very finely for that space. I tried at that time to have seen Mercury, which I cou'd not do, but by the Comet's distance from the Sun's body, I was sure that its perihelion wou'd be within the orbite of that planet.

If I had been in the possession of the new-invented [di?]urnal Telescope, I might have seen [the] Comet through the day, when the Sun was shining.[1]

That above the silver burn.

My son George and my chaplain, Mr. William Ainsley, and others, were with me.

[1] Probably the Baron here refers to the improved telescopes which James Short, acting on the suggestions of Professor James Gregory, had constructed in the rooms in the University of Edinburgh, which were placed at his disposal by Professor Colin Maclaurin. See *Encyclopædia Britannica*, vol. xxiii. p. 137 (Ninth Edition).

fol. 195. All this I saw without either fogs or clouds interveening. | If comets presage great alterations and Trubles in states, this comet may be thought a foreruner, and tho' it be a little superstitious to think so, yet I am tempted to think that as the moon in some cases influences our bodies, I know not how far the vapours which arise from a Comet may not have some influence on Men's minds. It is certain that before great Calamities hapning to a nation, Comets have been seen, hovering in the Aire, and other odd phenomena. All Histories are full of such accounts, and Josephus takes notice of a very remarkable one befor the destruction of Jerusalem.

Invasion from Dunkirk, 1744.

In february and March this year, 1744, we were alarmed with an Invasion from Dunkirk. A body of French was to be transported from thence, under the Command of the oldest son of the Pretender[1] and the Count de Sax,[2] a natural son of the late Elector of Saxony.

The ground of this intended Invasion was, no doubt, the noise and clamour of a discontented party in England, which still went under the name of patriots. Things were therefor represented at the Courts of France and Rome much worse than they were, for it was not doubted there but that all Britain was ready for a Revolt in favours of the persone we called the Pretender, but nothing was farther from the minds *fol.* 196. of the people, as the | French afterwards found, for tho' they sent a large squadron of Men of War from Brest, to come upon the English coast from the Mouth of the Channel down to Portsmouth, in order to sound the inclinations of the

---

[1] Prince Charles Edward reached Paris on the 20th January 1744, and sailed in the same ship with Marshal Saxe.

[2] Maurice, Count of Saxony, Marshal Saxe, was born in 1696, a natural son of Frederick Augustus II. of Poland, by Aurora, Countess of Königsmarke. He was a soldier from his earliest youth, and in the campaign of 1710 received the eulogies of the allied generals. After serving against the Swedes, 1711, and against the Turks, 1717, he, in 1733, entered the French service under the Duke of Berwick, and after the campaign of 1740 was appointed Marshal-General of the French armies. He commanded the army of Bavaria, and while defending Alsace he was summoned by Lous XV. to take part in the expedition against England; but his fleet was scattered by a tempest, and its remains blockaded by the English fleet. His defeat of the French and Hanoverians at Fontenoy, in 1745, was followed by the conquest of Belgium. After the capture of Laufeldt in 1747, Saxe retired into private life. He died in 1750.

people, yet they found them so much averse to this Roman-Catholick project, that they were glad to get back again to Brest, more especially when they found themselves ready to be attaqued by the British Fleet far superior to theirs. One night's favourable Wind from the nor'east protected them, and gave them the advantage of sailing off in the night. Sir John Noris,[1] who commanded this great British Fleet, was much blamed for a little delay in sailing after them, but he was always a very unlucky Admiral, and on that account got the name of Jack foulweather, and S^r. John no-risque.

The French transports were in the mean time in the road of Dunkirk, and ready to sail, but a Tempest overtook them, so that, with the loss of some of their ships and some hundreds of Men, they were forced to lay aside their Expedition.

The French knew very well the strength of the British Fleet, and that they were in no condition to force a passage over to England, but it seems they intended in the night time to have got over and tried their Fortune. I am of opinion that tho' they had landed they cou'd have done nothing, but must have been destroied or taken prisoners, for 'tis certain that there was not one of a hundred in Britain who had the least inclinations to favour them.

All this time we had been only Auxiliaries to the Queen of Hungary,[2] in defence | of that ballance of Power which was *fol. 197.* necessary to be keept up between the two great Families of Bourbon and Austria, but now we became principals in a War

The French declared War against us with great reluctance, but the Queen of Spain, who manadged the Affaires of that Kingdom, forced them to it after suspecting their fidelity in a sea fight in the Mediterranean between the English Fleet, under Admiral Mathews, and the combined fleets of France and Spain, who for two years [be]fore had been blockt up

[1] Admiral Sir John Norris, descended from an Irish family, for his conduct in the action off Beachy Head in 1690, was appointed commander of the 'Pelican' fire-ship. He distinguished himself under Sir George Rooke, Captain James Killegrew, and Sir Cloudesley Shovel. Having been knighted, he, in 1707, was advanced to the rank of Rear-Admiral of the Blue, and in 1732 became Admiral of the White. The expedition against the French fleet mentioned above was his last naval service; and he died, at an advanced age, in 1749.

[2] Maria-Theresa, daughter of the Emperor Charles VI., was born at Vienna in 1717, and in 1736 was married to Francis Stephen, Duke of Lorraine, who in 1737 became Grand Duke of Tuscany. On her father's death, in 1740, she ascended the throne of Hungary, Bohemia, and Austria; but Charles Albert, Elector of Bavaria (see note [1], p. 163; and note [2], p. 172) disputed her claim to the Austrian territories, and, simultaneously with Frederick the Great, invaded her states. She fled to Presburg, and, with her child in her arms, invoked the aid of the Hungarians. She obtained assistance from England and Holland, and her rights were confirmed by the treaty of Aix-la-Chapelle, 1784. She died in 1780.

[in] the Harbour of Thoulon ...s year they ventured out, and were attaqued by the British fleet, and in this engagement it was thought that the French did not support the Spanish fleet as they ought to have done, but sailed to the ...y of Alicant. We [ha]d the same complaint against our Fleet, that ... two divisions under Ad[l]. Mathews and Lestock [di]d not their endeavours [to] have destroied the united fleets of France and Spain. There was, I think, reasone on both sides of the Question, for I believe our Ministry did not care to destroy the French, and they did not care to assist the Spaniards to destroy us. my fears were but too just.

with France, for the French, at the earnest desire of the Court of Spain, first declared war against us, so that we were next in honour oblidged to declare war against them.

'Tis very remarkable that during the whole Trubles in Germany and several Campaigns in the years 1742 and 1743 and even at the time of a famous engagement at Dettingen on the Rhyn in 1743 where our King was present and where his Arms were victorious against the French, yet neither we nor the French nor the Austrians had declared War against one another. We fought for the Queen of Hungary as head of the Austrian family, and much blood was shed in Germany and Bohemia, but still we keept up a kind of correspondence with the Court of France, and no hostilities were committed at sea. In the mean time the cuning triming people of Holand lay by, and wou'd not engage as principals in any War, tho at the same time they sent 20,000 men to the field as Auxiliares to the Queen of Hungary, who was actually in War against both the French and the Emperor, but did not declare the War even in the campaign 1744, when her General, Charles of Lorrain,[1] past the Rhyn, and attaqued the French Territories in Alsace.

To return now again to my own Family concerns. My son
1744. Henry had returned in safety from the West Indies, and from
fol. 198. other cruses which he made as | first Liutenant of the Preston, commanded by the Earl of Noresk,[2] but in Aprile this year the sd Earl and 3 other Captains were ordered to fit out their ships for a long voyage. My son acquainted me of this by a letter but knew not to what place they were bound. At last they sailed, being in all 4 ships, one of 70, one of 60, one of 50, and one of 20 guns, under the command of one Commadore

[1] Charles of Lorraine, Maria Theresa's General, brother of the Duke of Tuscany; born 1712, son of Leopold, Duke of Lorraine; became Governor of the Low Countries; died in 1744.

[2] George Carnegie, attained the rank of a captain in the royal navy in 1741, and in the same year succeeded his brother as sixth Earl of Northesk. In January 1744 he sailed in the fleet, under Sir John Norris, to the East Indies, commanding the 'Preston,' a ship of fifty guns. On 25th January 1745 they captured, in the Straits of Banca, three very valuable French East Indiamen, bound from Canton to Europe. In 1755 he commanded the 'Oxford,' a ship of sixty-six guns; was promoted to a flag in 1756; rose, by seniority, to the rank of Admiral of the White; and died in 1792.

Barnet. I heard from my son when he sailed, but whether I am ever to see the poor Lad again, God only knows. I had a letter from him some weeks after from the coast of Africk, by a ship which met them there, but was inform'd that they knew not where they were bound for that their orders cou'd not yet be opened.

In may this year I carried my Wife and some of my Daughters to Bonhill,[1] where my Daughter jean lived, and with her and her spouse, Mr. Smollet, we went for 3 weeks and drank the goat-whey at Luss. From thence I myself made a trip to Inveraray, and took occasion to visite Mr. Clerk of Braelaken, who was married to my Niece Sarah Little, the daughter of my Sister Sophia Clerk, who had been married to Mr Little of Liberton.[2] There I staid with great pleasure for a day or two, and returned back to Luss.

N.B.—There is only one child of this marriage, John Clerk, a very pro[mising] Lad, who went this year, 1749, to Jam[aica].

On our return home we went and lived at Mavisbank in the months of june and july, and I attended the Exchequer as formerly.

During this summer the principal schem of publick Action was in Bohemia and Bavaria, for the Machivelian King of Prussia,[3] contrary to his engagements with the magnanimous Queen of Hungary, invaded Bohemia with an Army of above 60000 men, 'tho | he had received from that Queen all the best *fol.* 199.
parts of all the fine province of Silesia, in order to keep him quiet and preventing [*sic*] him from joining with the French. This was an unhappy stroke to the peace of Germany, and the ballance of power so much wisht and contended for, between the two Houses of Bourbon and Austria.

This Queen of Hungary was at this time only about 26 years of age.

Prince Charles of Lorrain, brother to the great Duke of Tuscany, and commander in chief of the Queen of Hungary's Army, had then past the Rhyn, and was in a fair way of

The Duke of Tuscany was formerly Duke of Lorrain.

---

[1] In Dumbartonshire.

[2] Sophia, youngest daughter of Sir John Clerk, first baronet of Penicuik, by his first wife, Elizabeth Henderson, was born at Newbiging, 29th August 1683, and was married to Gabriel Ranken of Orcharhead, Stirlingshire. Their son Walter, succeeding as heir of entail to the estate of Little of Liberton, took the name of Little; and their daughter, Sarah, married Dougal Clerk of Braekethan [Braelaken], Argyllshire.—Douglas's *Baronage* and MS. *Family Register*.

[3] Frederick II., the Great, born 1712; succeeded his father as King of Prussia 1741; died 1786.

recovering Alsace to the Empire of Germany, but on hearing of the progress which the king of Prussia had made in Bohemia, he was oblidged to repass that River, and return to protect the Queen's subjects in that country.

In his way he was oblidged to leave Garrisons in several Towns in Bavaria and the upper Palatinat, yet he was successful wherever he came, and the Prussians with vast losses were oblidged to surrender Prague, which they had taken, and retire out of Bohemia without ever offering to stand the hazard of a Battle. They knew indeed that they were far from having any chance of succeeding in an attempt of that kind, for the king of Poland,[1] who was at the same time Elector of Saxony, sent 22000 men to the assistence of Prince Charles. After this the Prussians with their King at their head retired to Silesia where they took up their Winter Quarters.

1744. About this time War was proclaimed by the Queen of Hungary against France, and the French King[2] turning his head to military affaires regained all the south parts of Germany and restored the Emperor to his Capital of Munich, from whence he had been forced the year before by the victorious Arms of the Queen of Hungary, for by the bye I must notice that this Emperor the Duke of Bavaria[3] had entered into a league with the Kings of France and Prussia for suppressing altogether the House of Austria.

This summer likeways the Ambition of the Queen of Spain,[4]
fol. 200. in order to procure | a kingdom in Italy to her second son Don Philip,[5] had raised a terrible coubustion there, her eldest son Don Carlos,[6] king of the two Sicilies, used his outmost efforts

---

[1] Frederick Augustus II. succeeded his father as King of Poland in 1734; died 1763. [2] Louis XV.

[3] Charles Albert, born 1697; succeeded his father as Elector of Bavaria, 1726; died 1745. See note [1], p. 163; and note [3], p. 169.

[4] Elizabeth Farnese, born 1692, daughter of Odoardo, eldest son of Duke Ranuccio of Parma, and Dorothea Sophia, daughter of Philip William, Elector Palatine. She became second wife of Philip V. of Spain, in 1714; and died 1766.

[5] Third (second surviving) son of Philip V. and Elizabeth Farnese, born 1720; became Duke of Parma and Piacenza in 1749; died 1765.

[6] Eldest son of Philip V. and Elizabeth Farnese, born 1716; succeeded as Duke of Parma and Piacenza, 1731; conquered Naples and Sicily 1735, and in the same year became King of Spain, as Carlos III.; died 1788.

for the same end, but as the king of Sardinia[1] was united in interest with the House of Austria, there were no considerable advantages gained by the Armes of France and Spain, but on the contrary they were oblidged to repass the Alps, and take up their Winter Quarters where they were the year before. In the mean time an Army of neapolitans and a handfull of Spaniards continued in Winter quarters on the confines of Bulognia and Tuscany.

In november this year the British parliament met, but the 1744.
Ministry under the Lord Carteret found themselves so weak as to be able to do nothing, wherefor his Lorp. was oblidged to resign contrary to the King's Inclinations, who was always steedy in his favours to those who served him well as he thought this Lord had done.

To him succeeded a Triumvirat who constituted jointly the prime ministry. The Duke of Newcastle,[2] the Lord Hardwick[3] who was Chancellor at the time, and Henry Pelham,[4] brother to the Duke, made up this Triumvirat. The Lord Hardwick was a great Lawer and an eloquent man, but good judges thought that all the Three had not the Qualifications of the late Sir Robert Walpole, created afterwards Earl of Orfoord as before mentioned.

The King's affaires had then but an indifferent Aspect; however, a new methode was introduced into publick management as set not only things to rights but outdid all the measures of Government that had hitherto been tried since the acces-

---

[1] Charles Emmanuel II., succeeded his father in 1730, and died in 1773.

[2] Thomas Pelham-Holles. Born 1693, succeeded as second Baron Pelham of Laughton in 1712; Secretary of State for the Southern Department 1724-26, and again 1746-54; First Lord of the Treasury 1754-56, when he was created Duke of Newcastle. Died 1768.

[3] Philip Yorke, born 1690; Solicitor-General 1720; Attorney-General 1724; Lord Chief-Justice of England 1733-7; created Baron Hardwicke of Hardwicke 1733; Lord High Chancellor of Great Britain 1737-56; created Earl of Hardwicke 1754; died 1764.

[4] Born 1696. After serving in the army and fighting at Preston, he entered Parliament, and became Secretary of State for War in 1724. In conjunction with his brother, the Duke of Newcastle, and the Opposition, he overthrew Walpole's administration, and in 1743 became First Lord of the Treasury, and, in the same year, Chancellor of the Exchequer. He resigned in 1744, but was recalled in a few days, and remained Prime Minister till his death in 1754.

sion of the family of Hannover to the Crown, but it had been tried in King William's time, and was like to have mared all his affaires: this was to incorporat the Whigs, Tories, and Jacobites in parliament into one Interest for preserving the
fol. 201. liberties of Europe. | It seem'd to be a very arduous undertaking, and yet it succeeded so well that the Royal Favours being equally dispenced the grand movement of the whole sisthem of politicks was called the Broadbottom.

These men were not to hang together for any long time, yet they were so well pleased with the distribution of the Royal Favours that they stuck at no expence for supporting the War abroad, and the liberties of Germany against the encroaching power of France; for after all the necessary subsidies were given for the support of every branch of the War, at sea and land, they gave 500,000 ℔. to the King more than was strictly necessary, at that time, so that about the begining of the year 1745 Great Britain furnished this year, partly for the War, partly for the subsistence of the Government, and partly to pay the interest of the publick Debts already contracted, at least 12 millions sterling, besides a debt of 50 millions which she lay under.

Our fleet at this time consisted of more than 220 Men of War.

Our seamen above 40,000, and our Land Troops at least as many.

1745. This year 1745 began in my family with some slight feavers of cold and indispositions which went quickly over, 'tho my Daughter jean, married to Mr. Smollet as above, recovered weakly of a Feaver she had in the begining of December last. I my self and my Wife continued pretty well, but both of us found old age aproaching very fast upon us. I attended the Exchequer in january and february as usually, and return'd to Pennicuik with my Family about the 22 of March. |

fol. 202. Upon the 26 of Aprile I went to Drumlanrig to attend the Duke of Queensberry's Affaires, from whom I never had the least Gratification, since friendship and the Remembrance of what I owed to his father were my only motives, remembring still *si ingratum dixeris omnia dixeris.*

By the way I called at Wanlockhead, where the Duke had

his lead mines, and staid there all night. I gave my advices about some of the works, and in going to Drumlanrig next day I took a new way, which I had advised, between Wanlockhead and the River Nith, from whence by the right hand one turns to Sanchar,[1] and by the left to Drumlanrig. This way lay down Minick Water, and was very crabed and steep, yet it being a much better pass into Nithsdale than by Entriken[2] Brae, I thought it might prove a benefite to the Lead trade in general if it cou'd be carried on as well at Dumfrise as at Leith; besides, I saw many other advantages by it which a little time wou'd certainly discover.

N.B.-The carts now emploied in the carriage of Lead from Wanlockhead to Leith, which chiefly belong to the shire of Lothian and T... prove a real loss to the Tenants, for they neglect fa[rm]ing of their ground in summer, which wou'd be of greater advantage to them.

I emploied about a week on the Duke's affaires at Drumlanrig, then went to make a visite to the Earl of Galloway,[3] his Father, my Brother in Law, and a most oblidging friend, being dead.

The way was monstrously bad for 30 miles. I went by New Galloway and Munigaff,[4] and found the Earl at Pouton,[5] a new House which he was just finishing. I visited my Brother in Law Brigadier General Stuart at Sorbie, staid with the Earl only two nights and a day, then returned back to Drumlanrig. I spent a day or two afterwards in revising some of the Duke's affaires, then returned home to Pennicuik house.

Here I staid for the remainder of the month of May, and in June I lived with my family as formerly at Mavisbank.

From this place I attended the Court of Exchequer dayly as often as it sat, on the 22 of june, during the vacation of the Court, I returned to Pennicuik, and in company of some of my friends took the diversion of the pouting till the 7 of july, when the Court sat again. | I continued as formerly at Mavisbank, but attended the court dayly till it rose. *fol.* 203.

Nothing remarkable hapned to me during the two months I

---

[1] Sanquhar. [2] Enterkin.

[3] According to Douglas, James, fifth Earl of Galloway, died 16th February 1746, when his son Alexander succeeded as sixth earl. He married Anne, second daughter of William, ninth Earl Marischal, and died at Aix in Provence, 1773, in his seventy-ninth year.

[4] Minigaff, a hamlet and parish in Kirkcudbrightshire, the former three-quarters of a mile north of Newton-Stewart.

[5] Powton.

spent at Mavisbank, all was peace and quietness, but in the month of Agust began such a scene of trubles over all Britain as shook the very foundation of its constitution, for about the end of July and begining of Agust the Highland Rebellion broke out, of which I shall here insert a short History.

The Rebellion ... afterwards ... took its rise ... England, but some of the Tories ...d at that time ... some services to the English ministry, they were desirous to turn the odium of the Rebellion on Scotland.

This Rebellion took its rise chiefly in Rome, for some of the Highland chiefs and others, as they traveled into Italy, never failed of visiting the pretender's family, and chiefly made their court to the two young princes, Charles and Henry, the sons of the s[d] pretender and the princess Sobieski, both in appearance handsome, sprightly young men.

It is probable that promises were not wanting on both sides, and I doubt not but several of the Highland chiefs, and even many in England, were very forward to engadge themselves and their friends so long as things seemed to be at some distance; however, the eldest of the two princes, whom I shall call the young chevalier, was impatient in his present situation at his Father's Court in Rome, and therefor wanted to try what his friends in Britain wou'd do for him. For this end he came into France in the begining of this year 1745 and offered himself to the Court of France as a proper instrument either to creat to the King of that country a new Aley in the persone of his Father, the Pretender, as King of Great Britain in case his schems should succeed, or otherways to foment such a disturbance in Britain by an Invasion as might facilitate the French conquests in Flanders.

This proposal took with that Court, wherefor preparations of some men, money, and arms were made in order to second
fol. 204. the intentions of the young Chevalier. | He embarked on the 14 of july from port Lasare[1] [*sic*] in Britanny, on board a frigate of 18 guns, and was afterwards joined by a Man of War of 66 guns. They soon fell in with some English ships, one of which, called the Lyon, a ship of about 60 guns, engaged the

[1] At seven of the evening of the 22d June (3d July N.S.) the Prince embarked at St. Nazaire, in the mouth of the Loire, in the 'Dontelle,' a brig of 18 guns, attended by seven friends. Proceeding to Belleisle, he was joined by the 'Elizabeth,' a ship of 68 guns, with 700 men aboard; and thence the expedition sailed on 2d July (O.S.). For an account of the action with the 'Lion,' a ship of 58 guns, commanded by Captain Brett, see Chambers's *Rebellion*, p. 21 (latest, undated, edition).

French Man of War for 9 houres, and disabled her, so that she was forced to return back to the coast of France. During this engagement the Frigate in which the young Chevalier was, got away, and after some days landed near the Isle of Sky, and the Chevalier was for some days entertained at the House of one Macdonald of Kinloch Moidart.[1] He had brought with him a few Officers, mostly Irish, and about 100 men. The money and arms intended for this Expedition were left in the Man of War, which had returned to France.

While the Chevalier tarried at Kinloch Moidart, several Highland chiefs came to him, particularly Locheal, the chief of the Camrons,[2] Glengarry,[3] and the Captain of Clan Ranold.[4]

[1] The Macdonalds of Kinlochmoidart were cadets of the Clanranald family, being descended from John, fourth son of Allan Macdonald, eighth of Clanranald. Donald, fourth in descent from the above Allan, married Isabel, daughter of Robert Stewart of Appin. With a hundred of his followers he accompanied the Prince through the whole campaign. His estates were confiscated, his house burned to the ground, and he was executed on the Gallows Hill, Carlisle, 18th October 1746. It was he who commanded the party of Highlanders who arrived at Rose Castle just after the birth of Rose Mary Dacre, afterwards wife of Sir John Clerk, fifth baronet of Penicuik, and who pinned his white cockade on the infant's breast in token of protection. See Note to Scott's *Monastery*; also Mackenzie's *History of the Macdonalds*, p. 463.

[2] Donald Cameron of Lochiel succeeded to the estate and style of 'Captain of the Clan Cameron' on the death of his grandfather Sir Ewen, his own father being attainted for his share in the Rebellion of 1715. He was active in preliminary negotiations for the Rebellion of 1745; and though, on the arrival of the Prince in Scotland, he anticipated the failure of the rising, yet the personal influence of the young Chevalier induced him to join his standard with 1400 of his clan. He behaved with great heroism, and was severely wounded at Culloden. After many adventures he escaped to France, where he commanded 'the Regiment of Albany,' composed of his exiled countrymen. He died in 1748.

[3] John Macdonell, twelfth of Glengarry, son of the celebrated Alastair Dubh Macdonell, was then chief. He did not take part in the Rebellion of 1745; but his son and succcessor Alastair carried an address from the Highland chiefs, signed with their blood, to the Prince in France, and on his return was captured and imprisoned in the Tower. His second son, Æneas, a colonel in the Prince's army, was slain at the battle of Falkirk. The Macdonalds of Glengarry greatly distinguished themselves by their bravery during the Rebellion. See Mackenzie's *History of the Macdonalds*, pp. 349, 354-5.

[4] Ranald Macdonald, fifteenth of Clanranald, was then chief. He had an interview with Prince Charles on his first arrival in the Long Island, and refused to take part in the Rebellion; but his son Ranald, afterwards his successor, was one of the first, along with his relative Kinlochmoidart, to join the Prince, with 500 men. He was wounded at Culloden, and with difficulty effected his escape to France, where he eventually became aide-de-camp to Marshal Saxe. His

Some likeways waited on him from the South Country, as Mr. Murry of Brughton[1] whom he made his Secretary. They endeavoured by letters and messages to get several others to joyn them, particularly the L[d] Fortrose[2] and Sir Alex. Macdonald,[3] but cou'd not prevail on them.

N.B.—L[d] Fortrose, son of the late Earl of Seaforth and chief of the Mackenzies.

These meetings, they knew, would give some disturbance to the Government, wherefor their friends gave out every where that the Chevalier had not landed in these bounds, but that some Highland Gentlemen intended only to take the diversion of hunting. By this means, for 2 or 3 weeks, there were few or no preparations made at Edin., till at last it came to be knoun that the Clans, to the number of 1500, had taken Arms, and

name being erroneously given as *Donald* in the act of attainder, his friends at length succeeded in recovering his estates; and he returned and lived quietly for the rest of his days on his property, a loyal subject to the king. See Mackenzie's *History of the Macdonalds*, pp. 428-35.

[1] John Murray of Broughton, in Peeblesshire, second son of Sir David Murray, second Baronet of Stanhope, by his second wife, Margaret, daughter of Sir John Scott of Ancrum, Baronet, was sent to the Jacobites in Scotland, to prepare them for the coming of the Prince, whom he joined on his arrival in Scotland, acting as his secretary during the Rebellion. At the proclamation of James VIII. at the cross of Edinburgh, his first wife, a lady of great beauty, appeared on horseback decorated with white ribbons, and with a drawn sword in her hand. After Culloden he escaped to Peeblesshire, and took refuge in the House of his brother-in-law, Hunter of Polmood, where he was captured. To save his life he basely turned King's evidence, and aided in the condemnation of his former associates. The abhorrence with which he was regarded even by his political enemies is well illustrated by the anecdote in Lockhart's *Life of Scott*, of how he had visited on business the novelist's father, a Hanoverian and Kirk elder, who, on his leaving, threw out of the window a cup from which he had drunk tea at Mrs. Scott's invitation, remarking—'I may admit into my house, on a piece of business, persons wholly unworthy to be treated as guests by my wife. Neither lip of me nor of mine comes after Mr. Murray of Broughton.' He sank into poverty, and sold his estate of Broughton in 1764. On the death of his half-brother, Charles, he became head of the family, and after the general Act of Reversal, assumed the title of Sir John Murray, Baronet, of Stanhope; and he died in 1777.

[2] Kenneth Mackenzie, eldest son of the fifth Earl of Seafield, who had been attainted for his share in the Rebellion of 1715. He was Member of Parliament for the burghs of Inverness, etc., in 1741, and for the county of Ross in 1747 and 1754; and displayed great zeal in support of the Government during the Rebellion of 1745. He married Lady Mary Stuart, eldest daughter of Alexander, sixth Earl of Galloway, and died in London in 1761.

[3] Fourteenth baron and seventh baronet of Sleat. He held aloof of the Rebellion of 1745, and aided the Government, though he had undertaken to join the Prince if he came to Scotland at the head of a French army. He and his second wife, Lady Margaret Montgomery, daughter of Alexander, ninth

that the Chevalier had set up his Standard not far from Fort William,[1] formerly called Innerlochy.[2] This was done about the middle of Agust, and immediately the clans went upon action.

Their first enterprise was the intercepting of about 100 souldiers belonging to the Regiment of Royal Scots, who were marching from Fort Augustus, at the head of Lochness, to Fort William. Some | of these souldiers were killed at a pass, *fol.* 205.
and some taken prisoners.[3] Their commanding officer was set at liberty on his parole of Honour, and upon his coming to Edin., and afterwards to London, all Britain was alarmed.

The king lost no time to provide against the impending storm, for he immediatly sent for 5000 Dutch troops, who landed in the north of England about the end of Agust, and some of them upon the first notice sent them. His Majesty was about this time in Hannover, but he quickly returned to England about the begining of September.

There were at that time in Scotland 2 Regiments of Irish dragoons and about 2500 regular Troops. One S^ir^ John Cope,[4]

Earl of Eglintoun, and a celebrated beauty, were distinguished for their hospitality, and were immensely popular in the Isles. Flora Macdonald resided in their house during the three years, from about 1739, that she spent in Edinburgh; and during her escape with the Prince, she visited Lady Margaret at her house of Monkstadt, her disguised companion taking shelter in the cave at Kilbride. He died 23d November 1746, and his funeral was attended by many thousands of the islanders, the procession, in which six men walked abreast, extending to a distance of two miles. Mackenzie's *History of the Macdonalds*, pp. 231-39; and see also Macgregor's *Life of Flora Macdonald*.

[1] In Glenfinnan, 'a narrow vale surrounded on both sides by lofty and craggy mountains, about twenty miles north from Fort William, and as far east from Borodale, forming, in fact, the outlet from Moidart into Lochaber.' The standard was unfurled by the Marquis of Tullibardine on the 19th of August. See Home's *Rebellion*, pp. 49 and 50.

[2] The old Inverlochy, formerly the seat of the Earls of Huntly, is two miles north-east of Fort-William; and the modern Inverlochy Castle, a seat of Baron Abinger, enlarged from a shooting-box in 1861, is three and a quarter miles north-east of Fort William. The town of Fort William was previously called Gordonsburgh, from its being built on the property of the Gordons.

[3] This occurred on the 16th of August, at the east end of Loch Lochy, three days previous to the raising of the Pretender's standard; the Government soldiers being two companies under the command of Captain (afterwards General) John Scott, who was wounded in the skirmish. They were overpowered by the Macdonalds; and Lochiel, who arrived at the conclusion of the skirmish, conveyed the prisoners to his house at Auchnacarie. See Home's *Rebellion*, pp. 46-48.

[4] Sir John Cope, K.B., was promoted in the army through the influence of

a little, dressy, finical man, had the command of them. He had already devoured the Rebels in his imagination, wherefor he wrote to Court for liberty to march immediatly into the Highlands to attaque them. Orders were accordingly given to him by the Ministry, but he had scarcely entered the Highlands when he found that he was mistaken in his schems, for that his little Army of foot was not sufficient to attaque the Rebels amongst the mountains, wherefor, to procure more assistence, he marched directly to Inverness, where Mr. Duncan Forbes of Culloden had got together some hundreds of men for the service of the Government. As this Gentleman, Mr. Forbes, was Lord President of the Session, Sir John Cope trusted to his power and authority, and never doubted but he should find in the Country about Inverness a sufficient number of men to his purpose, especially when a Regiment was to be levied there for Flanders.

While Sir John Cope was marching to Inverness, the Rebels took a Resolution of coming by the way of Blair in Athole directly to Edin. They were but half armed, being about 4000 in number, and by Letters from their Friends in Edin. *fol. 206.* they were assured | that the Town wou'd be surrendered to them, notwithstanding 5 or 600 volunteers who pretended to defend it. One provost Stuart,[1] a secret jacobite, was at the head of the Magistracy, but most of the Trades were more open and declared friends to the new intended Revolution. It is difficult to account for this change of temper, since most of them were presbiterians and Whigs in principles, but it seems a love to novelties, joined with a certain infatuation in their councils, was what most prevailed amongst them.

I believe this same spirit prevailed amongst many of our

Lord Strafford. In 1742 he was appointed one of the generals of the troops despatched to aid Maria Theresa, Queen of Hungary, and he was commander-in-chief in Scotland in 1745. A council of officers was appointed to inquire into his conduct during the Rebellion, but he was acquitted of all blame. In 1751 he was placed on the Staff in Ireland, and he died in 1760.

[1] Archibald Stuart, merchant, represented the city of Edinburgh in Parliament from 1741 to 1747. He was tried in 1727 for 'neglect of duty, misbehaviour in public office, and violation of the trust and duty of office' while Lord Provost of Edinburgh during the Rebellion, and 'after the longest trial recorded in the books of justiciary' (Arnot's *History of Edinburgh*, p. 222), was unanimously found not guilty. See an interesting volume of printed and MS. matter relating to the trial in the Signet Library, Edinburgh.

great folks in this Country, for there was little or no care taken to provide against the impending storm, no Lords Liutenants were appointed as in 1715, for by the contentions of two factions in Scotland, and even amongst the Ministry in England, it cou'd not be agreed who should be intrusted with Lieutenances, and therefor no body was named. The heads of the two factions were the Duke of Argyle and the Marquise of Twedale.

Under these disputes the Duke went to London, and with him the Duke of Athole[1] and several other persons of note and distinction, so that the country was entirely left to it self, for no doubt some of the ministry wanted that we in Scotland should worry one another, for their vanity and self-conceit was so great that they never thought that the Rebels dared to venture into the populous Country of England, where they had so few Friends and so many Ennemies. Thus the country people in the Southern and Western Shires of Scotland, many of whom wou'd have chosen to have died in defence of the Religion and Laws of their Country, were left to themselves, without Arms and without Leaders.

About the Time that the young Pretender was marching towards Edin. the Military state of the Country was this. S^ir John Cope had with him about 2500 men, there were in the Castle of Stirling about 100 men, and in its nighbourhood 2 Regiments of Dragoons, Hamilton's and Gardiner's. The Castle of Edin. had a Garrisone of about 200 men. In the Town of Edin. were about 100 men or under belonging to the Guard, and between 4 or 500 volunteers, all Gentlemen or Burgers. These last had begun to put themselves in Regular companies and to lairn their military Exercises. The Town Walls were good for nothing, but | were mounted with a few *fol.* 207.
cannon, and some barricads were made at the several ports, but all these preparations were a little too slow, for the young Pre-

[1] On the approach of the rebels 'the Duke of Athole fled from his castle at Blair, and it was immediatly occupied by Tullibardine [his elder brother, disinherited, by Act of Parliament, for his share in the Rebellion of 1715], who assumed the title of the head of the house,' and 'issued his commands to the feudatories and tenantry of the estates to rally round his banner.'—Hill Burton's *History of Scotland*, vol. viii. p. 442.

tender with his Highlanders, consisting chiefly of the clans in Lochaber, moved on and passed the Forth at the foord of the Freuis,[1] a little above Stirling.

As they advanced, the two Regiments of Dragoons were ordered to retire towards Edin., which they did and encamped near the Town, but so as to be frequently moved off for greater security to themselves, and by these means chiefly were intimidated and taught, as I think, to be notorious Cowards, for as the Highlanders were naturally affraied of Horse, they were sufficient to have put them all to the flight if they had keept their ground, but all our Military Councils were at that time infatuated. We were to be chastised for some time coming. About the time the Rebels had taken possession of Lithgow, these two Regiments, with the Town Guards of Edin., were ordered to advance to the Colt-bridge, about a mile west of the Town. I went and saw them there, the Dragoons placed on each side of the road. I was delighted to see their order, and never doubted but they wou'd prove sufficient to defend the Town. I spoke to severals of them, and found them, as I thought, very much resolved to stand their ground, but the Rebels no sooner came in sight than their officers commanded them off towards Musselburgh, where they went in pretty great hurry and confusion.[2]

At that time we had a very worthy man at the Head of our Military Affaires, one General Guest,[3] who in his time had been an Active, diligent Souldier, but being a Man of above 86 years of age he cou'd scarsely stir out of his room. In the Castle we

---

1 The Ford of Frew, a shallow part of the river formed by the efflux of the Boquhan Water, about eight miles above Stirling.

2 This retreat was afterwards styled *The Canter of Coltbrigg.*

3 Joshua Guest, born in 1660 in Yorkshire, commanded the party of dragoons who routed the fugitives at Perth, 21st January 1716. He was a commissioner to inquire into the Glasgow riots in 1725, and in 1745 he was sent from London to replace Preston as deputy-governor of Edinburgh Castle. According to Chambers, he proposed after the defeat of Prestonpans to surrender the castle, a proposal successfully opposed by Preston, who remained as a volunteer, and who, now in his eighty-seventh year, was wheeled round the guards every two hours during the hottest part of the blockade. According to other accounts, Guest refused a bribe of £200,000 to surrender the fortress, which 'he closed a service of sixty years by faithfully defending.' After the suppression of the Rebellion he returned to London in a horse-litter, and he died there 1747.

had another brave man of the same age, one General Preston,[1] so that the few Troops we had at Edin. were in a manner without heads or officers. The rebels were represented to be resolute and numerous, so that the Dragoons and other Troops we had were oblidged to shift for themselves, there was nothing to trust to in Edin. but the Castle, and that furnished no other defence for the Town than to oblidge the Rebels to march towards Bred's | craigs [2] to be without reach of the cannon. *fol.* 203.
There they incamped for a night, being then the 16 of September.

From their Camp, they sent a messenger to the Provost and Town Council of Edin. to surrender next morning, which, after some disputes, with no great tenaciousness, they agreed to, without any Terms at all. No promises or conditions were made in behalf of the Volunteers or Town Guard, so that every man did as he had a mind. The volunteers carried their arms to the Castle, whence they had got them, immediatly after they knew that the Town was to be given up, but the Town's Arms were, by connivance of the Lord Provost and Magistrats, to be left for the use of the Rebels.[3]

---

[1] Lieutenant-General George Preston, second son of Sir George Preston, first baronet of Valleyfield. He was a captain in the service of the States-General in 1688, and attended the Prince of Orange to England in that year. He served in all the wars of King William and Queen Anne, and was wounded at Ramillies. From 1706 to 1720 he was colonel of the Cameronian regiment; in 1715 he was sent from London as deputy-governor of the Castle of Edinburgh; and he was commander-in-chief of the forces in Scotland for several years after. He died 7th July 1748, in his eighty-ninth year.

[2] The Braid Hills.

[3] In reply to a deputation from the city the Prince had replied :—'. . . His Royal Highness supposes that, since the receipt of his letter to the Provost, no arms or ammunition have been suffered to be carried off or concealed, and will expect a particular account of all things of that nature. . . .' 'And much about the same time two of the officers of the voluntiers came to the council-chamber and insisted that the scheme of defending the town should be resumed. . . . To this the Lord Provost made several objections; but, at last, in appearance, yielded to the motion for defending the town, provided Gen. Guest would agree to let them have arms from the castle. This the General, when applied to, chearfully promised; and at the same time proposed that the city arms should be put into the hands of the well-affected. A wise proposal! for it had been a foolish measure from the beginning to call out and arm the trained bands, many of whom were well known to be professed Jacobites, and therefore very improper persons to be trusted with the defence of the city against the

Next morning by 5 a great body of the Highlanders entered the Nether Bow port and took possession of the Town Guard house, without opposition, and without offering any injury to those they found in the streets. As to the young Pretender, he and the bulk of his Savage Army marched about from Bred's craigs to the east side of Dudeston and the King's park, and took possession of the Abey of Holyroodhouse.

That same day the Pretender was proclaimed at the Cross of Edin. by Heralds and pursuivants in their formalities, which they had seised, and likeways on that day Sir John Cope, with the Troops he had carried to Inverness, landed at Dunbar. If

I and my family were at that time at Mavisbank, and my Wife being uneasy that I should continue in the nighbourhood of Edin., we, in company of my eldest daughter, left the house in the night time, lodged in a privat house within half a mile of my own house all night, and next day came in a coach to the Minister's[1] House of Mackerstone, near Kelso, for it hapned that both the Master and Mistress of the House had been long in my family.

Thus my Wife and I in our old Age came to be in exile,

---

pretender. When Gen. Guest's answer was reported to the council, the person who brought it was told, That as the person who had been sent to bring back the deputies had not come up with them, the Provost and Council, as they had entered upon a treaty, had come to a resolution not to defend the town.'—*The History of the Rise, Progress, and Extinction of the Rebellion*, second edition (London: R. Thomson, etc.), pp. 27-29. At the trial of Lord Provost Archibald Stuart, one of the charges was that, 'In the same evening of the sixteenth of September, One thousand seven hundred and forty-five, it was proposed and urged in Council, where the said Archibald Stuart was present, and presided, That the whole City Arms, being in Number about Twelve hundred Firelocks and Bayonets, should be lodged and secured within the Castle of Edinburgh, in order to prevent their falling into the Hands of the Rebels; but he, the said Archibald Stuart, refused or declined to give any order for their Purpose, neither in Fact were the City-arms so lodged and secured, but were seized by the Rebels upon their entring the City the Day following, who came to Edinburgh so imperfectly armed, that the Supply of Arms which they thus received appears to have been one principal Cause of the Disaster that befel our Forces near Prestonpans, on the twenty-first Day of the same month of September, One thousand seven hundred and forty-five.'—*Criminal Letters: His Majesty's Advocate for his Majesty's Interest against Archibald Stuart, late Provost of the City of Edinburgh*, p. 9.

[1] The Rev. William Walker, M.A., son of the minister of Kirkurd, was laureated by the University of Edinburgh in 1713, licensed 1720, and presented to the living of Makerston by John, Duke of Roxburgh, 1726. He was suspended by the Synod of Lothian and Tweeddale, *sine die*, 5th November 1741; and on 5th November 1744 they empowered the Presbytery of Peebles to take off the sentence if they saw cause. He died 1759, aged sixty-six; and his widow, Christian Fiddes, died in 1773.—Scott's *Fasti*.

which was often a melancholly reflexion to us both; however, we lived in hopes for some days that should soon return home, especially after we heard that S[ir] John Cope and the Troops under his command were come by sea from Aberdeen, and were landed at Dunbar. But these hopes soon vanished, for upon his approach to Preston pans, which was the third day after he landed, the Rebels being now well armed had the confidence to meet and fight him. The issue was that he | was shamefully beaten by the cowardice of the two Regiments of Dragons above mentioned, who run away without attempting any thing. About 800 [of] the King's Troops were cut to pieces or taken prisoners. The Dragons went off pretty entire, and never stoped till night that they got to the English borders, for one of them came that night to Cannall, where my Wife and I chanced to be, and the other to Coldstream, so that they made a march that day of above 35 miles. S[ir] John Cope, Lord Hume,[1] and some of their officers were with them, and next day they all retired to Berwick, as the only place in which they cou'd find safety for some time.

this had hapned 3 days sooner, the Town cou'd not have been taken by a handfull of Highlanders, who were not acquainted with the methods of taking towns, and even if the Town's people had been well inclin'd to preserve it, they might have disappointed the Rebels.

fol. 209.

This memorable route of the King's Troops was on the morning of the 21 of Sept. by day light. The Troops lay on their Arms all night, and the Rebels lurked about the dyks and ditches of Preston pans as if they had been to steal a drove of Cattle. Thus far I do believe that they had their Eyes mainly to the plunder they expected, for S[ir] John Cope and his Troops carried a vast deal of Baggage with them, being secure on their part of the victory. Few of our people behaved well in this Battle, except, perhaps, Colonel Gardiner,[2] who, en-

Battle of Preston, 1745.

---

[1] William, eighth Earl of Home, succeeded his father in 1720. After having served on the Continent, he joined Cope's army at Dunbar in Sept. 1745; and at the battle of Prestonpans endeavoured, unsuccessfully, to rally the dragoons. He commanded the Glasgow regiment which joined the royal forces at Stirling in December; in 1750 was appointed colonel of the 48th foot; and in 1752 of the 25th foot. In 1757 he became Governor of Gibraltar, where he died in 1761.

[2] Colonel James Gardiner, born 1688, served in a Scots regiment in Holland; and, entering the English army, was wounded at Ramillies. He greatly distinguished himself at the taking of Preston, 1715; and accompanied Lord Stair as aide-de-camp during his embassy in Paris. In 1743 he became colonel of a dragoon regiment; and he was slain at the battle of Prestonpans, fought beside his own house of Bankton, in 1745.

'The Colonel (Gardiner) was for a few moments supported by his men,

deavouring to stop his Regiment of Dragons, fell a sacrifice to the fury of the Rebels. His own house hapned to be within a quarter of a mile from the field of Battle, which the Rebels affected to call Gladsmoor,[1] to make it quadrat with a foolish old prophecy of Thomas the Rhymer,

'In Gladesmoor shall the Battle be;'

but Gladesmoor happens to be at least two miles from the field of Battle, which being just at the back of the Town of Preston cou'd in no time or age have been different from what it is at present, being one of the best fields in East Lothian for all kinds of Grain.

After I heard the melancholly news of the loss of the Battle I with my Wife and two of my Daughters went into England and lay by accident at Cannall,[2] when one of the Regiments of

fol. 210. Dragoons | came there as above.

---

and particularly by that worthy person lieutenant-colonel Whitney, who was shot through the arm here, and a few months after fell nobly in the battle of Falkirk; and by lieutenant West, a man of distinguished bravery; as also by about fifteen dragoons, who stood by him to the last. But after a faint fire, the regiment in general was seized with a panic, and though their colonel and some other gallant officers did what they could to rally them once or twice, they at last took to precipitate flight. And just as Colonel Gardiner seemed to be making a pause to deliberate what duty required him to do in such a circumstance . . . he saw a party of the foot who were bravely fighting near him, and whom he was ordered to support, had no officer to head them; upon which he said eagerly, in the hearing of the person from whom I had this account, "Those brave fellows would be cut to pieces for want of a commander," or words to that effect: which while he was speaking he rode up to them and cried aloud, "Fire on, my lads, and fear nothing." But just as the words were out of his mouth, a Highlander advanced towards him with a scythe fastened on a long pole, with which he gave him such a deep wound on his right arm that his sword dropped out of his hand; and at the same time several others coming about him while he was thus dreadfully entangled with that cruel weapon, he was dragged off his horse. The moment he fell, another Highlander, who, if the king's evidence at Carlisle may be credited, as I know not why they should not, though the unhappy creature died denying it, was one MacNought, who was executed about a year after, gave him a stroke, either with a broadsword or Lochaber axe, my informant could not exactly distinguish, on the hinder part of his head, which was the mortal blow. . . .'—See Doddridge's *Life of Gardiner*, where the account of the Colonel's death was carefully compiled from the narration of John Foster, his servant, confirmed by a corporal in Colonel Lascelles's regiment, who was also an eye-witness.

[1] The village of Gladsmuir is about four miles south-east of Prestonpans.

[2] Channelkirk in Berwickshire.

As many of their officers came to lodge under us in the same house, we thought Hell had broken louse, for I never heard such oaths and imprecations branding one another with Cowardice and neglect of duty. Here we left them next morning and proceeded directly to Morpeth, but night coming on within 2 miles of this place, we had a bad overturn in the coach, and my Wife was very ill bruised. Next morning, in the best way we cou'd, we crauled to the coach and got safely to Durham at night, by the way of Newcastle, which, on the news of the defeat of S[ir] John Cope, was in such a terrible consternation, that if the Rebels had followed their Blow I believe this important city had surrendered to them. Here at Durham, for the sake of good company, I took up my place of Exile, and continued there for above 6 weeks, only for diversion we made a Trip to Studley park in Yorkshire, near Rippon, and from thence to York. In this city we remained only a day and two nights, for we found the Roads were to be crowded with Troops under Marishal Wade,[1] designed to make head against the Rebels, and these Troops were already as far advanced as Ferry bridge and Wetherby. Lest therefor the crouded Roads should be quite spoiled, we made haste to get back to Durham, and staid there till the Highlanders were come south the length of Carlyle.

I must here observe in general that where I staid and traveled in England a most terrible pannick had possessed all the people to that degree that many rich people about Newcastle, Durham, and York, had sent off a great deal of their Effects to Holand and Hamburgh, and all their silver plate, jewels, money, and such like domestick necessaries were hid under ground, so that I had left England and returned to Scotland before these things appeared again. We did the same in Scotland, and I am affraied that many of us lost in that manner what will never be supplied.

While I staid at Durham I was daily acquainted with the

[1] Field-Marshal George Wade, born 1673, entered the army and became major-general in 1709. While commander-in-chief in Scotland, after the Rebellion of 1715, he constructed roads through the Highlands and a bridge over the Tay. He became field-marshal in 1743, and from 1745 to 1747 was commander-in-chief of the British army. He represented Hindon and after wards Bath in Parliament. Died 1748, and was buried in Westminster.

Transactions at Edin. The Highlanders were with difficulty keept in order, and in the Country many Robries were committed. They imposed contributions on the Town of Edin. to the extent of about 6000 ℔. ster., and uplifted the Cess wherever any was due. On privat Gentlemen they imposed contri-
fol. 211. butions of Hay | and Corns to a considerable valou. My impositions were 6000 stone of Hay and 76 bolls of oats, under pains of military Execution, which was understood to be the quartering of some Savage Highlanders upon us. As this denounciation frighted all our servants and Tenants, the contributions were readily paid, and the valou of my share in all amounted to about 200 ℔. ster. But besides these impositions they quartered themselves frequently upon us and our Tenants, so that the Family I left at Pennicuik was oblidged to entertain some of their Chiefs three several times, and frequently 16 or 20 at a time.

The Family I had then at Pennicuik consisted of my
1745. Daughter Babe,[1] and two young Ladies, Mrs. Holborn and Miss Brown, a grandson, a chaplain, Gentlewoman Stuart, and cook, with several servants. All my horses of any valou were carried off to England.

When the Highland parties came they were civilly used, and so committed no disorders about the House except that they eated and drank all they cou'd find, and called for everything as they thought fit, for they lookt on them selves to be the Masters of all the Country.

They continued for 3 weeks in and about Edin., and were so foolish as to think they cou'd take the Castle, 'tho they saw that besides the provisions laid up in it for a siege of 3 or 4 Months, they had every day fresh provisions brought to them. To prevent this, they made a sort of Blocade by puting Garrisons in some little houses between the West port and West Kirk, but this produced a threatning letter from the Governours of the Castle to the Inhabitants of the Town that if they did not procure the favour from the young Pretender to get the Blocade removed, these Governours wou'd order Bombs and hot bullets to be fired upon the Town. A limited day

[1] Barbara, the baron's sixth daughter. See page 120.

was given to this military Execution, and in the mean time the
Magistrates sent a petition to the King to beg that the
Governours of the Castle might be discharged to fire on the
Town. | To this there was an Answere sent that these Gover- *fol. 212.*
nours must do their best to preserve the Castle whatever the
consequence was. On hearing of this message the young Pretender, to shew his regard and compassion to the good Town, ordered the Blocade to be laid aside, and gave liberty to the importation of provisions as formerly,[1] yet this was not done so fully as was wanted, for still Highland guards, and particularly one at Livingston's[2] yards on the south side of the Castle was[*sic*] keept for some days by one Taylor,[3] a Shoemaker, who did a world of mischief till he was beaten and taken by a small party from the Castle. The Governour of the Castle of Edin. was at that time one Lord Mark Ker, unckle to the Marquise of Lothian,[4] but as he was absent in England the command fell on the Daputy-Governour, Brigadier General Preston, who was assisted by General Guest, both above mentioned.

At last the Rebels having recruited their Army with supplies from the North and provided for themselves a sufficient number of Arms, particularly new Targets, and having got together a great many Horses for their Cavalry and bagage, marched from

---

[1] The Prince did not issue this proclamation till after the cannonade from the Castle had begun on the afternoon of the 4th of October, and the garrison, after dark, had made a sally, setting fire to houses near the Castle, and constructing a trench between the fortress and the upper end of the Castle Hill, whence they fired down the street, killing and wounding some of the rebels and inhabitants.—Home's *Rebellion*, p. 126 (1802). Compare Chambers's *Rebellion*, pp. 158-60 (last, undated, edition).

[2] Livingston Yards lay to the west of the West Port of Edinburgh.

[3] This little incident of Taylor, the shoemaker, seems to have escaped the notice of Chambers, Home, Arnott, and other historians of the Rebellion. A 'James Taylor, Shoemaker,' from Newmills of Boyn is included, as having 'carried Arms as a private man,' and as being at the time in hiding, in the List of Rebels furnished by the Supervision of Excise at Banff. See *Lists of Persons concerned in the Rebellion*. (Scot. Hist. Society. 1890.)

[4] Fourth son of Robert, fourth Earl of Lothian, born 1676. Entering the army, he was wounded at Almanza, 1707; acted as brigadier-general at the capture of Vigo; commanded the 29th regiment of foot, 1712; the 13th foot, 1725; and the 11th dragoons, 1732-52. He was appointed governor of Edinburgh Castle, 30th July 1745, and died 1752. Of a punctilious disposition, he was noted for his success as a duellist.

Edin. on the[1] of[1] into England by the way of Carlyle. Their Army was divided in 3 bodies, one marched by the way of Kelso, one by Peebles, and one by Moffat. But at first no body knew whether they were to attaque the Army under Marishal Wade, then lying in the moor of Newcastle, or to march directly to Carlyle. This last route was what they chiefly intended, and at last, after some consultations, they took possession of Carlyle, with as little difficulty as they had taken possession of Edinburgh. But without insisting on the particulars that hapned at Carlyle, I shall only observe that it was very lucky for Scotland that the Rebels marched into England and found so little opposition there, for if this had not hapned, all Scotsmen wou'd have been reproached either with Cowardice or disaffection to the Government, for before the Highlanders entered England there was nothing heard in that country but the mighty things their very Militia wou'd do against the Rebels, 'tho by the bye it appeared very evident to me that 100 Highlanders wou'd have routed 1000 of their Militia. |

fol. 213. My only hopes, next to the assistence of almighty God, depended entirely on the Troops which his Majesty had sent for from Flanders, together with about 4 or 5000 Dutch and Swiss who landed near Newcastle. These in all might amount to above 30,000 men, and every day made new additions to their numbers, for the Dukes of Kingstone,[2] Bedford,[3] and others had raised no less than 13 Regiments of Horse and foot.

I observed while I staid in England a very great and unexpected alacrity amongst all degrees of people for defending our happy constitution, and 'tho but lately great pains were

---

[1] There are blanks here in the MS. The Highlanders left Edinburgh on the 1st and the 3d of October. See Chambers's *Rebellion*.

[2] Evelyn Pierrepont, born 1711; succeeded his grandfather as second Duke of Kingston 1726; invested a K.G., 1741; in 1745 raised 'Kingston's' regiment of light horse, of which he was colonel; died 1773. Walpole styles him 'a very weak man, of the greatest beauty and finest person in England.'

[3] John Russell, fourth Duke of Bedford, was born in 1710, and succeeded to the title in 1732. He became First Lord of the Admiralty in 1744; raised for the royal service a regiment of foot, of which he was appointed colonel in 1745; was Secretary of State for the Southern Department 1748-51; in 1762 was Plenipotentiary to France; and Lord-Lieutenant of Ireland 1756-61. He died in 1771.

used to reproach the Hannoverians and render them despicable in the eyes of the people of England, yet now things took another turn, especially since the last year's Battle at Fontenoy, for at that time the Hannoverians behaved so well that many of the English souldiers protested to me that they were willing to divide a Loaf with them. Thus matters stood at the begining of the Rebellion; however, the King thought fit rather to ask assistence from the Dutch than bring over any of his Hannoverians.

I noticed before that Marishal Wade with a great body of Troops was come the length of York and Wetherby. These consisted of about 10,000 Horse and foot. The Horse being 3 Regiments were quartered at Durham, and as their officers were mostly very brave deserving Men, I was constantly with them, till they were called off to attend Marishal Wade on his camp on the moor of Newcastle. It was then very bad weather, being in the month of November, and many of the souldiers indured great hardships by cold and fatigue; however, as the Rebels were then laying their schems for taking Carlyle there was a necessity for the Marishal to march to Hexam in his way to engage them, but bad weather and bad ways prevented his endeavours, for the Rebels marched south towards London, and the Marishal with his fatigued Troops was oblidged to return to Newcastle.

Then it was that I and my Family left Durham to return to Edin. We got to Newcastle before the souldiers under the Marishall returned, and next day in frost and snow through monstruous bad ways we set northwards, and by slow journies got to Berwick | and from thence back to Edin. where we found *fol. 214.*
things much in the same condition we left them, only that our friends were much divided in their principles, as to their Loyalty to King George and Jacobitism. I perceived plainly that all the poor shortsighted wrong-headed folks were jacobites, for they made no question but the Highlanders wou'd be able to beat the Troops in England, and had nothing to do but to take possession of London with all the ease imaginable. However, in a little time they found themselves vastly disappointed when they heard that after the Rebels had got the length of Derby they were so frighted for the Duke of Cumberland, his

majesty's second son, and the troops under his command, that they marched back to Scotland in a very great hurry, and got to Drumfrise where they halted for a day. The Duke had with him about 10,000 men in all, Horse and foot, which was indeed a force which the Rebels cou'd never pretend to resist, but after they began their retreat into Scotland the Duke made no difficulty to pursue them with about 4 or 500 Horse.[1]

I may here notice with regard to my privat family that the eldest son James on hearing that the Rebellion was begun left Holand and came to London. There he got recommendatory Letters to some of the officers of the Army, and marched to joyn the King's Troops as a Volunteer. I commended his zeal, but since he had not been bred in a military way I dissuaded him from the service, but rather to go home to Scotland and do what service he cou'd amongst the country people. He took my advice and left me at Durham. In the mean time, George, my second son, joined himself to a body of Yorkshire Gentlemen who went under the name of the Royal Hunters. These came to General Wade at Newcastle, and by his orders were sent on several exploits to recognoitre the Rebels. When the Marishal marched south to joine the Duke of Cumberland they went with him, and when the Highlanders were on their retreat to Scotland they left the Marishal and joined the Duke in his pursuit of the Rebels to Carlyle, and in taking that place.

No sooner we heard at Edin. that the Rebels were returning
fol. 213. than we gave up the Town for lost and | many of us were preparing to fly into England, for we never doubted but the Rebels wou'd return directly and take possession of their former quarters. We continued for some time in suspence, and at last heard that they had returned by Dumfrise and Drumlanrick to Glasgow, where they continued for some weeks[2] raising contributions and greatly oppressing the people.

---

[1] The Duke left London on the 24th of November, and superseded Sir John Ligonier in the command of the army of 10,000 men, chiefly veteran and experienced, that had been mustered in Staffordshire. He pursued the retreating Highlanders from Preston with a force of 3000 or 4000 horse. Having captured Carlisle he returned to London, to be ready to repel an expected invasion from France. See Chambers's *Rebellion*.

[2] The rebels entered Glasgow on the 25th and 26th December, and left on the 3d of January.—See Chambers's *Rebellion*, pp. 209 and 212.

About this time our fears at Edin. came to wear off by degrees, for about 13 Regiments of foot came to Edin., being part of the army which had been under the command of Marishal Wade, and the Generals Haley[1] and Husk[2] were sent to command them. The Duke of Cumberland, after the recovery of Carlyle from the Rebels, had returned back to London. About this time another affliction hapned in my family, for my Wife, my son John,[3] and daughter Joanna[4] fell ill of a feaver. They were long ill, and had several relapses, but it pleased God to recover them.

I my self was likeways seised with a cholera morbus flux and vomiting. I fainted, and was very ill for two days, but I got the better of my distemper by nature and the advice of my cousin, Doctor Clerk,[5] who had been likeways very assisting to the rest of the Invalides of my Family. January 1746.

I was very sensible that I had brought my distemper upon *N.B.*—besides fears and

[1] Lieutenant-General Henry Hawley, said to have been born about 1679, a grandson of the first Lord Hawley. He commanded the left wing of the royal army at Sheriffmuir, and was second in command of the horse at Dettingen and at Fontenoy. He was appointed to the command of the army, in the absence of the Duke of Cumberland. On the morning of the battle of Falkirk he breakfasted with the Jacobite Countess of Kilmarnock at Callander House; and first his negligence, and then his precipitate orders, contributed materially towards the disgraceful issue of the day. After the battle of Culloden he was most remorseless in his severities against the rebels. He afterwards accompanied the Duke to Flanders, in command of the cavalry, and in 1752 became Governor of Portsmouth. He died in 1759.

[2] General John Huske was born about 1692, and in 1708 was appointed ensign in Caulfield's regiment. He was present as a brigadier at Dettingen, where he 'behaved gloriously,' and was severely wounded. He commanded the five regiments and the dragoons and militia who, on the 13th of January 1746, left Edinburgh for Linlithgow; and, with Brigadier Cholmondeley, he commanded the right of the royal army at the battle of Falkirk, whose force checked the pursuing Highlanders and saved the English army from destruction. At Culloden he commanded Fleming's regiment, the 35th, and greatly distinguished himself. After serving in Flanders and Minorca, he became full general in 1756. He was appointed governor of Sheerness in 1745, and of Jersey in 1760, and died in 1761.

[3] See note [2], page 115, and note [3], page 135.

[4] The Baron's fifth daughter. See page 116.

[5] Dr. John Clerk, 'the most celebrated physician that has appeared in Scotland since Dr. Pitcairn, whom he is said to have resembled in sagacity and intuition.' Eldest son of Dr. Robert Clerk. See note [1], page 11; also Ramsay of Ochtertyre's *Scotland and Scotsmen*, vol. i. pp. 234-235.

Anxieties, the minds of my Wife and me were greatly sunk and overwhelmed by daily reflexions we had on the loss of our son Hary, and which brought us at the same time in remembrance of our son Patrick. In these two lads few family losses were equal with ours. Lord sustain us. They brought, particularly on me, a swiming; and pain in my head, which I never intend to complain of, nor no ailement, if but tollerable.

me by a large quantity of Green Kail which I chanced to eat at Dinner, nor is this the first time that I have felt the bad effects of Green Kail, for in cold, rainy Winters they are always unwholesome, and at this very time they brought an Epidemical flux upon many of the country people. From thence we may be instructed that there are few deseases that affect us but what enter our bodies by the mouth. Still some piece of Intemperance or other affects us especially at such times as this was, when our minds were filled with fears and Anxieties, as I believe every body's was during the time of the Rebellion, those of the Rebel party, in case they and their friends did not succeed in their Enterprise, and the Friends of the Government least the Rebels should succeed, for inevitable ruine hung over the one party or the other.

But to return to the military operations in Scotland, as soon as our Generals had the Troops in any tollerable condition | *fol.* 216. they marched to attaque the Rebels between Stirling and Falkirk. All men's Expectations were intent upon the Event, and the Generals were so secure of the victory that when they came in sight of the Highland Army, they contemned them so much that with all the calmness in the world they went to dinner, and at last suffered themselves to be attaqued, whereas they ought to have marched forward to meet the Rebels.

The neglect of this motion brought the Battle on much later in the afternoon than it ought to have been, and the consequence of this was fatal to our Troops, for there hapned such a storm, or rather, hurrycane of Wind and rain, that their Firearms were rendered useless, whereas the Highlanders relied most on their swords. But what was worst of all, a pannick got so much possession of the Souldiers, that some of them ran off without firing one shot at them, and left their officers exposed to the fury of the Rebels. Sir Robert Monro[1] and some other brave men fell a sacrifice here, but more to the

Sir R. Monro of Foules.

[1] Sir Robert Munro, sixth baronet of Foulis, rendered important service to the government in 1715, in delaying the rising of the clans Mackenzie and Macdonald till Argyll had collected a sufficient force to oppose them. In 1740 he became lieutenant-colonel of the Highland regiment commanded by the Earl of Crawford, which distinguished itself in Germany and Flanders; and he was slain by the Highlanders at the battle of Falkirk 1745.

cowardice of our own Troops than the bravery of the Rebels, for it is certain that the generality of them had no mind to fight at all. This appeared by what hapned to the right wing of our Army, for it was never attaqued; on the contrary, the Rebels marched to attaque the left of our Army, and very little wou'd have put them in confusion. We had two or three Regiments of Dragoons, not indeed compleat, on our left, and those, to regain their honour which they had lost at the Battle of Preston, attaqued the right of the Rebel Army with great bravery. Many of them were killed and put to the flight, which, when the Infantry on that side of our Army observed, they took to their heels, and whole Regiments ran off without firing or receiving a fire from the Ennemy. Thus our brave Army of Regular Troops which amounted to about 8000 men, and who had behaved well in Flanders, fled before an Army of no greater force than their own, to the shame and disgrace of all military discipline. Our Generals perceived this with great grief of heart, as may be supposed, and finding it impossible to raly their men, they took the Resolution to march that night back to Lithgou, which they did in good order, but left their Tents and most of their baggage, with 8 pieces of Cannon in the hands of the Rebels. | In the mean-time, it was very remarkable that tho the Rebels had gained the Battle they did not perceive it at first, for their loss was so small that they took it for some strategem of war that our Troops were retired. They were, as they thought, to be drawn into an Ambuscade, wherefor it was more than an houer before they wou'd venture to return to the field of Battle, but at last, understanding by their spies that our Army was retiring to Lithgou, they took Courage, and took possession of all the Tents and Baggage, and lay in and about Falkirk that night this unhappy Action hapned on.

N.B.—There were thousands of onlookers who did great harm, for as they came not there to fight, they ran off amongst the first, and came directly to Edin. However, my son James, who was there, continued till our Army retired.

fol. 217.

This Action at Falkirk was very oddly manadged on both sides, for the half of the Highland Army had fled away at the same time that ours had left the field of Battle.

In the mean time, by a singular Fortune, this unhappy Event turned out much to our advantage and the ruine of the Rebel Army, for it dreu down his Highness the Duke of Cumberland into Scotland, who absolutely restored the courage of our souldiery. He came to Edin. on [1] of 1745.

[1] There is a blank here in the MS. The Duke arrived in Edinburgh early in the morning of the 30th of January 1746.—Chambers's *Rebellion*, p. 247.

Nov^{r}., and after puting things in some order, which he did with that dispatch as to be finished in a day, he marched to Lithgou, and next morning to Falkirk to attaque the Rebels. They were confounded at the news of the Duke's arrival in Edin., but to that degree when they heard that he was come to Lithgou, that early next morning they resolved to abandon all their conquests in the south and retire northwards, where they expected to be joined by some French Troops and by a body of about 3000 men which L^{d}. Louis Gordon,[1] Brother to the Duke of Gordon, had got togither, for the service of the young pretender. In a word, they passed the Forth above Stirling, and in 3 bodies marched northward, one by the Blair of Athole, one by Dunkel and Brichen, and one by Perth and Dundee.

After the Battle of Falkirk the Castle of Stirling was closely besieged by the Rebels, supported by some French, who, with a few battering pieces, landed at Montrose. The Rebels and their Friends in Edin. placed great hopes on the success of this enterprise, for as all things were easy in their Imaginations, they never doubted but that Castle wou'd fall
fol. 218. into their hands in a feu days, after their | Trenches were opened, but they found themselves vastly disappointed, for the Governour of the Castle, General Blakeney,[2] and his Garisone, made so good a defence that the Cannon of the besiegers were dismounted, and most of the French Engeneers destroied before the Duke of Cumberland came the length of Falkirk.

The Highlanders in their retreat did one very brutal action, for they blew up their powder Magazine in the Kirk of St. Ninians near Stirling, and with it designed to have destroied

[1] Lord Lewis Gordon, third son of Alexander, second Duke of Gordon, was a lieutenant in the navy; but in the rebellion of 1745 he raised a regiment of two battalions for the Pretender, and defeated the royalists, under the Laird of Macleod, near Inverurie, 23d December. After Culloden he escaped abroad; was attainted; and died, unmarried, at Montreuil, in 1754.

[2] General William Blakeney, born 1672. Though he distinguished himself in Marlborough's campaigns, he was not promoted colonel till 1737. In 1745 he defended Stirling Castle, as mentioned above, and defeated the Highlanders by a sudden attack; and in 1756, at the age of eighty-four, he signalised himself by his gallant defence of Minorca. He died in 1761, and was buried in Westminster.

many innocent people. Some perished, but most part of those near the Kirk escaped.[1]

The Duke was received in Stirling with great joy, and next day the Dutchess of Perth[2] and some Ladies taken in that nighbourhood were sent prisoners to the Castle of Edin. This action was esteemed a little uncourtly for a young man like the Duke of Cumberland, but there was a necessity for this piece of severity, that women might understand that they might be punished for Treasone as well as others.

After this the Duke followed his blow and marched all his troops to Perth, which the Rebels abandon'd.

In this Town the Duke thought fit to refresh his Army, and in the meantime took care to provide them with money, Forrage, and all kinds of provisions in great plenty.

At this instant of time the prince of Hess,[3] Son in Law to our King, landed at Lieth, and with him 4800 foot and about 80 Hussars. We did not at that time want them, since the Duke had put the Rebels to flight, but as they were already on British pay it was thought proper to employ them in Scotland and spend their pay where they had it. The prince of Hess was received at the Abey of Holyroodhouse with all the marks of respect and esteem that were in our pouer. All those who had been in the Magistracy of Edin., all the Ministers in the Presbitry of Edin., all the heads of Colleges, and all Gentlemen of any fashion or account in the shire,

[1] 'In the hurry of the occasion, the powder belonging to the army, amounting to fifty barrels, was blown up in the church of St. Ninian's, killing ten country-people and also some of the Highlanders, besides endangering the person of the Prince and some other persons of note who were passing through the village at the time. It is not certain whether an order had been given to destroy this powder; but certainly its explosion at that particular moment must have been accidental, when the preceding circumstances are considered. . . . The Whig party papers represented the St. Ninian's accident in a light unfavourable to the Prince, alleging that he had ordered the explosion for the purpose of destroying the church and killing unoffending villagers. So ridiculous a charge is not worthy of notice.'—Chambers's *Rebellion*, p. 254.

[2] Lady Jean Gordon, daughter of George, first Duke of Gordon, and widow of James, second (titular) Duke of Perth. She was committed prisoner to Edinburgh Castle, 11th February 1746; liberated on bail, 17th November following; and died at Stobhall in 1773.

[3] Frederick, Landgrave of Hesse Cassel. He married the Princess Mary, fourth daughter of George II., in 1740.

waited on him. I was introduced to kiss his hands by the Earl of Crauford,[1] who had attended him over, and I was with his highness several times after this. I found him to be a Comely young Man of about 25 years of Age, of a middle stature, and of great benevolence and humanity. He behaved exceedingly well towards everybody, and went to our Musick
fol. 219. meetings and balls wherever he chanced to be invited. | He had not been at the Abey above two days, when the Duke of Cumberland, his brother in Law, waited on him from Perth, and staid with him for a day and two nights. I suppose they concerted togither their operations, and the result was that the Hessians were quartered in Edin., Leith, Musslebrugh, and Dalkieth, where they continued for several weeks, and behaved always well in their Quarters. They seemed all to be pickt Men, for I never saw a body of handsomer Men in my Life, most of them, if not all, were at least 5 feet 8 inches high, and very many above 6 feet, and of a very cleanly make.[2]

After the Duke of Cumberland had refreshed the Army and prepared all kinds of provisions necessary, he marched from Perth to Aberdeen, which the Rebels abandoned on his approach.

His highness continued in that place for several weeks as in a Winter quarter, but about the 1 of Aprile[3] he began his march to Inverness, where the Rebels keept their head quarters.

While the Rebels continued at Inverness they took Fort Augustus, formerly called Killichimy,[4] at the head of Lochness,

---

[1] John, eighteenth Earl of Crawford, succeeded his father in 1713. After the battle of Fontenoy he accompanied the Landgrave of Hesse Cassel from Antwerp, and took part in the operations against the rebels. Died 1749.

[2] These troops seem to have made an especially good impression on the Scots generally. See note in Chambers's *Rebellion*, p. 259.

[3] 'The Duke of Cumberland remained from 25th of February till the 8th of April in Aberdeen.'—Chambers's *Rebellion*, p. 275.

[4] The Rev. Father Hunter Blair, of St. Benedict's Abbey, Fort Augustus, informs me that Kilquhunan or Kilichuiman, 'the burial ground of the Cummins,' is the name still in use for Fort Augustus by the native Gaelic-speaking population of the district. The name 'Kilchuinan' appears in the original drawings made by Pont in his survey of Scotland, about 1608, and in the map of Inverness-shire, in Blaeu's *Atlas*, published at Amsterdam in 1662, for which these drawings were used.

and they laid siege to Fort William by the help of their French cannon, mortars, cohorns, and Engeneers. They never doubted of success, but the Garisone made such a resistence that in the end the Rebels were oblidged to abandon their enterprise. With the same bad success they laid siege to the Castle of Blair, which they battered for some days, but the Garrisone there, calling two Regiments of Hessians to their assistence, who, with the prince of Hess, had lately come to Perth, they no sooner appeared than the party who besieged that place under Ld. George Murry[1] retired towards Rivan in Badenoch.[2]

The Rebels in appearance had some better success at Dingwall, for a party under the Earl of Cromarty[3] passed the Murry frith in the night time, and oblidged the Earl of Loudon,[4] Duncan Forbes of Culloden, Prece|dent of Session, *fol.* 220.
with about 1500 men under his command, to disband and retire to their several habitations from whence they had come. Those of Sutherland and Strathneven retired towards Caithness, and the Earl of Loudon and the Precedent with Sir Alexdr

[1] Lord George Murray, fifth son of John, first Duke of Atholl, was wounded in the battle of Glenshiel in 1719, and, after making his escape, entered the Sardinian service. Receiving a pardon, he returned to Britain; but, engaging in the Rebellion of 1745, he acted as lieutenant-general of the rebel force. After Culloden he escaped to France, and then to Rome, where he was well received by the Prince. He died at Medemblik in Holland, in 1760. His son became third Duke of Atholl in 1764.

[2] 'Ruthven Barracks crowned a conical mound, the site of a castle of the Comyns, Lords of Badenoch, 1½ miles S. by E. of the village (Kingussie), on the opposite side of the Spey.'—*Ordnance Gazetteer of Scotland*, Article 'Kingussie.'

[3] George, third Earl of Cromarty, succeeded his father in 1731. Engaging in the Rebellion of 1745, he raised about 400 of his clan, and was present at the battle of Falkirk. On 15th April 1746, along with his son Lord Macleod, he was surprised and captured at Dunrobin by a party of the Duke of Sutherland's militia, and sent to London. He was condemned to death, but was pardoned in 1749, and died 1766.

[4] James, fourth Earl of Loudon, born 1705, succeeded his father in 1731. In the Rebellion of 1745 he raised a regiment of Highlanders, of which he was appointed colonel, and exerted himself greatly in the royal interest. In 1756 he was constituted general and commander-in-chief in America; but he was recalled by Pitt. He was second in command of the British troops sent to Portugal in 1762; and colonel of the 3rd regiment of foot-guards from 1770 till his death in 1782.

Macdonald and Lord Fortrose or Seaforth, as he was sometimes called, retired to the Island of Sky.

But this good success did not long attend the Rebels, for the L[d] Cromarty and his son[1] were shamefully beaten and taken prisoners by the sons of Lord Rae,[2] who a little before had taken a sloop from France with about 12,000 lib. ster. in it. This sloop belonged at first to his majesty King George, and was called the Hasard sloop. She was taken by the Rebels in the River of Montrose, and was afterwards called the Prince Charles. She had been a voyage into France with some messages from the Rebels, and, as I mentioned before, was returned with money at the time she was forced on shore by a ship of our Fleet. The loss of this little ship of war entirely disconcerted the measures of the Rebels, for having no money they were oblidged to stand the chance of a Battle with the Duke of Cumberland on the moor of Colloden, where they were severly chastised, 'tho they were in numbers superior to the Duke. The Battle was fought on the 10 of Aprile,[3] after his Highness had marched that morning from Nairn, at the distance of about 10 miles. They lost in the Battle and in the pursuit between 3000 and 4000 men,[4] with all their Cannon and Bagage. They were very regularly drauen up,

---

[1] John, Lord Macleod, son of George, third Earl of Cromarty, born 1727, was in 1748 pardoned for his share in the Rebellion. He entered the service of the King of Sweden, by whom he was created Count of Cromarty. Returning to Britain in 1777, he raised two Highland battalions, and became colonel of the 71st regiment; and, after a distinguished career, he died in 1781.

[2] Donald Mackay succeeded his father in 1748, as fourth Lord Reay, and died in 1761. His half-brother, the Hon. Colonel Hugh Mackay of Bighouse, died in 1770.

[3] The battle was fought on the 16th of April.

[4] 'The number of Highlanders slain upon the field of Culloden was never well ascertained, but it could not be much less than a thousand.'—Chambers's *Rebellion*, p. 310. 'The newspapers and magazines published at that time make the number amount to 2000 or 3000. Other accounts make the number to be less than 1000.'—Home's *Rebellion*, p. 238. 'Charles's army before Falkirk was at least 9000, and at Culloden perhaps not less than 8000. In that curious little book, *The Letters of a Volunteer with Cumberland's Army*, the author, on hearsay evidence, estimates the Jacobite loss at Culloden at 2000 killed, besides 222 French and 326 prisoners. . . . Lord President Forbes says they were supposed to have 8000 men at Culloden, "of whom one-half are probably destroyed or in custody." The Duke of Argyll, in an article published in 1883, alludes to a manuscript in the British Museum which states that the greatest number of men

and were in number between eght and nine thousand, including about 500 French or Irish whom the King of France had at different times sent from Ostend and Dunkirk to their assistence.[1] The Duke's loss did not exceed 250 killed and wounded.[2] The right of the first line of the Rebels behaved well, for they broke in upon Barrels Regiment,[3] and had cut it in pieces if it had not been supported by a Regiment which belonged to our second line, and was immediatly behind them.[4] However, they behaved, | in general, very ill, for the whole left wing of their first line, and all their second line, and their Corps de reserve with which was the young pretender, ran away without firing a shot. The whole action did not last for above 36 minuts, and the Rebels never attempted to raly again, but fled every way, and the far greatest number of their Army were taken prisoners, so that in a week or two after, all the prisons in Scotland were crouded with them. The young pretender, Lord Elcho,[5] Lord George Murry, Ld John Drummond,[6] and Lord Louis Gordon, Mr. Murry, the pretender's secretary, and many others retired to the Hills, in hopes of finding a vessel in the

Battle of Colloden.

fol. 221.

N.B.—Some of them [wen]t off in a ship [to] Berghen

in arms against the Government did not exceed 11,000. This points to a higher estimate than any that I had seen.'—The Earl of Rosebery's Preface to *A List of Persons concerned in the Rebellion* (Scottish History Society, 1890).

[1] Chambers estimates the rebel forces as about 5000 men (p. 285); see also note in Home's *Rebellion*, p. 228.

[2] 'A list of the killed and wounded (on the royal side), published by authority, makes the number amount to 310, officers included. Four officers were killed, fourteen were wounded.—Home's *Rebellion*, p. 237.

[3] Barrel or Burrel's grenadiers, now the 4th. It was in this regiment that Lord Robert Ker, second son of the Marquis of Lothian, and the most distinguished royalist who fell at Culloden, was a captain.

[4] See Home's *Rebellion*, pp. 232-33.

[5] David, Lord Elcho, eldest son of James, fourth Earl of Wemyss. He was born in 1721; engaging in the Rebellion of 1745, he was colonel of the first troop of the Pretender's life-guards; after Culloden he escaped to France, and was attainted. His next brother, Francis, succeeded as fifth Earl, on his death at Paris in 1787.

[6] John, second son of James, Lord Drummond, second (titular) Duke of Perth, was educated at Douay, and entered the service of the King of France, raising the regiment of Royal Scots, with whom, and other troops, he landed at Montrose, under the style of 'commander-in-chief of his most Christian Majesty's forces in Scotland,' and joined the Pretender on his return from England. After Culloden he escaped to France, and served with distinction, under Marshal Saxe, in Flanders, dying at Bergen-op-Zoom in 1747.

in Norway, but were there taken [by] order of the King of Denmark.[1] West coasts that might transport them to France. But the Marquise of Tullibarden,[2] the Earl of Cromarty and his son, the Earl of Kilmarnock, with several Knights and Gentlemen of the Rebel Army, were taken prisoners. The Duke marched that night into Inverness, and a few days afterwards the Earl of Loudon and the Ld Precedent returned from the Isle of Sky to his Highness.

The success of this Battle gave universal joy, especially to the friends of the Government, but there were even Jacobites who were at least content at what had hapned, for peace and quietness began now to break in, whereas Anxiety and distress of various kinds had possessed the breasts of most people ever since the Rebellion broke out. All Trade and business in this Country were quite at a stand; for my part, 'tho I never lost hopes of seing a speedy end put to our trubles, and possessed as much tranquillity of mind as I cou'd wish for, yet because I neither eated nor sleept so much as before the Rebellion broke out, I found my flesh sensibly decay, and I know not but there might be the same proportionable decay in the spirits, being now 70 years of Age on the 8 of feb. last. |

fol. 222. Thus our publick affaires stood on the 22 of May 1746, and my privat affaires as above, being now at Pennycuik house

---

1 'A party, in which were included Lord Ogilvie, Mr. Hunter of Burnside, Mr. Fletcher of Benshie, David Graham of Duntroon, and David Fotheringham, who had been governor of Dundee for Prince Charles, got on board a vessel riding off the Lights of Tay, and reached Norway in safety. The British Government had enjoined all friendly Powers to aid in apprehending the unfortunate adherents of the Prince. The King of Denmark had consequently ordered all vessels landing in his ports to be examined, and all persons not possessing passports to be apprehended. These gentlemen were accordingly seized and put into prison in the castle of Bergen, but were soon after allowed to make their escape to France. It may be added that Mr. Hunter was one of the five exiles whom Smollett describes in such touching terms in his novel of *Peregrine Pickle* as living at Boulogne, and going every day to the seaside in order to indulge their longing eyes with a prospect of the white cliffs of Albion, which they must never approach.'—Chambers's *Rebellion*, p. 323.

2 William, Marquis of Tullibardine, second son of John, first Duke of Atholl, was one of the first who joined the Earl of Mar and proclaimed the Pretender in 1715. He returned to Scotland in 1719, and fought at the battle of Glenshiel. In 1745 he accompanied Prince Charles to Scotland, and unfurled his standard at Glenfinnan. After Culloden, he surrendered himself, and died in the Tower of London in 1746.

with my Eldest son to put such papers and other things in order which the Rebellion had throwen into the greatest confusion, for most of my Effects were either hiden under ground or put in such secret places as gave me considerable thought and truble to set right again. But I go back to the time I left my Exile in England in novemb^r last.

On my return to Edin., my Wife and I were certainly informed of our great loss by the death of our son Henry, who was the Twin Brother of my son Patrick, who died two years before at Carthagena.[1] I had got some accounts of this great family disaster while I staid at Durham, but never firmly believed it, nor communicated it to my wife till we were got back to Edin. Thus afflictions on afflictions were heaped on us, but we were oblidged to submit to the providence of God, more especially when both of us reflected that by means of our approaching old Age we should soon be in these circumstances when no sorrous or Griefs cou'd attaque us.

Our deseased son was about the Age of 27 when he died in the East Indies of a lingring distemper; he had been bred to the sea since his Age of 14, and at the time of his death was first Liutenant to the Earl of Noresk, who commanded a Man of War of 50 Guns sent to the Indies with other 3 ships of War under the command of Commodore Barnet.[2] They had just before taken 3 French East India ships, and my son's share of the Capture was intrusted to the s^d Earl of Noresk.

The Earl was a mighty honest friendly man. He did all he cou'd to recover these effects for the use of my son John, and daughter Betty, to whom they were left.

The loss my family sustained by the death of this Lad cannot be remembered by me without tears, for he was one of that diligence and capacity, and that skill in navigation and the mathematical sciences, as wou'd have rendered him a blessing to his Relations.

---

[1] See page 162.

[2] Commodore Curtis Barnett, the son of a lieutenant who was lost in the 'Stirling Castle' in 1703, was in 1726 a lieutenant in Sir Charles Wager's flag-ship, the 'Torbay.' In 1730 he commanded the 'Spence' sloop on the coast of Ireland; and in 1731 the 'Bideford' frigate. In 1744 he sailed in the 'Deptford' for Porto Praya, where he captured a Spanish privateer; and cruised with the 'Preston' in the Straits of Banca, where, 26th January 1745, they captured three large French East Indiamen from China, which they sold to the Governor of Batavia for £92,000. After cruising in the Bay of Bengal, he died at Fort St. David's, 2d May 1746.

fol. 223. From that time I found a sensible decay | in my strength, for the loss of my two Lads came constantly in my mind night and day, 'tho I did all I cou'd to summon up my resolutions and behave with tollerable decency, few afflictions in Life but what were upon me at this time.

In Aprile and May 1746 my son Mathew fell ill of a Feaver at Dalkieth, and was many weeks before he recovered, and about the same time my Grandson John,[1] my son George's son, at Pennycuik, was ill of the measles. Some of his children at Drumfrise were inoculated of the small-pox, and one of them, William,[2] died of them. Inoculations of this kind were common in that place, and not one of a hundered died. Some complained of this practise, but I know not why it may not be as lawful and expedient to prevent a desease as to endeavour to cure one. God in his providence has ordained the particular means to be used in sickness as well as in health, and whatever our Deaths be as to their kind God has ordained them. However, I wou'd never advise to inoculat for the small-pox any but strong and seemingly healthy children; weak ones may probably die.

This boy is a fine schollar, and of great application to learning and business of all kinds.

Now to return to the Rebellion, 2 Men of War or privateers of force from France landed some money and arms on the Western Highland coast, about the Isle of Mull.[3] This encouraged some of the Macdonalds and Camrons to draw togither again, as some said, to the number of 2, 3, or 4000. On this news the Duke of Cumberland marched from Inverness with 12 Batalions towards Fort Augustus and Fort William on friday the 23 May 1746, and no body doubted of his success, 'tho the wild Clans behoved to labour for their French pay for some days, but these must be few and evil in all humane probability. However, as small helps are trusted to by those who are in

N.B.—The French Ships brought in a supply of 3500 pistols, but it will remain a question what became of it all.

N.B.—French promises and Highland Armies are never to be depended upon, as may be known from several Instances within

[1] Afterwards fifth Baronet. He married Mary Dacre of Kirklinton, Cumberland, and died without issue in 1798, when he was succeeded by his nephew, the Right Hon. Sir George Clerk, Lord of the Admiralty 1819-30, Master of the Mint and Vice-President of the Board of Trade 1845-46.

[2] The fourth son of George, afterwards fourth Baronet.

[3] Six casks of French gold, valued at £35,000, were landed in Burradale. Murray of Broughton's charge and discharge for this amount and other sums, amounting in all to £37,775, are printed in Chambers's *Rebellion*, pp. 514-525; see also pp. 324-326.

perril of drowning, the jacobites at Edin., and particularly the Ladies of that sort, gave themselves great Aires as if very important things were to happen, for by the Bye, those declared Ennemies to their Country plagued themselves vastly in the hopes that the French and Spaniards wou'd land and set all to rights again. | *fol. 224.* They either do not consider or do not care for the consequences which would be the landing of Hannoverian, Danish, and Saxon Troops to the assistence of our King and the Whig party in Great Britain, when as a necessary consesequence all this country should be rendered a desolation and field of Blood, for it is never to be thought that King George will suffer himself and his Family to be deprived of the Crown of Great Britain so long as he has powerful dominions abroad and faithful Allies who will support him, but what can we say of Men who are blind to reasone, except *quos Jupiter vult perdere eos dementat.*

In the months of june and july I attended the Court of Exchequer, and my Family for these 2 months lived at Mavisbank.

Prisoners were daily taken, for the unhappy Rebels knew not well where to retire or hide themselves, a strange reverse of their Fortune, and such as they wou'd never believe, for I must notice here that amongst them and their Friends the success of their enterprise was considered as certain and infallible. For my part, my thoughts were quite the reverse, and I cou'd have hazarded any thing against the success of it.

Amongst other prisoners, John Murry of Brughton, the Pretender's secretary, was one. He was taken at his Sister's House in Twedale, about 5 miles from his own, but some with great probability thought that he intended to be taken, and for that end had apprised an officer of Dragons at Brughton of his design. He was carried first to the Castle of Edin., and afterwards to London, where at last he obtained his pardon upon some discoveries he had made, and particularly for his promise to become an Evidence on the Trial of Lord Lovit, who had likeways been taken and carried to London, as shall be more particularly noticed hereafter.

Our affaires in Flanders went on this summer in a very bad way. The Emperor, as usual, neglected to send the quota of

the space of 102 years past; for instance, as to Highlanders, in the days of Montrose, under K. Charles the first, 'tho they fought many battles for him, yet they deserted him at last before the Battle of Philiphaugh, where he was ruined. A 2d Instance in the Highlanders, is when they dreu togither in defence of K. Charles the 2d, but left him on the borders, and suffered him to be beat by Cromwell at Worcester. A 3d Instance is when the year 1685 proved fatal to the Earl of Argyle, who thought to have supported his Rebellion by 3 or 4000 of them, but they deserted him, on which the Earl was taken prisoner, and suffered death. A 4th Instance was at the Revolution by King William. They fought the Battle of Killecranky, and did no more service to King James the 7th. A 5th Instance was in 1715, when the half of them ran away at the Battle of Sheriffmoor, and never appeared after. A 6th Instance was in 17[19] when at Glenshiels they deserted their Spanish auxiliares, and never appeared after. A 7th Instance [was] at the Battle of [Culloden] last Aprile, 1746, [when they] left of their first [line], all their second, line and corps de reserve deserted their friends.

As to the failure of French promises they are innumerable within these 100 years past, which is known to all the princes and states in Europe to that degree that no body c[ares] to trust them.

fol. 225.

Troops stipulated to the Allies, so that the best we cou'd do was to be on the defensive.

In Agust and part of Septem^r I and some of my family paid a visite to my sone George and his wife at Drumcrief. I had been at | Drumlanrig to wait on the D. of Queensferry, and from thence, after 3 days stay, I came to Drumcrief by Duresdeer, and by the moors, and the head of Evan Water, taking the diversion of shooting by the way. I continued there not above 8 days, for my Wife had been left at Pennicuik.

The rest of the vacation was spent at Pennicuik and Mavisbank as usually.

In Novr we came to Edin., and I attended the Court of Exchequer.

That which in forreign affaires took up the attention of all Europe was the siege of Genua [1] by the Emperor's and King of Sardinia's [2] Troops. This siege was in appearance as foolishly and Rogueishly manadged as it was entered upon, for it was evident that neither the Troops of the Emperor nor the K. of Sardinia, nor the ships of Britain, did what they might have done, otherways without loss of men the Genuese might have been oblidged to surrender. Provisions were allowed to pass to them without great opposition, so that they had all the opportunities they cou'd wish to defend themselves, and keep up a great Army from entering into the Kingdom of France. This, it seems, either the King of Sardinia had not a mind to do, nor were the Emperor's Generals fond to do anything that might too quickly put an end to the War. War is a Souldier's Harvest.

1747. This year, 1747, began with preparations on all sides for the next summer's campaign. Money was not wanted on reasonable funds to be granted in Parliament. That which gave us most truble in Scotland was the Window Tax. To aleviate

---

[1] Genoa had capitulated to the Marquis of Botta, who entered it in the name of the Empress-Queen Maria Theresa on the 5th September 1746: but an insurrection arose, and he was driven from the city and territory with a loss of 8000 men. The city was next invested by the Austrians and Sardinians, who retired on the approach of the French and Spanish army under Marshal Belleisle.

[2] King Charles Emmanuel I., in whose favour his father King Victor-Amadeus abdicated in 1730. He was born in 1701, and died in 1773.

this, many methods were taken, which disfigured many of the Houses through all Britain, such as the building up of Windows, etc. However, the Government was willing to acquiesce in all that was done by the Commissioners of Supply and justices of the peace, but all this Lenity did not signify much in this part of Britain, for, if I am not much mistaken, there is little or none of it paid to this day, being the 17 of january 1748.

On the return of the Spring the Armies on both sides | took *fol.* 226.
the fields, but little was done till the Battle which enseued at Val ten miles from Mastricht. The Duke of Cumberland commanded, and that part of the Army under him, which consisted of the British and Hannoverian Troops, behaved very well, but neither the Imperialists nor the Dutch did anything to purpose. This Battle was fought on ——[1] of ——[1], and on the defeat of our Army by Marshall Sax, the French General, it returned under the Cannon of Mastricht. The French had their chief views fixed on this City, which is one of the principal Garisone Towns belonging to the Dutch. The consequence was that the Army of the Allies came to be very safely posted, but the French, partly to pursue their victory at Val, and partly to humble the Dutch and force them into a reproachful and dangerous neutrality, laid siege to Berghen op Zoom. Another German General, Count Leuendale,[2] or rather a Dane by birth, commanded the siege.

One Cromstrom,[3] an experienced Dutch General, commanded in the Town, and most people considered that the siege was impracticable. Count Leuendal, it seems, had a different notion of the success of his Enterprise, since he had not only men and cannon at his command, but a sufficiency of money to bribe the whole Garisone. In short, it was taken at last, no body knows well how, but most men ascribe the misfortune to supine negligence and to the indolence and inactivity of old Cromstrom, for he was in bed when the Town was taken, and

---

[1] There are blanks here in the MS. The battle was fought on the 2d of July 1747, at the village of Val or Laufeldt, near Maestricht, which was four times taken and retaken.

[2] Count Löwendal.

[3] Baron Cronstrom.

very narrowly escaped. The Allies lost a multitude of Men there, but the loss of so famouse a barrier as this Town was, proved a mortal wound to the Allies and a vast encouragement to the French to attempt any thing under such experienced and fortunat Generals as Mareshall Sax and Count Leuendal were.

fol. 227. But this stab to the vitals of the Dutch | proved in the event very lucky for them and of bad consequence to the French projects in Holand, for that phlegmatick people, as awakened out of a dream, resolved to pursue the steps which had been taken in 1672, when Louis the 14 of France invaded Holand.[1] They declared the Prince of Orange not only Stadtholder, but heretable Stadtholder, making that great office to descend to his Female Heirs.[2] The province of Zealand began this measure, and by degrees it was followed by all the 7 provinces.

This year in the month of —[3] Lord Lovite was tried and condemned by his peers on the Evidences of John Murry of Brughton, the pretender's secretary, and his own secretary.[4] These two [Gent]lemen, as a Lady very pleasantly observed, at the Trial, were extream good evidences but very bad Secretaries. Lovite suffered on the Tower Hill as the Lords Kilmarnock and Balmerino had done the year before. I was well

This step was not only bold and advantageous to the Dutch, but extreamly honourable to our Reigning Family on the Throne of Great Britain. The French were amazed at the procedure of the Dutch, but much more at the Resolutions taken to anoy the French in all the Branches of their trade and forreign settlements. In the mean time, neither France nor Holand declared War against one another, 'tho' both seem'd to wish ardently that the one or the other should begin.

Yet nothing was wanted to an open war but the meer form of it for Hostilities went on between the two nations with the

---

[1] In 1672 William, Prince of Orange, was appointed Captain-General of Holland.

[2] This occurred before the battle of Laufeldt and the capture of Bergen-op-Zoom. The burghers of Vere, in Zealand, rose in insurrection, and obliged their magistrates to elevate William Henry Friso, Prince of Orange, to the Stadtholdership. The other provinces concurred, and on 15th May 1747 he was installed as Stadtholder, Captain-General, and Admiral of the Union. He had married in 1734 Anne, Princess Royal of England, daughter of George II., who in 1751 succeeded him as governor, during the minority of her son, till her death in 1759.

[3] There is a blank here in the MS. Lord Lovat's trial terminated on the 19th March 1747, when the sentence was pronounced.

[4] Both Hugh Fraser, who was Lord Lovat's secretary from 1741 to 1744, and Robert Fraser, who afterwards succeeded him, were examined as witnesses. See *State Trials*, vol. xviii. p. 698 (London, 1813).

same spirit and rancour, both by sea and land, as if War had been actually declared.

I now come to mention some of my own privat affaires during this year, 1747.

I was at Pennycuik till the 23 of january, when the Candlemass Term of the Exchequer began. I staid in Town from that day to the 10 of March thereafter, when I and my Family returned back to Pennicuik.

acquainted with L[d] Lovite. He was a man of a bold, nimbling kind of sense, very vain of his clan the Frazers, and ready to sacrifice everything for their Interest.

I emploied most of the time I staid there in planting and in studies, much in the same way I have lived these 47 years past, only about the end of Aprile I went to Drumlanrig and lookt after the Duke of Queensberry's affaires for some days.

I returned to Pennicuik and staid there with my | Family during the month of May, and amusing my self with books, for the most part. *fol.* 298.

In june I carried my Family to Mavisbank, and from thence every day attended the Court of Exchequer.

On the 22 of that month I returned to Pennycuik, and with some of my English friends took frequently the diversion of the pouting in my own moors, dineing sometimes at a little Hut I built, called the Spy, at the Head of the Dykenook Rig,[1] and sometimes at the [2] well on the west side of the great [2] moss.

N.B.—This little Hut at the west end of the Dykenook Rig is still in request for the diversion of pouting.

On the 7 of july I went back to Mavisbank, and from thence each day as usual I attended the Court of Exchequer.

In August I and my Wife went and paid a visite to my son George and his Wife at Drumcrief, in Anandale, where we staid about 3 weeks. My amusements here were generally shooting and Fishing in good Weather and in books when bad.

In september I returned back to Pennicuik, and from thence went for 2 weeks to Mavisbank. I was visited at this last place by Lord Drumlanrig[3] and his Brother, Lord

He was all his 1753. life a cunning [d]ouble man, but this dexterity left him a year or two before the Rebellion, for in drawing on to his age of 78, 79, and 80, he began to dream and dote, so that in his conduct he committed many great absurdities.

[1] Dykeneuk is about a mile and a quarter south-east of Penicuik House.

[2] The words here are illegible.

[3] Henry, Earl of Drumlanrig, eldest son of Charles, third Duke of Queensberry, was born in 1722, and educated at Winchester. He served in two campaigns under the Earl of Stair, and distinguished himself, at Conti, in the Sardinian service. In 1747 he raised a regiment in the Highlands for the service of the States of Holland, which he commanded. He married Elizabeth, eldest daughter of

At this time I caused clean out and repaire the large pond at Hurley, and began to plant the Brae facing Clermon Hill on the East side with young oakes.

Charles,[1] two very hopeful young Lords, sons of the Duke of Queensberry. I was at Pennycuik for the greatest part of October, and had a visite there from the Duke and Dutchess of Queensberry.[2]

In november, and till the 18 of December, I was with my family at Edin., and attended the Court of Exchequer.

After the s[d] 18 day I returned back to Pennycuik, and amused my self with Books and planting after the old way. My sones, James and George with his Wife, were with me both in the Town and Country for the months of novem[r] and d[r].

I shall now consider the state of my Health for the year 1747.

I found old Age advancing a pace, and frequently made use of Seneca's advice against old Age, *Obsta*, but it wou'd not always do, for I had several severe fits of sickness. They were, I thank God, but very short, but the pins of my Earthly Tabernacle were sadly | loused and chattered with them. These sicknesses were often attended with a little feaver, once with a Fainting, and always with vomitings. My digestion was for the most part very bad, and on that account I seldom wanted a Headach, 'tho it commonly went off about the time of breakfast. I did the best I cou'd to conceal these Infirmities from my friends, and especially from Strangers, who, I saw, were gaping for my office to some of their Friends. I expect nothing but bad days and bad health, yet I must keep up my mind and do the best I can to appear content, but how can this be when

Obsta, resist it.

fol. 229.

John, second Earl of Hopetoun; and died 19th October 1754, as described in page 230, having, according to Chambers's *Traditions*, shot himself in consequence of having entered into a previous contract with another lady.

[1] Charles, second son of Charles, third Duke of Queensberry, was born 1726. He represented the county of Dumfries in 1747 and again in 1754. He was at Lisbon during the famous earthquake of 1755, and died at Amesbury, Wiltshire, in 1756.

[2] It was at this time that Bishop Pococke's visit took place, as referred to by himself:—'Near this place [Roslin] I dined with the late Baron Clark, a great antiquarian, at his seat of Pennyline [*sic*], situated in a bottom on this river, a sweet spot, and here he had many valuable antiquities; among them a statue of the goddess Brigantiæ [*sic*], a deity of the Brigantes, supposed to be the Picts. It is four feet high, in a kind of toga, with a mural crown, a head in relief on the breast, with a spear in the right hand and a globe in the left.'—Letter from Bishop Pococke describing his visit to Scotland in 1747, in Pococke's *Tours in Scotland*, p. 314 (Scottish History Society, 1887). See also *ibid.*, p. 2.

I feel my body a kind of burden to me, and the pleasures I once had quite gone. How can I go about to divert myself when Exercise is a kinde of toile to me. Rest seems now more agreable to me than formerly Exercise and motion were. I feel it verified now that the greatest pleasure of an old Man is to be free of pain and sickness.

In the mean time, the habits and operations of my soul are not very much diminished, for tho' my Memory is not so strong as it was, yet I cannot complain of my judgement, for I read, write, and think in the very same way I ever did, and which I esteem as a very great blessing.

I use no Drugs, but sometimes, at the request of my Wife, a little Hyrapica[1] and Rhubarb, because of a continual, and I may say habitual, constipation.

I never used them, for my stomach ab-|horred them, so that when I was sick I only fasted till I was well, or took but little sustenance, and never was better than when I drank no wine or strong drink; warm water was always my | best medicine.

I sometimes sleap 5 or 6 Houres, but frequently less, and my sleaps are often broken and disturbed; however, I find one good effect from my Age and Infirmities, that I am sensibly weaned from the world and all its Enjoyments, for most things I had a relish for before, are now in a great measure quite insipide. I strive to amuse my self in different ways, but the efforts I use, for instance, to go a-fishing or shooting, are in a manner quite useless, | so that I am actually droping insensibly into the grave, but happy I am in this, that I resign my Life to God who gave it, and only wait patiently till my change come. *fol.* 230.]

1748.

I must begin this year, 1748, with the same accounts of my state of health in which I ended the former, conceiving it very useful and necessary that my posterity should knou all the particulars of my Life, that so they may obviat some things and prepare for others, especially the deseases and infirmities I was subject to in my old age. Even the weakest of the Human Species can look the King of Terrors in the face when they are duely prepared for that end, as we observe sometimes in Weak Criminals, particularly Women, whom I have seen behave with great decency and constancy on a scafold and the brink of Eternity. Few live as long as I have done, not one of a Thousand, and therefor I and those who come after me, at my

[1] Hiera Picra, a mixture of aloes and canella.

age, will have reasone to be thankful and contented that they have lived so long, particularly if through a long stage of Life they have been free of many acute and dangerous deseases, and a continual series of pain and Anguish, as those are under who are tormented with the Gout and the Gravel.

I have from my childhood been of a week and delicat constitution, had but a squeemish tender stomach, and was apt to throw up what I cou'd not easily disgest. I remember that on my return from abroad to my native country, about my age of 24, I was so bad a supper-man that I was scarsely able to digest a roasted Apple, but by degrees I got the better of this, yet never to be able to eat a flesh supper unless I had fasted most of the day.

I never choised to drink, so that I have not been any way intoxicated above tuice at most these 40 years, nor need I say I was intoxicated at any time, for my stomach wou'd never
fol. 231. bear so much drink as in the least to affect | my Head, for I always threu it up, and at last gave over drinking any strong liquor above 3 or 4 moderat glasses. So far my constitution curbed my desire for Drink, but nothing had more influence upon me than the character I bore as a judge, for I always thought that no man lookt so poor so contemptible and detestable as a drunken judge.

N.B.—I never had a desire for drink, and knew not once in 7 years what it was to have any thirst. Even at the hunting, and in very warm weather, I never had the least Thirst.

It was then no wounder that I was never trubled with the least fit of the Gout, nor had I ever a fit of the Gravel, except, perhaps, once in 7 years, when after riding I passed a little red sand.

I never had the Tooth-Ach except once, for 2 Houres in a very frosty day.

And on this account I never had a louse tooth till I was near 50 years of Age; however, these pins of my Earthly Tabernacle began at last to loosen and decay, so that now, near my Age of 72, I have but 3 or 4 in my head.

My Eyesight continued strong till my Age of 48, when I began to use Glasses; however, my sight is not so weakned but that I can sometimes both read and write without them.

My nerves were never strong. I had a little shaking in both my hands, which I contracted at first at Vienna when some young Frolicksome Gentlemen tempted me to lift great weights. I was affraied it should have incressed with my years, but as I greu older I rather greu firmer than weaker.

As all my parents were in some degree threatened with a Rupture, I began at 60 years of age to use a soft, broad belt about the underpart of my belly, haveing it tied with soft runds[1] down between my Thighs. I escaped by this timous precaution, tho' for these 10 years past I have had a Relaxation of the Peritoneum on both sides of the pubes. The Gut falls down with a sort of pretuberance, but I keep it up by a little cord under the bandage.

A Rupture feared for several years.

On revising this passage in 1753, I find myself much in the same case, and no worse, as I took care to use a bandage continually except in the night time.

I never knew what a Head Ach was till within these 2 years, but such fits are very gentle, and never continue above 6 or 7 houres. I am sensible that they proceed from Indigestion and weaknesses on my stomach. |

My deseases were chiefly Coghs especially in the Winter time, but I was seldom or never trubled with an Asthma or pains in my breast. I never threw up any blood, and when any such symptom appeared I was sensible it came either from my Head or my Stomach, yet my Coghs have often been so severe as that I was put under the apprehensions of a decay, particularly in 1710 when I travelled into England for my Health.[2] . . . . . .[3]

fol. 232.

I staid at Bath, but riding was the only thing that did me most service.

There is one phenomenon which I must notice here, viz., that after I lost most of my Teeth, there were few people, tho' never so young, whose breaths were not offensive to me. The reasone of this I take to be that their Teeth continued which often spoiled the breath, and mine were gone, so that nothing remained to put my breath and theirs in a kind of ballance.

I shall now mention a few things with regard to the constitution of mind. I was generally always in temper, few things rufled me, which kind of Tranquillity was partly oweing to my constitution, and partly to a phylosophick kind of guard which I endeavoured to preserve over all my words and actions.

I never was trubled with vapours or lowness of spirits but perhaps after a fit of sickness, and this but once or twice in my life, so far as I remember, and but for a day or a few Houres, if any time at all.

My Memory in my younger days was greater than I observed

---

[1] 'Rund—a border, selvage, shred, remnant.' Jamieson's *Dictionary*.

[2] See pages 76-78.

[3] I have here taken the liberty of slightly abridging the Baron's medical particulars.

it amongst those of my own age. I cou'd repeat sermons or any discourse of half an Houer without losing a Word, but it grew worse by degrees, yet still continues as entire as I observe it in any Man of my Age. I had a constant inclination for Books and Studies from my very childhood, and may truely say that I was never so happy as when I was learning something out of a book.

Yet this strong inclination to learning was tempered with a great relish for sport, particularly shooting and fishing. |

fol. 233. Amongst all the studies I followed I cou'd have preferred Mathematicks and Phylosophy, but as my Lot was calculated for publick business I was oblidged to follow such Studies as tended to improve me in this way, such as Law, History, and political Essays.

I had a strong inclination to be a scribler, and began to write books before I was 18 years of Age. I have reasone to believe that at this day, in some of the Colleges of Germany there are Compends of Logick, Physicks, and Moral phylosophy taught, which I wrote, because when I was in Holand, copies of the treatises I wrote were borrowed by those who actually taught them, intermixed, perhaps, with some things of their own.

I observed that there was one thing which those young projecting Professors took care of, which was to borrow all, till they left me no copies. There was one Sanguerdus, afterwards a professor at [Up ?]sall, who treated me in this way. For my part I was a little indifferent of these lucubrations, tho' they cost me much reading and truble, for I never intended to print any of them.

I have written several Treatises on the State of the British nation and on Trade,[1] which, however, I wou'd not venture to publish lest I had been mistaken in some Facts. If I had been living in London and near the Court, I should certainly have been daubling this way, but I came often to be sensible that an Edinburgh politician was not fit to treat of facts which he cou'd lairn only at the second or third hands.

These difficulties being considered, tho' I have spared many things, yet within these 3 years I have burnt and destroied at least a Thousand sheets of paper written with my own hand. I constantly inclined to follow Horace's advice, *nonumque prematur in annum*, and before the half of that time was over, several things which perhaps wou'd have relished with others,

Horat: *de Arte Poetica*, let your writtings be suppressed for 9 years.

I mean such things as were written by my self.

[1] In an inventory of the Baron's MSS. preserved in Penicuik, made in 1783, are mentioned, 'Observations on the Trade and Manufactures of Scotland, 1733,' and 'Arguments to prove that the Public Debts of 50 millions sterling is an advantage to Britain.'

had no relish with me. I was something squeemish in my Taste; and the longer I lived, the things thought tollerably well by others wou'd not at all go down with me. However, I read always the works of others with abundance of Complacency, | observing this Rule in Horace, *verum ubi plura nitent in carmine, non ego paucis offendar maculis.* I cou'd spare 100 dull things for the sake of one fine thought or expression.

fol. 234.

Hor: *de Arte Poetica*, when several things happen to be well expressed in a copy of verses, I am not offended with a few blemishes.

I had a great inclination to Poetry, both in Latine and English, but I curbed as much as I cou'd these salies of fancy as what I thought inconsistent with the gravity of a judge and a man of Business. However, I read the Greek and Latine classicks with great diligence, and still discovered new beuties in them.

This day, being the 19 of Jan. 1748, I read over Horace *de Arte Poetica*, which I am persuaded to have read 50 times before.

As to my Habits of piety and vertue, I leave them to others, only I may honestly affirm that as I was never greedy of money, I have been so far from wronging any body that I have often abatted my just rights to purchess peace of mind and an honest character. I have likeways, I thank God, had great inclinations to charity, agreable to my abilities and the care I thought my self oblidged to take of a very large Family of children. I have maintained many poor families and many poor workmen, which I thought was one of the best ways of being charitable.

Now I have done with this picture of my self, which to the best of my knowledge is perfectly agreable to truth, so I leave it with my posterity for their imitation or dislike, as they have a mind. I am very sensible of my wants, but very thankful to Almighty God that things are no worse with me

This year I rebuilt and repaired the Scobey Well at Pennicuik House, and added the Latine Inscription[1] on it, which

[1] Various versions of this inscription exist among the Baron's papers, but the following are the words actually inscribed:—

ἄριστον μὲν ὕδωρ

SCOBBEA DULCE FLUENS QUÆ NON SOLAMINA VITÆ
FUNDIT NECTAREUS RIVULUS ISTE TUUS
ET QUOT DELICIAS ETIAM DUM FERCULA NOBIS
FARREA COMPONIT RUSTICA SIMPLICITAS
SEU SEDARE SITIM CUPIMUS SEU LAVERE FESSOS
ARTUS RORE TUO SIS PANACEA MEA
SUSTINEAS SANOS ÆGRORUM CORPORA FIRMAS
EFFUGIANT MORBI DUM MEDICINA FLUIT.

The fountain is immediately below the new Penicuik House, which it still supplies with drinking water.

[...] made on account of the great respect paid to its Waters by my Father and Grandfather, tho' I knou no medicinal effects it has above other W[aters] of the same kind. The Inscription will be found amongst my Latine papers.

than they are, for by what I may observe in others, I have, I think, no reasone to wish my self one bit more inclined to Religion than I am. Enthousiastick notions, superstition, and singularity in Religious points are my utter aversion. In the mean time, may I dayly add to my vertues and growth in saving grace till it please God to call on me to give account of the few Talents he has been pleased to intrust me with.

I began this year, 1748, with a fit of an Ague, as I thought. I felt a shivering over my whole body, but it proved a slight fit of the Gravel, for after passing a little red sand I was well the second or third day after. |

fol. 235.

N.B.—In the Inscription above mentioned, the words *Farrea componit Rustica Simplicitas* relate to oatmeal potage, which the great Dr. Bouerhaven, on eating them with cream, used to call *nutrimentum divinum*.

The cold was a more Epidemick distemper at this time than ever it was known, and I and my Family had their share of it for 2 or 3 weeks. During this year the famous peace of Aix Lachapele[1] was made. All thought this peace a great condescension on the part of France, because Leuis the 15 was every where victorious, partly by the force of his Arms and partly by the influence of his Money. The Dutch were reduced to the same straits which the Romans some times felt when they had recourse to Dictators, by which their seperat powers and Interests were devolved on one persone. The Dutch had experienced the good of this very schem in 1672, and therefor they agreed, as I mentioned before, to constitute the Prince of Orange their Stadtholder and Captain General. This had so good an effect on the publick interest of Europe, that from that periode the King of France was willing to give peace to Europe, and restore all the Countries and Cities which he had conquered. In the mean time it was sufficiently known that France was very much reduced, and her Trade and navigation quite ruined.

I began this year, 1748, the Tower on the Head of the Knight's Law, near Pennicuik House.

During some time in Aprile and May I was at Luss, in the shire of Dunbarton, where I and my wife drank the Goat whey. Our quarters were in the Minister's House,[2] where I and some of my family had lodged some time before.

---

[1] In 1748 a general peace was made at Aix-la-Chapelle, every power restoring its conquests with the exception of Frederick, who kept Silesia for Prussia.—Gardiner's *Students' History of England*, p. 743.

[2] The Rev. James Robertson, A.M., a native of Sutherland. He studied and graduated at St. Andrews, and was called to the parish of Balquhidder in 1709,

The place is very agreable, and the Loch Lomond perfectly charming, but I soon weared of the place, and went home about the end of May.

It was this year that the military corps, by command of the Government, began in good earnest to make the highway to Inveraray from Glasgow, or rather from the Town of Luss, along the side of Loch Lomond. This way was carried on by 50 or 100 men at a time, and before Winter they brought it to Loch Skeen [Fyne?]. However, there were several beginings made to it, even in 1745, when the Rebels carried away some of the men prisoners.[1] |

I made a Latine Inscription to be put up at the Bridge of Luss, in memory of this High-way, but cared not to be at the expence of geting it cut into a Table of stone.

I left my daughter Jecke at Luss in the begining of june, *fol.* 236.
and she continued at the Goat whey with some other young Ladies for some time after, but this was so far from establishing her own health that I believe it did her harm, for on her returning from Banf, where she had gone to wait upon her sister, Mrs. Pringle, she sickned, and continued so at Edin. the remaining part of this year.

Mr. Robt. Pringle,[2] my Son in Law, was at this time Shiriff of Banff, where by Law he was oblidged to reside for 4 Months.

The year 1749 was begun in parliament by puting in execu- 1749.
tion the several articles of the Treaty of Aix la chapele, such as the evacuation of Cape Breton,[3] for which two peers had been sent as Hostages to France, namely, the Earl of Essex[4]

---

and in 1723 translated to Luss. He died, father of the Church, in 1772, in his ninety-sixth year. He had married Elizabeth Colquhoun, who died in 1773; and their son John became minister of Dunblane.—Scott's *Fasti*.

[1] See Hill Burton's *History of Scotland*, vol. viii. pp. 372-73; and Burt's *Letters from the North of Scotland*, vol. ii. pp. 284-350.

[2] See page 85, and note [4] there: also page 145, note [2].

[3] The surrender of Cape Breton was exceedingly unpopular in England, and when Prince Charles heard that the hostages had arrived in Paris he exclaimed: —'Shameful concession, unworthy of a ministry not abandoned to all sense of honour and virtue! but if ever I mount the throne of my ancestors Europe shall see me use my utmost endeavours to force France in her turn to send hostages to England.'—*Lockhart Papers*, vol. ii. p. 578. It was re-conquered in 1758, and its possession by Britain was acknowledged by France at the Peace of Paris in 1763.

[4] William, fourth Earl of Essex, was a boy of only sixteen at this time. It was George Augustus Yelverton, second Earl of Sussex, who was the joint-hostage. He was born in 1727; succeeded his father in 1731, and died in 1758.

and Ld. Cathcart. This the French had insisted on in case the Parliament of Great Britain had opposed the evacuation of that Fortress, as every body expected they wou'd.

During the months of january and february I attended the affaires of the Exchequer, and keept my health very well till about the end of february, that I catched a slight cold.

My Daughter Jeckie continued all this time confined to her bed by a kind of Ague and sweating, without any relief from her Phisitians by the Drugs she was oblidged to take.

In Aprile this year, 1749, I went to Strathearn for the Goat whey,[1] and carried my Wife and some of my Daughters with me. We were lodged at the Laers, a very good House, belonging to the son[2] of General Campbel,[3] who was killed at the Battle of Fontanoy. I had here very good fishing and other country diversions, but wearied very soon, and staid only about 4 weeks.

I rejoiced to find the Highlanders here and about Loch *fol. 237.* Earn very much improven, for they began to | sou great quantities of Lint seed, and as the estate of Perth lay here and in the nighbourhood of this country, I found that most of their Rents were paid by the Linnen yarn and Linnen wrought here. While I staid here I paid a visite to the Forrest of Glenelg,[4] belonging to the Estate of Perth. It is situated

---

[1] See Additional Note S,—Memoirs of a Goat Whey Campaign at Laers.

[2] James Mure Campbell, son of Lieutenant-General the Hon. Sir James Campbell of Lawers and Lady Jane Boyle, eldest daughter of David, first Earl of Glasgow; born 1726. He assumed the name of Mure on succeeding to the estate of his grandmother, the Countess of Glasgow. After a distinguished military career, he succeeded as fifth Earl of Loudoun in 1782, and died 1786.

[3] Lieutenant-General the Hon. Sir James Campbell of Lawers, K.B., third son of James, second Earl of Loudon, grand-uncle to John, fourth Earl. He greatly distinguished himself at Malplaquet and at Dettingen, and was mortally wounded when commanding the British horse at Fontenoy, May 1745.

[4] In the account of this expedition in 'Memoirs of a Goat Whey Campaign at Laers, in 1749' (Additional Note S), the name is left blank (thus 'Glen '); in the above, later, MSS. it is styled 'Glenelg,' evidently in error, for Glenelg is in the north-west of Inverness-shire, opposite the island of Skye. Probably Glenartney is the place referred to. The forest of Glenartney, or Glen-Orkney as it was then called, came into the possession of Sir John Drummond, 1400-1428, ancestor of the Earls of Perth, through his marriage with Lady Elizabeth Sinclair, daughter of Henry, first Earl of Orkney, from whom he obtained the lands of Muthlow and the whole forest of Glenartney.

amongst many wild hills and glens. I saw some flocks of Deer feeding at a distance, and 'tho we brought some young men with us to beat the woods and hills, yet we cou'd not bring them within half a mile of us. We dined here in a wood, and being extreamly hungry I eated too much, which occasioned a fit of vomiting after I returned.

I have, from my Infancy, fallen often into such fits of vomiting, my stomach haveing been always very unfit for a load of meat or drink.

I returned about the end of May, and in my way visited the Roman Camp at Ardoch,[1] where an Inscription was found which is now in the Castle of Drummond.

On my return I finished the little summer House at Hurley pond.

My design for making this house was to entice my friends and others about my House to walk for their diversion, and in this I my self have found great advantage. The natural beuty of the place, and the solitude which one finds here, are a great | help to studies and meditation. *fol. 238.*

I sometimes draw the Ponds where I have aboundance of Carp and Tench. Some of the first I observed had grouen to near 22 inches. In the mean time 'tho they, at least many of them, have been there for 7 or 8 years, yet they have not bred. They were brought from Corby in Northumberland at different times. Carp are long in breeding.

In the months of june and july I attended the Courts of Exchequer as usual, but in the short vacation from the 22 of june to the 7 of july I was at Pennicuik, and plied the shooting with the same satisfaction I ever enjoied on the Moors, 'tho I was not quite so good a Traveller on foot as I used to be. However, the accident of breaking my leg when I was young made it wearisome to me to travel above half a mile at one time, and since I began to grow old I find the broken leg weaker.

---

[1] 'The most entire and best preserved of any Roman antiquity of the kind in Britain.' Gordon's *Itinerarium Septentrionale*, p. 41, where the camp is figured, and also the stone at Drummond Castle, the inscription on which Gordon reads as '*Amonius Damionis cohortis primæ Hispanorum stipendiorum xxvii haeredes fieri curarunt.*'

This year, in june and the following summer months, I carried forward the Tower on the Top of the Knights' Law, and brought it about 16 or 20 feet higher than last year. It is a very substantial Building, 'tho it stands very much exposed.[1]

This Touer I now call the Touer of Belem ... t ...

In Agust I made a visite to my son George's Family at Drumcrief, and was several times at the country diversions.

About the middle of September I returned to Pennicuik, and from thence I carried my Family to Mavisbank, where we staid 2 or 3 weeks.

fol. 239. I find nothing more for my Health | than a *mutatio loci et aeris*, which Cornelius Celsus[2] so much recommends, and in the alteration of stations, I always live as if I was at Home, carrying books of all kinds with me. About the month of October my Daughter Jeckie began sensibly to recover, and was able to go abroad in a chair. *Laus Deo!*

I know nothing remarkable that hapned this summer in publick affaires. We had in Scotland many projects amongst us for establishing a publick Fishery in the form of a Company, which hitherto has been often tried, but never succeeded.

The High Ways in many places in the Highlands were repaired by Military assistence, particularly the Roads leading to Inveraray and Fort William.

The care of the Forfeited Estates was committed to the Barons of the Exchequer, and in the management of these nothing appeared clearer than that most of all the proprietors were Bankrupts before they entered into the Rebellion. If they had got any thing to lose by their conduct, I have reasone to believe that they, or many of them, had not hazarded their

---

[1] This is still a prominent object on the top of the Knight's Law, and bears above its door the inscription given by the Baron in his marginal note on page 225. It was formerly used as a dove-cot, and is now called Terregles Tower.

[2] Aurelius Cornelius, or Aulus Cornelius Celsus, styled the Medical Cicero, appears to have lived in Rome about the time of Augustus or Tiberius, and he wrote on law, history, philosophy, rhetoric, etc., but his work *De Medicina*, in eight books, is his only production now extant. It is written in an elegant style, with the purity of the Augustan age, contains much information regarding the sects of physicians, and is regarded as the most complete body of medicine that has come down to us from the ancients. The *editio princeps* was printed at Florence in 1478, and an English translation by Dr. James Grieve was published in London in 1756.

persons and Estates in such a desperat schem, for nothing in life is less to be trusted than French promises and Highland Armies. The whole world | knows the first by experience, and *fol. 240.*
as to Highland Armies, 'tho they have Courage in aboundance, yet their poverty and desire of plunder make them commonly retire home when they should keep the field. Whatever personal bravery men may have, yet they are not to be compared with Regular Troops, for 'tho they may make a furious burst by runing in columns with great weight and impetuosity, yet in the end all this Heat and fury will succumb to the regular and sedate behaviour of Regular Troops. This observation has been verified by what hapned to the Marquise of Montross on his defeat at the Battle of Philiphaugh, and to the late viscount of Dundee after the battle of Kilecranky, for 'tho he had survived the Battle, yet his Army, without waiting to know whether he was dead or alive, run off with the plunder.

This hapned at the Battle of Coloden, in 1746.

In november I went to Edin. in the ordinary way, and attended the Court of Exchequer, where nothing uncommon was transacted.

On the 20th of December I returned to Pennicuik, and lived in a solitary, peaceable way with my family and some of my friends, who came to visite me.

In the same way I lived in the month of january 1750, till 1750.
the affaires of the Court of Exchequer called me to Edin.

I find every day I live puting me in mind of Æternity, for I am sensible of a great decay of Spirits, Strength, and Memory. Mean time I keep up as well as I can, and as a remedy to advancing old Age I follow Seneca's advice, which is, as before mentioned, Ostare; therefore I use as much exercise as my Bodily strength will allow of, for I generally walk a Mile or two | every day. My constant walk is to my pond of Hurley *fol. 241.*
and Grotto, where I take great delight. I have seldom any sickness that lasts above an Houer or two, and this sickness comes always upon transgressing the strictest Rules of sobriety, or eating such meats as my stomach wou'd never agree with, such as greens and fat heavy meat. In drinking I never transgress, being rather too sober and abstemous, but this Regimen has notwithstanding been of great use to me, for 'tho my

Memory be not so good as formerly, yet I feel no manner of decay in my judgement when I think proper to exert it either in speaking or writing Letters. In studies I am as ardent as ever, only I weary sooner in my applications to any thing.

I am now begining to enter on the 75 year of my Age, an Age I never expected to arrive at, and I accustome myself to think on Death without the least disturbance. On this account I live with great Tranquillity, and eat and sleap as well as ever I did in all the course of my Life. Mean time I reflect with some Melancholly that 'tho I have lived soberly and manadged my affaires with tollerable œconomy, yet I have not laid any thing considerable to the fore for my children. But this misfortune was oweing mostly to themselves, for I was generally the worst provided in the Family. My annual journals will shew that I have not been a hard Father to them, nor have I lived nigardly with my Relations. Every body got a part of what I had, and many poor Workman have been supported by me.

I may be allowed here to mention that in the year 1750 I published a Latine dissertation de Monumentis ... Romanis, etc., this I did only to preserve these monuments which I have in my possession at Pennicuik House. The copies of this dissertation were never sold, but some were given away to my particular friends.[2]

On the 7 of feb. this year, 1750, died my dear Brother Hugh,[1] merchant in Edin. He was in many respects a very desirable persone, and beloved by every body. He left 5 children behind him, 2 Boys and 3 Girls. | *fol. 242.* Amongst other Qualifications which my sd Brother was possessed of, he play'd on the violencello with all the perfection of the greatest Master, and rather too well for a Gentleman.

On the 16 of Aprile this year, I married my Daughter Jennie to Mr James Carmichel,[3] Clerk to the Signet, and son to Mr William Carmichel, a son of the Earl of Hyndfoord, and I have reasone to hope that this marriage will prove happy to

---

[1] Hugh Clerk, eighth son of Sir John Clerk, first baronet of Penicuik, was born on 25th October 1709. He married Mary Beaumont. His eldest son John married and had issue. His second son Hugh served in Germany and died soon after the battle of Minden. His eldest daughter was named Susan; his second, Euphemia, married Thomas Dallas, and had issue; and the youngest was named Mary.

[2] See marginal note, pages 138, 139, and note [3] to 139.

[3] Jennet, the Baron's seventh daughter (see folio 150), was married on the 9th of April 1750 (according to the *MS. Family Register*) to James Carmichael of Hailes, second son of the Hon. William Carmichael of Skirling, the second son of John, first Earl of Hyndford. He was admitted a Writer to the Signet in 1741, and died in 1781.

my s[d] Daughter, for he sets out with the general approbation of all my Friends and acquaintances as a very good Lad and a Man of business.

In this month, about the 26, I went to Drumlanrig and attended the Duke of Queenberry's affaires, in company with Lord Sewalton, formerly Mr. Boyle, one of the Duke's Commissioners.

We continued there for some days, and found the Tenants as formerly, some very well, and others in distress, according as they manadged their affaires.

In june, I attended the Court of Exchequer after the ordinary way. I was with my Family all nights at Mavisbank, and every day went to Edinburgh, as I found this medicine of traveling and Exercise did me great service. On the 22 of june I returned to Pennicuik, and with some of my friends took the diversion of pouting till the 7 of july, when the Term of the Exchequer began again.

The affaires of the Court chiefly related to the Forfeited Estates, about which some Acts in the last session of parliament gave us directions.[1]

This management of the forfeited estates affected me greatly with melancholly.

About the meddle of Agust I went with my Wife to visite my son George's Family at Drumcrief. I staid there till the 8 of september, and then returned | to Pennicuik.

N.B.—My visits to my son George were not to his loss.

fol. 243.

About the meddle of sep. I carried most of my Family to Mavisbank, where I continued the rest of this month.

On my return to Pennicuik I emploied my self, as usually I did, partly with Books and partly diversions, amongst other studies I revised the 2nd book of my Latin History.[2]

N.B.—Here I had the diversion of shooting every other day, and cannot but notice that, according to my old practice, I shot 22 times and killed 21 partridges and moorfowl, but this number includes all the massacre I made both in june, july, and september, both

In november I attended the Exchequer as usually, in the absence of the Chief Baron. In December I and my Family returned to Mavisbank for some days, and towards the 20th I and my Family came to Pennicuik. Here I amused my self in revising the 3[d] book of my Latine History, and am hopeful that at last it will make a tollerable good appearance.[2]

Nothing very remarkable hapned to me and my Family

[1] 'The management of the Forfeited Estates in Scotland was intrusted to the Barons of the Court of Exchequer by 20 Geo. II., cap. 41. See Additional Note T,—The Court of Exchequer and the Forfeited Estates.

[2] See page 85, and note [1] there.

about Pennicuik and Mavisbank. In the mean time I acknowledge my self very faulty in murdering so many of God's creatures by way of sport. except what related to my Daughters. The 2 and fourth had been at the Bath for their health, and had returned safe. The youngest had been married to Mr Ja. Carmichel as above.

The Winter proved very fine weather, and I had keept my health the whole year without the least disorder or accident, for which I endeavour to be thankfull to Almighty God.

1751. Tho' they are made for our use, yet I think they have as good a right to Life as I my self have. I began this year in very good health and spirits, but yet I find the symptoms of old Age advancing a pace; however, I eat and sleap well, and the decays of nature are very little different from what they were a year ago. I endeavour to make myself easy. I go on in preparing for death in my fol. 244. Temporal affaires by puting things in the best methode and order I can.

At this time all Europe was in peace, nor did there seem any intentions to make War in haste. However, as the French saw their error in the last war, by entering into it without preparing such a Fleet as was necessary to protect their Trade, they began to build Ships of War in all the ports of France.

On these preparations, all the friends of the Family of the Stuarts began to build great hopes. Trade was about this time much cultivated in Britain, and here in Scotland we set up for cultivating several branches of Trade, as particularly companies for carrying on the Whale and Herring Fisheries.[1]

formerly. I had joined in several projects of this kind, but with no success, therefor I only encouraged all my sones to become partners in these Fisheries, and furnished them with suitable stocks for making trials, as I was satisfied that nothing contributes more for the Honour and Intrest of any Country than Trade honestly carried on, in all its branches.

Last year and this I carried on the Tower on the Top of the Knight's Law, and as I propose an ornament to the country by it, I likeways have it in my view to make it beneficial to my family as a Dovecoat, that which I have near the House of

[1] 'A subscription for a whale-fishery is going on in Aberdeen; and before the end of March the subscriptions amounted to between £3000 and £4000 sterling.'—*Scots Magazine*, 1752, p. 155.

'At a meeting of the Edinburgh Whale-fishing Company in October, it was resolved to purchase a fourth ship for the Greenland fishing.'—*Scots Magazine*, 1752, p. 462.

See also many other references in the same journal.

Pennicuik being hurt by too many Trees, where Hawks and Gleds destroy the pigeons when they come out.

N.B.—Above the do[or] of this Tower I caused cut these words, *Tibi sit prudentia Turris.*

Here I may observe that I have on many occasions carried on several expensive projects, at least such as were too heavy for a Privat Man, who had a large Family of children; but this I thought a kind of duty, for as I received yearly about 500 lib. ster. of the king's money, so I seemed to be under an obligation to bestow a good part of it on his subjects who were Masons, Wrights, and other workmen. *fol.* 245.

To this the building of Mavisbank and a good many other things are oweing, but such who receive no publick money, I advise them to be a little more sparing in their Expenses. However, in all my Projects I have studied either to do useful things, or such as would ornament my Country as well as my Estate.

N.B.—If all the world were as frugal as by the dictates of good oeconomy they ought to be, the half of Mankind wou'd starve. The poor must always live by the prodigality and extravagances of the Rich, at least every man who can afford to spend a little might do it for the benefite of the poor, and indeed this is the best way I know for bestowing of charity, except it be carried to a hight that must do manifest prejudice to our children and poor Relations who cannot work for their bread.

In 1750 I found my self very ill used by some whom I trusted at Lonhead in the management of my Coal affaires, therefor I put them in the hands of my son James, who had more strength of Body and more leisure to look after them, for in the management of coal I judged that there was a necessity frequently to go below ground, and not to trust to those called oversmen, cheques, and coalgrives. Besides, as to the choise of my son for chief Manadger, there was a necessity to breed him up a little in the management of these matters. |

This experiment I found succeeded to my Wishes, for the profits of my coal began to be doubled. About this time I sent my youngest son Adam to the sea, for as he seemed to have a great inclination this way, there was a necessity to try how far his Genius wou'd carry him. The first trial I made was by sending him in a Merchant Ship to N. Carolina, from *fol.* 246.

thence to Lisbon, and from this place to Lieth. The experiment succeeded so well that this Boy seemed confirmed in his Inclinations to sea affaires, but whether to breed him for the navy or the merchant service was what remained to be determined.

I was oblidged at the same time to dispose of my fourth son, Matheu who had his head no less turned on the Military service, therefor I bought for him in 1751 a Commission of Ensigncy in the Lord Panmure's[1] Regiment,[2] which was then in Ireland, but because this lad had always showen a particular inclination for the Engineering Trade, I procured from his Colonel liberty to absent himself for 6 months, and in that time to visit the Accademy at Woolwich, and afterwards to travel into France and Flanders for his improvement in that Trade till a proper opportunity should happen to provide for him.

I paid for it 400 guines.

In our publick affaires a very mortifying Event hapned to Great Britain by the Death of the Prince of Wales,[3] who was much beloved by every body, and on his death an Act of Parliament past for constituting the Princess of Wales[4] Regent, on the event of the King's death and minority of her son. This Lady was thought every way equal to this great office, 'tho it is hoped that the king may live for many years.

1751.

fol. 247. This year a very great Misfortune hapned to the whole protestant interest, and particularly to our Royal family, for the Prince of Orange, created Stadtholder of the united provinces, died, and the Authority devolved on his mother,[5] the eldest daughter of our King George the 2d.

[1] William Maule, grandson of the fourth (attainted) Earl of Panmure, was born about 1700, and created Earl of Panmure of Forth, in the Peerage of Ireland, in 1743, and in 1764 purchased the Panmure estates. He was present at Dettingen and Fontenoy, and became a general in 1770. On his death in 1782 his titles became extinct.

[2] The twenty-fifth regiment of foot.

[3] Frederick Lewis, Prince of Wales, born 1707; died 20th March 1751 N.S.

[4] Augusta, younger daughter of Frederic II., Duke of Saxe-Gotha. As George II. survived till 1760, she never became regent; but she did much to instil into the mind of her son, afterward George III., that love of prerogative, and hatred of the Whigs, which afterwards distinguished him.

[5] His *widow*; see note [2], page 208.

In my own family there were no extraordinary occurrences, only my son Adam returned from Carolina, and after this trial at sea he continued resolved to return to the sea and serve in the Navy.

NOTE—On the 17 of Decembr[1] 1751, about 8 in the evening, there was an eclipse or occultation of the planet of jupiter by the moon, which lasted about 40 minutes. The night very clear.

This year my health began to decline considerably, 'tho still without any form'd sickness, particularly in 1752 I began to feel a languor and a kind of *satietas vitæ*, so that I may say, as J. Cæsar did, *emori nolle sed de vita nihil curo.* In the mean time I shall wait God's time with patience and submission.

My son Adam went to London about the middle of February, being recommend by Captain William Holborn[2] to a Captain of a Man of War now lying at Debtfoord, near London.

My son Matheu continued at the Accademy at Woolwich, and happily fell into the favour of all who knew him, and I in particular had much reasone to be satisfied with him.

In Aprile 1752 I grew sickly and tender, but walkt or rode out dayly. I thought likeways that my memory was a little affected, so that business grew uneasy to me. My strength seemed to decay dayly; in a word, I felt, as I thought, the approaches of death. Lord help me for I know not well my own complaints! |

N.B.—I believe that all this indisposition proceeded from imagination only, for I grew very well in summer thereafter.

fol. 248.

1752. My son Matheu had the happiness of being in favour with his Colonel, Ld Panmure, and he was allowed to attend his Ldp. to Ireland, for at Cork the Regiment was to be revieued.

One of these days I got notice of the death of my old and intimat friend, Mr. Scrope,[3] who had at first been one of the Barons of Exchequer, and afterwards one of the clerks of the Treasury. He died near a dussan of years older than I was,

N.C. Œ [?].

---

[1] The name of the month here is rather indistinctly written but appears to be 'December.' An eclipse of Jupiter by the moon, 'which will happen on the 21st of *November*,' is computed in the *Scots Magazine* for October 1751, p. 489.

[2] The second son of Sir James Holburne, first baronet of Menstrie (see note [2], page 148). He was a post-captain in the navy; and at the time of his death, in 1760, was captain of the 'Newark.' His younger brother was Admiral Francis Holburne.

[3] See note [1], page 71. Scrope resigned his office in the Exchequer, 25th March 1724.

yet his death was very shocking to me, and much lamented, as our acquaintance began in 1709.

Here lived my son George and his family. In the begining of Agust this year I went with my Wife and a friend or two to Drumcrief, where we staid near a month in great happiness and tranquillity of mind.

My son Matheu about this time was allowed to go to Paris and prosecute his studies, in the Engineering Art, and was very

In Novem. 1752. happy in his Masters. I and my family went to Edin., and I attended the Exchequer as formerly.

The affaires in Parliament and other public affaires went on as usually.

In the spring of this year my son James began to build the Library and to add a few Rooms on the west side of the House, but as there was no pressing occasion for these things, the work proceeded slowly.

This was from jelousy of the House of Austria's governing power. Abroad the election of a king of the Romans[1] was carried on, but not finished, opposed chiefly by the Intrigues of the French court and by the Intrigues of the king of Prussia.

In feb. 1753 I enter into the 78 year of my Age, yet found my self very well, but my sight not a little decayed, yet I reckon it no small happiness that consequently the pleasures of the world decayed likeways and turn'd insipide.

25 March this year I observe a great decay of bodily strength and of my memory, yet I endeavour to keep a good heart and to bear with patience and resignation what I cannot help.

fol. 249. In publick affaires I observe but little alteration. However, it wou'd seem as if the King of Prussia was preparing for some attempt on his nighbours, since at present he keeps up an Army of above 100,000 men, and is reputed to be a very rich Prince.

But to return to my self, I continue to have a great relish

Some at my age are angry at all the world. for books, 'tho I seem to forget as fast as I read. Where then can I have my best refuge but in God himself, to whom I commit all my concerns.

10 June 1753. I decline much in my Memory, 'tho I be pretty well in

[1] Newcastle and the English Government supported the claims of the Arch-Duke Joseph II., son of Francis I. and Maria Theresa. He was at length elected King of the Romans in 1764, after the Peace of Hubertsburg, which terminated the Seven Years' War.

Health, and am always in a serene good temper of mind. I am so far very happy that I get dayly accounts from all hands that my son Matheu is in great favour with several considerable men abroad, and that he will turn out to be a fine Engeneer.

My daughter Jeckie relapsed into the same kind of Ague with which she had been affected in 1749.

My son George and his Wife came in the beginning of july and staid with us a feu days in their way to Drumcrief.

My son Adam is now on board a 20 gun ship commanded by one Leg in the West Indies.

My daughter Jeckie, after languishing for some time, recovered her health again. *Laus Deo!*

In Agust and September I staid for some time at Drumcrief with my Wife and Daughter Anna. Here I was very easy and happy. Mr. Alan Ramsey,[1] a very pleasant companion, staid with us. We returned to Pennicuik in October.

1754.

About the begining of this year I was trubled with a vomiting, but grew well in a day. This was by a little surfeit, for indeed very little affects my stomach, because I commonly practise too much Moderation.

The great old physitian Cornelius Celsus gives this advice, *interdum plus justo interdum non amplius assumere*, Lib. i. cap. 1., but I cannot approve of *plus justo* at any time.

In March I had a visite from my son Matheu, who is appointed an Engineer, and to go over to Gibralter for 2 or 3 years. However, I was greatly refreshed to see him, and especially to find him a sensible young lad, and | who may, I hope, make some figure in the World.

fol. 250.

I continue to divert my self with reading or in having

[1] Curiously enough, this is the only reference in the MS. to Allan Ramsay, who has been always stated to have been an intimate friend of the Baron's. It has been frequently asserted that the obelisk to his poet's memory at Ravensneuk, on the Penicuik estate, was erected by the Baron. This, however, is incorrect, as Ramsay survived him till 1758; it was erected by his son, Sir James Clerk, in 1759. A portrait of Allan Ramsay, painted by Aikman, is preserved at Penicuik House. It is inscribed on the back, in the Baron's autograph as follows:—

'*A Roundlet in Mr. Ramsay's own way.*

Here painted on this canvas clout,
By Aikman's hand is Ramsay's snout,
The picture's value none may doubt,
For ten to one I'll venture,
The greatest critics could not tell
Which of the two does not excel,
Or in his way should bear the bell,
The poet or the painter.

J. C., Pennicuik, 5 May 1723.'

Beside it is a portrait of the artist, the Baron's cousin, marked in his handwriting, 'Mr. Aikman, painted by himself when dying, and left as a legacy to me, J. C., anno 1733.'

others to read to me. My Meditations are likeways very diverting to me, for, as I have read and studied much in my time, the calling these things to mind gives me very great pleasure.

5 Ap. 1754. I must record here a very providential escape from a very great danger. As I was returning from the Howgate mouth[1] homewards, my Horse took a fright on the top of the Bridge of Pennicuik and threu me. I was stuned with the fall but got no other harm, whereas I was in danger either of being throuen over the Bridge or breaking a bone on the Caseuay. However, it pleased God that I escaped, 'tho I cannot call to mind this event without Horror and a great thankfullness to Almighty God who has preserved me in many dangers.

In May 1754 I continued well, 'tho sometimes trubled with a swiming in my head. In the mean time I complain to no body. There is no helping of old Age and the infirmities which always attend it.

26 june this year, my son Matheu was called for to attend the Garrisone at Gibraltar, and accordingly he went from Edin. post to London.

This month I went to the pouting in my own Moors on Dykenook Rig, dined at the little House, and shot as well as ever, 'tho I seldom wish to see above 3 or 4 pouts killed.

In july this year, 1754, I had 3 visits from my friends; one from the Duke and Dutchess of Queensberry, accompanied with one Mr. Macgie,[2] a Gallouay Gentleman; another from the Earl of Galloway with his Lady and Daughter, Lady Hendretta;[3] and the 3d was from L^{d}. Drumlanrig, son of the Duke of Queensberry, and his new married Lady, a daughter fol. 251. of the Earl of Hopton. They were | accompanied by L^{d}.

---

[1] Howgate, a village about a mile and a quarter south-east of the town of Penicuik.

[2] Probably John M'Ghie of Balmaghie, Kirkcudbrightshire; or his son Alexander, who married Grizell, only daughter of James Gordon, second son of Alexander, Viscount Kenmure, and predeceased his father.

[3] Lady Harriet, fifth daughter of Alexander, sixth Earl of Galloway, by his second wife, Lady Catherine Cochrane, third daughter of John, fourth Earl of Dundonald. She married, in 1765, Lord Archibald Hamilton, afterwards ninth Duke of Hamilton and Brandon, and died in 1788.

Areskin and his Lady.[1] Two of these companies staid with me at Pennicuik only a night, but L[d]. Drumlanrig staid with me only till dinner was over, and then went and lay at the Brighouse in their way to Drumlanrig.

A little while after, a most melanchollly accident hapned to my L[d]. Drumlanrig, for as he was traveling with the Duke and Dutchess to London, and had come a little beyond Batry,[2] in Yorkshire, he was shot dead by himself in putting out his pistols to try if they were loaded with ball, as the Report of Highwaymen near that place made necessary.[3]

'Tis impossible to describe the consternation of his Parents and of his Lady, who were all in a coach near him, and I doubt much if ever they will recover their loss and consternation upon such a terrible occasion.

In Agust and September for 3 weeks I staid with my son George at Drumcrief, and was very happy. In Novemb[r]. I attended the Court of Exchequer for some days, but on the return of our Chief Baron from England, and as my attendance was not very necessary, I absented during the rest of our Term.

In decemb[r]., being at Pennicuik with the rest of my Family, I fell ill of a flux, but blessed be God, this continued only for a day or two. My distress was occasioned by eating too much cabage broth. *N.B.*—All Greens affect me in the same way, and for the future must be avoided.

---

[1] Thomas, Lord Erskine, only son of John, the attainted Earl of Mar. He married, in 1741, Lady Charlotte Hope, eighth daughter of Charles, first Earl of Hopetoun; and died in 1766.

[2] Bawtry.

[3] See note [3], page 209.

APPENDIX

A LIST OF IMPROVEMENTS MADE BY ME AT PENNICUIKE AND MAVISBANK, LIKEWAYS AT CAMMO, IN THE PARISH OF CRAMOND, BEFORE I SOLD[1] THE SAME TO ONE JOHN HOG, A RELATION OF MINE, AND COLLECTOR OF THE CESS AT EDIN.

From the year 1714.

I insert this List, not at all from any principle of vanity, but to incite those who succeed me to attempt the same things according to their circumstances.

I have always thought that my salary as a Baron of the Exchequer was publick money and a gratification I owed to my Country, and therfor I laid out the whole of it and some more of my privat patrimony for the Improvement of my Country; and besides I was constantly of opinion that since his Majesty King George the First, and before him Queen Ann, supported me not only in necessaries but in superfluities, it was my duty to support several of my poor Country-men.

Agreable to this principle I, for the most part, supported at least a dussan of them, and several times above a score, so that I hope the publick will not think the money unprofitably spent which was bestowed on me. Many poor families were maintained by me, so that I doubt not but of young and old I supported for many years near to fifty or sixty. Nor was my care confined to able bodied Men who served me in these improvements, but extended likeways to the old, for several of such Men were supported by me when they were between 70 and 80 years of Age at the rate of 6 sh. 8 d Scots pr day when they never were able to work to me above what I might have expected from Boys of 12 or 14 years of Age; yea, severals of those were maintained by me to their deaths, for 3 or 4 years after they cou'd work no more.

---

[1] See Additional Note K,—Cammo.

These Improvements were made at Pennicuik.

All the plantations on both sides of the Water of Esk from Ravenshaugh burn down to the Damhead of Pennicuik, being at least a mile.

The Inclosures on both sides of that Water down to the said Damhead.

Several Inclosures upon the grounds of Hurley and many plantations.

The Inclosure of Clermont Park, the ponds there stocked with Carp and Tench, together with the plantations there.

Carp and Tench were brought from England.

The Cave of Hurley.

The Inclosure and plantation opposite to it.

The great square Loch or pond on the north west side of Pennicuik House, with all the plantations there.

The plantations on the South side of the same House and above Montesine's Cave.

The stone Bridge at Montesine's Cave.

The Avenue through Coldshoulders park.

Eskfield house. Garden and plantations at the Damhead of Pennicuik.

The Hedges, ditches, and plantations at Cooking and Glaskills, which include about 230 Acres of ground.

The House and Mains of the Eastfield of Pennicuik, being formerly all outfield grounds.

The great Isle of Pennicuik Kirk over against the pulpet, for the use of my Tenants.

The Steeple from the ground, both on my own charges.

The Town House of Pennicuik.

The Avenue and Bridge over the East burn to the House of Pennicuik, which was the greatest improvement that ever was done to the House.

N.B.—Before this Avenue was made, which was begun in 1728, there was no road nor access to the House but on the North side the Knight's Law round the Park dykes to the north Avenue.

At Lonhead and Mavisbank.

The Level to the coal seams, which begins on the East side of the Garden at Mavisbank, and runs above 300 fathoms under ground.

The whole Inclosures in the moor of Lonhead, with the moor Houses, there having been nothing in this moor but whins.

The House, offices, Gardens, and inclosures of Mavisbank, there having been nothing there before but a little farm-house 300 elles farther east, which likeways was called Mavisbank.

Water to Lonhead, brought in by me in Timber pipes, there having been nothing there before but what was brought from the Mavis Well, under the House of Mavisbank.

The Town House of Lonhead, not built by me, but bought from the masone who built it.

At Cammo.

Here I lived from the year 1710 to 1723. I was constantly doing something about it and all the plantations; the dyks and inclosures which were at that time, were done by me.

X

ARMORIAL BOOK-PLATE

of the Clerks of Penicuik

ADDITIONAL NOTES

NOTE A, p. 5. *Barony of Penicuik.*—In Chambers's *Peeblesshire* it is stated that Dr. Alexander Pennicuik, in 1646, sold the estate of Penicuik to John Clerk, and purchased the smaller estate of Newhall. This, however, is incorrect, as is proved by the interesting account of the estate and its successive owners given in Wilson's *Annals of Penicuik* (Edinburgh, 1891), which should be consulted. The family of Pennicuik had possessed the barony from a remote period, and in 1298 John de Kingston, Constable of Edinburgh, writes to Walter de Langton, Lord Treasurer of England, that 'intelligence has come to me that the Lady of Penicok (which is 10 leagues from our Castle) has received her son, who is against the peace, and that other evil-doers are there harboured and received.' The estate remained in the family till the beginning of the seventeenth century, and on 19th December 1603, Alexander Penycuke of that Ilk entered into a contract with John Prestoun of Fentonbarns regarding the sale of the lands and barony, and, on 22d March 1604, granted procuratory of resignation in his favour. On 29th March 1604 Prestoun received a charter of the lands from the Crown. John Prestoun, who was knighted by King James, and in 1609 appointed Lord President of the Court of Session, was succeeded in 1616 by his eldest son, John Prestoun, who was Solicitor-General, and was created a baronet in 1628. By him the estates were sold, in 1646, to Dame Margaret Scott, Countess of Eglintoune, wife of the sixth earl, eldest daughter of Walter, first Lord Scott of Buccleuch, and relict of James, sixth Lord Ross; and the records from the Register of Sasines, dated September 1st, 1646, and September 4th, 1647, are given by Mr. Wilson in full. According to Douglas, the Countess died in 1651; and on 19th October 1653 her youngest daughter, Jean Ross, married to Sir Robert Innes of Innes, Bart., and her granddaughter, Margeret Hepburn, were served heirs-portioners to the lands of Pennycook. To quote Wilson's *Annals of Penicuik*, page 149, 'Their Sasines are recorded on 31st March 1654. Prior to that date, however, Sasine proceeding upon bond and obligation is granted by Robert Innes, elder of that ilk, and Sir Robert Innes, younger thereof, as principals; Alexander Brodie of that ilk, and Alexander Douglas of Spynie, as cautioners for them, and also by David Dunbar of Binnies, and other cautioners for them, whereby, for the sum of £6000 Scots, then borrowed and received by the said Sir Robert Innes, elder and younger, from John Clark, merchant, burgess of Edinburgh, the said Sir Robert Innes, younger, bound him duly and lawfully to infeft and seise the said John Clark, his heirs and assignees whomsoever, in all and haill an annual rent of £360 out of the lands and barony of Pennycook and lands of Hailles, with the whole parts, pendicles, and pertinents thereof, to be holden of the said Sir Robert Innes, younger, in free blench. This document is dated at Mylnetoun of Ross Innes, and Edinburgh, the 29th September, 9th and 10th April and May, 1653, and Sasine given on 10th February 1654. The above record is interesting as showing the first connection of the ancestor of the present owner with the barony of Penicuik. His final acquisition took place shortly afterwards, when Jean Ross and Margaret Hepburn, who were infeft in equal halves of it, granted charter of the lands and barony to the said John Clerk, Merchant, burgess of Edinburgh, and he was infeft therein heritably and irredeemably, his Sasine being recorded on 3d June 1654.' According to Mr. Wilson, it was about 1646 that the Creichtounes sold the estate of Newhall to Dr. Alexander Pennycuick, the lineal descendant and representative of the Penycukes of that ilk, who was succeeded by his eldest son of the same name, the poet, and author of a *Description of Tweeddale* (Edinburgh, 1715). The arms of 'Pennycuke of that Ilk' appear in Sir David Lindsay's MS. as Argent, a fess between three hunting-horns sable; and the arms of 'Pennicook of Newhall,' representative of the Pennycukes of that Ilk, are marticulated in the Register of the Lyon Office in 1672 as 'Or, a fess betwixt three hunting-horns, sable, garnished and stringed gules,' with the crest of 'a stag lodged under ane oak-tree proper and the motto *Ut resurgam*.'

NOTE B, pp. 6-18. *Description of Estate and Old House of Penicuik, in a Letter from the Baron to Boerhaave.*—I may here give an abbreviated English version, kindly furnished by Mr. T. Graves Law, of a draft of a Latin letter to Boerhaave, preserved among the Clerk papers, giving a quaint, and in parts curiously grandiloquent, account of the house and estate of Penicuik. The Baron notes that the letter was 'afterwards much shortened, all or most of the redundances being laid aside before it was sent,' and that the paragraph describing the Cave of Hurley, made in 1741, was added long after.

After some general prefatory remarks the Baron proceeds to satisfy his friend's desire to have a full description of his house and estate.

'The villa is seven or eight miles from Edinburgh. This distance is particularly pleasant to me, and would be, as I suppose, to all men immersed in public affairs, more agreeable than a retreat nearer to the city. For, as Pliny, the younger, says of his Tuscan home, here is the most profound and undisturbed ease, there is no need to sport fine clothes, no neighbour calls, and all things give rest and quiet. Here I have lived from my cradle. There is not a corner, not a tree, not a stream, which has not been a witness of my juvenile studies and games.

'But to describe the estate: On the west stretches a plain for some miles, varied with hills, valleys, streams, springs, and shrubberies. Parts are uncultivated and marshy, but this gives work for my tenants and servants, who are daily improving it. Meanwhile there is no part, however swampy, which has not its use, for the moors are suited for sport. There is an abundance of hares. The birds thrive in the heather. Wild geese, partridges, quails, etc., abundantly provide for the conviviality of guests.

'All these animals and birds I regard in the light of neighbours; and, to speak my own mind, I think nothing more conduces to the tranquillity and charm of a country house than the fact that one sees (with the exception of one's farmers and servants) nothing in the neighbourhood but flocks and cattle and birds. The society of men, however useful and pleasant, is fitted for the town rather than the country. On the east lies the most fertile and, as I believe, most cultivated region of all Scotland—the greater part, that is, of the counties of Edinburgh and Haddington, where some noble estates render the prospect varied and agreeable.

'On the north are the Pentland Hills—most healthy—moderating the current of the glacial winds in winter, and in summer increasing the heat of the sun. For in these northern regions of ours the rays of the sun, as a rule, are found even in summer-time to be useful. These mountains are covered with herds and flocks, and the herbs scattered everywhere supply rich materials for the delightful researches of the botanist.

'Now you will easily form a guess as to the temperate character of the climate. Although the atmosphere is cold in winter, yet in summer its mildness is a blessing to the inhabitants. And, indeed, throughout the British island it is a general rule that the climate is more temperate in winter as well as in summer than with you in Holland. So, here in our Scotland, many old men, grandfathers and great-grandfathers, are to be seen, enjoying the greatest felicity. The greater part of them die rather of old age than of disease.

'This country domain of mine is distinguished by many enclosures and preserves, and is everywhere fed with springs and rivulets. Some 500 acres give employment to my servants. Part is destined for pasturage, part for hay, and part for grain. Here, too, the variety greatly pleases the eye—plantations of timber, forest trees, hills and rocks interspersed, covered with shrubs and thickets. Nor are there wanting rugged and contorted boulders, those relics of an ancient world which, if not terrible of aspect, adorn the face of nature. . . .

'This in general must suffice. Now for a more particular description of my villa; and meanwhile I pray you, most illustrious sir, not to believe that I have been so blinded as not to be able to distinguish what is true from what is imaginary. . . .

'I therefore make a beginning with my house and its conveniences. It is ample rather than magnificent, useful and convenient rather than sumptuous or splendid. It shows an aged and wrinkled brow, for here my father and grandfather lived and died; but it is clean and bright, and more suited to the wants of my family than if it had been finished with all the arts and ornaments of Vitruvius.

'In the upper part of the house is the library, by no means to be despised either for the number of its volumes or the fame and dignity of their authors. There you will find books in all departments of literature—theological, legal, philosophical, mathematical, historical, medical. There is plenty of the classics, nor are there wanting various editions of them, although I should have disregarded some of them as too ponderous, and others on account of the dreams and hallucinations of their editors. The first fruits of the typographical art I venerate rather than cherish. Therefore I leave the rarer works of John Fust, Pannartz, and Sweinheym to public libraries, and would that in these libraries there could rest in peace those great commentaries of literati which have brought to the human race more disgust than utility.

'But lest my library should be quite empty of the monuments and delights of the arts, you may see there certain ancient bronze and marble statues, altar-pieces, inscriptions, and that sort of thing, as far as the slenderness of my fortune permitted. There are also in the museum a number of Greek and Roman coins, incised vases, traces of a picture of ancient workmanship. There also are objects notable for beauty or rarity, such as the bones, limbs, or skins of wild beasts, birds, and fishes; for so I would imitate Julius Cæsar and Augustus (according to Suetonius), and even if I had not the example of such great men, I should regard it as a mean thing to build up a library of huge volumes on antiquities, and yet to disdain as useless the very objects which the most learned men, as Graevius, Gronovius, and Montfaucon, have explained with such expenditure of time and toil. The things themselves speak and for the most part explain themselves; but descriptions, however accurate, present to the mind only confused or shadowy ideas. . . .

'But to continue. In the lower part of the house I have a chamber fitted up with my private and domestic things, and consecrated to study and quiet, that is, remote from the noise of my children and servants. I have here many books to be read, and read often. For I even provoke my friends and guests, and allure them by my example, by this variety to studies, each according to his bent. Therefore there is something learnt here daily. . . .

'For the basement of the house are cellars, where, in addition to plenty of our British wine made from barley, other better kinds may be found—not, indeed, Falernian nor Massic wine, but what the neighbouring nations, France, Spain, and Portugal, bestow. Moreover, what is most rare—unless this be imputed to my too great frugality or moderation—I have what sometimes Horace himself thought worthy of Mæcenas, *i.e.* wine nine years old. But, to confess the truth, if it were not for my guests I should seldom trouble my cellars, for thus I have learnt from Cornelius Celsus to want neither physician nor druggist, and to accept as a celestial oracle that first chapter of his first book on medicine. As to my tables, for the most part they are furnished with unbought feasts, for I should think it most disgraceful that a countryman such as I profess myself to be should not imitate that old man of Virgil, the Corycian.

'Throughout the other parts of the house, the hall, supper-room, dining-room, etc., are seen certain pictures, most elegant of their kind. Not, indeed, those painted by the hands of the Greeks, of Apelles, Parrhasius, Zenzides, or Protogenes, but such as others, I hardly believe of less note, have produced, such as Raphael of Urbino, the Rhenish Guido, Rubens, Vandyck, Paul Veronese, and Francis Imperialis, all of whom, as you well know, in certain matters of ornament proper to their age, could rival the Greeks and Romans, and in certain others were far their superiors, as may be easily demonstrated from fragments of ancient monuments.

'Other things upon my walls I pass over as of small moment, unless perchance my votive offering engraved on stone may for a little arrest your curiosity.'

[Here follows an inscription of twelve lines, beginning—

'Rustica sed mihi chara domus,'

and ending—

'Hæc precor utque tibi dominos gens clerica semper
Suppleant eximios qui tua rura colant.']

'Now, about my gardens, preserves, fish-ponds, and other parts of my villa, a few words must be said. The gardens are rather rustic than cultivated, according to modern elegance; and pleasant rather than sumptuous. . . . All vegetables useful for cooking are sedulously cultivated, and the trees fixed to the garden-walls might give delight to Pomona herself, for here are all the species of fruits which our Scottish land produces.

'In these gardens I think the chiefest ornament is the apiary. It gives me daily an example of industry and frugality. Heavenly gifts are there prepared, while the bees in the summer collect the honey in their waxen granaries. From their slender but courageous breasts men may learn military discipline. . . . Such rich matter for philosophising occurs to me as I watch them. . . .

'Among other gardens there is one, or rather an aviary, near the window of my chamber, where sometimes I feed the various birds with my hand. Here ducks, Guinea fowls, partridges, and occasionally pheasants, daily look for my help. In the midst is a fountain, whence water flows from an urn supported on the shoulder of the statue of a man; and by its gentle sprinkling the grass below is refreshed. Moreover, round the basin are numerous little runnels, which sometimes allure you to sleep with their pleasant murmur.

'I have various fish-ponds, and one especially which forms a lake rather than a pond. It is situated in the midst of a wood, which is dissected by a number of paths. Four little islands covered with shrubs adorn it, and afford hiding-places and protection for ducks and aquatic birds of the sort. It supports a great multitude of fish which, either from natural joy or with the desire of catching flies, are seen continually to skip and play and throw themselves about. Here, therefore, for walking, or fishing, or hunting, my whole family at times take exercise. . . .

'Nor can I omit another fish-pond, or lesser lake, noteworthy for its position and solitude, which a poet only could describe. It is surrounded by hills and steep rocks, and no one can get access to it but by the mouth of a frightful cave. To those who enter, therefore, first occurs the memory of the cave of the Cuman Sibyl, for the ruinous aperture, blocked up with stones and briars, strikes the eye. Then there comes upon the wayfarers a shudder, as they stand in doubt whether they are among the living or the dead. As, indeed, certain discords set off and give finish to musical cadencies in such a way as to render the subsequent harmony more grateful to the ear, so does the form of this mournful cave, with its long and shady path followed by the light and prospect, make the exit more delightful. For suddenly the darkness disappears, and as it were at the creation of a new world. . . .

'Further, among the aquatic adornments of this villa is conspicuous the fountain called Scobea, more lustrous than glass, or even than the Horatian fountain of Blandusia itself, surrounded on all sides by trees, and so umbrageous that Diana herself, with her nymphs, might use it for a bath. It is incredible what joys this fountain provided for my youth, and still, as often as I pass by its margin, I recall to memory those tokens of puerile innocence. It is decorated with a certain rustic piece of architecture, upon which is cut this inscription— . . . (Given before, in note to page 215.) The meadows are adorned with game preserves, woods, caves, and pleasant hills, but above all by the river Esk; and of these I must say a few words.

'The meadows are filled with every kind of field herbs, and watered with perennial streams. Therefore a multitude of tame animals, especially horses and oxen, are seen, not so much to graze as to disport themselves. The woods are in leaf with every kind of tree. Wild animals, whether quadrupeds or birds, not only endure the sight of man, but, as it were, court his society. . . .

'We have often noticed on one tree, or at a short interval, birds rapacious and tame, harmless and trustful, building their nests and cherishing their young, hawks, pigeons, woodpeckers, thrushes, crows, blackbirds, and the whole tribe of songsters. Often, also, in the same preserve, foxes, sheep, weasels, hares, wild cats, and rabbits delight to dwell.

'Among the caves, that which is called Montesina is held in renown with us, rocky and umbrageous, hidden with thick filbert bushes and various shrubs. Therefore certain wonders are told about it, and by the credulous it is taken for a seat of the subterranean gods, or dryads of the wood. Superb elms overshadow the entrance. . . .

'As to the river Esk, it has its source in the Pentland Hills, referred to above, and, after traversing many fields with serpentine twists, flows with placid rather than tumultuous waves into the estuary of the Forth, to the German Sea. Throughout its whole course it is embellished with timber, planted by art or by nature, for it is graced with many seats of the nobility, etc. Where it waters my estates it is distinguished with every gift of nature. Springs bubble up on both banks, which, with their rivulets placidly murmuring, soothe the ear and attract to solitude. . . . Among the valleys which this river adorns is one called "Turrita," which gives the picture of an immense amphitheatre, such as only the Parent of Nature could frame. . . .

'Higher up, those who walk by the bank meet a bridge, built for the private use of the house, and on the bank a certain roofed summer-house lets you see the windings and cataracts of the river. There a square stone serves for a table, and bears this inscription—

"Hic interdum studiis," etc.

Other inscriptions may be seen here and there on my estate, but these must not delay your studies and occupations. Therefore I will make an end, with this prayer only, that God, the most good and most great, may preserve and increase for a long time for us and our posterity these our joys and the desires of our home, and that you may bear with patience and indulgence this missive, more than usually verbose. Farewell.'

NOTE C, p. 7. *Wrightshouses.*—From the charter of 1664, mentioned by Douglas, it would appear that the lands of Wrightshouses had been acquired by John Clerk from William Napier of Wrightshouses, Robert Menzies of Glassie, and Robert Urie, writer in Edinburgh, subject to the reversionary interest of Napier—which may account for the fact, recorded by Stair, that a claim to the estates of Napier of Wrightshouses was made by persons of that name so late as 1680.

The present proprietors of Wrightshouses are the Governors of the Trades-Maiden Hospital, Edinburgh, who acquired it in 1762, as appears from the only title-deed in their possession, a charter of sale from the Crown, as superior, following upon a judicial sale, and dated 6th August in that year. This document throws no light upon the statement in Douglas as to the disposal of the estate by John Clerk. The oldest deed referred to in it is a procuratory of resignation by Colin Mackenzie in favour of Sir John Clerk of Pennycuick, dated 1689, by whom the estate seems to have been conveyed to a Robert Clerk on 6th January 1710. It passed from a James Clerk (probably the heir of Robert) in 1720, under a decree of sale, into the hands of Sir William Menzies of Gladstanes. In 1754 it was the property of James Hamilton of Gilkerscleugh and Robert Ramsay of Blackcraig. From them it went to James Mitchelson, jeweller in Edinburgh, and from him to the present proprietors.—M.

NOTE D, p. 8. *The Court Book of the Baronies of Lasswade and Loanhead.*—Amongst the documents preserved in the Clerk family there is an interesting record of the barony courts for Lasswade and Loanhead commencing in 1664, a date some thirty-two years before the acquisition of these estates by the first Sir John Clerk, and continuing down to 1740. There must be many similar records preserved in old charter-chests, and they are of considerable value not only in illustrating the manners, customs, and superstitions of the time, but also in giving us a good idea of the mode in which petty justice—both criminal and civil—was administered at a period when the modern Sheriff Court (which, under the fostering care of the Legislature, has extinguished its former rivals) was practically non-existing. The barony court was certainly an anomalous institution; and although, when its powers were wisely made use of, it must have benefited the district, it certainly gave wide scope for injustice and tyranny. The baron was an exception to the sound rule that no one ought to be judge in his own cause, for a large proportion of the business in his court must have consisted in proceedings at his instance against his vassals and tenants, in which he either gave judgment himself or by means of the bailie, who was his creature. Baron courts have never recovered the cruel blow struck at them by the Act of George II. putting an end to heritable jurisdictions. The baron's jurisdiction, both civil and criminal, although not abolished, was so limited by that Act that it was hardly worth the trouble of administrating it, while he, his bailie and his prison were put under the humiliating supervision of the Sheriff and Sheriff-Clerk. The glory of the baron courts has vanished for ever, and they have, along with other institutions, had to give way to the progress of civilisation.

At the date when this record commences, the court is described as being held at Lasswade, Sir John Nicolson, baronet of Lasswade, being the baron. In 1670, however, there is a court described as that of the barony of Nicolson. Later, in 1687, the name Loanhead of Lasswade is introduced, and about this date a factor for the estate of Nicolson appears on the scene, to be followed in due time by a new baron in the shape of Sir John Clerk (the first baronet), whose first court, set forth as that of the 'baronie of Laswade holden at Loanhead,' bears date 23d October 1696. On and after this date we hear no more of 'Nicolson.'

It is impossible within the compass of a brief note to give an adequate idea of the number of matters dealt with in such a court. Its work may be said to fall under the divisions of legislative and judicial. It made laws, *inter alia*, for the regulation of the drink traffic, observance of the Sabbath, and the protection of the baron's estate, and punished persons for breaches of these laws, and it also acted as a tribunal for the disposal of minor criminal trials and civil actions. Sir John seems to have set about a vigorous reformation of his little community at the very outset. Drunkards were to be punished with a fine of one shilling Scots for the first offence, with a further threat of an abode in the 'jogs' until caution be found for future 'peaceable and Christian behaviour.' The sale of drink within the barony was apparently entirely prohibited, as also the supply of drink in private houses to excess, under the terrible sanction of the names being given up to the Kirk-session of Lasswade.

Persons failing to keep the church or to sanctify the Lord's Day, or whoever came home betwixt sermons without a weighty cause, were to be looked upon as profane and unworthy of Christian fellowship, and if a rebuke did not serve to correct their ways, banishment from the barony was to follow. Home life upon the Sabbath was strictly watched. Those who were not at church (for some weighty cause) were to keep within doors all day, and not even to sit at their doors. The barony officers were at intervals to go through 'the heill houses of Loanhead in tyme of public worship and mark who are at home and what is their carriage.' Children gathering of a Sunday together, 'as ordinarly they do,' to play on the high roads, were to be beaten privately by their parents for the first and second offence and publicly for the third, upon the following Monday morning.

These provisions were made, be it observed, by a man whose moderation had enabled him to escape all molestation during the years following upon the Restoration.

All masters of families were to set up the worship of God in their houses, and to pray, read the Bible, and sing psalms morning and evening with their children and servants. But there is much kindness in the intimation to the coaliers (the serfs of the barony) which follows, and in terms of which Sir John undertakes to educate at his own expense the children of those who are not able to do this themselves.

As a specimen of the judicial work performed in the court the following case, decided 11th March 1697, may suffice:—We find John Gilles complaining against Margrat Miller that the latter had slandered his mother a few days previously by calling her, in her absence, a witch, offering to prove this by famous witnesses, and consigning in the bailie's hands the sum of five pounds Scots 'as his fyne in case he succombd in ye probatione.' Then follows the names of the witnesses, and the purport of their evidence, which was to the effect that the defender was heard on one occasion addressing the pursuer's daughter with the expression 'witche's brood,' and using similar terms, but without naming any person. The bailie found the libel not proven, 'but y^t^ ye said Marg^r^ Miller gave great offence to Margrat Gilles and others by her rash speeches, ordained her to crave pardone, to finde caution for her futor and peaceable behaviour, and to pay five pound of fyne, qh she did; as also decerned ye s^d^ John Gilles to have lost ye s^d^ five pounds which he consigned in respect he succombd in ye probatione.'—M.

NOTE E, p. 53. *The Act of Security and Liberty of the Plantations.*—England having refused to Scotsmen equal mercantile privileges to those enjoyed by Englishmen and equal right to trade with foreign colonies and 'plantations,' Scotland retaliated by the Act of Security. In the Parliament of 1703 there was much dispute from 21st till 26th July over the clause indicated in the Baron's side-note, and in the Parliamentary Minutes of the last-named day it was re-adjusted, inserted, and agreed to as follows:—'It is hereby specially Statute, Enacted, and Declared, that it shall not be in the power of the said meeting of Estates to name the Successor to the Crown of England, to be Successor to the Crown of the Realm, nor shall the same Person be capable in any event to be King or Queen of both Realms, unless a free communication of Trade, the freedom of Navigation, and the liberty of the Plantations be fully agreed to.' In the Act as passed in the following Session, 5th August 1704, the clause is made more general, and the phrase 'liberty of the Plantations' is omitted:—'. . . unless that in the present session of this or any ensuing Parliament during her Majestie's reign there be such Conditions of government settled and enacted as may secure the Honour and Sovereignty of this Crown and Kingdom, the freedom, frequency, and power of Parliament, the Religious Liberty and Trade of the Nation, from English or other foreign influence.'

NOTE F, p. 54. *The Rev. John Hepburn.*—John Hepburn, A.M., son of James Hepburn, farmer in Morayshire, had his degree at the University and King's College, Aberdeen, in 1669, ordained by the Presbyterian ministers at London in 1678. He was accused of intruding into the ministry, 'thereby debauching weak men and women, drawing them into rebellious methods in Ross-shire, 6th March 1680, and declared fugitive, 5th May 1684; called hither in 1680, 1685, and 1689. He was suspended by the General Assembly, 4th January 1696, for disorderly courses, which sentence was taken off by the Assembly, 30th January 1699, on his promising to confine his ministry for to the parish. In 1696, he was also tried before the Privy Council not taking the oaths to Government, and adjudged to confine himself to the town of Brechin, and two miles around, and in case he find not caution, to be imprisoned in the Tolbooth of Edinburgh, which was changed after to the Castle of Stirling, where he remained about three months, but was prevented for nearly three years from returning to the parish. He was suspended by the Commission of Assembly in 1704, served with a long libel, and deposed, after many warnings, 9th April 1705, "after having neither dispensed the Lord's Supper to others, nor partaken thereof himself, for more than sixteen years, and been guilty of a continuous tract of erroneous, seditious, and divisive doctrines, and schismatical courses, wherein he is obstinate, and refuses to be reclaimed." He was reponed, however, 12th August 1707, partly by reason of a protest from the heritors, elders, and inhabitants of the parish, and partly by his conciliatory declaration. He formed a presbytery with another disaffected brother about 1713, which lasted a very short while, and died 20th March 1723, aged about 74, in the forty-fifth year of his ministry. Remarkable effects sometimes attended his ministry, especially in prayer, which sometimes continued for hours together, while he was equally fervid in preaching. He was strenuously opposed to the Union of the kingdom in 1707, to the Act of Toleration, and to the ambiguous character of the Oaths of Abjuration and Supremacy. So zealous was he against Popery that books on the subject which he could find in the parish were collected and set fire to on the Corse Hill; and when the Protestant Succession to the Throne was endangered in 1715, he raised a volunteer corps of 300, and marched at their head, having on their standard an inscription, "For the Lord of Hosts." He married, in April 1701, Emila, daughter of Alexander Nisbett of Craigentinny, and had a son, Mr. John, who became one of the ministers of Edinburgh. Publications: *True Copy of a Letter sent to the Rev. Will. Vetch, min. of Dumfries, Answering some Gross Calumnies in his Pamphlet entitled "A short History of Rome's designs, etc."* (In Vetch's answer it is asserted that the real authors were Riddoch and Hunter, and other Popish emissaries.) *Some Additional Rules for Fellowship Meetings* (Smith's *Directory*, Edin. 1738, 12mo).'—Scott's *Fasti.* Part II. pp. 607-8.

In *Humble Pleadings for the Good Old Way* (*s.l.* 1713), a manifesto of Hepburn's adherents will be found, at pp. 2-5, a list of six 'principles,' 'for the most part read in almost the same words at the committee held at *Sanquhar*, *anno* 1705, and approven by the Ministers Members of the same.' These are briefly—I. Adherence to the Scriptures and the Confessions of the Church of Scotland; II. Adherence to the Forms of Worship of the Church of Scotland; III. Adherence to the Presbyterian Form of Church Government; IV. Belief in the Headship of Christ and Independence of the Church upon any Foreign Civil Power, whether Supreme or Subordinate: V. Approbation of the Reformation from Popery and Prelacy; VI. Adherence to the National Covenants. Then follows a list of twenty-six specified grievances against Church and State; and the first part of the volume concludes with the statement that 'we resolve to dissent no longer if our grievances were Redressed, or honestly sought to be Redressed.'

The second part of the volume deals more particularly with the life and 'contendings' of Hepburn. See also *The Last Testimony of the Reverend, Pious, and Painful Servant of Christ, Mr. John Hepburn* (*s.l.* 1723).

It will be remembered that it was at Sanquhar that the celebrated Declaration of Cameron, Cargill, and their adherents—modelled, with alterations, on the Queensferry Paper found on the dead body of Cargill—was affixed to the market-cross, on 22d June 1680. See Hetherington's *History of the Church of Scotland*, vol. ii. p. 109; and Wodrow, vol. iii. p. 218.

NOTE G, p. 66. *Pamphlets attributed to Baron Sir John Clerk.*—I have not been able to discover a pamphlet with the title given above, but a copy of *A Letter to a Friend giving an Account how the Treaty of Union has been received here, and wherein are contained some remarks upon what has been written by Mr. H. and Mr. R., Edinburgh, Printed in the year* M.D.CCVI., in the Advocates' Library, is inscribed in a contemporary hand 'By Mr. John Clerk of Pennycook, younger,' which, taken in connection with the statement above—'these pieces were known to be mine'—seems to be evidence of considerable weight as to its authorship. Wilson includes this pamphlet in his list of De Foe's works (*Memoirs*, vol. i. p. 32), and identifies the 'Mr. H.' of the title-page as James Hodges (a Presbyterian minister, author of an *Essay upon the Union, etc.*, Edinr., 1706), and the 'Mr. R.' as George Ridpath (author of *Considerations upon the Union of the Two Kingdoms*, n. p. 1706), but in vol. ii. p. 491, he merely states that 'this seems to have been written by an Englishman, and probably by De Foe.' Lee (*Life and Recently Discovered Works of Defoe*, vol. iii. p. 133) notes that 'Mr. Wilson attributes this to Defoe, although he does not appear to have seen a copy. Not having myself been more successful, I adopt a saying of our author's and "leave it as I find it."' But all doubt as to the authorship of the pamphlet is set at rest by a copy preserved at Penicuik House, which is inscribed on the title-page, in the Baron's own handwriting, 'Written by J. C. of P., afterwards B. of E.' It is a vigorous and readable pamphlet of forty-four pages, and contains a clear exposition of the same opinions upon the Union as are expressed in the present MS. That Clerk was practically at one with De Foe on the subject may be gathered from his good opinion of the Englishman's *History of the Union*, given in his side-note to folio 75 above (page 64): 'There is not one single fact in it that I can challenge.' As an example of the style of the pamphlet I may quote two passages:—

'In a corner of the Street one may see a *Presbyterian Minister*, a *Popish Priest*, and an *Episcopal Prelate*, all agreeing together in their discource against the Union: but upon quite different views and contradictory Reasons. The *Minister*, because he fears the Presbyterian Church Government will be ruined, and so great encouragement will be given to Popery and Prelacy. The *Priest*, because his Darling Hopes will be disappointed, by the settling the Succession in the Protestant Line. And the *Prelate*, because he knows the Parliament will make such a Security for the Presbyterian Church Government, as that it cannot be altered in *Scotland* without saping the Fundation of the Union, and shaking the whole Fabrick of the *British* Constitution,' p. 7.

'We have the Honour indeed to pretend to *Chastity* (as some call it) having never been Conquered; but this should serve only to entice us to imitate the Conduct of a chaste Virgin, who, because she fears her own Weakness, and want of Resolution to continue long in that Condition, prudently enters into Wedlock: by which sort of Union, she acquires indeed the Name of being one flesh with her Husband, yet at the same time she remains that very numerical Honourable Person that she was before,' p. 9.

It may be noticed that a pamphlet on *Money and Trade considered, with a Proposal for supplying the Nation with Money*, 4to, Edinr., 1705, has been incorrectly attributed to Clerk in the *Dictionary of National Biography*. In the Advocates' Library this pamphlet is twice indexed, in immediately succeeding entries: the first copy being correctly assigned to John Law, of the Mississippi Scheme, under whose name the second edition, published in 1750, was issued; but the second copy being erroneously assigned to Clerk, on the authority of a MS. note on its title-page, in a contemporary hand (different from both of those that appear in the two jottings referred to above)—'By John Clerk of Pennicook, yr.'

NOTE H, p. 77. *Edinburgh Residences of the Clerks of Penicuik.*—By disposition dated 23d June 1697, John Clerk (the author of these Memoirs), with the advice and consent of his father, Sir John Clerk, and Sir John Clerk for his own right and interest, conveyed this house or lodging to Andrew Patersone of Kirktoun, 'wright, burges' of Edinburgh, and Patrick Steel, vintner, burges, jointly, the purchase money being six thousand merks Scots, with five guineas in gold. John Clerk, junior, who was the proprietor, is described as the heir to the umquile Mr. Hendry Hendersone, doctor of medicine, 'my goodsir on the mother's syde.' Sir John's interest in the property may have arisen under his marriage-contract. The description of the property, which affords an idea of what constituted an aristocratic dwelling at that period, is as follows:—'All and haill that lodgeing lying on the south syde of the high street of Edinburgh, at the head of Blackfriars wynd, presently possessed by Lady Susanna Campbell, consisting of one outer roome, kitchen, and dining-roome, bed-chamber, and closet, and one fore chamber towards the high street of Edinburgh, all in the third storrie from the street, with two bed-chambers above the s[d] dining-room and laigh chamber, with ane closet in the fourth storrie, with ane cellar at the foot of the turnpick, belonging to the s[d] lodgeing.' There is further conveyed what is described as 'a little lodgeing presently possessed by me, the s[d] Sir John, consisting of ane large room towards the s[d] high street of Edinburgh, ane little bed-chamber, with three closets, in the fourth storrie, and two garrets above the samen, as also ain laigh house in Blackfriars wynd, with ane little timber shop at the door thereof, presently possessed by widow Mossman . . . all which are ane pairt of that tenement of land sometyme waist and burnt by the Englishmen, fore and back, under and above, sometyme pertaining to umquile Mr. John Prestoune, President of the College of Justice, and thereafter to Sir Michael Prestoune of Fentonbarns, his sone.' Dr. Wilson, in his *Memorials*, describes Lord President Fentonbarns' house as one of the finest specimens of ancient style of building in Edinburgh, having the main timbers of its open façade richly carved in the fashion of some of the magnificent old timber fronts of the opulent Flemings in Bruges or Ghent. He also quotes from a disposition by Sir Michael, dated 1626, in which there is the same reference to 'the waist and burnt land' as is given in that of the Clerks, and points out that this shows the erection to have been subsequent to 1544. The house seems also to have suffered from the siege in 1572. John Preston of Fentonbarns was appointed Commissary of Edinburgh in 1580, and a Lord of Session in 1595, Lord President in 1609, and died in 1616. It would thus appear that even at the end of the seventeenth century this fine mansion had undergone the process of division amongst various possessors. Dr. Wilson, upon the authority of Chambers, refers to another fine old house in Blackfriars Wynd as the town residence of the Clerks. It is that which was known as Cardinal Beaton's house. In 1756 Sir James Clerk (the son of Sir John) had a lodging in the head of Blackfriars Wynd either as proprietor or tenant. If in the former capacity, he must have contemplated a further acquisition, as amongst the Clerk papers there is preserved a search for encumbrances, evidently made with a view to purchase. The fact that the disposition in favour of Paterson and Steel also forms one of these papers may point to Dr. Henderson's house having become again the possession of the Clerks at a later period, perhaps by the year 1710, when the Baron states that he was residing at the head of Blackfriars Wynd 'in my own home.'

Dr. Wilson says that Sir James Clerk purchased the family mansion of the Sempills in Sempill Close in 1755. Another old house which is associated with the Clerk family is that of Bailie Macmoran in Riddell's Close, but this was at an earlier date.—M.

Wilson, in his *Memorials of Edinburgh* (pp. 168 and 169, ed. of 1872), states that the last-named residence, after passing through several generations of the Macmorans, 'was acquired by Sir John Clerk of Pennycuick. By him it was sold to Sir Robert Mackenzie of Preston Hall;' and in his *Reminiscences of Old Edinburgh*, vol. ii. pp. 166, 170, he states, without giving his authority, that in the year when Gordon's *Itinerarium* was published (1726) the Baron wrote a letter to Gale from that address, referring, *inter alia*, to Gordon's scheme for cutting a canal between the Clyde and Forth. The letter, however, is printed in *Reliquiæ Galeanæ*, and is there headed simply 'Edinburgh, August 29, 1726.' The present owners of the Riddell's Court property have courteously permitted an examination of the title-deeds in their possession; but these afford no information as to its having been the property of the Clerks.

NOTE I, p. 77. *Elixar Proprietatis.*—'*Elixi. Proprietat. nost.* resists putrifaction, opens the Spleen, helps Digestion, purifies the Blood: it is very cordial,' etc.—P. 20 of *The Direct Method of Curing Chymically*, by Geo. Thomson, M.D.: London, 1675.—L.

NOTE K, p. 78. *Cammo.*—In J. P. Wood's 'Parish of Cramond' (Edinburgh, 1794), will be found a view of the House of Cammo or New Saughton, and an account of the various owners of the estate:—

From a charter dated 1345, it appears to have belonged to the abbot and convent of Inchcolm: and by an indenture, dated 30th March 1409, Bishop Cardney, who had obtained Cammo heritably by an excambion and contract of sale from John, Abbot of Inchcolm, gave and granted the lands to John de Nudre; the descendant of whose daughter, John Mowbray of Cammo, sold the estate in 1637 to William Wilkie, merchant in Edinburgh, of the family of Foulden in Berwickshire. John Menzies of Coulteraller married Wilkie's grand-daughter, who, on her death, in 1688, bequeathed Cammo to her husband; who built a mansion-house, and in 1710 sold the 'estate to Sir John Clerk of Pennycuick, a gentleman whose antiquarian knowledge has been much and justly celebrated. . . . His long residence at Cammo, and his connection with Sir John Inglis, were the means of enriching his museum with innumerable coins and other remains of antiquity found at Cramond.'

In 1726 Sir John sold Cammo for £4333, 6s. 8d. to John Hog of Ladykirk,[1] in Berwickshire (nephew of Sir Roger Hog of Harcarse, Senator of the College of Justice), who, in 1741, sold it for £4252, 10s. to James Watson of Saughton, who changed its name to New Saughton; and who was succeeded in 1778 by his only surviving son, Captain Charles Watson of Saughton.

For the more recent history of Cammo I am indebted to Mr. Archibald Steuart, W.S.:—Charles Watson was succeeded by his eldest son James, who was infeft in 1805; James was succeeded in 1833 by Charles his eldest son, who was followed in 1837 by William Ramsay Watson, and in 1841 by Helen Watson, afterwards Lady Aberdour. She, in 1851, was succeeded by her only child, the Honourable Sholto George Watson Douglas, Lord Aberdour, who sold the property in 1873 to the late Alexander Campbell, Esq., of 6 Charlotte Square, Edinburgh, by whose trustees it is now held. In the same year Mr. Campbell acquired by purchase from Lady Aberdour's trustees and added to the estate the adjoining lands of Braehead Mains.

NOTE L, pp. 108 and 113. *The Rev. Alexander Moncrieff of Culfargie.*—The Rev. Alexander Moncrieff of Culfargie was the son of Matthew Moncrieff of Culfargie, a grandson of the Rev. Alexander Moncrieff, minister of Scoonie, a prominent ecclesiastic in the 17th century, who narrowly escaped with his life after the Restoration.

Moncrieff was born in 1695, and studied at St. Andrews and Leyden, and at the latter University distinguished himself. He was licensed in 1717, and ordained minister of his native parish of Abernethy in 1720. In 1732, he, along with three other ministers, including Ebenezer Erskine, took up an antagonistic position towards the majority of the Church, which led to their suspension and the formation of the Associate Synod.

His wife, Mary Clerk, died within a few years of her marriage, and their only surviving issue was a son, Matthew, who afterwards succeeded to the estate of Culfargie, and who became a minister of the sect which his father had assisted in founding. Alexander Moncrieff married a second time, in 1728, Jean Lyon (daughter of the Rev. William Lyon of Ogil, minister of Airlie), by whom he had a very large family. He died in 1761. He was the author of numerous pamphlets and sermons, chiefly of a controversial nature.

Sir John Clerk seems to have had but little sympathy with his brother-in-law's 'seceding scheme,' and endeavoured to bring him to a more reasonable mind. In notes of a letter dated June 28, 1739, preserved at Penicuik, the worthy baronet complains that although Culfargie comes to preach in the neigh-

---

[1] See page 116 above; where the date of the sale is given as the summer of 1724, and the price received as '4200 lib. ster., or thereby.' John Hog's son, of the same name, died in 1744, and his widow, second daughter of Sir Christopher Musgrave of Edenhall, Cumberland, married, in 1749, the Right Hon. John Idle, Chief Baron of the Court of Exchequer. See page 133 above, and note [1] there.

bourhood he never comes near him. True religion, he contends, consists 'not in forms, but in acts of charity, benevolence, and brotherly love as well as of faith.' He also holds up the example of Whitefield, whose friendly intercourse, by the way, with the Establishment gave much offence to the infant Secession. Another matter referred to is the position taken up by the dissenters against the Government in the matter of the Porteous murder. The former refused to read the Act referring to it from the pulpit, and to communicate with such as did. Sir John is very indignant, and characterises this conduct as abominable.

To this letter, extending to seven quarto pages, Mr. Moncrieff seems to have replied in such a spirit that Sir John, in the following month of July, dating from Mavisbank, writes: 'Your open way of corresponding with me was so agreeable that I fancy if we were more together I could get you to laugh at your seceding schemes; but to get you to have a better opinion than you entertain of our Church government at present is what I do not expect.' He again refers to Mr. Whitefield: 'I wish you would only imitate him in the main thing—to wit, in a peaceable, charitable disposition.' At the same time he finds fault with Whitefield for inducing men to neglect their business and 'goe a gading after conventicles as they doe at present,' and estimates the loss thus endangered to the nation of one day's work in the week at eight millions of sixpences. He has to confess to having passed by Culfargie's house on the last occasion of a visit to Fife, disgusted apparently by the crowds of idle people whom he had witnessed flocking to Abernethy on the Friday before the Sacrament. The rest of the letter is taken up with the question of the Porteous Act and of the Abolition of Patronage. 'Is it not an absurd thing,' he argues, 'that a tenant or servant who may be removed at a certain term should have a vote in choosing a minister for life to his master?' To him it seemed inconceivable that patronage should ever be abolished, and wrong to stir people up to wish for what they cannot obtain. The tone of the letter is, on the whole, an irritable one, and hardly consistent with the charity which he preaches.—M.

NOTE M, p. 115. *Mavisbank.*—The estate of Mavisbank, including the mansion-house, was conveyed by Sir James Clerk, third Baronet, to Robert Clark or Clerk (grandson of Dr. Robert Clerk, the youngest son of John Clerk, first owner of Penicuik) in July 1763. In 1815 his disponees sold it to Mr. Græme Mercer, from whose trustees it was acquired by the late George Clerk Arbuthnot, merchant in Liverpool, in 1842. The Crown Charter in his favour is dated 23d January 1843. By his trustees it was afterwards sold to the Messrs. Annandale, who re-sold it in 1876 to the Heritages Association, Limited, and by them in 1876 it was disposed of to the present proprietors, the Mavisbank Company, Limited, and the house is now used as an asylum.—M.

In its general effect of frontage Mavisbank House is much as the Baron left it; for the additions of recent date have been made quite independently as an extension of the wing to our right, and the modern porch at the back does not obtrude itself upon our notice. The two old projecting wings have charmingly pitched concave Georgean roofs; that of the central portion being convex. The central block has a fine massive effect, with its bold pediment, its windows enriched with carved fruit and leafage, and its sculptured decoration above the main entrance, which is shaped like a classical altar and admirably designed, and now shows armorial bearings.

Above one of the windows appears the date 1724; and the front bears two Latin inscriptions by the Baron. On one side is—

'HANC IN GREMIO RESONANTIS SILVAE
AQUIS HORTIS AVIUM GARRITU
CAETERISque RURIS HONORIBUS
UNDIQUE RENIDENTEM VILLAM
NON MAGNIFICAM NON SUPERBAM
AT QUALEM VIDES.
COMMODAM MUNDAM GENIALEM
NATURÆ PAREM SOCIANS ARTEM
SIBI SUISQUE.
AD VITAM PLACIDE
ET TRANQUILLE AGENDAM
DESIGNAVIT INSTRUXITQUE
D
I C
ÆRARII TRIBUNUS
M.DCC.XXIV.'

And on the other side appears the following:—

'PARVA DOMUS, NEMOROSA QUIES, SIS TU QUOQUE NOSTRIS
HOSPITIUM LARIBUS, SUBSIDIUMQUE DIU,
POSTES FLORA TUOS ORNET, POMONAQUE MENSAS,
CONFERAT ET VARIAS FERTILIS HORTUS OPES,
TE VOLUCRES PICTÆ CINGENTES VOCE CANORA,
RETIA SOLA CANANT QUAE SIBIT TENDIT AMOR,
FLORIFERI COLLES, DULCES MIHI SÆPE RECESSUS
DENT, ATQUE HOSPITIBUS GAUDIA PLENA MEIS.
CONCEDATQUE DEUS, NUNQUAM VEL SERO SENESCAS
SEROQUE TERRENAS EXPERIARE VICES
INTEGRA REDDANTUR, QUAE PLURIMA SAECULA RODANT
DETUR ET UT SENIO PULCHRIOR ENITEAS.'

Behind the house rises, in green abruptness, a trenched Roman camp, which must have been dear to the Baron's reverently antiquarian soul.

Lower, to the left, beneath the slopes, is the large level space of the gardens, enclosed with walls of mellow red brick, which have their own point of stately classicism in the touches of rich carving on the stone pilasters of the entrance. Venerable yew-trees make a duskier note of green against the grass, as they gather round the ornamental pond, with its spouting Cupid of bronze; and there is a wide inner enclosure, where beyond the stretch of emerald sward we catch sight of the classic shape and the embossed convex roof of the summer-house built by the Baron, as appears by the date, 1731, with which it is inscribed.

NOTE N, pp. 130 and 135. *Dumcrieff and Craigieburn.*—The lands of Dumcrieff (formerly spelt Drumcreich or Drumcrief), in the parish of Moffat and county of Dumfries, belonged to a family of Murray from anterior to 1632 up to 1724, when John Murray and Grizel Douglas, his spouse, conveyed to Lord George Douglas, brother-german to Charles, Duke of Queensberry and Dover, who got a Crown Charter in that year. The Duke was served heir in special to his brother, and was infeft on a Precept from Chancery in 1726. On 29th November 1726 he conveyed to Sir John Clerk of Pennycuik. In 1737 Sir John disponed the lands to George Clerk, his second son, afterwards Sir George Clerk, who had a Crown Charter in 1738. Sir George Clerk, by Disposition 1782, registered in Books of Council and Session 15th January 1783, in which he is designed George Clerk Maxwell, Esq. of Dumcrieff, one of the Commissioners of His Majesty's Customs, conveyed with consent of Mrs. Dorothea Clerk Maxwell, his spouse, *inter alia*, these lands to Alexander Farquharson, accountant in Edinburgh, as trustee for his creditors. Farquharson, as trustee, with consent of Sir George, disponed on 22d May 1783 to Lieutenant-Col. Wm. Johnston, of the Royal Artillery. He, on 1st March 1792, disponed to Dr. James Currie, physician in Liverpool, who had a Crown Charter, dated 2d July in that year. Dr. James Currie's testamentary trustees disponed in 1806 to Dr. John Rogerson, who was succeeded in the Dumcrieff Estate by his grandson, John Rogerson Rollo, now Lord Rollo and Dunning, who had a Crown Charter 3d February 1840, and is the present proprietor of Dumcrieff and adjoining lands.

By Sasine dated 12th April and registered at Dumfries 6th May 1729, Sir John Clerk was infeft in the half of the lands of Craigieburn, purchased by him from William Johnston, son of Archibald Johnston of Girthhead. The other half belonged to Archibald Tod, son of John Tod, in Craigbeck, who, with Archibald Johnston, was heir-portioner of Robert Murray. By Contract of Division and Disposition between Sir John Clerk and Thomas Tod, minister of the gospel at Durrisdeer, dated 13th December 1733, the lands of Craigieburn or Cragyburn were divided, and the portion conveyed to Sir John Clerk became incorporated with the Dumcrieff property.

NOTE O, pp. 142 and 152. *Baron Clerk and the Restoration of Rosslyn Chapel: Date of its Foundation.*—When Gale visited Scotland in the autumn of 1739 the Baron furnished him with 'Memorandums for travelling from Edinburgh to Glasgow' (Nichols' *Bibliotheca Topographica Britannica—Reliquiæ Galeanæ*—No. 2, Part III. pp. 320-2). In Gale's letter to Maurice Johnston, dated 'Scruton, 18 Aug. 1739' (*ibid.* pp. 323-6), he mentions that he was at Penicuik House, and twice at Mavisbank; and he further gives such particulars as enable us to add to the list of the Baron's good deeds the preservation of Rosslyn Chapel, that richest example of Gothic in Scotland. Gale writes:—'We were twice at Mavisbank, four miles to the south of Edenborough, built by Sir John Clerk, in a true Palladio style, one of the most elegant I ever saw, for situation, wood, and water, though the house is small. We went four miles farther to another seat of Sir John's, that is called Pennycuick (*Mons cuculi*), built in the ancient style, but not without its natural beauties, particularly a vast pond or lake, with two islands in it, and full of fish. In the way to it we saw Roslin-chapel, a most noble Gothic structure, exceeded by few: founded, as appears by an inscription cut the whole length of it over the windows, by William Sinclair, Earl of Orkney and Zetland, A.D. 1453. It has laid open to the weather ever since the Reformation, but has withstood all its effects, by the goodness of the materials, and the excellency of its work to a miracle; however, the rain now penetrating through the roof, which is vaulted with stone, would in a few years have dissolved it entirely, had not that true lover of antiquities and all the liberal arts, Sir John Clerk, persuaded the present Lord Sinclair to put it into compleat repair. The workmen have been upon it all this summer, and as Sir John has the whole direction of it, in a year more it will not be only secured from ruin, but be made as beautiful and stately as most of that sort of edifices in the kingdom, though it is like to be used as only a burying-place for that noble family of whom there is only one tomb in it now, and that in the same wretched condition as the rest of the fabric, which brings to my mind the forlorn state of Holyrood-house in the palace of Edenborough, a most magnificent building, having been the east end of the Abbey-church, the burying-place of their kings and nobility, but now much like a dog-kennel, the tombs laid open or destroyed, the whole full of dirt and rubbish.' Among the Baron's papers are two sketches, evidently made by him at the time when he was superintending the repairs at the Chapel. They preserve the inscription along the top of the north clerestory wall, which shows, on square compartments, between grotesque heads and shields bearing the engrailed cross of the Sinclairs, the letters 'W. L. S. F. Y. C. Y. Z. O. G. M. iiij. L.' In our own time, when the Chapel was restored by the late Andrew Kerr, F.S.A. Scot., he also transcribed the inscription, and engraved it in his account of the Chapel (*Proceedings of the Society of Antiquaries of Scot.*, 14th May 1877). It was then read by Dr. T. Dickson of the Register House as standing for 'William Lorde Sinclaire Fundit Yis College Ye Zeir Of God, M. iiij. L. (1450),' thus, apparently, settling the exact date of foundation. The Baron's sketches and accompanying notes, however, are interesting not only as showing that he had deciphered the beginning of the inscription as standing for 'William, Lord Sinclair,' but also as preserving the fact that three other compartments follow those figured by Mr. Kerr, two of them showing shields bearing the engrailed cross, with between them a square similar to the others that are inscribed with letters but with a blank surface, having possibly been originally inscribed with a continuation of the date. An examination of the Chapel wall shows that this blank compartment still holds its place at the top of the clerestory wall. It should be noted that Gale—as quoted above—gives the date 1453 as that appearing on the inscription: but it is curious that the Baron, in his transcript of this inscription, gives the year as 1450, followed by a blank square.

NOTE P, p. 144. *The Estate of Middlebie.*—Dorothea Maxwell and George Clerk were married in 1735; and in order to simplify their affairs the baron obtained a decree of the Court of Session, followed by an Act of Parliament, by which (notwithstanding the entail of 1722) Middlebie proper was sold to liquidate the Maxwell debts, and was bought in for George Clerk, whose title was thus freed from burdens, and, so far, from the conditions of the entail. George Clerk Maxwell sold portions of Middlebie to various purchasers, principally to the Duke of Queensberry, and the estate was thus reduced to something like its present area. See Campbell and Garnet's *Life of James Clerk Maxwell*, p. 23.

The courtesy of Alexander Wedderburn Maxwell of Middlebie has supplied us with the following facts about that estate. It was a possession of the Lord Maxwells, and was bestowed by Robert, tenth lord, to John Maxwell, his half-brother. From him it went by direct descent to his great-granddaughter Agnes, who married William Clerk. Their daughter, an heiress, Dorothea, married her cousin George Clerk, afterwards third baronet. The property was entailed in 1722, and under the deed any heir adopting another title than that of Maxwell of Middlebie was declared to forfeit the right to succeed. When the late Sir George Clerk was served heir to Penicuik, his younger brother, taking the name of Clerk Maxwell, was served heir to Middlebie. Upon the death of his son, Professor James Clerk Maxwell, without issue, the estate went to the present proprietor through his mother, Isabella Clerk, wife of James Wedderburn.—M.

NOTE Q, p. 145. *Letter from the Baron when sending Patrick and Henry to School.*—Among the Clerk papers is a copy in the Baron's autograph of 'A Letter by me to Mr. Lesley, schoolmaster of Haddington, 30th October 1730, when my sons Patrick and Henry were sent to him:'—

'Sir,—I send you two of my sones, and committ them to God and your care.

'I have no particular thing to recommend save one on which all parents ought to joyn with me, that is, that our boys should be brought up in the old Greek and Roman way, in the constant exercise of Eloquence. This sort of Education fitted all their youth to the management of their sacred and civil concerns. The jesuits abroad, who understand the education of youth to a very great nicety, bring up their boys in this way.

'I approved much of your methode to make your boys once a year act a play in publick. This gave them a decent behaviour and seem'd to prepare them for the business of the world, but if this has been found troublesome or expensive, I would earnestly recommend to you that once a week you wou'd cause one or more of your boys pronounce in English from a pulpet in the most publick manner you can think of. This exercise will fit them either for the pulpet or the barr and doe much honour to your school. You will find abundance of speeches ready made to your hand in Quintillian's declamations in English will furnish you with severals. I disapprove of speeches in Latine, and so do the best judges in the education of youth abroad. Those who can speak in English will always be able to declame in Latine when there is any occasion for it, especially if they be any way conversant in Cicero and Quintilian.

'As to their diet, I have likeways but one thing to recommend to you, that is, that your boys at every mail should at least accustom themselves to one glass of water. They are very unhappily bred who cannot at all times satisfy their thirst with water: Ἄριστον μὲν ὕδωρ, as Pindar begins his book.

'I send 8 lib. stg. as their first quarter's board, the rest and other dues of the School shall be sent to you when you please, &c.—I am, &c., J. C.'

Allan Ramsay wrote 'A Prologue before the Acting of Aurengzebe at Haddington School,' in 1727, concluding—

'"Get seven score verse of Ovid's Trist by heart,
To rattle o'er, else I shall make ye smart,"
Cry snarling dominies that little ken;
Such may teach parrots, but our Lesly men.'

In a note the poet refers to the teacher as 'Mr. John Lesly, master of the school of Haddington; a gentleman of true learning, who, by his excellent method, most worthily fills his place.'

NOTE R, p. 160. *Scheme for Improvement of the Barony of Penicuik.*—Among the Clerk Papers is a MS. of fifty-six folio pages, in the Baron's handwriting, titled 'Scheme of Improvements in the Baronie of Penicuik and in the Lands of Lauhead, Utershill, and Montlothian, belonging to me, S. J. C., Pennicuik, 12 May 1741:'—'That which induces me to give this Schem of Improvements is a persuasion that if any of my Posterity make money it will be better laying it out in improving the ground they are in possession of than in buying more Lands. . . . I know very little ground in the Lothians so cheap set and so improvable as the Baronie of Pennicuik, for I dare say that if it was measured it would be found that I do not receive for it above two shill. ster., or half a crown at most, the Aicre; the rent being at this time very little above 500 lib. ster. It is true that for some Aicres I receive 10 or 12, 15 or 20 shillings stg.: but for others I do not receive 6 pence. As to the best methode of making Hedges and ditches, I have said enough in a paper by itself. Several people have various ways, but I mention only such as seem to me to have answered best in this High, cold ground, which must be at least 150 fathoms above the level of the sea at Lieth or Musselburgh.' He enters minutely into all improvements desirable in the various 'rooms'[1] of the Barony, viz.:—'Cooking,' 'The Touer,' 'Coats,' 'Lukenhouses,' 'Carsewell,' 'Silverburn,' 'Satir's Syke,' 'Brunstane,' 'Wallstone,' 'Concraig,' 'Loan Stane,' 'Rhodes,' 'Pomathorn,' 'Puttingstane Law,' 'Clickhim or Noble Hall,' 'Utershill,' 'Halls,' 'Fahills,' 'Montlothian Grounds,' 'Herberstain,' 'Montlothian Mains South,' 'Easter Ravensnook,' 'Wester Ravensnook,'[2] 'Dyknook,' 'Hurley,' 'Brunstane Rigg,' 'Achencorth.'[3] Upon the 'room' of Cooking he remarks that he enclosed a portion of the land 'with Hedges and ditches, I think about 80 Aicres in all, and made an advance of my rent. I lost by markets when I kept this Room in my own hands, and when I let it I was oblidged to take one of our own young bungling, disorderly, county fellowes for a Tenant, James Willsone, who was never bred to know any thing about the improvement of ground by inclosures, and thus it happens that the Hedges there are neglected and will go to ruin unless the Genius of the Tenant improve. By calling so much ground into one man's hand, I thought he might live better and pay his rent better, but I now find by experience, from several observations I have made in the Duke of Queensberry's lands, as well as my own, that small Tenants near a Royal Burgh Town or near Coal, pay their rents best. I obtained this likeways at Moffat, in my own Lands of Drumcrief, which I have now given to my son George. When

---

1 'Rowm, a possession, or portion of land; whether occupied by the proprietor or by a tenant.—Jamieson's *Scot. Dictionary* (ed. of 1882). Room is still commonly used for a farm.

2 'I have seen Ravensnook Tower 40 or 50 feet high, and it was against my inclination that it was pulled down; but as my father, who wanted stones for the park dyke, found here the readiest provision, I submitted. The touer of Pennicuik was pulled down on the same account, but if I had stones in readiness I would repair them both. Old houses and Touers are, I think, the Honour and pride of a Country.'

3 'As goats have commonly been kept on Achencorth, I have several times thought that if an Active diligent Farmer would build Goat Milk Huts or small Houses near a Spring which is on the East side of Achencorth houses on the side of a glen or within 50 paces of the fine stone Quarry, he might have abundance of business from Edinr. in the summer-time.'—See note 1, p. 116. As the reader will have noticed, the Baron makes frequent reference to expeditions to the Highlands and to Northumberland for the benefit of the goat whey. The custom continued long after the Baron's time. Ramsay of Ochtertyre mentions (*Scotland and Scotsmen*, i. 31, notes) that 'In the summer of 1770 I was at the goat-whey in Rannoch.'

these were in the hands of 5 or 6 little Tenants, there was more rent paid and much better than when they were brought into one or two Farms. Small Tenants have other methods to live by than their lands, for these they make only a help to them. However, there is a vast distinction to be made in countries which abound in wood, or are near Sea Ports where forraigne timber may be easily got, and countries where there is a scarsity of these conveniences, for when timber abounds Houses can be made and kept up at a small expense, whereas a multitude of houses is never to be thought of where Timber is expensive in itself or difficult in its carriage.'

He also draws up a scheme of improvements for the mansion, gardens, and policies of Penicuik. 'The House, which I think should have been called by any other name than Pennicuik House or Newbiging, might be made more commodious and handsome. I had done this, but the Roof and other parts of it were too new and entire to be taken down, and therefor I built and embelished Mavisbank between 1723 and 1746 more than was absolutely necessary. However, if Pennicuik House wants hereafter to be taken down as defective in either Roof or walls, but I hope not till then, it will be necessary to make a double house fronting the East with one very large Room in it to fill up the whole length of the present closs. A Family House without one Large Room in it is, in my opinion, very defective and ridiculouse.' He further sketches a plan and elevation of a library which he intended to have built by the side of the long walk on the south side of the large pond to the north-west of the house; an elevation of the 'Gothick touer' which in 1748-50 he erected on the Knight's Law; and various other proposed embellishments: and he is careful to add: ''Tis a beuty to see things natural and at little or no expense. All expensive ornaments about gentlemen's houses are so shocking that those who see them commonly bless themselves that they do not belong to them. The reparation or new modelings of the house of Pennicuik, with the Library above sketched, are never to be attempted but with a superfluity of money;' and he concludes the 'schem' by again advising caution:—'What I have mentioned above are, so far as I know, the best ways of improving the Estate of Pennicuik and for preserving it to posterity. I have no better prescription than for the possessor who lives in Pennicuik House to take care not to do anything, even in the way of improvement, upon borrowed money: let him always have ready cash before he attempts any thing,' etc.

Under date of June 1742, he notes that he has revised the MS., 'and altered a few things, but in general I am still of opinion that my proposals are right, one particularly by which I advise the planting all the Barren, steep, whinny, Hathery braes with Timber, and with oak in particular.' He had previously remarked that 'warmness and shelter at Pennicuik is chiefly what is wanted.' He now adds:—'*Nota.*—Under the improvement of the Baronie of Pennicuik I cannot but recommend the Improvement of the Town of Pennicuik. I have done something this way by building a Court-house to serve likeways for a good Inn, and likeways a House for a Linnen Weaver,[1] but the chief improvement ought to be by Manufactories of all kinds, and, amongst the rest, care should be taken to introduce serge manufactories, now about Stirling, by transplanting journey Men or getting some of our young Lads bred to the Trade at St.

[1] Doubtless in connection with the schemes of the Board of Manufactures.

Ringans near that place. Such woolen manufactories might thrive at Pennicuik, because the coarse wool, of which so much is wrought up at the above-named places, comes from the Southern shires, Peebles, Selkirk, or the Forrest, Tweedale, and others. Build the houses at Pennicuik regularly, and at least of 2 stories or rather 3.' On the final page is a later note, stating that in 1743 he bought Harlawmuir from the Trustees of John Forbes of Newhall, and in the same year found a seam of coal 'upon the west brae about 200 Elles from the houses.' 'My reasons for not working it were two: first, I was unwilling that it should be said that I purchased the lands with a view to the coal; next, I had a view of getting a confirmation of my purchase from young Mr. Forbes, who was to be Major 2 years hence, viz., in 1745, but this I could not expect in case the coal had proven good, and for removing all objections I was resolved to have made a present to the young gentleman of 20 or 30 guineas.' Next he notes that on 20th October 1744 he discovered another coal-seam 'to the westward of the glen which makes the March between the Lands of Auchincorth and Harlaw moor;' and finally, he states: 'I see now that there are above a dussan of coal seams of one kind or another in Harlaw moor ground.'

NOTE S, p. 218. *Memoirs of a Goat Whey Campaign at Lawers in* 1749.—An unpublished manuscript in the Baron's handwriting.—The House of Lauers belongs to the sone[1] of the deceased General Campbel,[2] unckle to the present Earl of Loudon.

The s^d^. son of the General takes the surname of Muir from his Mother, who was Heiress of Rouallan, the family from whom all the princes in Europe are depended, by the Marriage of Robt. the 2 of Scotland to Eliz. Muir. About this marriage many disputes have hapned, see the dissertations of Mr. Rudiman and Mr. Logan, a Minister in Ed.[3]

came to Lauers on the Recommendation of Mr. Patrick Boyle, Lord Seualton, unckle to the proprietor, Captain Muir.

The company consisted of myself, my wife, my daughters Ann and Bettie, my son James, and Brother Hugh Clerk.

We came there on the 29 of Aprile and found a very kind reception by Mr Campbel the chamberlain and the House keeper on L^d^. Sewalton's account.

Our Quarters were very fine, for the House is 120 feet in front, and very well finished.

We began to drink the whey on the 2^d^ of May, but it did not agree with my stomach at first. It was very scarse because there were few Goats ready for milking.

---

1 See note 2, page 218. See note 3, page 218.

3 The Rev. Dr. George Logan's *Treatise on Government; showing that the right of the Kings of Scotland to the Crown was not strictly and absolutely hereditary: against the Earl of Cromarty, Sir George Mackenzie, Mr. John Sage, and Mr. Thomas Ruddiman*, 8vo, Edinr. 1746; and his *Second Treatise on Government* . . ., 8vo, Edin. 1747; and Thomas Ruddiman's *Answer to Mr. Logan's Treatise on Government* . . ., 8vo, Edin. 1747: and his *Dissertation concerning the competition for the Crown of Scotland betwixt Lord Robert Bruce and Lord John Balliol in the year* 1291 . . ., 8vo, Edin. 1748.

See note 1, page 222.

The Chamberlain furnished us with good Corn and Hay for our Horses. Our diversions were fishing and Hare hunting.

The Water of Earn yielded the first in sufficient plenty.

The Salmon were very good and the Trouts excellent, all red in the flesh, but not many; they were generally between 14 and 18 inches long.

I had a fishing-Rod there, but did little good with it, for I knew not the right streams, but at last found that one above Lauers about half a mile never wanted Salmon, for at one draught we got 4 or 5, tho we had a bad net, besides Trouts.

There is another fine stream under the foord to Strouan where there are trees growing along the water side, on the south side of the River.

There is a 3d stream under the kirk and boat of Strouan, which is excellent for the Rod.

We went always to the Kirk of Comry on Sundays, but Achtertyre[1] is the parish kirk.

The way we took to Lauers was by Lithgow, Falkirk, Stirling, Dumblain, and so by the great Highland road to Crief, from whence Lauers lay 3 miles to the westward.

The Gentlemen's seats I visited were not many, but I saw some of them at a distance.

I was one day invited by Lord Monzie[2] to his House of Monzie. This is a warm low seat near the great High Road. My Lord was a great Encourager of the Linnen Manufactories, and by his example I found that the country people had made a very great progress, for most of their Rents, especially on the great Estate of Drummond, are paid by the produce of their Linen Manufactories.

Another day he and I visited his Lint Mill about a mile under Loch Earn. It was then building and promised well.

This Lord has a considerable Estate in this country, made for the most by himself.

He carried me one day to see the design and stance of a House for a publick Library at the kirk of .[3]

---

1 Ochtertyre.

2 Patrick, second son of Colin Campbell, of Monzie, was retoured heir to his brother Duncan in 1706. He was admitted advocate in 1709, and raised to the bench, as Lord Monzie, in 1729; and was one of the original Commissioners of the Board of Trustees for Improving Fisheries and Manufactures in Scotland, constituted in 1727. He died in 1751, aged seventy-six.

3 Blank in the MS. here.

The Library of Innerpeffray was left as a family endowment. In 1691 David Drummond, third Lord Madertie, left his library and a sum of money for maintaining the Library and a School for the benefit of Innerpeffray and surrounding district. In 1696 his nephew and heir William Drummond, second Lord Strathallan, made the annual rent of this money chargeable on the estate of Innerpeffray,—'Provided always that I and my heirs and successors in the lands and barony of Innerpeffray shall be sole and undoubted patrons in presenting the Library keeper and Schoolmaster in all time coming,' . . . 'as also reserving full power . . . to determine what part of the annual rent shall be applied for building a new house for containing the aforesaid Library, etc. Lord Madertie erected a house for a library beside the chapel of Innerpeffray, and afterwards a room in the said chapel (kirk) was used for the same purpose. In 1739 the Hon. Robert Hay Drummond, afterwards Archbishop of York, succeeded to the estate of Innerpeffray. He decided to build a new house, the present library, which was erected between the years 1747 and 1751. Pennant (*Tour in Scot.*, vol. iii.) mentions having visited the library

The situation is very pleasant, but the fund small; it was left by [1].

From thence I saw his land improvements on the great Moor of Crief which may in time turn to great account, the soile being very capable of meliorations. We dined that day at Monzie and saw his Lordships Library, where are many good books. Amongst other Excursions I went one day to the fishing at Loch ,[2] about 4 miles from Lauers. I saw nothing by the way but a bad mountanous country and villanous road. We should have catched trouts at this Loch by the Rod, but had very bad sport and saw much snow.

In the afternoon I and some of my company return'd by Achtertire[3] and saw the Enclosures. The situation of this House is very high, but the Loch below it and the woods make it a very agreable place. It belongs to Sir Patrick Murry.[4]

I was once and again at Crief, which is a miserable village. The Houses lie scattered about in it, and the trees which once embellished it were cut down by the Hessian troops, at the Rebellion in 1745. Want of fire made this a necessary evil.

I saw the Castle of Drummond at a distance as I have done on former occasions. The House is very great, and the plantations of Fir and other trees very numerous.

N.B.—It is now a Question whether it be forfeited by the Rebellion in 1745, or will belong to the protestant Heir, for the late proprietor, the Duke of Perth, as he was called, was in the Rebellion, but died before the Attainder in July 1746.[5]

I was to see Loch Earn, but had little fishing upon it. I found that the ground about it was very wild and full of Mountains.

My son and Brother made a Touer on foot along by the side of this Loch and from the head of it they went over to the head of Loch Tay, which they reported to be no bad way, and that the people on the side of Loch Tay were very numerous and dealt a great deal in the Linnen Manufactories.

These people belong to the family of Bredalban and live for the most part on these lands which were inhabited by the antient Caledonii. A good many of them have red Hair as they were described by Tacitus in *Vita Agricolæ*.

From Loch Tay runs the River of Tay, which enters the sea at Dundee.

I was one day at Arbruchill, which belongs to Sir James Campbel.[6] The

---

in 1772, 'when books were still being added.' When the late Hon. Robert Hay Drummond succeeded to the estate of Innerpeffray in 1852, and his brother, the Hon. A. Hay Drummond, the present proprietor, in 1855, many new books were added, and a large number of the old ones repaired and re-bound. Books are still lent out, and the library is visited by parties from all quarters, upwards of 500 names being entered in the visitors' book during the past twelve months. It now contains about 2700 volumes.

1 Blank in the MS. See preceding note.

2 There is a blank in the MS. here. Probably Loch Turret is meant.

3 Ochtertyre.

4 Sir Patrick Murray, fourth Baronet of Ochtertyre, succeeded his father in 1739, and died 1764.

5 The Court of Session and House of Lords pronounced the estate of Perth forfeited to the Crown; and it remained forfeited till 1785, when James Drummond, lineal descendant of John, Earl of Melford, in virtue of an Act of Parliament passed in the previous year, obtained from the Crown a grant of the estate. See Douglas's *Peerage*, vol. ii. p. 366 (ed. of 1813).

6 Sir James Campbell, second Baronet of Aberuchill, eldest son of Sir Colin Campbell and his second wife, Catherine, daughter of Sir John Mackenzie of Tarbet, succeeded his father in 1704, and died about 1754.

House is bad, but the Grounds about it very pleasant. Here grew a Walnut Tree, lately cut down, which sold at 45 lib. ster. I saw several large Trees here, and amongst others an Ash of about 7 feet in diameter with 32 crows nests on it.

I was once here in 1723 for the Goat whey, which is excellent. At Lauers the Whey is no less excellent, for the Goats feed in large woods where they have abundance of fine Herbs, particularly the Capilli Veneris, Wild Garlick, etc., but I observed that their chief food is the tops of young Oak.

One day I made an Excursion to the great Forrest belonging to the family of Perth called Glen [1]. It is about 5 miles from Lauers. Here we saw some flocks of Deer of the great red kind, but they keept the high grounds, so we had no great satisfaction in the visite we made them but to see a very high, wild country on both sides of a narrow Glen.

At night by fasting and afterwards a very great mail I turn'd very sick and with faintings vomited much, but this was over by next day. *Laus Deo!*

On the 29 of May I began my journey homewards by the way I came, only that I keept on the side of Strouan till I came on the great high road to Stirling. I came next day to Edin. before dinner.

The curiosities I saw in my stay at Lauers and by the way were chiefly two: the great Roman Camp [2] at a place south of Comry described by Mr. Gordon in his *Itinerarium Septentrionale.*

The other was the camp of Ardoch,[3] which I had seen once before, and this last is pretty strong and I doubt not but Agricola's Army had been encamped here. The ditches are large about the prætorium and there is a square place in the middle where I believe they have had a Temple, for there was a chapel built here, and the ground about serves still for a burrial place to the country people. There was once a stone with an Inscription on it found here, which is now in the Castle of Drummond. The Inscription is *Diis Manibus Ammonius Damionis centurio cohortis primæ Hispanorum stipendiorum viginti septem heredes FC,* that is, faciendum curarunt. See Horsley's *Britannia Romana*, page 192 and page 205.

N.B.—Our Forefathers used to say that Scotland had 6 Knights to defend it from its Ennemies

viz

Sir Moor, Sir Moss, Sr. Mountain,
Sir Hunger, Sir Cold, Sir Dunt on.

NOTE T, p. 223. *The Scottish Court of Exchequer and the Forfeited Estates.*—The Court of Exchequer was in a special sense the court of the Crown, having charge of all matters relating to the revenue and the rent and casualties due to the sovereign as owner of Crown lands or as feudal superior. Persons employed in collecting the revenue were under this court, and were subject to penalties imposed by it in the event of failure of duty or contempt of its jurisdiction. The duties relating to the revenue were transferred by 3 and 4 William IV., c. 13, to the Treasury. Certain deeds relating to Crown holdings were

---

[1] Probably Glenartney. See page 218, note [4].

[2] The name omitted here seems to be the Stragaeth Camp, near Innerpeffray. See Gordon's *Itinerarium*, p. 42, where this camp is figured.

[3] See page 219, note [1].

granted by the Barons of Exchequer as the King's Commissioners, although the effect of such deeds could only be determined in the Court of Session. Various nice questions relating to the jurisdiction of these two courts have arisen. It has been found competent, for example, to interdict in the Court of Session the granting of a deed in Exchequer—while a declarator of immunity from taxes was held incompetent in the former court. Nor could a charge for Crown feu-duties be suspended by Court of Session judges.

The rebellions of 1715 and 1745 must have had the result of bringing a good deal of work into the Court of Exchequer in the shape of the recovery and administration of estates belonging to rebels and the granting of gifts of escheat, etc. Baron Clerk seems to have been most industrious as a judge of this court, and numerous papers relating to the powers and duties of his office, apparently drawn up by him, are still preserved. One which may perhaps be classed with these is entitled, 'Memorial concerning the Forfeited Estates of Scotland,' and is dated 1747. In this paper he criticises unfavourably the rules which had been laid down by statute for the management and sale of these lands. He expected a very small profit to be available to the Crown, because, in the first place, of the privileges conferred upon the superiors, and the tenants of the rebels. Superiors and tenants alike had only combined to benefit the rebel and his family. He objects also to the appointment of connections of the rebel as factors. Such persons seemed to him only capable of deceiving and concealing to the prejudice of the Crown. He therefore advocates the appointment of a different class of factors, for whom, however, he does not anticipate a pleasant life. For he admits that in the case of the Highland forfeitures the attachment of the inhabitants 'to the family of the forfeiting person which they consider as their Sovereign, their God, and their All, joined with their savage dispositions,' might endanger the factor's person and property. Nor could these unfortunate men expect any assistance from their neighbours, it being a maxim among the Highlanders not to engage in a quarrel with one another except for their own sakes. But civil and military power were to do their utmost to protect them. He seems to have rightly recognised one of the causes of Highland destitution when he says, 'The smallness of the possessions and the precarious tenure under which they are held is one principal cause of the poverty, the slavery, and the consequent barbarity of these parts.' Accordingly, he suggests that factors should be prohibited from granting leases under a certain rent and a certain endurance.—M.

BARON SCROPE.

See pp. 71, 227.

As the last pages of this volume were going to press, I received from Mr. G. L. Ryder of the Treasury some information regarding Baron Scrope, 'one of our most distinguished Secretaries,' the result of a careful search by Mr. J. J. Cartwright in the Public Record Office. John Scrope appears to have been born in 1662, for in his evidence before the Commission of Inquiry into Secret Service Expenditure in 1742, he mentioned that he was then eighty years old. He was appointed 'one of the Secretarys to the Commissioners of Our Treasury, or High Treasurer for the time being' previous to 20th May 1724, as appears from a warrant of that date in the *Treasury Records: Entries for North Britain*, vol. vii. p. 161, in which it is stated that he had been appointed a Baron of the Court of Exchequer in Scotland 'with a salary of £500 per annum as Baron, and £1000 per annum in consideration of his having left his Practice at the Barr in England,' and that, though he had surrendered his office of Baron, the latter sum of £1000 per annum 'shall continue to be paid to the said John Scrope or his Assigns from the time the same was last paid, Quarterly from time to time in like manner as the same should and ought to have been paid in case he had continued in the said office of Baron, and no such Surrender had been made.' His predecessor in the Secretaryship was William Lowndes; and, from entries in the *Treasury Fee Book*, 1723-24, it would appear that the exact date of Scrope's appointment was 21st January 1724. Scrope died in 1752, at the age of ninety; his tenure of office having ended, as is indicated by the *Treasury Fee Book*, on 21st April 1752, when he was succeeded by Mr. Harding.

INDEX

Printed by T. and A. CONSTABLE, Printers to Her Majesty,
at the Edinburgh University Press.

Scottish History Society.

LIST OF MEMBERS.

1891-92.

3

LIST OF MEMBERS.

Abernethy, James, 11 Prince of Wales Terrace, Kensington, London, W.

Adam, Sir Charles E., Bart., Blair-Adam.

Adam, Robert, Brae-Moray, Gillsland Road, Edinburgh.

Adam, Thomas, Hazelbank, Uddingston.

Adams, William, 28 Ashton Terrace, Hillhead, Glasgow.

Agnew, Alex., Procurator-Fiscal, Court-House Buildings, Dundee.

Aikman, Andrew, 27 Buckingham Terrace, Edinburgh.

Airy, Osmund, The Laurels, Solihull, Birmingham.

Aitken, Dr. A. P., 57 Great King Street, Edinburgh.

10 Aitken, James H., Gartcows, Falkirk.

Alexander, William, M.D., Dundonald, Kilmarnock.

Allan, A. G., Blackfriars Haugh, Elgin.

Allan, George, Advocate, 56 Castle Street, Aberdeen.

Allen, Lady Henrietta, Tusculum House, North Berwick.

Anderson, Archibald, 30 Oxford Square, London, W.

Anderson, Arthur, M.D., C.B., Sunny-Brae, Pitlochry.

Anderson, John, jun., Atlantic Mills, Bridgeton, Glasgow.

Andrew, Thomas, Doune, Perthshire.

Armstrong, Robert Bruce, 6 Randolph Cliff, Edinburgh.

20 Arnot, James, M.A., 57 Leamington Terrace, Edinburgh.

Arrol, William A., 11 Lynedoch Place, Glasgow.

Baird, J. G. A., Wellwood, Muirkirk.

Balfour, Right Hon. J. B., Q.C., 6 Rothesay Terrace, Edinburgh.

Ballingall, Hugh, Ardarroch, Dundee.

Barclay, George, 17 Coates Crescent, Edinburgh.
Barron, Rev. Douglas Gordon, Dunnottar Manse, Stonehaven.
Begg, Ferdinand Faithfull, 13 Earl's Court Square, London, S.W.
Bell, A. Beatson, Advocate, 2 Eglinton Crescent, Edinburgh.
Bell, Joseph, F.R.C.S., 2 Melville Crescent, Edinburgh.
30 Bell, Robert Fitzroy, Advocate, 7 Ainslie Place, Edinburgh.
Bell, Russell, Advocate, Kildalloig, Campbeltown.
Beveridge, Erskine, St. Leonard's Hill, Dunfermline.
Black, James Tait, 33 Palace Court, Bayswater Hill, London, W.
Black, Rev. John S., 6 Oxford Terrace, Edinburgh.
Blaikie, Walter B., 11 Thistle Street, Edinburgh.
Blair, Patrick, Advocate, 4 Ardross Terrace, Inverness.
Bonar, Horatius, W.S., 15 Strathearn Place, Edinburgh.
Boyd, Sir Thomas J., 41 Moray Place, Edinburgh.
Brodie, Sir T. D., W.S., 5 Thistle Street, Edinburgh.
40 Brookman, James, W.S., 16 Ravelston Park, Edinburgh.
Broun-Morison, J. B., of Finderlie, The Old House, Harrow-on-the-Hill.
Brown, Professor Alex. Crum, 8 Belgrave Crescent, Edinburgh.
Brown, J. A. Harvie, Dunipace House, Larbert, Stirlingshire.
Brown, P. Hume, 25 Gillespie Crescent, Edinburgh.
Brown, Robert, Underwood Park, Paisley.
Brown, William, 26 Princes Street, Edinburgh.
Brownlie, James R., 10 Brandon Pl., West George St., Glasgow.
Bruce, Alex., Clyne House, Sutherland Avenue, Pollokshields.
Bruce, James, W.S., 23 St. Bernard's Crescent, Edinburgh.
50 Bruce, Hon. R. Preston, Broom Hall, Dunfermline.
Bryce, James, M.P., 54 Portland Place, London, W.
Bryce, William Moir, 5 Dick Place, Edinburgh.
Buchanan, A. W. Gray, Parkhill, Polmont, N.B.
Buchanan, T. D., M.D., 24 Westminster Terrace, West, Glasgow.
Burns, George Stewart, D.D., 3 Westbourne Terrace, Glasgow.
Burns, John William, Kilmahew, Cardross.
Burns, Rev. Thomas, 2 St. Margaret's Road, Edinburgh.
Bute, The Marquis of, Mountstuart, Isle of Bute.

CALDWELL, JAMES, Craigielea Place, Paisley.
60 Cameron, Dr. J. A., Elgin.
Cameron, Richard, 1 South St. David Street, Edinburgh.
Campbell, Rev. James, D.D., the Manse, Balmerino, Dundee.
Campbell, James A., Stracathro, Brechin.
Carne-Ross, Joseph, M.D., Parsonage Nook, Withington, Manchester.
Carrick, J. Stewart, 58 Renfield Street, Glasgow.
Chambers, W. & R., 339 High Street, Edinburgh.
Chiene, Professor, 26 Charlotte Square, Edinburgh.
Christie, J., Breadalbane Estate Office, Kenmore, Aberfeldy.
Christie, Thomas Craig, of Bedlay, Chryston, Glasgow.
70 Clark, G. Bennet, W.S., 57 Queen Street, Edinburgh.
Clark, George T., Talygarn, Llantrissant.
Clark, James, Advocate, 4 Drumsheugh Gardens, Edinburgh.
Clark, James T., Crear Villa, Ferry Road, Edinburgh.
Clark, Robert, 42 Hanover Street, Edinburgh.
Clark, Sir Thomas, Bart., 11 Melville Crescent, Edinburgh.
Clouston, T. S., M.D., Tipperlinn House, Morningside Place, Edinburgh.
Cochran-Patrick, R. W., LL.D., of Woodside, Beith, Ayrshire.
Coldstream, John P., W.S., 6 Buckingham Terrace, Edinburgh.
Constable, Archibald, 1 Nelson Street, Edinburgh.
80 Cowan, George, 1 Gillsland Road, Edinburgh.
Cowan, Hugh, St. Leonards, Ayr.
Cowan, J. J., 38 West Register Street, Edinburgh.
Cowan, John, W.S., St. Roque, Grange Loan, Edinburgh.
Cowan, John, Beeslack, Mid-Lothian.
Cowan, William, 2 Montpelier, Edinburgh.
Cox, Edward, Lyndhurst, Dundee.
Craik, James, W.S., 9 Eglinton Crescent, Edinburgh.
Crawford, Donald, M.P., 60 Pall Mall, London.
Crole, Gerard L., Advocate, 1 Royal Circus, Edinburgh.
90 Cunningham, Geo. Miller, C.E., 2 Ainslie Place, Edinburgh.
Cunynghame, R. J. Blair, M.D., 18 Rothesay Place, Edinburgh.
Currie, James, 16 Bernard Street, Leith.

Currie, Walter Thomson, Rankeillour, by Cupar-Fife.
Currie, W. R., 28 Holyrood Quadrant, Glasgow.
Cuthbert, Alex. A., 14 Newton Terrace, Glasgow.

Dalgleish, John J., of Ardnamurchan, 8 Atholl Cres., Edin.
Dalrymple, Hon. Hew, Lochinch, Castle Kennedy, Wigtownshire.
Davidson, Hugh, Braedale, Lanark.
Davidson, J., Solicitor, Kirriemuir.
100 Davidson, Thomas, 339 High Street, Edinburgh.
Davies, J. Mair, C.A., Sheiling, Pollokshields, Glasgow.
Dickson, Thomas, LL.D., Register House, Edinburgh.
Dickson, Dr. Walter G. W., 3 Royal Circus, Edinburgh.
Dickson, William K., Advocate, 19 Dundas Street, Edinburgh.
Dickson, Wm. Traquair, W.S., 11 Hill Street, Edinburgh.
Dixon, John H., Inveran, Poolewe, by Dingwall.
Doak, Rev. Andrew, M.A., 15 Queen's Road, Aberdeen.
Dodds, Rev. James, D.D., The Manse, Corstorphine.
Dods, Colonel P., United Service Club, Edinburgh.
110 Donald, C. D., 172 St. Vincent Street, Glasgow.
Donaldson, James, LL.D., Principal, St. Andrews University.
Donaldson, James, Sunnyside, Formby, Liverpool.
Douglas, Hon. and Right Rev. A. G., Bishop of Aberdeen and Orkney, Aberdeen.
Douglas, David, 9 Castle Street, Edinburgh.
Dowden, Right Rev. John, D.D., Bishop of Edinburgh, Lynn House, Gillsland Road, Edinburgh.
Duff, T. Gordon, Drummuir, Keith.
Duncan, James Barker, W.S., 6 Hill Street, Edinburgh.
Duncan, John, National Bank, Haymarket, Edinburgh.
Dundas, Ralph, C.S., 28 Drumsheugh Gardens, Edinburgh.
120 Dunn, Robert Hunter, Belgian Consulate, Glasgow.

Easton, Walter, 125 Buchanan Street, Glasgow.
Ewart, Prof. Cossar, 2 Belford Park, Edinburgh.

Faulds, A. Wilson, Knockbuckle, Beith, Ayrshire.

Ferguson, James, Advocate, 10 Wemyss Place, Edinburgh.
Ferguson, John, Town Clerk, Linlithgow.
Ferguson, Rev. John, Manse, Aberdalgie, Perth.
Findlay, J. Ritchie, 3 Rothesay Terrace, Edinburgh.
Findlay, Rev. Wm., The Manse, Saline, Fife.
Firth, Charles Harding, 33 Norham Road, Oxford.
130 Fleming, D. Hay, 16 North Bell Street, St. Andrews.
Fleming, J. S., 16 Grosvenor Crescent, Edinburgh.
Flint, Prof., D.D., LL.D., Johnstone Lodge, Craigmillar Park, Edinburgh.
Forrest, James R. P., 32 Broughton Place, Edinburgh.
Forrester, John, 29 Windsor Street, Edinburgh.
Foulis, James, M.D., 34 Heriot Row, Edinburgh.
Fraser, Professor A. Campbell, D.C.L., LL.D., Gorton House, Hawthornden.
Fraser, W. N., S.S.C., 41 Albany Street, Edinburgh.

Gairdner, Charles, Broom, Newton-Mearns, Glasgow.
Galletly, Edwin G., 7 St. Ninian's Terrace, Edinburgh.
140 Gardner, Alexander, 7 Gilmour Street, Paisley.
Gartshore, Miss Murray, Ravelston, Blackhall, Edinburgh.
Geikie, Sir Archibald, LL.D., Geological Survey, 28 Jermyn Street, London, S.W.
Geikie, Prof. James, LL.D., 31 Merchiston Avenue, Edinburgh.
Gemmill, William, 62 Bath Street, Glasgow.
Gibson, Andrew, 3 Morrison Street, Govan.
Gibson, James T., LL.B., W.S., 28 St. Andrew Sq., Edinburgh.
Giles, Arthur, 107 Princes Street, Edinburgh.
Gillies, Walter, M.A., The Academy, Perth.
Gordon, Rev. Robert, Mayfield Gardens, Edinburgh.
150 Goudie, Gilbert, F.S.A. Scot., 39 Northumberland Street, Edinburgh.
Goudie, James Tulloch, Oakleigh Park, Nithsdale Drive, Pollokshields.
Goudie, Robert, Commissary Clerk of Ayrshire, Ayr.
Gourlay, Robert, Bank of Scotland, Glasgow.

Gow, Leonard, Hayston, Kelvinside, Glasgow.
Graeme, Lieut.-Col., Naval and Military Club, 94 Piccadilly, London.
Grahame, James, 93 Hope Street, Glasgow.
Grant, William G. L., Woodside, East Newport, Fife.
Gray, George, Clerk of the Peace, Glasgow.
Greig, Andrew, 36 Belmont Gardens, Hillhead, Glasgow.
160 Gunning, His Excellency Robert Haliday, M.D., 12 Addison Crescent, Kensington, London, W.
Guthrie, Charles J., Advocate, 13 Royal Circus, Edinburgh.
Guy, Robert, 120 West Regent Street, Glasgow.

HALKETT, MISS KATHERINE E., 2 Edinburgh Terrace, Kensington, London, W.
Hall, David, Elmbank House, Kilmarnock.
Hallen, Rev. A. W. Cornelius, The Parsonage, Alloa.
Hamilton, Hubert, Advocate, 55 Manor Place, Edinburgh.
Hamilton, Lord, of Dalzell, Motherwell.
Hamilton-Ogilvy, Henry T. N., Prestonkirk.
Harrison, John, 36 North Bridge, Edinburgh.
170 Hedderwick, A. W. H., 79 St. George's Place, Glasgow.
Henderson, J. G. B., Nether Parkley, Linlithgow.
Henderson, Joseph, 11 Blythswood Square, Glasgow.
Henry, David, 2 Lockhart Place, St. Andrews, Fife.
Hewison, Rev. J. King, The Manse, Rothesay.
Hill, William H., LL.D., Barlanark, Shettleston, Glasgow.
Hislop, Robert, Solicitor, Auchterarder.
Hogg, John, 66 Chancery Street, Boston, U.S.
Honeyman, John, A.R.S.A., 140 Bath Street, Glasgow.
Howden, Charles R. A., Advocate, 25 Melville Street, Edinburgh.
180 Hunt, John, Fingarry, Milton of Campsie, Glasgow.
Hunter, Colonel, F.R.S., of Plâs Côch, Anglesea.
Hutcheson, Alexander, Herschel House, Broughty Ferry.
Hutchison, John, D.D., Afton Lodge, Bonnington.
Hyslop, J. M., M.D., 22 Palmerston Place, Edinburgh.

Imrie, Rev. T. Nairne, Dunfermline.

Jameson, J. H., W.S., 3 Northumberland Street, Edinburgh.
Jamieson, George Auldjo, C.A., 37 Drumsheugh Gardens, Edinburgh.
Jamieson, J. Auldjo, W.S., 14 Buckingham Ter., Edinburgh.
Japp, William, Solicitor, Alyth.
190 Johnston, David, 24 Huntly Gardens, Kelvinside, Glasgow.
Johnston, George Harvey, 6 Osborne Terrace, Edinburgh.
Johnston, George P., 33 George Street, Edinburgh.
Johnston, T. Morton, Eskhill, Roslin.
Johnstone, James F. Kellas, 3 Broad Street Buildings, Liverpool Street, London.
Jonas, Alfred Charles, Poundfald, Penclawdd, Swansea.

Kemp, D. William, Ivy Lodge, Trinity, Edinburgh.
Kennedy, David H. C., 69 St. George's Place, Glasgow.
Kermack, John, W.S., 10 Atholl Crescent, Edinburgh.
Kincairney, The Hon. Lord, 6 Heriot Row, Edinburgh.
200 Kinnear, The Hon. Lord, 2 Moray Place, Edinburgh.
Kirkpatrick, Prof. John, LL.B., Advocate, 24 Alva Street, Edinburgh.
Kirkpatrick, Robert, 1 Queen Square, Strathbungo, Glasgow.

Laidlaw, David, jun., 6 Marlborough Ter., Kelvinside, Glasgow.
Laing, Alex., Norfolk House, St. Leonards, Sussex.
Lang, James, 9 Crown Gardens, Dowanhill, Glasgow.
Langwill, Robert B., Manse, Currie.
Laurie, Professor S. S., Nairne Lodge, Duddingston.
Law, James F., Seaview, Monifieth.
Law, Thomas Graves, Signet Library, Edinburgh, *Secretary.*
210 Leadbetter, Thomas, 122 George Street, Edinburgh.
Leslie, Lieut.-Colonel, Cameron Highlanders, Malta.
Livingston, E. B., 9 Gracechurch Street, London, E.C.
Lorimer, George, 2 Abbotsford Crescent, Edinburgh.

Macadam, W. Ivison, Slioch, Lady Road, Newington, Edinburgh.
Macandrew, Sir Henry C., Aisthorpe, Midmills Road, Inverness.

Macbrayne, David, Jun., 17 Royal Exchange Square, Glasgow.
M'Call, James, F.S.A., 6 St. John's Ter., Hillhead, Glasgow.
M'Candlish, John M., W.S. 27 Drumsheugh Gar., Edinburgh.
M'Cosh, J. M., Clydesdale Bank, Dalry, Ayrshire.
220 Macdonald, James, W.S., 4 Greenhill Park, Edinburgh.
Macdonald, W. Rae, 1 Forres Street, Edinburgh.
Macdougall, James Patten, Advocate, 16 Lynedoch Place, Edinburgh.
M'Ewen, W. C., W.S., 2 Rothesay Place, Edinburgh.
Macfarlane, George L., Advocate, 14 Moray Place, Edinburgh.
Macgeorge, B. B., 19 Woodside Crescent, Glasgow.
Macgregor, John, W.S., 10 Dundas Street, Edinburgh.
M'Grigor, Alexander, 172 St. Vincent Street, Glasgow.
Macintyre, P. M., Advocate, 12 India Street, Edinburgh.
Mackay, Æneas J. G., LL.D., 7 Albyn Place, Edinburgh.
230 Mackay, Rev. G. S., M.A., Free Church Manse, Doune.
Mackay, James F., W.S., Whitehouse, Cramond.
Mackay, James R., 37 St. Andrew Square, Edinburgh.
Mackay, John.
Mackay, Thomas, 14 Wetherby Place, South Kensington, London, S.W.
Mackay, Thomas A., 14 Henderson Row, Edinburgh.
Mackay, William, Solicitor, Inverness.
Mackenzie, A., St. Catherines, Paisley.
Mackenzie, David J., Sheriff-Substitute, Wick.
Mackenzie, Thomas, M.A., Sheriff-Substitute of Ross, Old Bank, Golspie.
240 Mackinlay, David, 6 Great Western Terrace, Glasgow.
Mackinnon, Professor, 1 Merchiston Place, Edinburgh.
Mackinnon, Sir W., Bart., 203 West George Street, Glasgow.
Mackinnon, William, 115 St. Vincent Street, Glasgow.
Mackintosh, Charles Fraser, 5 Clarges Street, London, W.
Mackintosh, W. F., 27 Commerce Street, Arbroath.
Maclachan, John, W.S., 12 Abercromby Place, Edinburgh.
Maclagan, Prof. Sir Douglas, M.D., 28 Heriot Row, Edinburgh.
Maclagan, Robert Craig, M.D., 5 Coates Crescent, Edinburgh.

Maclauchlan, John, Albert Institute, Dundee.

250 Maclean, Sir Andrew, Viewfield House, Balshagray, Partick, Glasgow.

Maclean, William C., F.R.G.S., 31 Camperdown Place, Great Yarmouth.

Maclehose, James J., 61 St. Vincent Street, Glasgow.

Macleod, Rev. Walter, 112 Thirlestane Road, Edinburgh.

Macniven, John, 138 Princes Street, Edinburgh.

M'Phee, Donald, Oakfield, Fort William.

Macray, Rev. W. D., Bodleian Library, Oxford.

Macritchie, David, 4 Archibald Place, Edinburgh.

Main, W. D., 128 St. Vincent Street, Glasgow.

Makellar, Rev. William, 8 Charlotte Square, Edinburgh.

260 Marshall, John, Caldergrove, Newton, Lanarkshire.

Martin, John, W.S., 19 Chester Street, Edinburgh.

Marwick, Sir J. D., LL.D., Killermont Ho., Maryhill, Glasgow.

Masson, Professor David, LL.D., 58 Gt. King St., Edinburgh.

Mathieson, Thomas A., 3 Grosvenor Terrace, Glasgow.

Maxwell, W. J., M.P., Terraughtie, Dumfries.

Millar, Alexander H., Rosslyn House, Clepington Rd., Dundee.

Miller, P., 8 Bellevue Terrace, Edinburgh.

Milligan, John, W.S., 10 Carlton Terrace, Edinburgh.

Milne, A. & R., Union Street, Aberdeen.

270 Mitchell, Rev. Professor Alexander, D.D., University, St. Andrews.

Mitchell, Sir Arthur, K.C.B., M.D., LL.D., 34 Drummond Place, Edinburgh.

Mitchell, James, 240 Darnley Street, Pollokshields, Glasgow.

Moncrieff, W. G. Scott, Advocate, Weedingshall Ho., Polmont.

Moffatt, Alexander, 23 Abercromby Place, Edinburgh.

Moffatt, Alexander, jun., LL.B., Advocate, 45 Northumberland Street, Edinburgh.

Morice, Arthur D., Fonthill Road, Aberdeen.

Morison, John, 11 Burnbank Gardens, Glasgow.

Morries-Stirling, J. M., Gogar House, Stirling.

Morrison, Hew, 7 Hermitage Terrace, Morningside.

280 Morton, Charles, W.S., 11 Palmerston Road, Edinburgh.
Muir, James, 27 Huntly Gardens, Dowanhill, Glasgow.
Muirhead, James, 10 Doune Gardens, Kelvinside, Glasgow.
Murdoch, Rev. A. D., All Saints' Parsonage, Edinburgh.
Murdoch, J. B., of Capelrig, Mearns, Renfrewshire.
Murray, Rev. Allan F., M.A., Free Church Manse, Torphichen, Bathgate.
Murray, David, 169 West George Street, Glasgow.

Norfor, Robert T., C.A., 30 South Morningside Drive, Edinburgh.

Oliver, James, Thornwood, Hawick.
Orrock, Archibald, 17 St. Catherine's Place, Edinburgh.

290 Panton, George A., F.R.S.E., 73 Westfield Road, Edgbaston, Birmingham.
Paton, Allan Park, Greenock Library, Watt Monument, Greenock.
Paton, Henry, M.A., 15 Myrtle Terrace, Edinburgh.
Patrick, David, 339 High Street, Edinburgh.
Paul, J. Balfour, Advocate, Lyon King of Arms, 32 Great King Street, Edinburgh.
Paul, Rev. Robert, F.S.A. Scot., Dollar.
Pearson, David Ritchie, M.D., 23 Upper Phillimore Place, Phillimore Gardens, London, W.
Pillans, Hugh H., 12 Dryden Place, Edinburgh.
Pollock, Hugh, 25 Carlton Place, Glasgow.
Prentice, A. R., 18 Kilblain Street, Greenock.
300 Pullar, Robert, Tayside, Perth.
Purves, A. P., W.S., Esk Tower, Lasswade.

Rampini, Charles, LL.D., Advocate, Springfield House, Elgin.
Rankine, John, Advocate, Professor of Scots Law, 23 Ainslie Place, Edinburgh.
Reichel, H. R., University College, Bangor, North Wales.
Reid, Alexander George, Solicitor, Auchterarder.

Reid, H. G., 11 Cromwell Cres., S. Kensington, London, S.W.
Reid, John Alexander, Advocate, 11 Royal Circus, Edinburgh.
Renwick, Robert, Depute Town-Clerk, City Chambers, Glasgow.
Richardson, Ralph, W.S., Commissary Office, 2 Parliament Square, Edinburgh.
310 Ritchie, David, Hopeville, Dowanhill Gardens, Glasgow.
Ritchie, R. Peel, M.D., 1 Melville Crescent, Edinburgh.
Roberton, James D., 1 Park Terrace East, Glasgow.
Robertson, D. Argyll, M.D., 18 Charlotte Square, Edinburgh.
Robertson, J. Stewart, W.S., Edradynate, Ballinluig.
Robertson, John, Elmslea, Dundee.
Robson, William, Marchholm, Gillsland Road, Edinburgh.
Rogerson, John J., LL.B., Merchiston Castle, Edinburgh.
Rosebery, The Earl of, K.G., Dalmeny Park, Linlithgowshire.
Ross, T. S., Balgillo Terrace, Broughty Ferry.
320 Ross, Rev. William, LL.D., 7 Grange Terrace, Edinburgh.
Ross, Rev. William, The Manse, Polmont.
Roy, William G., S.S.C., 28 Broughton Place, Edinburgh.
Russell, John, 7 Seton Place, Edinburgh.

Scott, Rev. Archibald, D.D., 16 Rothesay Place, Edinburgh.
Scott, John, C.B., Seafield, Greenock.
Shaw, David, W.S., 1 Thistle Court, Edinburgh.
Shaw, Rev. R. D., B.D., 21 Lauder Road, Edinburgh.
Shaw, Thomas, M.P., Advocate, 17 Abercromby Pl., Edinburgh.
Shiell, John, 5 Bank Street, Dundee.
330 Shiells, Robert, National Bank of Neenah, Neenah, Wisconsin.
Simpson, Prof. A. R., 52 Queen Street, Edinburgh.
Simpson, Sir W. G., Bart., Stoneshiel Hall, Reston, Berwickshire.
Simson, D. J., Advocate, 3 Glenfinlas Street, Edinburgh.
Sinclair, Alexander, Glasgow Herald Office, Glasgow.
Skelton, John, Advocate, C.B., LL.D., the Hermitage of Braid, Edinburgh.
Skene, W. F., D.C.L., LL.D., 27 Inverleith Row, Edinburgh.
Skinner, William, W.S., 35 George Square, Edinburgh.

Smart, William, M.A., Nunholm, Dowanhill, Glasgow.
Smith, G. Gregory, M.A., 9 Warrender Park Cres., Edinburgh.
340 Smith, Rev. G. Mure, 6 Clarendon Place, Stirling.
Smith, Rev. R. Nimmo, Manse of the First Charge, Haddington.
Smith, Robert, 24 Meadowside, Dundee.
Smythe, David M., Methven Castle, Perth.
Sprott, Rev. Dr., The Manse, North Berwick.
Stair, Earl of, Oxenfoord Castle, Dalkeith.
Steele, W. Cunninghame, Advocate, 21 Drummond Place, Edinburgh.
Stevenson, J. H., Advocate, 10 Albyn Place, Edinburgh.
Stevenson, Rev. Robert, M.A., The Abbey, Dunfermline.
Stevenson, T. G., 22 Frederick Street, Edinburgh.
350 Stevenson, William, Towerbank, Lenzie, by Glasgow.
Stewart, Major-General Shaw, 61 Lancaster Gate, London, W.
Stewart, James R., 31 George Square, Edinburgh.
Stewart, R. K., Murdostoun Castle, Newmains, Lanarkshire.
Stewart, Prof. T. Grainger, M.D., 19 Charlotte Sq., Edinburgh.
Stirling, Major C. C. Graham, Craigbarnet, Haughhead of Campsie, Glasgow.
Strathallan, Lord, Carlton Club, Pall Mall, London, S.W.
Strathern, Robert, W.S., 12 South Charlotte St., Edinburgh.
Strathmore, Earl of, Glamis Castle, Glamis.
Stuart, Surgeon-Major G. B., 7 Carlton Street, Edinburgh.
360 Sturrock, James S., W.S., 110 George Street, Edinburgh.
Sutherland, James B., S.S.C., 10 Windsor Street, Edinburgh.

Taylor, Benjamin, 10 Derby Crescent, Kelvinside, Glasgow.
Taylor, Rev. Malcolm C., D.D., Professor of Church History, 6 Greenhill Park, Edinburgh.
Telford, Rev. W. H., Free Church Manse, Reston, Berwickshire.
Tennant, Sir Charles, Bart., The Glen, Innerleithen.
Thoms, George H. M., Advocate, 13 Charlotte Sq., Edinburgh.
Thomson, John Comrie, Advocate, 30 Moray Place, Edinburgh.
Thomson, Rev. John Henderson, Free Church Manse, Hightae, by Lockerbie.

Thomson, John Maitland, Advocate, 10 Wemyss Pl., Edinburgh.
370 Thomson, Lockhart, S.S.C., 114 George Street, Edinburgh.
Thorburn, Robert Macfie, Uddevalla, Sweden.
Trail, John A., W.S., 30 Drummond Place, Edinburgh.
Trayner, The Hon. Lord, 27 Moray Place, Edinburgh.
Tuke, John Batty, M.D., 20 Charlotte Square, Edinburgh.
Tweedale, Mrs., Milton Hall, Milton, Cambridge.
Tweeddale, Marquis of, Yester, Gifford, Haddington.

Underhill, Charles E., M.D., 8 Coates Crescent, Edinburgh.

Veitch, Professor, LL.D., 4 The College, Glasgow.

Waddel, Alexander, Royal Bank, Calton, Glasgow.
380 Walker, Alexander, 64 Hamilton Place, Aberdeen.
Walker, James, Hanley Lodge, Corstorphine.
Walker, Louson, Westhorpe, Greenock.
Walker, Robert, M.A., University Library, Aberdeen.
Wannop, Rev. Canon, Parsonage, Haddington.
Watson, D., Hillside Cottage, Hawick.
Watson, James, Myskyns, Ticehurst, Hawkhurst.
Waugh, Alexander, National Bank, Newton-Stewart, N.B.
Weld-French, A. D., Union Club, Boston, U.S.
Will, J. C. Ogilvie, M.D., 379 Union Street, Aberdeen.
390 Wilson, Rev. J. Skinner, 4 Duke Street, Edinburgh.
Wilson, John J., Clydesdale Bank, Penicuik.
Wilson, Robert, Procurator-Fiscal, County Buildings, Hamilton.
Wood, Mrs. Christina S., Woodburn, Galashiels.
Wood, Prof. J. P., W.S., 16 Buckingham Terrace, Edinburgh.
Wood, W. A., C.A., 11 Clarendon Crescent, Edinburgh.
Wordie, John, 49 West Nile Street, Glasgow.

Young, David, Town Clerk, Paisley.
Young, A. J., Advocate, 60 Great King Street, Edinburgh.
Young, J. W., W.S., 22 Royal Circus, Edinburgh.
400 Young, William Laurence, Solicitor, Auchterarder.

PUBLIC LIBRARIES.

Aberdeen Free Public Library.
Aberdeen University Library.
All Souls' College, Oxford.
Antiquaries, Society of, Edinburgh.
Baillie's Institution Free Library, 48 Miller St., Glasgow.
Berlin Royal Library.
Bodleian Library, Oxford.
Boston Athenæum.
Boston Public Library.
10 British Museum.
Cambridge University Library.
Copenhagen (Bibliothèque Royale).
Dollar Institution.
Dundee Free Library.
Edinburgh Public Library.
Edinburgh University Library.
Free Church College Library, Edinburgh.
Free Church College Library, Glasgow.
Glasgow University Library.
20 Gray's Inn, Hon. Society of, London.
Harvard College Library, Cambridge, Mass.
Leeds Subscription Library.
London Corporation Library, Guildhall.
London Library, 12 St. James Square.
Manchester Public Free Library.
Mitchell Library, Glasgow.
National Liberal Club, London.
National Library of Ireland.
Nottingham Free Public Library.
30 Ottawa Parliamentary Library.
Paisley Philosophical Institution.
Philosophical Institution, Edinburgh.
Procurators, Faculty of, Glasgow.
Royal College of Physicians, Edinburgh.
St. Andrews University Library.
Sheffield Free Public Library.
Signet Library, Edinburgh.
Solicitors, Society of, before the Supreme Court, Edinburgh.
Speculative Society, Edinburgh.
40 Stonyhurst College, Blackburn, Lancashire.
Sydney Free Library.
Vienna, Library of the R. I. University.

REPORT OF THE FIFTH ANNUAL MEETING OF THE SCOTTISH HISTORY SOCIETY

The Fifth Annual Meeting of the Society was held on Tuesday, October 27, 1891, at Dowell's Rooms, George Street, Edinburgh,—Sheriff Mackay in the Chair.

The Secretary read the Report of the Council as follows:—

The Council regrets that *Major's History of Greater Britain*, and two other volumes now due to Members, are not yet ready for issue. The annotations to Major's book have demanded considerable care, and have involved researches which could not be hurried. All, however, but a few pages of the text, and all of the introduction, are in type, and it may confidently be stated that the volume, extending to over 500 pages, will be in the hands of Members within a month from this date.

The first volume of the *Minutes of the Commission of the General Assembly* (1646-1662), edited by Professor Mitchell and Dr. Christie, only awaits the completion of the Index and Professor Mitchell's Preface. It is hoped it will be issued with *Major's History*.

Owing to a variety of causes Mr. J. M. Gray has been unable to fulfil his promise to edit the *Diary of Sir John Clerk of Penicuik* for this year. It will, however, form one of the Society's publications for next year, Meanwhile, to take its place, the Rev. D. G. Barron has pushed forward the preparation of the *Court Book of the Barony of Urie.* A portion of this work is already in type, and the whole will be published in a few months, when all the arrears of the Society will be cleared off.

Another book of importance not hitherto brought before the notice of the General Meeting is ready for press, and will form the first publication belonging to the issue of 1891-92. It will be entitled *The Jacobite Rising of* 1719, which rising ended in the battle of Glenshiel, in Ross-shire. It has hitherto been an obscure episode in Scottish history, and the correspondence in the forthcoming volume will, it is believed, throw fresh light upon it. The correspondence, which is partly in French and partly in English, consists of letters written by James, second Duke of Ormonde, with regard to the projected Spanish invasion of Great Britain in the interest of the Stuarts in 1719. The existence of these letters was only made known to the public by their description in an auction catalogue of Messrs. Sotheby, in which the volume containing them, entitled 'The Alberoni MS.,' was offered for sale, and eventually was acquired by the British Museum. The Council took steps, with the kind co-operation of the authorities of the Museum, to have the letters transcribed at once, and Mr. John Russell undertook to prepare them for publication.

In view of its historical importance it was thought that this work should take precedence of the other projected publications of the Society. The volume contains 199 letters addressed to the Chevalier James, to Cardinal Alberoni, the Duke of Mar, and others, by the Duke of Ormonde, between November 4, 1718, and September 27, 1719, written mostly from various towns in Spain, or from on board the Spanish Fleet. A few of the letters refer to the project of Charles XII. of Sweden, who had arranged with Alberoni to land in Britain at the head of 10,000 Swedish troops.

Mr. A. G. Reid of Auchterarder will shortly have ready for the press his *Diary of Andrew Hay of Craignethan Castle*, 1659-60, for which the introduction and most of the notes are already written.

Fresh matter offered for publication by the Society is under the consideration of the Council. The Rev. Robert Paul proposes to edit a collection of letters of the Honourable Sir Charles Erskine of Alva, written from London chiefly to his wife, the daughter of the Lord Advocate, Sir Thomas Hope of Craighall, in the years 1644-47, when Sir Charles was concerned with the business of the Commissioners to the Westminster Assembly of Divines.

Colonel H. W. Feilden of Wells, Norfolk, also offers a portion of the Correspondence of the Earl of Albemarle during the month of August 1746, containing some interesting particulars regarding the suppression of the Jacobite rising of that date.

The publications of the Society continue to be highly prized.

There have been intimated during the year eight vacancies by death or resignation, and when these have been filled up there remain about twenty candidates still waiting for admission.

A vacancy in the Council occurs through the death of Mr. T. G. Murray, and two Members retire, viz., Mr. J. R. Findlay and Dr. Dickson.

The Council proposes to the Society that the vacant places should be filled by the re-election of Mr. J. R. Findlay, and by the appointment of Mr. P. Hume Brown and Mr. Gregory Smith.

In the absence of Mr. Ralph Richardson, Mr. John Milligan, W.S., has kindly consented to act as auditor along with Mr. Traquair Dickson.

The accompanying Abstract of the Treasurer's Accounts shows that the income for 1890-91 has been £490, 13s. 7d., and the expenditure £410, 10s. 2d., leaving a balance for the year in favour of the Society of £80, 3s. 5d. The Reserve Fund of £300 remains intact.

The CHAIRMAN, in moving the adoption of the Report, suggested that new matter for publication might be found if search were made in the archives of the chief towns of the Continent for documents relating to Scottish history, and that valuable memorials might exist in the Colonies, in the shape of journals of early Scottish settlers.

The Report having been adopted, Mr. J. BALFOUR PAUL, Lyon King of Arms, moved 'That the Council of the Scottish History Society would respectfully represent to the University Commissioners the importance of recognising the special claims of historical study, and particularly the study of the history of the British Islands, in the arrangements they may make for future teaching and graduation in the Scottish Universities.' Professor KIRKPATRICK, in seconding the resolution, dwelt on the impossibility of any one man teaching more than one branch of what he (the Professor) considered the greatest of all educational subjects. He contrasted the high place given to historical study in the universities of Germany and Italy with the little attention paid to it in this country, and expressed his hope that the Commissioners would see their way to founding a more complete Chair of History in the Universities.

The Resolution was agreed to, and it was further decided to send copies of it to all the University Councils of Scotland.

ABSTRACT OF HON. TREASURER'S ACCOUNTS

For Year to 22d October 1891.

I.—Charge.

Balance from last year, ...				£139	6	2
19 Subscriptions in arrear for 1889-90, . . .				19	19	0
400 Subscriptions for 1890-91 at £1, 1s., ...	£420	0	0			
Less 26 in arrear for 1890-91, . .	27	6	0			
				392	14	0
38 Libraries at £1, 1s., ...				39	18	0
Copies of previous issues sold to new Members, .				23	12	6
Interest on Bank Account, . .	£0	17	1			
„ Deposit Receipts, .	13	13	0			
				14	10	1
Sum of Charge, .				£629	19	9

II.—Discharge.

I. *Incidental Expenses*—

Printing Circulars and Cards, .	£6	15	6
„ Annual Report of Council,	1	6	6
„ List of Subscribers, . .	1	10	0
Stationery, ...	2	1	0
Carry forward,	£11	13	0

Brought forward,	£11	13	0			
Making up, and delivering copies,	15	17	8			
Postages of Secretary and Treasurer,	4	2	5			
Clerical work, ...	3	8	9			
Charges on Cheques, ...	0	12	0			
Hire of Room for Meeting, 1889 and 1890, ...	0	10	0			
				£36	3	10
II. *Index to List of Rebels*—						
Composition, Presswork, and Paper, ...	£12	5	4			
Proofs and Corrections, . .	2	3	0			
Binding, ...	0	17	6			
Addressing Labels for Post, .	0	11	0			
				15	16	10
III. *Major's History, Expenses to Date*—						
Composition, Presswork, and Paper, ...	£86	11	6			
Proofs and Corrections, . .	36	12	0			
Transcribing, ...	1	5	0			
				124	8	6
IV. *Acts and Proceedings of General Assembly, Expenses to Date*—						
Composition, Presswork, and Paper, ...	£116	9	0			
Proofs and Corrections, . . .	48	4	0			
Transcribing, ...	29	0	0			
				193	13	0
V. *Court Book of Barony of Urie*—						
Expenses to date, ...				6	2	0
VI. *Glamis Papers*—						
Outlays by Editor, ...				14	6	0
VII. *Craig's De Unione*—						
Transcribing, ...				5	0	0
VIII. *Ormonde Letters*—						
Transcribing, ...				15	0	0
Carry forward,				£410	10	2

			£	s.	d.
Brought forward,			£410	10	2
IX. *Balance to next Account*—					
Sum due by Bank of Scotland as at 22d October 1891, . .	£222 12 7				
Less 3 Subscriptions for 1891-92 paid in advance, ...	3 3 0				
			219	9	7
Sum of Discharge, .			£629	19	9

Edinburgh, 29th October 1891.—Having examined the Accounts of the Treasurer of the Scottish History Society for year to 22d October 1891, we have found the same correctly stated and sufficiently vouched, and that the balance in Bank at the close of the Account amounts to Two hundred and twenty-two pounds, twelve shillings, and seven pence stg., whereof Three guineas represent subscriptions paid in advance.

WM. TRAQUAIR DICKSON, *Auditor.*
J. MILLIGAN, *Auditor.*

Scottish History Society.

RULES

1. The object of the Society is the discovery and printing, under selected editorship, of unpublished documents illustrative of the civil, religious, and social history of Scotland. The Society will also undertake, in exceptional cases, to issue translations of printed works of a similar nature, which have not hitherto been accessible in English.

2. The number of Members of the Society shall be limited to 400.

3. The affairs of the Society shall be managed by a Council, consisting of a Chairman, Treasurer, Secretary, and twelve elected Members, five to make a quorum. Three of the twelve elected Members shall retire annually by ballot, but they shall be eligible for re-election.

4. The Annual Subscription to the Society shall be One Guinea. The publications of the Society shall not be delivered to any Member whose Subscription is in arrear, and no Member shall be permitted to receive more than one copy of the Society's publications.

5. The Society will undertake the issue of its own publications, *i.e.* without the intervention of a publisher or any other paid agent.

6. The Society will issue yearly two octavo volumes of about 320 pages each.

7. An Annual General Meeting of the Society shall be held on the last Tuesday in October.

8. Two stated Meetings of the Council shall be held each year, one on the last Tuesday of May, the other on the Tuesday preceding the day upon which the Annual General Meeting shall be held. The Secretary, on the request of three Members of the Council, shall call a special meeting of the Council.

9. Editors shall receive 20 copies of each volume they edit for the Society.

10. The owners of Manuscripts published by the Society will also be presented with a certain number of copies.

11. The Annual Balance-Sheet, Rules, and List of Members shall be printed.

12. No alteration shall be made in these Rules except at a General Meeting of the Society. A fortnight's notice of any alteration to be proposed shall be given to the Members of the Council.

PUBLICATIONS

For the year 1886-1887.

1. BISHOP POCOCKE'S TOURS IN SCOTLAND, 1747-1760. Edited by D. W. KEMP. (Oct. 1887.)

2. DIARY OF AND GENERAL EXPENDITURE BOOK OF WILLIAM CUNNINGHAM OF CRAIGENDS, 1673-1680. Edited by the Rev. JAMES DODDS, D.D. (Oct. 1887.)

For the year 1887-1888.

3. PANURGI PHILO-CABALLI SCOTI GRAMEIDOS LIBRI SEX.—THE GRAMEID: an heroic poem descriptive of the Campaign of Viscount Dundee in 1689, by JAMES PHILIP of Almerieclose. Translated and Edited by the Rev. A. D. MURDOCH. (Oct. 1888.)

4. THE REGISTER OF THE KIRK-SESSION OF ST. ANDREWS. Part I. 1559-1582. Edited by D. HAY FLEMING. (Feb. 1889.)

For the year 1888-1889.

5. DIARY OF THE REV. JOHN MILL, Minister of Dunrossness, Sandwick, and Cunningsburgh, in Shetland, 1740-1803. Edited by GILBERT GOUDIE, F.S.A. Scot. (June 1889.)

6. NARRATIVE OF MR. JAMES NIMMO, A COVENANTER, 1654-1709. Edited by W. G. SCOTT-MONCRIEFF, Advocate. (June 1889.)

7. THE REGISTER OF THE KIRK-SESSION OF ST. ANDREWS. Part II. 1583-1600. Edited by D. HAY FLEMING. (Aug. 1890.)

For the year 1889-1890.

8. A LIST OF PERSONS CONCERNED IN THE REBELLION (1745). With a Preface by the EARL OF ROSEBERY and Annotations by the Rev. WALTER MACLEOD. (Sept. 1890.)
   Presented to the Society by the Earl of Rosebery.

9. GLAMIS PAPERS: The 'BOOK OF RECORD,' a Diary written by PATRICK, FIRST EARL OF STRATHMORE, and other documents relating to Glamis Castle (1684-89). Edited by A. H. MILLAR, F.S.A. Scot. (Sept. 1890.)

10. JOHN MAJOR'S HISTORY OF GREATER BRITAIN (1521). Translated and Edited by ARCHIBALD CONSTABLE, with a Life of the author by ÆNEAS J. G. MACKAY, Advocate. (Feb. 1892.)

For the year 1890-1891.

11. The Records of the Commissions of the General Assemblies, 1646-47. Edited by the Rev. Professor Mitchell, D.D., and the Rev. James Christie, D.D., with an Introduction by the former. (May 1892.)
12. Court-Book of the Barony of Urie, 1604-1747. Edited by the Rev. D. G. Barron, from a ms. in possession of Mr. R. Barclay of Dorking. (October 1892.)

For the year 1891-1892.

13. Memoirs of the Life of Sir John Clerk of Penicuik, Baronet, Baron of the Exchequer, Commissioner of the Union, etc. Extracted by himself from his own Journals, 1676-1755. Edited from the original ms. in Penicuik House by John M. Gray, F.S.A. Scot. (December 1892.)

The Jacobite Rising of 1719. Letter Book of James, Second Duke of Ormonde, Nov. 4, 1718—Sept. 27, 1719. Edited by John Russell. (*In active progress.*)

To be issued for the year 1892-1893.

Diary of Col. the Hon. John Erskine of Carnock, 1683-1687. From a ms. in possession of Henry David Erskine, Esq., of Cardross. Edited by the Rev. Walter Macleod.

The Diaries or Account Books of Sir John Foulis of Ravelston, (1679-1707), and the Account Book of Dame Hannah Erskine (1675-1699). Edited by the Rev. A. W. Cornelius Hallen.

In preparation.

The Diary of Andrew Hay of Stone, near Biggar, afterwards of Craignethan Castle, 1659-60. Edited by A. G. Reid, F.S.A. Scot., from a manuscript in his possession.

Sir Thomas Craig's De Unione Regnorum Britanniæ. Edited, with an English Translation, from the unpublished manuscript in the Advocates' Library.

Papers relating to the Military Government of Scotland, and the Correspondence of Robert Lilburne and General Monk, from 1653 to 1658. Edited by C. H. Firth.

A Selection of the Forfeited Estate Papers preserved in H.M. General Register House.

Continuation of the Records of the Commissions of the General Assemblies, 1648-1662.